Get the eBooks FREE!
(PDF, ePub, Kindle, and liveBook all included)

We believe that once you buy a book from us, you should be able to read it in any format we have available. To get electronic versions of this book at no additional cost to you, purchase and then register this book at the Manning website.

Go to https://www.manning.com/freebook and follow the instructions to complete your pBook registration.

That's it!
Thanks from Manning!

Using the TI-83 Plus/TI-84 Plus

CHRISTOPHER R. MITCHELL

MANNING

SHELTER ISLAND

For online information and ordering of this and other Manning books, please visit
www.manning.com. The publisher offers discounts on this book when ordered in quantity.
For more information, please contact

> Special Sales Department
> Manning Publications Co.
> 20 Baldwin Road
> PO Box 261
> Shelter Island, NY 11964
> Email: orders@manning.com

Manning Publications Co.
20 Baldwin Road
PO Box 261
Shelter Island, NY 11964

Development editor: Jeff Bleiel
Copyeditor: Linda Recktenwald
Proofreader: Tiffany Taylor
Typesetter: Dennis Dalinnik
Cover designer: Leslie Haimes

ISBN: 9781617290848
Printed in the United States of America
3 4 5 6 7 8 9 10 – SP – 19 18

brief contents

contents

preface

When I was 13 years old, I received my first graphing calculator. It was Christmas, and my biggest present under the tree turned out to be a TI-83 I had ardently wanted. I was thrilled. I first used it just for math, but over the course of a few months, I became more curious and discovered that I could write programs directly on the calculator. I explored increasingly more complex programs and games, first written in the calculator's built-in TI-BASIC language and then later in z80 assembly. I started an online community called Cemetech (pronounced "KEH-meh-tek"), first to showcase my own programs and later to teach others how to use and program TI calculators. Cemetech thrives to this day, driven by a core of dedicated volunteers of all ages who are passionate about math, science, computer science, engineering, and programming.

I have been fortunate to have received many opportunities to get an early start with teaching. My first teaching experience was in third grade, when I taught my classmates how to build a battery and light bulb circuit out of thumbtacks, paperclips, and wires. Aside from my ongoing self-imposed teaching on Cemetech for over a decade, I taught Java to professional engineers as an undergraduate engineering student at Cooper Union. I later served as the graduate teaching assistant for a C programming and computer architecture course at the Courant Institute of NYU. My career as a student has led to two degrees in electrical engineering and one in computer science; I'm now working toward my doctorate. I credit much of my love of programming and engineering to those first faltering steps with my graphing calculator.

Although I first fell in love with graphing calculators as a programming and engineering tool, I simultaneously came to appreciate their value as powerful teaching tools. The number of undergraduates pursuing science, technology, engineering, and math (STEM) majors in the United States has been steadily declining; I believe comprehension and interest in math and science have been declining as well. Although nothing can replace enthusiastic teachers and engaged students in the classroom, I feel that graphing calculators can help students learn math and science more effectively. With calculators, students can more readily visualize graphs and functions, calculus, statistics, and more. If students learn to use their calculators properly, they (or you!) can build a more intuitive understanding of the subject matter without sacrificing the ability to do all the math by hand. Ideally, students should understand that graphing calculators solve problems just like them, and that it's not a magic "black box" that pulls answers from thin air. What you do by hand when you solve out a problem is exactly what your calculator does; the only difference is that it can manipulate the numbers much faster and has infinite patience for repeatedly solving problems.

Because I've been so enthusiastic about graphing calculators as a teaching tool, for programming and for math and science, it was with excitement that I accepted Manning's invitation to write *Programming the TI-83 Plus/TI-84 Plus* last year, which is now widely available to teach beginner programmers. With the successful completion of that first book, we discussed where I might want to go next with my writing career. Canvassing the available books on using graphing calculators for their primary intended purpose, math and science instruction, left me underwhelmed by many of the current offerings. I set off on writing this book with the goal of making graphing calculators as simple and approachable as possible via a multitude of examples. If students are going to be solving specific problems in class, what better way to prepare them than to show them many specific problems solved out?

Of course, any book on graphing calculators also has to be an effective quick reference guide for students who are in a hurry to complete a homework assignment or prepare for a test, and the 13 chapters of this book are peppered with sidebars for quick reference. Appendix B compiles many of these sidebars into a broad reference. Because many students also buy their Texas Instruments graphing calculators for taking the SAT, I included a guide to solving SAT math problems with graphing calculators, complete with many example problems, as appendix A. Occasionally something goes wrong and appendix C offers suggestions for solving problems big and small.

I hope that you enjoy reading and using this book as much as I enjoyed writing it. Of course, there's always more that I can learn about teaching (and using and programming!) graphing calculators, so I hope to hear from you. Don't hesitate to drop me a line if you find this book helpful or if you have any comments or suggestions. Perhaps you'll want to show off calculator projects and programs of your own on Cemetech.

Good luck!

acknowledgments

Thanks must first go to the friends, family, and other loved ones who have supported my teaching, programming, and engineering career throughout the years. I'd especially like to acknowledge my mother, Maria Mitchell, for giving me my first calculator, for always supporting my education, and for offering selfless moral support during this book's creation. My friends and loved ones have been patient with my hobbies and projects and have always been ready with words of encouragement; Sara Nodroff in particular encouraged me to undertake this project and was supportive through the many hours I spent on it. I'm also grateful to teachers and advisers current and past who helped me get where I am today, especially to Jinyang Li, who was understanding of me threading the writing of this book around my PhD research.

Although my first forays into using and understanding calculators took place on my own, the members of the worldwide graphing calculator enthusiast community have been my colleagues and friends for over a decade. It is impossible to name all of the individuals who have made a difference for me here, so if I don't specifically acknowledge you, know that I treasure your help, inspiration, and camaraderie nonetheless. I must first tip my hat to my Cemetech administrators, staff, and friends, who have stood by me through my technical and personal struggles and achievements. Thomas "Elfprince13" Dickerson and Daniel "TIFreak8x" Thorneycroft have been with Cemetech since its early days and have encouraged my projects for more than seven years, though more recent additions, Shaun "Merthsoft" Mcfall and Jon "Jonimus/TheStorm" Sturm have become my valued friends and colleagues. Other Cemetech staff past and present have been my teachers, students, and friends, including

Theodore Davis, Alex Glanville, Kenneth Hammond, Catherine Hobson, Peter Marheine, Jonathan Pezzino, and many more. I'm grateful to all of the Cemetechians who provided feedback and corrections for this book, especially Ryan "Phero" Boyd, this book's technical proofreader and an unassailably enthusiastic ticalc.org news editor.

The following reviewers also provided invaluable feedback during the development of the manuscript: Alejandro Cabrera, Elisabeth Adams, Erwan Martin, Jonathan Walker, Linda Nelson, Louis Becquey, Nikky Southerland, Parker Reed, Sam Gockel, Tammy L. Jones, Thomas Dickerson, and Travis Evans.

Texas Instruments provided encouragement that helped make this book a more thorough resource, including providing an early TI-84 Plus C Silver Edition so that I could explore the device. A special tip of the hat goes to Dale Philbrick, Gayle Mujica, Margo Mankus, and Marianne Hancock, among many others. The staff of ticalc.org have over the years been advisers and friends, including Travis Evans, Nikky Southerland, Michael Vincent, Ryan Boyd, and Duncan Smith.

This book would have been impossible without the tireless efforts of many at Manning. Thanks to my publisher, Marjan Bace, and to Michael Stephens, who first found me for this project. In chronological order, Elizabeth Lexleigh, Maureen Spencer, and Jeff Bleiel contributed a great deal of their time and effort to make this book the best that it could be. My gratitude also goes to the Manning marketing, editorial, and production teams for every aspect of their contributions that combined to make the virtual or physical pages you now hold in your hand a reality.

about this book

Graphing calculators are a useful tool for students, teachers, SAT test-takers, professionals, and just about anyone who needs to work with numbers and graphs. You can use a graphing calculator to help solve math and science problems or to check your work, to draw graphs and manipulate statistics, and even to write programs. But all this power can make your graphing calculator an intimidating device. With all the features it offers, you might have difficulty figuring out where to start. And that's where this book comes in. It focuses primarily on the TI-83 Plus and TI-84 Plus-family calculators but also can help you with any TI-83, TI-83.fr, TI-82, or TI-82 Stats.fr calculator. In the coming chapters, you'll see almost everything your calculator can do, from the simplest arithmetic to complex graphing, statistics, calculus, and programming.

Before you begin chapter 1, I'd like to give you some background material about this book and how you can use it. First, I'll show you a roadmap for the book, in which I'll introduce the material in each of the four parts, 13 chapters, and three appendices. Of course, you can also use the index or table of contents to find specific material. Next, I'll discuss who should use this book and how you can use it, whether you're a student, a teacher, a professional, or simply learning to use graphing calculators. I'll present the typographic conventions used throughout the book, point you to online resources that might help if you get stuck, and conclude with a few words about myself.

Let's get started with a roadmap of the material in this book.

Roadmap

This book consists of 13 chapters, divided into four parts, plus three appendices for quick reference. Part 1 focuses on introductory TI-83 Plus/TI-84 Plus skills for arithmetic, algebra, and graphing.

- Chapter 1 introduces graphing calculators, starting with five sample problems picked from a cross-section of what your calculator can do. It explains what you'll need to use this book, and it highlights the similarities and differences between the existing TI-83 Plus and TI-84 Plus-family calculators.
- Chapter 2 presents the basics of math and algebra on the graphing calculators, from arithmetic, square roots, fractions, and exponents to solving algebraic equations and using logic.
- Chapter 3 covers the basics of graphing functions in the form $y=f(x)$ on your calculator, complete with plenty of real-world examples. You'll also learn to draw graphs, find maximum and minimum points on graphed functions, and determine exactly where functions cross other functions or the x axis.
- Chapter 4 teaches variables, lists, and matrices, three different ways to store numbers. Variables store single values, lists store one-dimensional sets of numbers, and matrices store two-dimensional arrays of numbers. Through many examples, you'll discover how to manipulate variables, lists, and matrices, as well as how to do math with them.

Part 2 teaches precalculus and calculus skills. You'll start with more ways to graph, cover all the calculator precalculus skills you didn't see yet, and then work with your calculator's calculus toolset.

- Chapter 5 teaches you how to graph in parametric, polar, and sequence modes. You'll work through many example problems showing where these new graphing modes are vital. The chapter also introduces drawing on the graphscreen and saving and recalling annotated graphs and diagrams.
- Chapter 6 rounds out the precalculus skills you already gleaned from the first five chapters with a few new skills. It shows you how to work with imaginary and complex numbers on your calculator, discusses more about trigonometry, and shows you how to compute limits, logarithms, and exponentials.
- Chapter 7 covers the TI-83 Plus/TI-84 Plus calculus tools. You'll learn how to find numeric (definite) integrals and derivatives at a point. The chapter also shows the applications of integrals and derivatives on your calculator, including finding the area under a curve, the slope of a function, and the minima, maxima, and inflection points of functions.

Part 3 introduces statistics, probability, and finance.

- Chapter 8 explores your calculator's statistics tools. It starts with how you can calculate statistics over sets of data and then moves on to plotting one-variable and two-variable statistics as graphs. The chapter concludes with regression, which you use to fit a function or curve to your data.

- Chapter 9 introduces tools and functions for probability. The bulk of the material focuses on probability distribution functions (PDFs) and cumulative distribution functions (CDFs) and how you can calculate and plot them on your graphing calculator. The chapter also demonstrates the calculator's combinatoric functions and the types of random numbers it can generate.
- Chapter 10 touches on an often-overlooked set of functions, the Finance tools. In particular, it shows how you can calculate properties of investments, mortgages, loans, and more with the Time-Value of Money (TVM) Solver. Each concept is made concrete with plenty of examples.

Part 4 goes into advanced concepts and details that don't fit anywhere else in the book.

- Chapter 11 gives you a thorough introduction to the powerful programming tools built into your calculator. You'll see sample math programs and games in action, learn about the programming commands in the TI-BASIC language, and find out about additional books and resources you can use to learn more.
- Chapter 12 is a complete reference to the new color-screen TI-84 Plus C Silver Edition calculator. Although almost all of the examples and skills taught in the book apply directly to this new calculator, it has a few new tools, plus the ability to draw graphs and plots in color. By the end of this chapter, you'll know how to use all of the new features.
- Chapter 13 concludes with a look at the nonmath things you can do with your calculator, from downloading and running programs and Apps to controlling robots and connecting to sensors. It ends with a look forward at the future of graphing calculators.

The appendices provide a quick reference to material, supplementing and coalescing the contents of the chapters:

- Appendix A walks you through how your calculator can help you solve typical SAT math problems quickly and easily.
- Appendix B summarizes important calculator skills. You can find the same material threaded throughout the book, but this appendix crystallizes summaries of each skill for quick and easy reference.
- Appendix C should be your first stop when something goes unexpectedly wrong and you can't figure out how to fix it. It provides a brief but thorough troubleshooting guide to common and rare calculator issues.

CALCULATOR CRASH COURSE   If you only have time to read two or three chapters, especially if you're using this book to help you with the SATs, chapters 2 and 3 should be where you start. Chapter 2 teaches you to use your calculator to calculate, and chapter 3 introduces the basics of graphing. For a quick reference to many of the calculator's skills, flip to appendix B. If you're focusing on the SATs, appendix A is also a must-read.

Who should read this book

If you are learning to use a TI graphing calculator for the first time, you probably are a student. You might be in junior high school or high school, or you might be a college student. Graphing calculators are, of course, also used by teachers, and they remain useful tools for other professionals, especially scientists and engineers. If you are learning to use a TI graphing calculator for the first time, then no matter who you are or how much math and science you know, this book will be a friendly guide that works at your pace, introducing every new skill with plenty of examples. If you have some experience with graphing calculators, or you're just in a hurry, this book is an effective quick reference for finding a specific skill fast.

As a student, this book will help you use your graphing calculator as a tool for math, science, and more. Whether you're dealing with algebra, trigonometry, precalculus, calculus, statistics, probability, finance, or programming, your graphing calculator can help. The coming chapters will teach you how to use your calculator efficiently, to avoid common pitfalls, and to understand new skills by way of examples. Although it teaches calculator use, not math or science, it's the perfect companion for a math or science curriculum. If you're studying for the SATs, you'll probably bring a TI-83 Plus or TI-84 Plus-family graphing calculator, and this book will show you how to quickly and accurately use the calculator.

This book can also help you if you're a teacher, no matter how much or how little graphing calculator experience you have. Even if you're a pro, you're likely to find new features and gotchas that you never knew about in these pages. This book features lessons on the new MathPrint tools as well as the quirks of the color-screen TI-84 Plus C Silver Edition, so if you or your students have any calculator in the TI-84 Plus family, this book is a particularly apt companion.

How to use this book

There are two ways to use this book, and you'll probably end up blending the two. The first way is as a comprehensive guide to graphing calculators, where you read whole chapters at a time. Alternatively, you might be in a lesson or working on a homework assignment where you need to know one specific skill fast.

In an ideal world, you'd have the leisure time to read this book cover to cover. You'd be able to sit down with your calculator and read chapter by chapter, trying each example as you learn each new skill. But I've been a student recently enough to know that's not realistic. Some students and teachers might have time to read from cover to cover, but others will only have time to focus on single chapters relevant to what they're currently covering in class. Still others might need to jump directly to learning a new skill; for example, graphing polar graphs, to complete a math assignment. Perhaps you can read through a page or three to go through an example or two, or perhaps it's so late in the evening that you only have time to read one paragraph that summarizes what you need to do for tomorrow.

In any of these cases, this book has you covered. The chapters are laid out linearly, progressing from the most basic of calculator skills, doing calculations, up through calculus, probability, and finance. If you read it from cover to cover, you'll learn more and more advanced skills as you go. The parts and chapters are also written to be as clear as possible even without reading surrounding material, and major skills are summarized in sidebars. If you jump directly the polar graphing material in section 5.2, for instance, you'll see a sidebar that succinctly describes changing modes, entering your polar equation, and viewing the graph. If you read more of the prose, you'll find an example, and if you read through the rest of the chapter, you'll understand how polar graphing fits in among the other precalculus features your calculator offers.

Typographic conventions and style

Because this book is aimed at the absolute beginner, significant effort was put into making the distinction between prose, math, and text typed on the calculator as clear as possible. Examples are woven liberally throughout the calculator skills taught, most of which are firmly grounded in math or science concepts. All of these conventions are followed:

- Math is written in normal font, with variables like x, c, and θ italicized.
- All calculator keys are represented by images like ③, (ALPHA), (▶), and (ZOOM). When a string of keys is shown, such as (ALPHA) (STO▸) (+) (1) (ENTER), you release each key before pressing the next one. The TI-83 Plus/TI-84 Plus-family calculators don't support holding more than one key together.
- Any text that appears on the calculator's screen is written in monospaced font, like `1+1` or `sin(3.5X)` or `fnInt(X²,X,0,4)`. In early chapters, the keys that type out the given sequence will be shown; in later chapters, readers are expected to know how to type out math on the calculators.
- Most lessons herein apply to the following calculators:
  - TI-83 Plus
  - TI-83 Plus Silver Edition
  - TI-84 Plus
  - TI-84 Plus Silver Edition
  - TI-84 Plus C Silver Edition

- A few of the lessons are specifically targeted at the TI-84 Plus C Silver Edition, a new (at publication time) color-screen graphing calculator from Texas Instruments. Such lessons are labeled with the "C" icon shown next to this paragraph. Many of the concepts and almost all of the examples also apply to the TI-82, the TI-82 Stats.fr, the TI-83, and to a lesser extent the TI-85 and TI-86. The TI-89 and TI-Nspire are sufficiently different from the TI-83 Plus/TI-84 Plus calculators for this book to not apply to them.
- The term *TI-83 Plus family* refers to any TI-83 Plus or TI-83 Plus Silver Edition. *TI-84 Plus family* means any TI-84 Plus, TI-84 Plus Silver Edition, or TI-84 Plus C Silver Edition.

- Newer versions of the TI-84 Plus-family calculators include a math display system called MathPrint. MathPrint makes the math on your calculator look more like the equations you'd see in a math textbook. Unfortunately, it also means that some skills require different keystrokes on calculators with MathPrint enabled. Chapter 1 will teach you how to tell if your calculator supports Math-Print and how to turn it on and off. Throughout the rest of the book, you'll see the "MP" symbol next to this paragraph whenever a MathPrint-specific detail is mentioned.

All screenshots in this book were taken with the jsTIfied emulator (http://www.cemetech.net/projects/jstified) and adjusted and annotated in GIMP. All source code listings were generated from the original programs by SourceCoder and checked in jsTIfied.

Sample programs

Chapter 11 teaches TI-BASIC programming; all three sample programs from the chapter can be found on the book's Manning web page, http://manning.com/mitchell2. If you wish to pursue programming further, there are more example programs in *Programming the TI-83 Plus/TI-84 Plus* and on that book's web page, http://manning.com/mitchell. Each program can be tested on your calculator or emulator; a list of the top TI calculator emulators is included in chapter 13. You can also view the source of programs on your computer using SourceCoder, at http://sc.cemetech.net.

Online resources

The purchase of *Using the TI-83 Plus/TI-84 Plus* includes free access to a private web forum run by Manning Publications, where you can make comments about this book, ask technical questions, and receive help from both the author and from other readers. The forum can be reached via www.manning.com/UsingtheTI-83Plus/TI-84Plus or www.manning.com/mitchell2. This page contains sample content from this book as well as information about the help that the book's forum provides.

Manning's commitment to our readers is to provide a venue where a meaningful dialogue between individual readers and between readers and the author can take place. It's not a commitment to any specific amount of participation on the part of the author, whose contribution to the forum remains voluntary (and unpaid). We suggest you try asking the author some challenging questions lest his interest stray!

The Author Online Forum and the archives of previous discussions will be accessible from the publisher's website as long as the book is in print. You can also ask technical questions on the author's forum, Cemetech, which has a special subforum for this book at www.cemetech.net/forum/f/73 (or http://cemete.ch/f73). Chapter 13 lists other resources, including emulators and discussion forums.

About the author

Christopher Mitchell is a PhD candidate in computer science and electrical engineering, a teacher, and a recognized leader in the TI and Casio graphing calculator communities. Christopher has pursued passions for programming, math, and teaching since an early age. He picked up his first calculator at the age of 12 and within a few years was teaching others to use and program the devices on his website, Cemetech. Today, he is the graphing calculator community's most prolific programmer, with well over 300 completed programs. He teaches programming at an undergraduate level and as one of hundreds of experts on Cemetech. Christopher is proud to be a born-and-raised New Yorker. He has a bachelors and masters of engineering in electrical engineering from Cooper Union and is now pursuing a PhD in computer science at the Courant Institute of NYU.

About the cover illustration

Manning has a long tradition of using figures from an 1805 edition of a compendium of contemporary French regional fashions for book covers. Feedback from many students in my previous book's target audience indicated that something more contemporary would be preferred. For that book, *Programming the TI-83 Plus/TI-84 Plus*, a cover was designed that combined the classical "Vitruvian Man" by Leonardo da Vinci with three graphing calculators. This book's cover continues the theme but features a TI-84 Plus Silver Edition rather than a TI-84 Plus in the center. It also sports a distinctive red-orange cover, easily distinguished from *Programming the TI-83 Plus/TI-84 Plus*'s yellow parchment-like cover.

Part 1

Basics and algebra on the TI-83 Plus/TI-84 Plus

Your graphing calculator is a powerful tool and helpful ally for math, science, and more. Part 1 of this book lays the foundation for you to use your calculator effectively. It begins by immersing you head-first in five examples demonstrating what your calculator can do, and it touches on performing arithmetic and basic math, graphing, using variables, and manipulating lists and matrices. By the end of this part, you'll have a toolkit of basic skills for using your calculator, and you'll be prepared to learn the specialized skills taught throughout the rest of the book. Each chapter grounds the skills taught in exciting examples and also includes sidebars for quick reference if you're in a hurry.

Chapter 1 begins with five examples of the tools your calculator includes to help you solve difficult problems, from computing the volume of a box to finding the area under a curve. It discusses what your calculator is and what you'll need to use this book effectively. It concludes with a discussion of the recent MathPrint operating systems included on the latest TI-84 Plus-family calculators and how those features will affect how you use your calculator.

The real start of your introduction to your calculator begins in chapter 2 with how to do basic math. You'll learn about arithmetic, exponents, fractions, functions, and even solving algebraic equations. Chapter 3 adds another vital set of graphing calculator skills: graphing equations. Beyond basic graphing, you'll discover how you can manipulate and format graphs, find properties of graphed functions, and compute where functions intersect.

Lessons on variables, lists, and matrices in chapter 4 round out the remainder of part 1. I'll show you how to use variables on the homescreen and then move on to using lists, matrices, and the functions used to manipulate each. You'll learn how to store lists and matrices for later use in variables.

If you have the leisure to see what your calculator can do, or you're not sure what calculator to buy, start with chapter 1. If you're in a hurry and need to start learning how to do math on your calculator right now, I'll meet you at the beginning of chapter 2.

What can your calculator do?

This chapter covers

- Hands-on examples of your calculator's features
- Using your calculator faster and better
- MathPrint and why you might need it

A graphing calculator is one of the most powerful tools you can use in school or at work. From the name, you can guess that it's great at math, from the simplest arithmetic like 2 + 2, to calculating statistics and multiplying matrices. It's also a pro at graphing and helping you understand its graphs. You can use your graphing calculator for algebra, trigonometry, precalculus, and calculus; you can even use it to write programs and games. If you're a student or teacher, a graphing calculator can be used in every math subject from middle school to college, as well as in science and computer classes. Many graphing calculators are available from Texas Instruments, HP, and Casio; this book focuses on the TI-83 Plus, TI-84 Plus, TI-83 Plus Silver Edition, TI-84 Plus Silver Edition, and TI-84 Plus C Silver Edition, but it can help you use all the calculators shown in figure 1.1.

Your calculator can also be an intimidating device, with so many functions and buttons. It certainly looks harder to use than other familiar gadgets, like a cell phone or a handheld game console. Instead of a mouse or touchscreen, you use

Figure 1.1   Calculators covered in this book (from left): TI-82, TI-83, TI-83 Plus, TI-83 Plus Silver Edition, TI-84 Plus, TI-84 Plus Silver Edition, and TI-84 Plus C Silver Edition. The focus is on the TI-83 Plus and TI-84 Plus models, although most of the skills and examples also apply to the TI-82, TI-83, and TI-82 Stats.fr.

the keyboard to navigate through its features. Fear not—complicated though it might look, you can easily become a calculator expert, and this book will hold your hand every step of the way. Whether you use this guide as a quick reference to do something specific or do a thorough read to learn how to use your calculator well, you'll find lessons taught with simple steps and fun examples. This chapter will immediately show you some calculator skills and demonstrate the variety of tasks a graphing calculator can help you do.

We'll start with five examples of what you can use your calculator for: algebra, geometry, graphing, calculus, and statistics. You can go through them one by one, trying them on your own calculator, skip around, or just peruse them. You'll find a section describing more about this book and how it can help you use your calculator and then a discussion of which calculators this book will teach. You'll learn the difference between MathPrint and non-MathPrint calculators (this book covers both) and end with a look forward at the basic calculator skills you'll discover in chapter 2. Let's get started with five fun examples and see how easy and powerful a graphing calculator can be.

1.1   *Five examples of what your calculator can do*

Your calculator can solve countless different kinds of math and science problems and help you double-check your work while doing homework or during tests (even the SAT!). To help you jump right into using your calculator, let's start with five complete examples, picked from exactly the sort of problems you might encounter in class. If you'd prefer to start learning specific math skills immediately, you might want to skip this section, skim the rest of chapter 1, and then begin with the arithmetic and algebra skills in chapter 2. If you want to see some examples of what your calculator can do, here's what this section will cover:

    1   Calculating the volume of a cube and then cutting off the top of the cube and finding the new volume

    2   Finding solutions to the Quadratic Formula, a method for solving $ax^2 + bx + c = 0$

3 Graphing the sine and cosine functions

4 Graphing a curve and then figuring out the area under a portion of the curve

5 Fitting a line of best fit to a series of data points

These examples are arranged in order from easiest to hardest and are taken, respectively, from algebra, geometry, precalculus, trigonometry, and statistics.

> **BEFORE YOU BEGIN** All five of these examples should work well on your calculator without any special setup. If you're getting different answers for some of the examples, consider resetting your calculator to its default settings. Section 2.1 explains how to do that.

Let's get started with the first example, finding the volume of a cube. Besides being a nifty demonstration that might come in handy during a geometry class, it's a great way to begin doing useful arithmetic on your graphing calculator.

1.1.1 *Calculating the volume of a cube*

Your calculator is a pro at arithmetic like addition, subtraction, multiplication, and division. It can also raise numbers to powers and perform lots of mathematical operations like logarithms and trigonometry. For our first example of what your calculator can do, imagine a cube of which every side is 9 inches, like the one on the left in figure 1.2.

> **VOLUME OF A BOX** To calculate the volume of a box, multiply its width, length, and height together. If it's a cube, then the width, length, and height are all the same.

To calculate the volume of the 9-inch cube, you need to multiply $9 \times 9 \times 9$. Turn on your calculator, and you should be at the homescreen, the area of your calculator's software where you do math. If you're not, press 2nd MODE to quit to the homescreen, which should have a blinking cursor and either be blank or show the previous calculations you performed.

Next, type 9 × 9 × 9 to get 9*9*9 on the screen. Your screen should match the left side in figure 1.3. There's no = key on your calculator; instead, you calculate

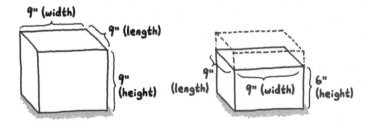

Figure 1.2 Measuring the volume of a cube. On the left, a cube with 9-inch sides. You can calculate its volume by multiplying width × length × height. On the right, the top 3 inches of the cube are cut off, and you want to find the volume of the new box that is 6 inches high instead of 9 inches.

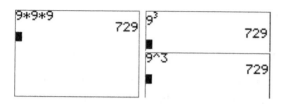

Figure 1.3   Two different ways to calculate the volume of a cube with 9-inch edges. On the left, multiply width × length × height to get the volume, 729. You can also cube 9 by raising it to the third power, which means multiplying the number by itself three times (right). Depending on what calculator type and version you have, your results will look like either the top or bottom; section 1.3 will explain more.

the result of the arithmetic you typed by pressing (ENTER). You'll see the result of the calculation printed at the right side of the screen: 729 cubic inches.

SCREENSHOTS   Throughout this book, I use TI-83 Plus/TI-84 Plus screenshots to demonstrate most problems, interspersed with occasional TI-84 Plus C Silver Edition screenshots. No matter which calculator you're using, all the examples and skills in this book will work on any TI-83 Plus or TI-84 Plus–family calculator, even if what you see on the screen is a bit different.

Another way you can find the volume of a 9-inch cube is to take the length of one side, 9, and cube it. Cubing a number is raising it to the third power, written 9^3. On your calculator, you type this as (9) (∧) (3) and then press (ENTER). As you might expect, and as the right side in figure 1.3 confirms, the result is still 729. Note that depending on whether you have a MathPrint operating system on your calculator, the key sequence (9) (∧) (3) might display different (but equivalent) math on your screen.

As a final exercise, imagine slicing the top 3 inches off the box. Perhaps you needed to open it, or perhaps the cube was actually a 6-inch-tall box with a 3-inch lid that you just took off. Either way, as the right side in figure 1.2 shows, you now have a 9-inch by 9-inch by 6-inch box, and you want to calculate the new volume. This time, you must multiply $9 \times 9 \times 6$, which is very similar to your previous experience multiplying $9 \times 9 \times 9$. Figure 1.4 shows what the equation will look like when you type (9) (×) (9) (×) (6); as before, the (ENTER) key acts like an = key to make the volume of the shorter box appear: 486. Because 9×9 is 9 squared, you could even be clever and type $9 \times 9 \times 6$ as $9^2 \times 6$, which once again (as the right side in figure 1.4 demonstrates) produces the correct volume of the shorter box: 486. To type the squared symbol, you could type (∧) (2), but it's faster to use the (x^2) key. Thus, to calculate $9^2 \times 6$, press (9) (x^2) (×) (6) (ENTER).

That's a quick introduction to using your calculator for math. You type in the expression to calculate with the number keys and operators like (+), (−), (×), and (÷).

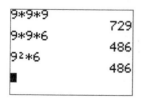

Figure 1.4   Calculating the volume of the 9-inch cube with the top 3 inches sliced off. The last line shows the same calculation using the (x^2) key instead of typing 9 × 9.

You then ask your calculator to produce the result with (ENTER). Section 2.2 will teach you more about basic arithmetic and your calculator.

A more complicated math example is solving the Quadratic Formula, which will require using a few tools you haven't seen yet.

1.1.2 Solving the Quadratic Formula

The Quadratic Formula is used to figure out values of the variable x that make a quadratic equation $0 = ax^2 + bx + c$ true, once you pick three constant numbers a, b, and c. If you're not familiar with the notation, you can read it as "0 equals a times x squared, plus b times x, plus c." You square x, multiply the result by a, add that to b times x, and add c. If you use a value of x that is a correct solution for the given a, b, and c, you'll get 0. For an x value that isn't a solution, the result of that multiplication and division will be a number other than 0. Even if you haven't worked with this type of math before, fear not! Follow along, and in later chapters (and math classes) you'll learn more about the Quadratic Formula.

MEET THE QUADRATIC FORMULA

You don't need to guess values for x and plug them in. The Quadratic Formula is a tool to find the 0, 1, or 2 values of x that satisfy (solve) $0 = ax^2 + bx + c$ for a given set of three constants a, b, and c. The Quadratic Formula is shown and demonstrated in action in figure 1.5.

We'll try solving for the roots of $0 = 2x^2 + 8x + 2$, where the roots are values of x that make the right side of the equation equal to 0. In this case, $a = 2$, $b = 8$, and $c = 2$. The top of figure 1.5 shows the Quadratic Formula, into which you'll plug values for a, b, and c. Your calculator can handle named variables, so you can store 2 into A, 8 into B, and 2 into C (your calculator only has uppercase variables like A, B, X, and M). You've seen the squared symbol (as in b^2) in the previous example, finding the volume of a box. But there are two new symbols that you might be unfamiliar with.

The ± symbol means you can put either a plus sign or a minus sign at that position. In other words, the Quadratic Formula is actually two different equations, one with a plus and one with a minus. When you plug in a, b, and c, you get two solutions: one for the equation with a plus and one for it with a minus. The other symbol that might be

$$x = \frac{-b \pm \sqrt{b^2 - 4ac}}{2a}$$

SOLUTION WITH DOUBLE ROOT
$a=1, b=2, c=1$

$$x = \frac{-2 \pm \sqrt{2^2 - 4*1*1}}{2*1} = \frac{-2 \pm \sqrt{0}}{2}$$

$$x = -1$$

SOLUTION WITH REAL ROOTS
$a=2, b=8, c=2$

$$x = \frac{-8 \pm \sqrt{8^2 - 4*2*2}}{2*2} = \frac{-8 \pm \sqrt{48}}{4}$$

$$x = -2 \pm \sqrt{3}$$

Figure 1.5 The Quadratic Formula (top) solved for two sets of a, b, and c constants. On the left, we set $a = 1$, $b = 2$, and $c = 1$, and get the double root –1, –1. On the right, setting $a = 2$, $b = 8$, and $c = 2$ yields two difference roots, –2 plus and minus the square root of 3.

new (but hopefully not!) is the radical or square root symbol, √. It indicates that you should take the square root of everything inside.

STORING VALUES FOR A, B, AND C

Let's set up your *a*, *b*, and *c* values into the A, B, and C variables on your calculator first and then type the two different forms of the Quadratic Formula to find the solutions. We'll try solving the case on the left in figure 1.5, where *a* = 1, *b* = 2, and *c* = 1. From the figure, you can see that you should get two (identical) solutions, *x* = −1 and *x* = −1.

First, make sure you're at the homescreen. You may have to press 2nd MODE to get there or CLEAR to start with a blank line. The first thing you'll do is assign (store) values to the variables A, B, and C. The STO▸ key prints the → symbol, which takes whatever is on its left side and stores it into whatever is on its right side. For example, 3→A stores the number 3 into the A variable, whereas ⁻4.5→X stores −4.5 (negative 4.5) into the X variable. You can then use those variables in expressions; so if you calculated A+4 after storing 3 into A, it would be like 3 + 4, and you would get 7 as the answer.

With that in mind, try these steps:

1   Type 1 STO▸ ALPHA MATH ALPHA . Don't press ENTER yet. You should see 1→A: on the screen, as in figure 1.6.
2   Continue by typing 2 STO▸ ALPHA APPS ALPHA . 1 STO▸ ALPHA PRGM. You should now have 1→A:2→B:1→C on the screen.
3   Press ENTER to store values to A, B, and C.

Although the calculator will just print 1 at the right edge of the screen, as you can see on the left side in figure 1.6, you executed three commands at once. You simultaneously put values in the three variables A, B, and C. On your calculator, you can separate multiple commands or calculations with a colon (:); and when you press ENTER, all the commands or calculations will be performed from left to right. The calculator only shows the result for the last operation, so if you typed 1+1:2+2:3+3 and pressed ENTER, the result would be 6. Why bother using colons instead of putting each store command on a different line? Because as you'll learn in chapter 2, you can go back to lines

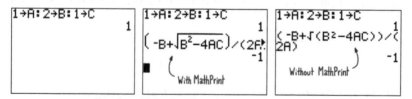

Figure 1.6   On the left, storing values *a* = 1, *b* = 2, and *c* = 1. These values can be used in the Quadratic Formula, as shown in the center and right. The center screenshot applies to TI-84 Plus, TI-84 Plus Silver Edition, and TI-84 Plus C Silver Edition calculators running one of the MathPrint operating systems. The right screenshot shows the same equation entered on a calculator without MathPrint. In section 1.3, I'll explain more about the MathPrint operating systems. Throughout this book, I'll show you how to do things both with and without MathPrint.

you already entered and run them again; and if you set A, B, and C on the same line, you can change them all by modifying one line instead of three.

Now that you have values in A, B, and C, it's time to calculate the two solutions to the Quadratic Formula. This is going to get a bit tricky, because depending on whether you have a calculator with a MathPrint operating system (newer TI-84 Plus/Silver Edition calculators) or a non-MathPrint operating system (TI-82, TI-83, TI-83 Plus/Silver Edition, and some TI-84 Plus/Silver Edition calculators), you'll have to enter a different series of commands.

SOLVING THE QUADRATIC FORMULA

Before we can continue, you need to figure out whether you have a MathPrint operating system and, moreover, whether the MathPrint mode is enabled. If you just stored values to A, B, and C, you should still be at the homescreen. Press the (∧) key, right under the (CLEAR) key:

- If the cursor is a dark square blinking inside a dotted square, next to and slightly above the word *Ans*, you have MathPrint installed and enabled.
- If the cursor is a dark rectangle blinking normally next to the text *Ans∧*, with no dotted line around the cursor, you either don't have MathPrint installed or have it disabled.

Without MathPrint: Type in the "plus" version of the Quadratic Formula (remember the ± symbol?) with the following key sequence: (( ) ((–)) (ALPHA) (APPS) (+) (2nd) (x^2) (ALPHA) (APPS) (x^2) (–) (4) (ALPHA) (MATH) (ALPHA) (PRGM) ( )) ( )) (÷) (( ) (2) (ALPHA) (MATH) ( )). Your screen should look like the right side in figure 1.6. If you made any mistakes, you can press (CLEAR) to clear the line and start over, or you can use the (◄) and (►) arrow keys to move the cursor through the line, press (DEL) to delete extra symbols or numbers, and press (2nd) (DEL) to switch into Insert mode. When you've finished, and your screen matches the right side in figure 1.6, press (ENTER). You should see the answer, –1.

> **NEGATION AND IMPLICIT MULTIPLICATION**   Notice that to type the negative symbol, you don't press the subtract key. On your calculator, negative and subtract are two different keys. Notice also that your calculator does implicit multiplication: 4AC is like 4*A*C.

With MathPrint: Type in the "plus" version of the Quadratic Formula with the following key sequence: (( ) ((–)) (ALPHA) (APPS) (+) (2nd) (x^2) (ALPHA) (APPS) (x^2) (–) (4) (ALPHA) (MATH) (ALPHA) (PRGM) (►) ( )) (÷) (( ) (2) (ALPHA) (MATH) ( )). Your screen should look like the right side in figure 1.6. The only difference from the non-MathPrint instructions is that you need to press (►) to get out of the square-root radical symbol, instead of pressing the ( )) key. As with the non-MathPrint instructions, you can use the arrows, (DEL), and (2nd) (DEL) to move the cursor around, delete errors, and insert missing numbers and symbols. When your entry looks like the center screenshot in figure 1.6, press (ENTER), and you should get –1.

GETTING THE OTHER ANSWER

I told you the Quadratic Formula has two answers, one for the + case of the ± operator and one for the – case. To get the minus answer, press (2nd) (ENTER), which pastes the previous line again. Use the (◄) key to move the blinking cursor over the first + sign, and press (–) to replace it with a subtraction symbol. You can press (ENTER) to get the second solution without needing to move the cursor to the end of the line: it should be –1 again.

This example was fairly simple, but you had to press a lot of keys. Let's save your fingers some work with the next example, in which you'll graph the sine and cosine functions.

1.1.3   *Graphing sine and cosine*

Sine and cosine are two trigonometric functions. They're periodic, which means that they repeat over and over again. Both look like a wave, repeatedly curving between $y = 1$ and $y = -1$ as you go left to right along the x axis. On your calculator, sine() is abbreviated sin(), and cosine() is abbreviated cos(). The parentheses mean you're taking the sine or cosine of whatever number or variable is inside the parentheses. Individually, the two equations $y = \sin(x)$ and $y = \cos(x)$ look something like the left and right sides of figure 1.7, respectively.

In this example, you'll be superimposing one sine graph and one cosine graph. Both sine and cosine only alternate between $y = 1$ and $y = -1$. This looks tiny with the calculator's standard graphing window, so you'll multiply both functions by a coefficient of 5 to make the functions taller. You'll be graphing these two functions together:

```
Y₁ = 5sin(X)
Y₂ = 5cos(X)
```

Before you can graph these, you should make sure all your graph settings are set to reasonable defaults.

First, press (Y=), use the (▼) and (▲) keys to move the cursor to any of the Y= equations that are filled in, and press (CLEAR) to erase them. Next, to make sure the graph

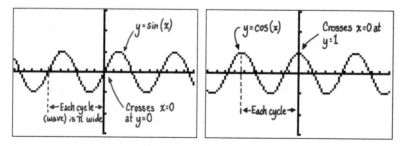

Figure 1.7   Graphs of sin(x) (left) and cos(x) (right). These are both graphed from x = –10 to x = 10, with limits of y = –3 at the bottom and y = 3 at the top. If you know how to graph curves, and you can't figure out why graphing sin(x) or cos(x) on your calculator doesn't look like these screenshots, try pressing (WINDOW) and setting Ymin to –3 and Ymax to 3.

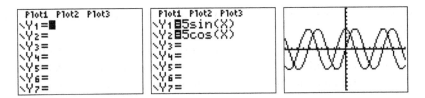

Figure 1.8   Screenshots of graphing sine and cosine from a TI-83 Plus or TI-84 Plus. On the left, the empty Y= menu, the same menu with the two functions you're graphing in this example filled in (center), and the result when you press GRAPH (right). Read the section to learn how to enter the equations and graph them, and read the sidebar "Problems with graphing?" if anything goes wrong. Take a look at figure 1.9 for the TI-84 Plus C Silver Edition versions of these screenshots.

window is set to useful values, press (ZOOM) (6) to select 6:ZStandard (Zoom Standard) in the Zoom menu. Finally, you can enter the equations for Y₁ and Y₂. Press (Y=) again to get back to the screen where you can enter equations to the graph, which should look like the left side in figure 1.8. If it doesn't, refer to the sidebar "Problems with graphing?" for help.

Next, enter the equations. With the cursor flashing next to Y₁=, press (5) (SIN) (XTθn) ( )). You should see 5sin(X) appear. Press (▼) to move to Y₂=, and press (5) (COS) (XTθn) ( )). Now you should have 5cos(X) under the first equation. If you want, double-check against the center in figure 1.8 to make sure you and I have the same equations.

We're ready to graph now: press the (GRAPH) key. You should see the two lines shown on the right side in figure 1.8 appear. If you have a TI-84 Plus C Silver Edition, your graph will look like figure 1.9 instead. You've graphed your first equations! If you want to be adventurous, you can press the (TRACE) key to examine points along each line or (2nd) (GRAPH) to see the table view of *x* and *y* values.

What just happened? Your calculator graphed sine and cosine on the graph screen. It can graph up to 10 different functions at the same time, so 2 is a breeze. When you choose ZStandard, you set the top of the screen to *y* = 10 and the bottom to *y* = –10. You multiplied both the sine and cosine functions by 5 so that the resulting

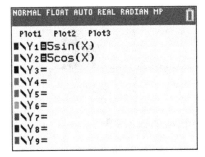

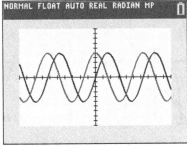

Figure 1.9   The same graphing operation as in figure 1.8 but on a TI-84 Plus C Silver Edition. The left side shows entering two trigonometric functions for graphing; the right side shows the result.

lines would alternate between $y = -5$ and $y = 5$ instead of -1 and 1. This makes them much easier to see.

For our fourth example, we'll move from precalculus to calculus to find the area under a simple curve. This will build on the graphing example you just worked with, so make sure you understand the basics of graphing before you continue.

Problems with graphing?

If you get `ERROR:DIM` when you try to graph, press (Y=), use the arrow keys to move to whichever of `Plot1`, `Plot2`, or `Plot3` is in white text on a black background, and press (ENTER). This will disable that statistics plot, and you should then be able to graph.

If you press (Y=) and you don't see $Y_1=$, $Y_2=$, and similar options, press the (MODE) key to enter the Mode menu, use the arrow keys to move the cursor to the word `FUNC`, and press (ENTER). You should then be able to press (Y=) and see what the left side in figure 1.8 shows.

If you're missing the vertical and horizontal axes when you graph, or you have a grid of dots over the graph screen, press (2nd) (ZOOM) and use the arrow and (ENTER) keys to modify the graph format settings. `AxesOn` turns on the axes; `GridOff` removes a grid of dots.

1.1.4   *Calculating the area under a curve*

Two of the most important skills you'll learn in calculus are taking the derivative and integral of functions. These might at first seem like abstract, confusing concepts, but they have some important real-world purposes. When you take the derivative of a function, you can choose any point along the function and calculate how steep the function is at that point, as the left side in figure 1.10 demonstrates. An integral lets you calculate the area in any area bounded by two *x* values, the *x* axis, and any function (as the right side in figure 1.10 and figure 1.11 show). In this example, you'll see how your calculator can find the area under a curve using an integral.

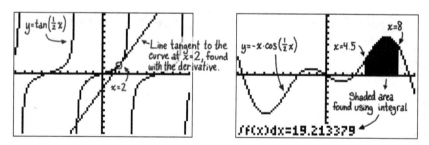

Figure 1.10   Using calculus skills to find information from graphs. On the left, the derivative lets you calculate the slope of a line that exactly touches a function at a given point. On the right, the integral helps you calculate the area of an oddly shaped region. Your calculator is capable of doing both. In this example, you'll get the area of the region on the right.

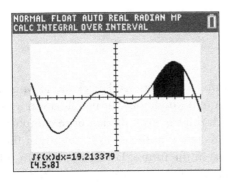

Figure 1.11 Calculating the area of a bounded area under a curve, also called a *definite integral*, using a TI-84 Plus C Silver Edition. As you can see, you get the same answer as a TI-83 Plus or TI-84 Plus (see figure 1.10).

As with the previous example, you'll start by clearing any functions you already have defined in the Y= menu. Press ⌈ Y= ⌉, move the cursor to any functions that are filled in, and press ⌈CLEAR⌉ to erase them. If you followed the instructions for the previous example, you should have already set the graph window to the calculator's defaults. If not, press ⌈ZOOM⌉ ⌈ 6 ⌉ to select the 6:ZStandard option in the Zoom menu. Returning to the Y= menu with the ⌈ Y= ⌉ key, enter the following sequence of keys with the cursor next to Y_1=: ⌈(–)⌉ ⌈XT𝜃n⌉ ⌈COS⌉ ⌈0⌉ ⌈ · ⌉ ⌈5⌉ ⌈XT𝜃n⌉ ⌈) ⌉.

This should type the expression you see on the left side in figure 1.12, ¯Xcos(0.5X). You can now press ⌈GRAPH⌉ to see the result, which will resemble the center in figure 1.12 (but without the extra text). Where you *will* get that extra text is by pressing ⌈ 2nd ⌉ ⌈TRACE⌉ to access to the Calculate menu and choosing 7:∫f(x)dx. You can move the cursor left and right along the curve with the arrow keys, but I'll ask you to type ⌈ 4 ⌉ ⌈ · ⌉ ⌈ 5 ⌉ to enter the exact lower limit, $x = 4.5$.

Press ⌈ENTER⌉, and the calculator will ask for the upper (right) limit. You can again move the cursor side to side; but you should type the exact value, ⌈ 8 ⌉, shown on the right side in figure 1.12, and press ⌈ENTER⌉. The calculator will silently divide the area into lots of tiny trapezoids, sum their individual areas, and present the result: about 19.21, as figure 1.10 and figure 1.11 show.

The method the calculator uses to perform integration, called the Trapezoid Rule, is something you might even learn to do by hand in your calculus class. Another skill your calculator can automate is the painstaking process of finding a

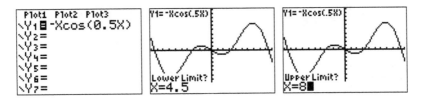

Figure 1.12 Calculating the area under a curve. On the left, entering the equation for the curve in Y_1. In the center, graphing the equation and choosing the left side of the area to be measured. On the right, choosing the right side of the area to measure. Once you choose both sides, the calculator returns the total area in that region, as shown on the right side in figure 1.10.

line that fits a collection of data points. The fifth and final example in this chapter shows you how.

1.1.5   *Fitting a line to data*

In math and especially science, you can make predictions. For example, you can figure out the equation for the acceleration of a wooden car as it rolls down a ramp or the arc of a cannonball fired across a field. You can even model more complicated situations, such as the number of people infected by a disease as it spreads or the population of the human race at specific points in the future. For these sorts of problems, you start with a bunch of data points, called *observations* or *samples*, and try to fit a line to the data to find trends or predict other data.

Consider a car driving at a steady speed down a highway. Along the road, you add students standing with stopwatches and notebooks. Each student looks at their stopwatch when the car passes and writes down the time. Later, they compare notes to compute how fast the car was going. But they're only human, so their measurements aren't perfect.

The data points they collected are shown on the left side in figure 1.13, and a graph of those points, with time on the x axis and distance on the y axis, is on the right side. In the table, L_1 is a list containing items representing numbers of seconds since the experiment began. L_2 is a list holding the number of meters between where the car started and where that student was standing (1 meter is a little over 3 feet).

You can see by glancing at figure 1.13 that the points don't form a perfectly straight line. You might be able to start at the table and see that the time measurements are spaced about 30 seconds apart, while the distances are about 600 meters apart. But you can get a much more accurate estimate than that.

ENTERING THE DATA

First, just in case you've worked with the lists on your calculator before, you'll want to start with fresh, clean lists. You'll use the ClrList command. Press (STAT) (4) to paste ClrList to the homescreen; then type (2nd) (1) (,) (2nd) (2). You'll have ClrList L_1, L_2 on the screen, so press (ENTER) to clear L_1 and L_2.

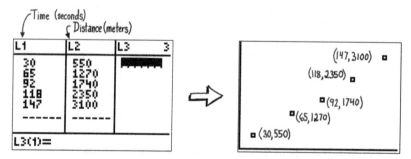

Figure 1.13   A table and graph of data points for estimating the speed of a car. Five students stood along a road, and each recorded both the time (in seconds) when the car passed them and how far (in meters) they stood from where the car started. They didn't do a perfect job, so the points aren't exactly in a straight line.

 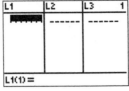

Figure 1.14 Clearing old lists and using the `SetUpEditor` command to set up the List Editor (left), and entering the List Editor (right). These are the first three steps to fitting a line to some data.

In case you've used the List Editor before, you press [STAT] to enter the Statistics menu, and in the Edit tab (that is, the first screen you see), choose 5:SetUpEditor. You'll see SetUpEditor pasted to the homescreen; press [ENTER] to run it. When it completes, it will have re-created L_1 and L_2 as empty lists and printed Done on the screen. Your screen will look a lot like the left in figure 1.14.

The next step is to enter the lists of times and distances. Go back to the Statistics menu by pressing [STAT], this time choosing 1:Edit…. You'll end up at the blank List Editor, like the right side in figure 1.14. Using the arrow and number keys, type in the five times and five distances shown in figure 1.13. Make sure your numbers match. When you have the same table, press [2nd] [MODE] to return to the homescreen.

PLOTTING THE DATA

Before you analyze this data, you probably want to plot it. Follow these steps:

1 Press [Y=] to go to the Y= menu. As in the previous examples, use the [CLEAR] key to erase any existing equations.
2 Move the flashing cursor up to the Plot1 text, and press [ENTER]. It should turn from black text on a white background to white text on a black background.
3 Press [2nd] [Y=], the Stat Plot menu, and choose option 1. Make sure Plot1 is set On by moving the cursor over On and pressing [ENTER]. Set Plot1 to the Scatter (first) type, use L_1 for the Xlist, and use L_2 for the Ylist. Figure 1.15 shows what that should look like on a TI-83 Plus, TI-83 Plus Silver Edition, TI-84 Plus, or TI-84 Plus Silver Edition.
4 Press [GRAPH]. But wait! Where is everything? The problem is that the edges of the graph are way too small, and all the points are far off the right and top edges of the screen.
5 Solution: press [ZOOM], and scroll down to 9:ZoomStat. When you press [ENTER] on it, you're brought back to the graph screen.

There are your points! As you might have expected from figure 1.13, which shows roughly what you should be seeing now, they don't exactly line up. The right side in figure 1.15 is what you'll see once you fit a line to the data.

But what is the best way to fit that line to the data? Let's perform the final step.

FINDING A LINE OF BEST FIT

Your calculator can fit all kinds of lines—from straight (linear) lines to polynomial curves to logarithmic and exponential curves. It's up to you to give the calculator a hint about what sort of fit it should try. Here, because it looks like the data almost

Figure 1.15   On the left, setting up a Stat Plot for display on your calculator's graph screen. The result of turning this feature on was shown on the right in figure 1.13. In the center, the numbers calculated from linear regression (fitting a straight line to a data set) on a MathPrint calculator. On the right, that line, Y₁=21.5X-141.7, graphed over the five data points it was fit to. Pretty close!

defines a straight line, we'll try *linear regression*, which means to try to fit a straight line to the data.

Press 2nd MODE to return once more to the homescreen. Press STAT for the Statistics menu, but this time press the ▶ key to get to the Calc tab. Choose 4:Lin-Reg(ax+b):

- On some calculators (the non-MathPrint ones), you'll see LinReg(ax+b) pasted to the homescreen; just press ENTER. Your calculator will assume that you mean to perform regression with *x* values in L₁ and *y* values in L₂ unless you tell it otherwise. You should get a=21.5 and b=⁻141.7, meaning the best-fit line is y=21.5x-141.7. Want to graph it? Press Y= and then VARS 5 ▶ ▶ 1 to paste the RegEQ (the regression equation) into Y₁. Finally, press GRAPH, and you'll see the best-fit line graphed over the points. The right screenshot in figure 1.15 is the result you'll be looking at. If you have a TI-84 Plus C Silver Edition, you'll see the result shown in figure 1.16 instead.

- On MathPrint calculators, you'll see another menu when you choose 4:Lin-Reg(ax+b). Leave the defaults (that is, don't change any of the options the calculator fills in for you), move the cursor to Calculate, and press ENTER. You'll get a slightly fancier display of the resulting line of best fit than the non-MathPrint folks, as in the center in figure 1.15, but you should still get a=21.5 and b=⁻141.7. To graph y = 21.5x – 141.7 quickly, press Y= and then 5 ▶ ▶ 1 to paste the RegEQ into Y₁. Press GRAPH to see this best-fit line graphed over the data points. The right screenshot in figure 1.15 (or figure 1.16 for a TI-84 Plus C Silver Edition) is still the result you'll be looking at.

FIX YOUR GRAPH SETTINGS   To prevent confusion when you go back to using your calculator for normal graphing, be sure to turn off the Stat Plot. Press Y= again, move the cursor up to Plot1, and press ENTER to turn it back to black text on a white background. Lists L₁ and L₂ are still in your calculator's memory, but they take up little space. You can delete them if you want to.

Now you've seen five different examples of what your calculator can do, ranging from arithmetic to calculus to statistics. Throughout this book, you'll learn many more cool

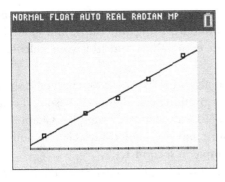

Figure 1.16   Fitting a line to a set of five points on the TI-84 Plus C Silver Edition. Compare this to the right side in figure 1.15, which shows the same result on any other TI-83 Plus or TI-84 Plus–family calculator. The only differences are color and higher resolution.

things it can do, applicable to your classes and to life in general. Before we dive into the material, let me tell you more about what exactly this book will teach you and why you need it to accompany you on your journey with your calculator.

1.2 *This book and your calculator*

Your calculator is a powerful and versatile tool. It's basically a pocket computer that you can use for many math and science classes, for financial calculations, and else-where in your life. But if you don't have the time or the experience to experiment and discover all of its features on your own, you might be missing out on a lot of the stuff it can do. I'd like to step in as your guide, showing you the many things your calculator can do.

In this section, I'll tell you about how your calculator can help make your math and science classes simpler and more understandable. I'll mention how this book will guide you toward using each of those features. I'll also explain that I don't assume you know anything about graphing calculators when you start reading. I'll talk about which calculators this book covers and, if you don't yet have one, which one you should get. Let's take a look at what your calculator can do for your classes.

1.2.1 *Your calculator, a multipurpose tool*

As you go through school, you'll encounter many classes that require math skills. Math classes are the obvious ones, but there are also science classes, finance and eco-nomics classes, computer classes, and more. Your calculator can help you learn more and learn faster in each of these types of courses. I'll take you through each of them and what your calculator and this book can do together to help you. This book is *not* a math book and isn't an adequate substitute for a class or textbook in each subject. But it *is* a complete calculator reference that can help you understand subjects better as you explore them on your calculator.

Math classes range from the simplest arithmetic up through complex college cal-culus and further. Your graphing calculator can do arithmetic from $2 + 2$ to advanced matrix math, as well as algebra, trigonometry, statistics, calculus, and more. This book is the perfect accompaniment to each subject:

- *Arithmetic*—Chapter 2 will teach you how to do basic calculations on your calculator, including arithmetic, exponents, using functions, and changing the modes that control how you enter expressions and how your calculator displays answers.

- *Algebra*—Your calculator can solve algebraic expressions; chapter 2 shows you how. Graphing is one of the things graphing calculators do best, and chapter 3 details creating and examining graphs with plenty of examples. Chapter 4 introduces how your calculator can store and use named variables, something you saw in the Quadratic Formula example in section 1.1.2.

- *Precalculus*—First you'll see how to use lists and matrices in chapter 4. Next are different types of graphing, including Polar and Parametric modes, in chapter 5. Chapter 6 fills in the remaining precalculus odds and ends you might want to know how to work with, from complex numbers and trigonometry to limits and logarithms.

- *Calculus*—The TI-83 Plus/TI-84 Plus can't do symbolic differentiation and integration, but as you saw in the example in section 1.1.4, your calculator can do numeric differentiation and integration. Chapter 7 is a methodical introduction to how to use these features and how they can help you find things like the slope, minima, maxima, and inflection points of functions.

- *Statistics*—One of the biggest differences between the TI-83 Plus/TI-84 Plus calculators and earlier graphing calculators is that the newer ones can manipulate statistics. The example in section 1.1.5 showed you how to enter lists of data, fit a line, and graph it; chapter 8 will show you lots more. You'll learn how to calculate properties of data like the average, mean, median, and maximum on your calculator and how to draw all different kinds of plots using data, and you'll see the types of regression (line-fitting) the calculator can do.

- *Probability*—You can calculate probability distribution functions (PDFs) and cumulative distribution functions (CDFs) with your calculator, as well as generate random numbers and work with combinatorics. Chapter 9 explains it all with plenty of examples.

- *Finance*—An often-overlooked function of your calculator, the financial tools can be used to calculate interest, depreciation, and much more. The tools and illustrative problems are introduced in chapter 10.

- *Programming*—Your calculator is such a powerful programming tool that I've written a whole book about it. You can write little math programs to help you check homework answers, test answers, and SAT questions. Although one chapter is only enough for a brief introduction, chapter 11 will give you a good framework for exploring programming on your own.

- *Physics*—Depending on what level of physics you're learning, you may need algebra and graphing to study kinematics and projectile motion, and you can use calculus to simplify solutions. Chapters 3, 4, 7, and others will help you there.

Once again, although this book will succinctly teach you the menus and keystrokes to use for each of your calculator's features, it also provides tons of illustrated examples to drive the skills home and make you feel more comfortable using your TI-83 Plus/ TI-84 Plus.

Now that you know what this book can offer you, I'll tell you what you need to bring with you to use this book to its full potential.

1.2.2 *What you'll need*

What do you need to use this book? The shorter answer is that you need almost nothing, other than your brain, this book, and a graphing calculator. The slightly longer answer is that you shouldn't try to use this book as a math textbook, because it isn't one. I do my best to refresh your memory about details of the math you're applying, as you saw in the five examples in section 1.1. But we'll be covering such a broad swath of math, science, and other subjects that it would be impossible to teach them all from scratch in one or even two or three books. Therefore, I strongly recommend that you use this book while you take the relevant courses and ideally pair it with the textbooks that are teaching you the particular math or science material.

That's not to say you can't use this book as an independent reference. If you're already well into high school or college, or no matter where you are in life, a graphing calculator is still an important tool. As long as you have a vague recollection of your schooling, you should be able to follow most of the lessons and examples in this book. Even if you aren't that far into your classes, all the examples in this book are laid out in detail from start to finish and don't require that you have to solve anything on your own to get the same answers I get.

The other important prerequisite is a graphing calculator. The TI-84 Plus Silver Edition, TI-83 Plus, and TI-84 Plus C Silver Edition all appear on the front page of this book, and they're three of the many calculators this book can help you use. Table 1.1 and its accompanying calculator pictures show all the graphing calculators you can use with this book. Every example in this book and every calculator feature taught will work on the TI-83 Plus, TI-83 Plus Silver Edition, TI-84 Plus, TI-84 Plus Silver Edition, and TI-84 Plus C Silver Edition. Almost everything will also work on the TI-83 and the TI-82 Stats.fr calculators, and most even apply to the TI-82.

If you don't already have a calculator, you should really buy one before continuing with this book! If you can afford it, the TI-84 Plus Silver Edition (black-and-white screen) or TI-84 Plus C Silver Edition (color screen) is your best choice, but any of the calculators in the TI-83 Plus and TI-84 Plus series can perform all the functions discussed in this book. If you prefer the MathPrint features, which I'll tell you more about in section 1.3, you need a TI-84 Plus, TI-84 Plus Silver Edition, or TI-84 Plus C Silver Edition calculator. There are also many emulators that let you use a virtual calculator on your computer, but they all legally require a ROM image from your real calculator to function. I prefer Wabbitemu (http://wabbit.codeplex.com/),

Table 1.1   Calculators you can use with this book

TI-83 Plus, TI-83 Plus Silver Edition	TI-84 Plus, TI-84 Plus Silver Edition	TI-84 Plus C Silver Edition	TI-82, TI-83, TI-82 Stats.fr
Introduced in 1999	Introduced in 2004	Introduced in 2013	Introduced in 1993–2002
Graphing, math, statistics, probability, finance, calculus features. Upgradeable operating system and Flash applications.	Adds a fast processor and more Flash memory to the TI-83 Plus series. Only calculators that can run Math-Print operating systems.	First color-screen TI-84 Plus model.	Similar in features to the TI-83 Plus but lacking Flash applications and an upgradeable operating system.

which runs under Windows, or jsTIfied (http://www.cemetech.net/projects/jstified/), an online emulator.

We'll soon start scrutinizing your calculator, and you'll learn the basics of it for simple arithmetic and math. Before we do, I want to teach you the difference between MathPrint (MP) and non-MathPrint operating systems and how that difference will affect how you use this book.

1.3   *MathPrint vs. non-MathPrint calculators*

From the 1990s until 2010, entering math on TI graphing calculators like the TI-82, TI-83, TI-83 Plus, and TI-84 Plus stayed basically the same. All these calculators have a home-screen 16 characters wide and 8 characters tall. On each one, you entered math expressions at the left side of the screen, and the results of your calculations appeared on the right side of the screen. More important, you entered every expression as a straight line of numbers and symbols, regardless of whether it included fractions, square roots, integrals, or matrices. You needed to carefully count opening and closing parentheses to make sure you didn't make a mistake.

> **OPERATING SYSTEM**   The operating system (OS) is the built-in software on your calculator that makes it do math, plot graphs, and even show text on the screen. Without the OS, your calculator would be just a hunk of plastic and circuits.

In February 2010, TI introduced something new, called MathPrint. An operating system upgrade for the TI-84 Plus, TI-84 Plus Silver Edition, and TI-84 Plus C Silver Edition calculators (and only those calculators), MathPrint makes the equations that you

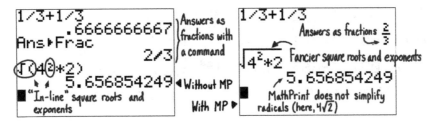

Figure 1.17 Working with fractions, square roots, and powers (exponents). The left side shows the same operations without MathPrint that the right side shows with MathPrint.

enter look more like what you might see in your math textbook. For example, as you can see on the right side in figure 1.17, now square-root symbols extend over the entire contents of the radical. On older calculator operating systems, you enclosed the contents in parentheses.

Figure 1.17 also shows how exponents got fancier, appearing above and to the side of the expression. Fractions now look more like fractions, as illustrated in figure 1.17 and especially on the right in figure 1.18.

It's easier to see what you're doing while entering matrices, demonstrated in figure 1.19.

Figure 1.18 Several screenshots of MathPrint-only features. On the left, pressing [2nd] [Y=] through [2nd] [TRACE] to access context menus. In the center, one of the new statistics wizards for regression. On the right, some of the most complex stuff you can do with MathPrint, including fancy fractions, absolute values, integrals, square roots, exponents, and fancy equation entry. You can still enter the same equations on non-MathPrint operating systems and graph them, but they won't look as fancy.

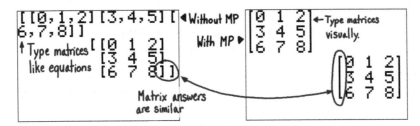

Figure 1.19 Entering matrices without MathPrint (left) and with MathPrint (right). The display of the matrix answer is similar with and without the MathPrint features, except for slightly cleaner square brackets in the MathPrint version. It's easier (but slightly slower) to keep track of the row and column for which you're entering a number when using the MathPrint version.

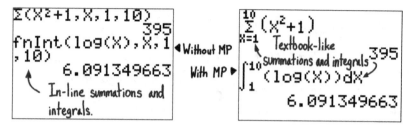

Figure 1.20 **The differences between summations and integrals when performed without MathPrint (left) and with MathPrint (right) on a TI-84 Plus or TI-84 Plus Silver Edition. Although the non-MathPrint version is slightly faster to type, you need to remember the correct order for the arguments to the Σ() and fnInt() functions. With the MathPrint version, entering summations and integrals is more like writing them on paper.**

You don't have to memorize the order of arguments (or parameters) to summations and integrals, as shown in figure 1.20.

The goal of MathPrint operating systems is to make entering equations and matrices easier and more intuitive. By making what you see on your calculator screen closer to what you see in your textbook and what your teacher writes on the board, TI hoped to make your calculator easier to use. But MathPrint has a few caveats:

- It has more options to configure, all found in the Mode menu.
- It can only run on TI-84 Plus, TI-84 Plus Silver Edition, and TI-84 Plus C Silver Edition calculators.
- It was slightly rushed, and if you get into graphing calculator programming, you'll discover several annoying bugs and quirks in the MathPrint operating systems. If you just use MathPrint for math and science class, you won't run across these bugs.

This book will cover both the MathPrint and non-MathPrint ways to do things. When you're learning something new and your screen looks different depending on whether you have a MathPrint operating system, I'm always careful to point out the differences and show you screenshots of both versions, and you'll see the MP symbol in the margin. The sidebars that succinctly explain the steps for each new skill always clarify differences between MathPrint and non-MathPrint instructions. The only remaining task for you is to decide whether you want to use MathPrint:

- *Can I use MathPrint?* If you have a TI-84 Plus, TI-84 Plus Silver Edition, or TI-84 Plus C Silver Edition, you can use MathPrint. If you have any other calculator model, you can't.

- *Am I using MathPrint now?* If you don't have a TI-84 Plus, TI-84 Plus Silver Edition, or TI-84 Plus C Silver Edition, you're not. If you have one of those three models, though, you might be. Press (2nd) (MODE) to quit to the homescreen, and then press (2nd) (+) (1) to get to the About section of the Memory menu. If your OS version has an MP suffix, like 2.53MP or 2.55MP, or it's version 4.0 or higher, then you're running a MathPrint operating system. But even if you have a Math-Print operating system, you might not have MathPrint enabled. Press (MODE) and scroll down until you see MATHPRINT CLASSIC. If MATHPRINT is highlighted (white text inside a black box), you have it enabled. If CLASSIC is highlighted, Math-Print is disabled.

- *How can I enable MathPrint?* If you have a MathPrint operating system installed (see previous entry), you can press (MODE), scroll down (or up) to MATHPRINT, and press (ENTER). If you don't have a MathPrint operating system installed, you need to install one to use MathPrint. If you want to *disable* MathPrint, press (MODE), move the cursor down to CLASSIC (on the second page of the menu), and press (ENTER).

- *How do I upgrade to a MathPrint OS?* If you have a TI-84 Plus or TI-84 Plus Silver Edition, install TI-Connect from http://education.ti.com on your computer, plug your calculator into your computer with a mini-USB cable, and then run the TI OS Downloader application. It will provide you with further instructions. Other calculator models can't be upgraded to run MathPrint. TI-84 Plus C Silver Edition calculators always come with MathPrint operating systems.

TI-84 PLUS C SILVER EDITION: CHECK MATHPRINT MODE   If you have a TI-84 Plus C Silver Edition, check the status bar (the gray area at the top of the screen). MP means you're in MathPrint mode, and CL means you're in Classic (MathPrint disabled) mode. Chapter 12 explains more about what the status bar shows.

The upshot of all this is that you can choose to enter equations the newer, fancier way, or you can use the older, established way. You may want to try both and choose for yourself, or your teacher may tell you which mode to use. Throughout this book, I'll occasionally point back to this section to refresh your memory about how to turn MathPrint on and off.

Now that you've learned about what your calculator can do and how this book can help, I'll leave you with a few final thoughts before we dive into the first complete steps in using your calculator.

1.4   *Summary*

In this chapter, you got a cross-sectional view of your calculator's power and how this book can unlock it. You saw five examples from geometry, algebra, trigonometry, calculus, and statistics that covered a range of things you might want to use your calculator for. I discussed the many different calculators this book will help you use, and you learned how to use this book:

- To prevent confusion as you venture into the next chapter, you now also know what MathPrint is, and you should be clear whether your calculator has it.
- If you don't yet have a calculator, I recommend that you get one (or an emulator with a legal ROM image), as discussed in section 1.2.2, before you continue.

- Remember that you can use this book as an instant reference, finding what you need in the index or table of contents and jumping to that section, or you can read it chapter by chapter.

In chapter 2, you'll officially meet your calculator, including learning how to use the keyboard, how to care for the device, how to do basic math on it, and how to solve simple algebraic equations. I look forward to taking this journey with you, so let's get started!

Get started
with your calculator

2

This chapter covers

- How to type on your calculator, do basic math, and navigate menus
- Functions and arguments and how to use them
- Changing calculation modes
- Using your calculator's equation-solving tools

Your graphing calculator is first and foremost a calculator. It can graph, calculate statistics and calculus, and run programs, but its primary job is to be great at math. The core of your calculator is the homescreen, the main area where you type math equations and read results. In this chapter, you'll learn about performing math on the homescreen. I'll teach you everything from finding the results of simple arithmetic like $2 + 2$, to using mathematical functions like sine, e^x, and absolute values, to solving an algebraic equation for an unknown variable.

In chapter 1, you saw five complete but specific examples of math, graphing, and statistics on your calculator. I walked you through the explanations, telling you exactly what buttons to press and what to do if you encountered any problems. This chapter will start out the same way. You'll learn the simplest things, such as turning on your calculator and changing the brightness of the screen. You'll learn how to use the keypad (keyboard) and what the (2nd) and (ALPHA) modifier keys do. I'll ease you into simple and later more advanced math, with plenty of examples sprinkled among the new skills. I'll also point out any important differences between skills on MathPrint and non-MathPrint calculators.

As we get into arithmetic and math on the homescreen, I'll gradually assume that you remember more and more. Don't worry: the previous content will always be there, and the vital skills are encapsulated in sidebars. If you get stuck, relax and flip back to the section that explains what you missed, or check the index in the back of the book for any relevant entries. One of the great things about learning from a book is that you can go at your own pace, and you can easily review material that you feel rusty on.

Later in the chapter, I'll show you some of the mathematical functions your calculator can apply for you, from trigonometry to exponents to roots. We'll finish the chapter with the often-overlooked Solver feature, which can help you solve algebraic equations for an unknown variable. By the end of this chapter, you'll be comfortable with basic math on your calculator, and you'll have a more intuitive feel for typing and navigating through menus.

We'll start with a few basics that aren't about doing math on your calculator. You should know how to change your calculator's batteries, reset it to factory defaults, and a few other housekeeping details.

2.1   *Before you begin*

Like any piece of technology, a graphing calculator requires that you know a few skills not directly related to what it does. For example, to use your laptop, you need to know how to run programs, but you also need to know how to plug in its charger and where the power button is. For your calculator, you need to know how to change the batteries, turn it on, and reset it. We don't need to spend much time on these straightforward tasks, but they're important to know nonetheless.

 TI-84+CSE'S RECHARGEABLE BATTERY   The TI-84 Plus C Silver Edition doesn't take AAA batteries. Instead, it has a rechargeable battery, so you need to plug it into a computer or charger via USB to charge it.

First, your calculator needs power to turn on. Unlike a cheap four-function solar calculator, which is so simple that it can run off power sucked from the ambient light in a room, your graphing calculator needs four AAA batteries. They must be installed with the correct polarity, and they should all be equally fresh. You can use either alkaline or rechargeable batteries; alkalines tend to work better.

To install the batteries, flip over your calculator, and look for the latch in the middle of the case. If you pull the latch down and out, you'll remove the battery cover and expose the battery compartment, as shown in figure 2.1. When you change the batteries, make sure the new batteries have the negative (flat) end against the springs in the compartment and the positive (bumpy) end against the flat pieces of metal.

Figure 2.1   The battery compartments of TI graphing calculators, from left to right: the TI-84 Plus Silver Edition, the TI-84 Plus, and the TI-83 Plus. Each calculator uses four AAA batteries to power the device, as well as a small coin cell battery (the silver circle in the left calculator, and under a small cover on the other two calculators) that keeps you from losing your settings while you're replacing the main batteries. The TI-84 Plus C Silver Edition has an internal rechargeable battery instead of AAAs.

There are also diagrams of the batteries at the bottom of the compartment to help guide you.

Your calculator will make a fuss any time the batteries are starting to get low, as illustrated on the left side of figure 2.2. If you ignore the suggestion to change the batteries long enough, the calculator will begin showing the message on the right side in figure 2.2 and will force you to replace the batteries before you do things like archive programs or install Applications. In the worst case, your calculator might not even turn on until you replace the batteries.

The round silver backup battery shown in figure 2.1, and present in every TI-83 Plus and TI-84 Plus, can last a decade or more. It isn't used during normal calculator operation, but it is used to keep your settings and programs safe while you change the main batteries. If you decide to change it, you'll have to unscrew a single Phillips-style screw and lift off the backup battery's cover. Pop the battery out and replace it; the TI-83 Plus series takes a CR1616 or CR1620 battery, and the TI-84 Plus series takes an SR44 battery.

Check out the "Essential basic calculator key sequences" sidebar for a summary of the keys to turn the calculator on and off and change the screen darkness.

A final introductory skill you should know is how to reset your calculator. You won't need to do this unless your settings become discombobulated and you can't figure out how to fix them, but it's a good thing to know. Resetting RAM sets things

```
Your batteries
are low.

Recommend
change of
batteries.
```

```
Batteries
are low.
Change is
required.
```

Figure 2.2   When your calculator's batteries start dying, you'll get a message like the one on the left, urging you to replace the batteries. When they get too low for the calculator to work properly, the screen will switch to the message on the right. Just turn off the calculator, replace all four AAAs with new ones, and turn it on.

Essential basic calculator key sequences

Remember these four important keystrokes, used to turn your calculator on and off and change the contrast (darkness/brightness) of the screen. If you turn the calculator on and the screen is still blank, try making the screen darker; the contents might just be too light to read:

(ON) —Turn on your calculator.

(2nd) (ON) —Turn off your calculator.

(2nd) (▲) —Make the screen darker (hold the arrow key).

(2nd) (▼) —Make the screen lighter (hold the arrow key).

like the graph settings and MathPrint modes back to the defaults that were set at the factory. It erases any variables, history, and programs stored in RAM, but it doesn't erase archived programs and apps in the Apps menu. The steps are simple:

1   Enter the Memory menu (shown on the left in figure 2.3) by pressing (2nd) (+). Use the arrow keys to move the cursor down to 7↓Reset... and press (ENTER), or just press (7).

2   You arrive in the Reset menu, shown in the center in figure 2.3. It has three tabs: RAM, Archive, and All. In most cases, you'll want to choose Defaults... or All RAM... under the RAM tab. If you just want to reset graph and math settings, choose 2: Defaults.... If you also want to delete history, variables, and programs, choose 1: All RAM.... Apps, special types of programs found under the (APPS) key, are preserved across RAM resets.

3   If the calculator asks for confirmation, which looks like the right side in figure 2.3, choose 2:Reset to perform the actual reset. You can also choose 1:No or press (CLEAR) if you change your mind at the last minute.

Now you know how to change your calculator's batteries, turn it on and off, make the screen darker and lighter, and reset it to factory settings. That's slightly boring but important background information that will become second nature to you as you proceed, if it's not already. With those housekeeping details out of the way, let's push onward to the real meat of this chapter: using your calculator to perform calculations.

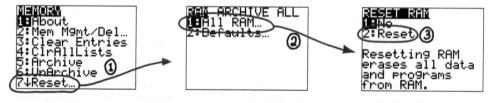

Figure 2.3 Resetting your calculator. This restores it to the state it was in when it left the factory, except that your Apps and any archived programs/variables are still there. If you *really* want to wipe it clean, press the left arrow twice in the RAM/Archive/All menu to choose ALL, and proceed from there.

2.2 *Performing basic calculations*

From your graphing calculator's name, it should come as no surprise that it's great at being a calculator. If you've ever used a four-function calculator—the simplest kind that can only do addition, subtraction, multiplication, and division—then performing those same operations on your TI-83 Plus or TI-84 Plus should be relatively easy for you. As you get into more complex operations like logarithms, exponents, square roots, and functions, you may be a bit more baffled. But that's why we're going through this together!

> **THE HOMESCREEN**   The main screen of your calculator that you see when you turn it on, the space where you perform calculations, is called the *home-screen*. If you're in menus, on the graph screen, or in the program or list editor, ⌈2nd⌉ ⌈MODE⌉ (Quit) quits back to the homescreen. Think of it as your computer's desktop.

Performing relatively simple calculations is the easiest thing you can do with your calculator and will probably be what you use it for most often over its lifetime. Even though the device you hold in your hand is essentially a complete computer, capable of running complex programs and graphing convoluted functions, its portability makes it an apt choice for day-to-day math.

In this section, we'll proceed from example to example as you pick up the skills for simple math on your calculator. We'll go through

- Simple arithmetic
- Using grouping parentheses
- Calculating exponents
- Taking the square root or *n*th root of a number
- Using Ans to continue a calculation

Let's jump right in with the first of these five examples, using simple arithmetic.

Calculations in a nutshell
- Type your calculation; then press ⌈ENTER⌉ to get the answer. ⌈ENTER⌉ is the equivalent to = on simpler calculators.
- You can clear a line and start over with ⌈CLEAR⌉.
- You can go to a previous equation to modify or recalculate it with ⌈▲⌉ (MathPrint only) or ⌈2nd⌉ ⌈ENTER⌉ (all calculators).
- Delete characters from anywhere in an equation with ⌈DEL⌉, move the cursor around with ⌈◄⌉ and ⌈►⌉, and insert characters in the middle of a line by pressing ⌈2nd⌉ ⌈DEL⌉. Normally, typing in the middle of a line will overwrite the characters that are already there, not push them over.

Any function that starts with an opening parenthesis must also have a closing parenthesis (with exceptions that would only muddy this explanation).

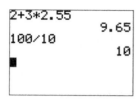

Figure 2.4   Two simple arithmetic expressions calculated on a TI-84 Plus calculator. The first consists of addition and multiplication and includes a decimal. The second is integer division.

2.2.1   Simple arithmetic

Forgive me if this part is obvious to you: I want every reader to start on the same mental page, and for some, these skills may not be intuitive. Glance for a second at figure 2.4, which shows the two calculations we'll perform in this section. The first is 2+3*2.55, which the calculator says is 9.65. If you're familiar with PEMDAS (parentheses, exponents, multiplication, division, addition, subtraction), formally called the order of operations, you should know that multiplication must be done before addition. In this case, 3×2.55 is 7.65, and $7.65 + 2$ is 9.65, just as the calculator says.

> **NEGATIVE NUMBERS**   On your calculator, negation and subtraction are not the same. To subtract, press ⎽ on the right side of the keypad, near the other three arithmetic operators. The negative sign before a number like ⁻3 or ⁻402.1 is a smaller minus; you type it with the ⎽ key.

To enter this equation on your calculator, use the number keys plus the arithmetic operators on the right side of the keyboard. Although your calculator's multiplication key looks like ⊗, it prints a * character to represent it on the screen. Likewise, the division key looks like ÷ but prints a / character. The sequence 2+3*2.55 corresponds to the keys ② ⊕ ③ ⊗ ② ⊙ ⑤ ⑤, as you might have guessed.

Press (ENTER), and the result appears: 9.65. If you get an ERR:SYNTAX message, then you made a typo. Whenever you type an expression that doesn't make any mathematical sense, like 2+*4 or 5/, your calculator will show an ERR:SYNTAX message. Appendix C explains more about troubleshooting.

> **PEMDAS**   Your calculator obeys the correct arithmetic order of operations, also called PEMDAS (parentheses, exponents, multiplication, division, addition, subtraction). This means it first simplifies everything inside parentheses down to a single number, then applies exponents, then performs all multiplication and division, and finally performs all addition and subtraction. In the end it simplifies a whole numerical expression down to a single number.

How about the second operation, dividing 100 by 10? As you might expect, the result is 10. Type ① ⓪ ⓪ ÷ ① ⓪, press (ENTER), and there's your answer, 10. So far, so good? Now let's talk more about PEMDAS and parentheses.

2.2.2   Dividing sums: demonstrating the importance of parentheses

In your math classes, you may have learned when to use parentheses in mathematical expressions. Long story short, they change the order of operations (see the "PEMDAS"

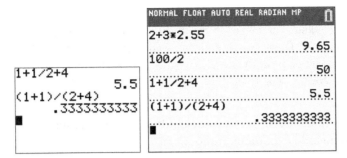

Figure 2.5 Why is it important to tell your calculator exactly what you mean? Because of PEMDAS (order of operations), the calculator interprets 1 + 1/2 + 4 as 1 + (1/2) + 4, so parentheses properly group things. The left side shows a TI-83 Plus or TI-84 Plus, and the right side shows the same operations on a TI-84 Plus C Silver Edition.

callout) and group operations together. Normally, the order of operations dictates that multiplication comes before addition, so 2 + 3 × 2 = 2 + 6 = 8. If you want to do the addition first, you need to group it, like (2 + 3) × 2 = 5 × 2 = 10.

One particular place where parentheses are important and often overlooked is in division. Hopefully you'd agree with me that 1 + 1 = 2 and that 2 + 4 = 6. If you saw the division problem 1 + 1/2 + 4, you might calculate it as 1 + (1/2) + 4 (which is 5½ or 5.5), or you might ask me if it should have been written (1 + 1)/(2 + 4) = 1/3 (or 0.333). Your calculator won't hesitate. It will confidently assume that you remember PEMDAS and produce the answer 5.5; check out figure 2.5 for the proof. You must be very clear about telling your calculator what you mean: the only downside of using excessive grouping parentheses is more typing, whereas if you omit necessary parentheses, you risk getting the wrong answer.

Figure 2.5 shows 1 + 1/2 + 4 and (1 + 1)/(2 + 4). Just as we discussed a moment ago, you get a different answer depending on whether you include the parentheses. Try some similar calculations on your own, with and without grouping parentheses, and notice the differences. The lesson is to be careful to keep the order of operations in mind when typing in calculations, or you may not get the right answers.

Answers as fractions

Your calculator prefers to display all answers as decimals. But it can also try to simplify them to fractions for you; depending on whether you're using MathPrint, you'll go about it different ways.

On any calculator, MathPrint or not, enter your equation as usual and press (ENTER). If a decimal appears at the right edge of the screen that you want to convert to a fraction, press (MATH) to open the Math menu and select 1:▶Frac. Ans▶Frac will be pasted to the homescreen; press (ENTER) to generate the fraction. If no fraction appears, then your calculator can't figure out a fractional equivalent.

Have a MathPrint calculator, and want to make your calculator always display fractions instead of decimals? Get to the Mode menu by pressing (MODE), scroll down until you see the ANSWERS: line, move the cursor over to FRAC, and press (ENTER). To undo this later, switch ANSWERS: back to AUTO or DEC.

Let's now move on from basic arithmetic to a slightly more challenging task: performing calculations that include exponents and powers.

2.2.3 Using exponents

Beyond simple arithmetic, one of the mathematical operations you'll use in many subjects is raising a number to a power, called an *exponent*. Your calculator can raise any number (or expression) to any power. Check out figure 2.6 for some examples.

Using exponents

To type an exponent, you type the number to raise, press (∧), and then press the power to raise it to. If the exponent is an expression instead of a number, you might want to wrap it in parentheses.

For the first line in figure 2.6, to raise 2 to the 8th power, press (2)(∧)(8). On non-MathPrint calculators, you can then immediately continue the expression if you have more to type. For example, if you enter 2^8, you get 256; if you enter 2^8+1, you get 257. Notice that this is (2^8)+1, rather than 2^(8+1), which would be 512! Once again, parentheses are important, and when in doubt, use them too much rather than too little.

On MathPrint calculators, pressing the exponent key ((∧)) moves the cursor to the top of the current line and makes it smaller, so everything you type is part of the exponent from that point onward. To type $2^8 + 1$, you have to press (2)(∧)(8)(▶)(+)(1), as shown in figure 2.7. Pressing the right-arrow key ((▶)) makes you leave the exponent-entry field with the small cursor and return to entering normal-size, non-exponent characters.

Figure 2.6 also demonstrates a special key, (x^2). When you want to square a number, you don't have to press (∧)(2). Instead, type the number or equation that you want to square and then press (x^2), which will insert the squared symbol ^{2} at the cursor. You also need to be careful with powers, negative numbers, and parentheses. If

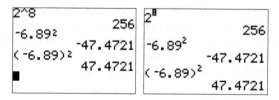

Figure 2.6 Using exponents (powers) on a normal calculator (left) and on a MathPrint calculator (right). The answers are the same in both cases; the only differences are whether exponents appear to be above the number they're raising.

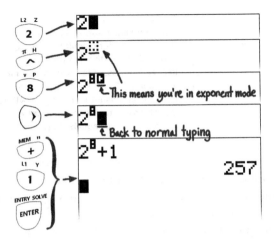

Figure 2.7 Typing an exponent on a MathPrint calculator. You enter exponent-entry mode by pressing the ⌃ key and leave it by pressing the ▶ key. This doesn't apply to non-MathPrint calculators.

you type a negative number and then raise it to a power, like ⁻3^5 or ⁻6.89², you may think you're raising the full number ⁻3 or ⁻6.89 to that power. Not so! Instead, the calculator will raise 3 to the 5th power or square 6.89 and then negate the result. This will give you the wrong answer (or at least not the answer you expect) in most cases. Keep the following in mind:

- To raise an entire number to a power, including the negative sign, wrap the number in parentheses and then add the exponent. For example:

  (⁻6.89)²

- If you want to negate the result of raising a number to a power, leave off the parentheses (or enclose the exponent operation in parentheses). Both of these will work:

  ⁻(4.5^4)
  ⁻4.5^4

Don't forget about the differences between odd and even exponents. If you're using odd exponents, you can use or omit the parentheses, because $-(x^y)=(-x)^y$ for odd exponents. If you want a good rule of thumb: when in doubt, use parentheses to make the order of operations explicit.

Now that you know exponents and arithmetic, we'll move on to taking a square root or nth root.

2.2.4 Roots of numbers

Taking the roots of numbers is another important basic math skill that your calculator can do well. You'll most often take the square root of a number, but you can also do cube roots and nth roots. As with exponents, this looks a little different on MathPrint and non-MathPrint calculators, but the steps are mostly the same.

Figure 2.8 demonstrates taking a square root (top line) and 4th root (second line) on a graphing calculator. The left screenshot is from a TI-84+SE with a MathPrint OS,

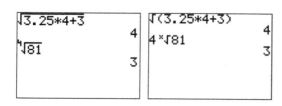

Figure 2.8   Square roots and *n*th roots on a graphing calculator. The left screenshot is from a MathPrint calculator; the right screenshot is without MathPrint. The first line in each screenshot is taking the square root of 16, because 3¼ × 4 + 3 = 16. The second line in each screenshot is finding the 4th root of 81, which means the number that when raised to the 4th power equals 81 (namely, 3).

whereas the right screenshot is without MathPrint. I'll tell you how to type the square root symbol and the *n*th root symbol, but this time, I'll assume you know how to type the expression 3.25*4+3 and the numbers 4 and 81. If you're having trouble, try reviewing the examples we've looked at up to this point.

The square root symbol is the ⬡2nd⬡ function of the ⬡x^2⬡ key, so to type it, press ⬡2nd⬡ ⬡x^2⬡. You'll notice that the square root symbol (called a *radical*) is above the ⬡x^2⬡ key in the same color as the ⬡2nd⬡ key, a hint that you press and release ⬡2nd⬡ before pressing and releasing ⬡x^2⬡ to type that symbol. On non-MathPrint OSs, you type the contents of the radical symbol (what you want to take the square root of) and then press ⬡) ⬡. The calculator takes the square root of only the part enclosed in the parentheses.

On a MathPrint calculator, typing square roots is a lot like typing exponents. Once you type the square root symbol, the radical keeps extending over everything you type until you press ⬡▶⬡, which is just like closing the parentheses on non-MathPrint calculators. You can then continue to type other parts of the equation that are outside the radical, if any, or press ⬡ENTER⬡ to get the result.

Figure 2.8 also shows calculating a 4th root, but you can take any *n*th root. Type the index of the radical (which you might also know as the *degree*), in this case 4. Then, go to the Math menu and choose 5:ˣ√. Type the contents of the radical, and then, as before, end the radical. On a MathPrint calculator, press ⬡▶⬡; otherwise, continue typing or press ⬡ENTER⬡. Notice that unlike the square root symbol, you don't need parentheses (but as always, by all means use them to avoid ambiguity!).

A final example in our parade of homescreen math immersion: let's look at what Ans is and how to use it.

2.2.5   *Continuing a calculation: Ans*

Your calculator has a special variable called Ans. In a nutshell, this is a little bin where the calculator puts the result of the last calculation you did. Type 2+2 and press ⬡ENTER⬡, and the calculator will put 4 into Ans. Any time you do a calculation and an answer appears in the right margin of the screen, that number (or list or matrix, as you'll see in chapter 4) is put into Ans. Why do you care? Because you can reuse the result of the last calculation without having to manually type it.

Say you're calculating an average. As you probably know, an average is the sum of the numbers you want to average divided by how many numbers you have. If you want

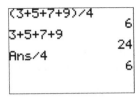

Figure 2.9 Calculating an average in a single line (top), or summing the numbers to be averaged and then dividing by 4 on another line. By pressing (÷) at the beginning of a new line, you force the calculator to automatically insert Ans before the division symbol.

to average 3, 5, 7, and 9, you could enter (3+5+7+9)/4 on your calculator, using the parentheses for grouping. To save yourself using the parentheses, though, you can use Ans. Figure 2.9 shows the two methods.

On the top line, you put the sum of the numbers to be averaged between (and) and then divide that by 4, all in one line. As expected, the average is 6. The second and third lines in figure 2.9 show an alternative. You type the sum (without parentheses) and press (ENTER). At the beginning of the next line, you press (÷) (4). When you press the division key, the calculator types Ans/, automatically recognizing that you need something to divide by 4 and assuming you want to divide the previous answer. Lo and behold, you get the correct average, 6.

If you press (×), (÷), (−), (+), (∧), or (x^2) at the beginning of a line (among a few other commands), the calculator automatically inserts Ans before it, meaning it will take the previous answer and multiply (or divide or subtract) whatever you type next. You can even type the Ans token yourself anywhere you need to use the value of the previous answer in a calculation: press (2nd) and then press ((-)).

EXAMPLE: USING ANS TO DIVIDE A NUMBER BY A SUM
Say you want to divide 300 by 4+2+1+.5. One way to do this would be to use grouping parentheses: 300/(4+2+1+.5). The other option would be to use Ans. You can first add 4+2+1+.5, which sets Ans to the sum of the numbers (7.5, incidentally). On the next line, divide 300 by Ans to get the final result, 40. Figure 2.10 shows this example on a TI-84 Plus C Silver Edition, although it would look nearly the same on any other TI-83 Plus or TI-84 Plus calculator. You can use Ans anywhere in a calculation, not just at the beginning, and you can use it as many times as you want.

Now that you have seen six full examples of using your calculator for arithmetic, let's go through a few more vital skills that you'll need for homescreen math. We'll look at the (2nd) and (ALPHA) keys, editing an equation you've typed, and repeating previous calculations. I'll also show you a few tricks that only apply to MathPrint calculators.

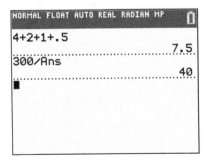

Figure 2.10 Another way to use Ans, this one demonstrated on a TI-84 Plus C Silver Edition. You can use Ans anywhere in a calculation.

2.3   *More homescreen skills*

In all five of the examples in section 2.2, you used the homescreen to practice your math skills on your calculator. You learned about arithmetic, exponents and roots, grouping parentheses, and Ans. In this section, you'll learn more of the vital skills you need to work with math on your calculator. For clarity, this section is organized according to specific skills, rather than by examples.

We'll start with the (2nd) and (ALPHA) keys, also known as the *modifier keys*. You'll need to use these to access a lot of the important functions and menus on your calculator, to type letters, and more. Next, I'll show you some equation-editing features, like moving the cursor around in whatever you're typing, deleting pieces of an equation, and inserting other pieces. I'll show you how to flip back to previous calculations, and I'll end with a look at entering fractions on MathPrint calculators.

We'll start with the modifier keys, which let you access up to three functions per key on your calculator's keypad, not just the one printed on the front of the key.

2.3.1   *More on 2nd and ALPHA*

In the square root example in section 2.2.4, you learned that to type the square root (radical) symbol, you had to press (2nd) and then (x^2). The (x^2) key has a small √ symbol above it in blue, the same color as the (2nd) key (if you have a TI-83 Plus, the key and text are orange instead of blue). When you press (2nd), release it, and press (x^2), you type the √ symbol. By the same token, there's a green *I* above the (x^2) key, the same green as the (ALPHA) key. As you might expect, if you press and release (ALPHA) and then press (x^2), you type an uppercase *I*.

Almost every key on your calculator's keypad has three functions: whatever is printed on the key itself, a (2nd) function, and an (ALPHA) function. Take a look at table 2.1 for another example of using the (2nd) and (ALPHA) modifier keys.

Table 2.1   **A recap of the (2nd) and (ALPHA) keys. Unlike pressing Shift or Ctrl on a computer, on your calculator you press the modifier key ((2nd) or (ALPHA)), release it, and then press the key to modify. Everything is color-coded, so when you press (2nd) or (ALPHA) and then another key, you activate whatever is above the other key in the color of the modifier key. (ALPHA) is green, so (ALPHA) (2) types a z, because there is a green z at upper-right over the (2) key.**

	Using the (2nd) key	Using the (ALPHA) key
What you see on the screen	⌐⌐ L₂	⊡ Z
What you press (TI-84+)	2ND **+** (2)	ALPHA **+** (2)
What you press (TI-83+)	2nd **+** (2)	ALPHA **+** (2)

Using Alpha-Lock to type letters

One special combination is [2nd] [ALPHA]. When you press and release [2nd] and then press [ALPHA], you turn on Alpha-Lock mode. This means you can type with the [ALPHA] mode stuck on, as if you were pressing [ALPHA] before every subsequent key (without actually doing so!). This is useful for typing text, because the [ALPHA] function for most keys is a letter, space, or other symbol. To turn off Alpha-Lock mode, press [ALPHA] again.

Table 2.2 shows a few other important key combinations for math that we won't go through in detail, but that you might find useful.

Table 2.2 Some special key combinations and what they do

Key combination	Types	What is it?
[(-)]	-	The negative symbol placed before negative numbers.
[2nd] [∧]	π	The constant pi (3.14159...).
[x^{-1}]	$^{-1}$ (exponent)	Takes the inverse of a number or expression.
[2nd] [x^2]	√(	Takes the square root of a number or expression.
[2nd] [,]	E	Multiplies a number by 10 to a power. 4.5E3=4.5*10³=4500; E4=10⁴=10000. For the related topic of how your calculator displays numbers with exponents as answers, check section 2.5.
[2nd] [÷]	e	The constant e (2.71828...).
[2nd] [LOG]	10^(	Raises 10 to a power.
[2nd] [LN]	e^(	Raises e (2.71828...) to a power.
[2nd] [.]	i	The imaginary number i, √-1.
[2nd] [(-)]	Ans	The result of the last calculation performed.

Let's look at what happens if you make a mistake while trying to edit an equation or if you want to modify a line you're currently typing.

2.3.2 *Editing an equation*

In a perfect world, you would never make mistakes. You don't live in a perfect world, though, and often you'll want to edit the equation you just entered. You might want to go backward in the current line, clear the whole line, or even clear the entire homescreen to give yourself a fresh slate to work with. I'll show you how to do all this in this section.

The easiest of the skills you'll see here is moving the cursor around. The cursor is the dark blinking rectangle that indicates where you're currently typing. If you type

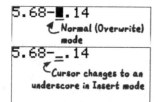

Figure 2.11 **The Overwrite cursor (top), a blinking black rectangle. The Insert cursor (bottom), a blinking underscore. To enter Insert mode, press** [2nd] [DEL]**; to return to Overwrite mode, press the left- or right-arrow key or** [ENTER]**.**

something, whatever you type appears where the cursor is currently flashing. Press the [◄] and [►] keys to move the cursor back and forth along a line.

If you try to type in the middle of a line, you'll notice that you replace what was there before. If you want to instead insert some new pieces of the equation while leaving the old stuff in place, you need to switch from overwriting text to inserting text. Press [2nd] [DEL], which despite its scary-sounding second key ([DEL]) switches you to Insert mode. As you can see from figure 2.11, the cursor will switch from a black rectangle to an underscore, indicating that you're in Insert mode. Continue by typing anything you want to insert, and then press an arrow key (or [ENTER]) to return to the normal Overwrite mode).

EXTRA MATHPRINT INSERT MODE   On MathPrint calculators, there's a special Insert mode that you can't control. It happens when you're editing a square root, an exponent, or a fraction (which you'll see in section 2.3.4). If you see the ▯ or ▯ cursor appear, it means what you type next will be inserted instead of overwritten. If you want to replace the text after the cursor, press [DEL] and then type the new text.

What if you want to delete characters instead of insert them? This one is easier: press [DEL], and whatever is currently under the cursor is deleted. What about backspace? Sorry, there's no backspace on your calculator! Your calculator can only delete things directly under and to the right of the cursor (like the Delete key on your computer). It can't delete things to the left of the cursor (like the Backspace key on your computer).

To clear an entire line, press [CLEAR]. The current contents of the line will be deleted, and the cursor will be back at the left edge of the screen. Want to clear the whole screen? Press [CLEAR] a second time, and voila. But wait! What if you just cleared the screen and an answer that you hadn't finished copying disappeared? Fear not—you can get back the equation that generated that answer, as you'll learn next.

2.3.3   *Repeating a calculation*

Your calculator can not only perform complex calculations; it can also remember those calculations for later use. Your calculator's history stores up to the last 10 equations that you entered. To access one of these previous calculations, press [2nd] and then [ENTER]; notice that ENTRY is written in blue (or orange) above the [ENTER] key.

The first time you invoke the Entry function, you get the previous calculation you performed; press [2nd] [ENTER] again, and the calculation before that will appear. If you keep pressing the combination, you'll go farther and farther back. If you get to the oldest item in the history and keep going, you'll loop back to the most recent entry.

Once you pull up a previous entry, you can rerun it as is by pressing (ENTER) immediately. If you want to change it a bit, you can do that too and then press (ENTER) when you're finished with your edits.

You now know just about everything you need to use the homescreen effectively for general math. In section 2.4, I'll teach you about special math functions that your calculator can use, but first we've reached the perfect point for a look at how Math-Print handles fractions.

VIEWING PREVIOUS ENTRIES ON MATHPRINT CALCULATORS On MathPrint calculators, you can press the (▲) key to access previous entries. Once you find the one you want, press (ENTER) to paste it and edit it. Be careful about (CLEAR): it will erase that entry from your history.

2.3.4 *MathPrint focus: entering and displaying fractions*

The recent MathPrint operating systems, as you learned in section 1.3, are an attempt to make calculations on your calculator look more like what you might see in a textbook. Square roots look fancier, exponents are above numbers, and you can enter real-looking fractions. In this section, I'll teach you the two types of fractions the calculator lets you type and what you can use them for. If you don't have a MathPrint OS or you have MathPrint disabled (see section 1.3 if you're not sure), then you can skip to section 2.4.

The Math menu, as you'll discover in section 2.4, has a lot of useful treasures to explore. Once you press (MATH) to get to the Math menu, you'll see four tabs at the top of the screen: Math, Num, Cpx, and Prb. If you have a TI-84 Plus C Silver Edition, you have a fifth tab labeled Frac, which contains the same items as the F1 ((ALPHA) (Y=)) menu. You can use the (◄) and (►) keys to move among the tabs and the (▼) and (▲) keys to move the cursor up and down the items in each tab. If you have a TI-84 Plus or TI-84 Plus Silver Edition, the bottom four items of the Num tab are the ones relevant to this discussion; you can see the menu in figure 2.12. If you have a TI-84 Plus C Silver Edition, go to the fifth tab, Frac, illustrated in figure 2.13.

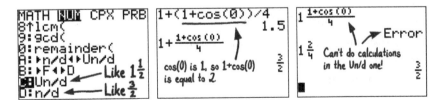

Figure 2.12 Typing fractions on MathPrint calculators. On the left, the bottom of the Num tab of the Math menu, where you can select the type of fraction you want to enter. In the center, entering a fraction without these MathPrint tools and then entering the same fraction using the n/d option. On the right, trying to do the same thing with Un/d and discovering its limitations.

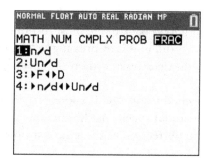

Figure 2.13   **The new Frac tab of the Math menu on the TI-84 Plus C Silver Edition. It contains the same options as the F1 menu under** ⎡ALPHA⎤ ⎡ Y= ⎤ **on MathPrint calculators.**

QUICK FRACTION ACCESS   To quickly get to MathPrint fraction tools, press ⎡ALPHA⎤ ⎡ Y= ⎤, the F1 key combination. You can access the fraction templates and conversion options here.

From top to bottom, these four options are

- ▶n/d◀▶Un/d—Take a fractional answer on the right edge of the screen and convert it from a proper/improper fraction to a mixed number or vice versa. This command should be run on a line by itself.
- ▶F◀▶D—Convert the latest answer to either a fraction or a decimal.
- Un/d—Insert a special MathPrint mixed fraction, like the one on the far right in figure 2.12. You get three blank spaces: one for the number in front of the fraction, one for the numerator, and one for the denominator. Unfortunately, you can't put expressions (calculations) in this; you can only use numbers.
- n/d—Insert a special MathPrint fraction, like the one in the center in figure 2.12. You get only two blank spaces: a numerator and a denominator. You can put calculations into this, unlike the mixed fraction (Un/d).

The center screenshot in figure 2.12 demonstrates the function that will probably be most useful for MathPrint users: typing a natural-looking fraction with a numerator and a denominator. You can cram any sort of calculation in there or, if you prefer, regular numbers. As the top of that screenshot shows, there's nothing stopping you from typing the same fraction as division, wrapping both the numerator and denominator in parentheses for safety, but the MathPrint fraction is much easier to read.

Want to type one yourself? It's easy:

1 Press ⎡MATH⎤ and then ⎡▶⎤ to get to the Num tab of the menu. Press ⎡▲⎤ once and then ⎡ENTER⎤.

2 You're in the numerator of the fraction, so type any value or expression you want there.

3 Press either ⎡▶⎤ or ⎡▼⎤ to get to the denominator of the fraction; it doesn't matter which.

4 Type your number or expression for the denominator; then press ⎡▶⎤ to leave the fraction.

You can add any sort of math on one or both sides of the fraction; look for the small cursor in the numerator/denominator versus the bigger "normal" cursor to tell if you're typing in the fraction or outside of it. As always, press (ENTER) once you're happy with your calculation to get the answer. If you get a SYNTAX error, make sure you filled in both the numerator and denominator.

You've now seen some extra skills past doing basic math on your calculator, and you should be starting to get more comfortable with the initially baffling keyboard. You've seen algebra, addition, subtraction, multiplication, and division; and you've explored the (2nd) and (ALPHA) functions of keys, how to edit and correct equations, repeating calculations, and typing fractions. What about more complex math functions, like taking absolute values, rounding, finding the remainder from division, and more? In the next section, we'll look at the basics of where you can find those sorts of functions. For the functions that I'll need more space to explain, such as calculus and trigonometry functions, I'll point you to the chapters where you can learn more.

2.4   Finding functions

Your calculator contains tons of functions. Although the word has many meanings, I mean something very specific by *function*: a word followed by an opening parenthesis. For example, abs (is a function you use to find an absolute value, and Circle (is used to draw a circle. Part of any function is one or more *arguments*, numbers, or mathematical expressions separated by parentheses, as shown in figure 2.14. You can even nest functions by putting them inside each other, also shown in figure 2.14.

In this section, you'll learn by way of examples how to find and use the many functions your calculator offers. I'll also show you a concise table of the menus in which you can find the most useful functions, plus a guide to the Catalog, which contains an exhaustive list of every function.

> **Functions 101**
>
> - A function performs some calculation or algorithm on one or more arguments.
> - Arguments are either numbers or more complex mathematical expressions, which can include other arguments.
> - Most functions can be found in menus.

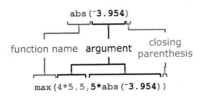

Figure 2.14   **A simple function with one argument (top); and a two-argument function with a nested function (bottom). On top, abs (is the name of the function, ‾3.954 is the single argument, and the closing parenthesis matches the opening parenthesis that is part of the function name. On the bottom, the two arguments to the max (function are 4*5.5 and 5*abs(‾3.954), which itself is a function with an argument. Notice that the arguments are separated by a comma. On MathPrint calculators, the abs function is represented by vertical bars │like this│ instead of by abs (.**

```
MATH NUM CPX PRB    NAMES MATH EDIT    CATALOG
1:▶Frac             1:det(            ▶abs(
2:▶Dec              2:T                and
3:3                 3:dim(             angle(
4:3√(               4:Fill(            ANOVA(
5:ˣ√                5:identity(        Ans
6:fMin(             6:randM(           Archive
7↓fMax(             7↓augment(         Asm(
```

Figure 2.15 Examples of menus where you can find functions. The left screenshot is the Math menu, accessed with the (MATH) key. Press the left- and right-arrow keys to move to the Num, Cpx, and Prb tabs. The center screenshot is the Matrix menu (accessed with (2nd) (x⁻¹)). The right screenshot is the Catalog, which collects all the functions from other menus and puts them in one place, arranged alphabetically.

Take a gander at figure 2.15, which shows three of the menus on your calculator. The left and center screenshots are what most menus look like. Each menu has one or more tabs, each containing a different set of items. In general, you'll want to paste functions onto the homescreen, into the Y= graph editor, or into other tools. To do so, follow these steps:

1 Go from the homescreen, Y= editor, or other tool into the menu you want: for example, by pressing (MATH).

2 Move to the tab that contains the function you want, switching between tabs with the (◄) and (►) keys.

3 Move the cursor up and down the list of functions by pressing the (▼) and (▲) keys.

4 When you find the function (or symbol) you want, press (ENTER) to paste it back onto the homescreen, Y= editor, or other tool. You can also press the number next to the item you want, such as (4) in the Math menu to get the cube root (³√ ()) symbol.

Once you have the function you want on the screen, you need to add arguments. As figure 2.14 shows, every function needs one or more arguments, which are either numbers or expressions that the calculator can reduce (simplify) into numbers. Arguments are separated by commas, and you need to put a closing parenthesis after the last argument to match the opening parenthesis in the function name. Almost every function requires a fixed number of arguments, but you must remember what the arguments are for each one. For example, max(takes two arguments and returns the larger of the two, whereas abs(returns (calculates) the absolute value of a single argument.

That's fine for an abstract introduction, but how about a few functions used in some concrete examples? Let's look at three different examples.

2.4.1 *Examples of homescreen math functions*

To get you started with using functions, let's look at three specific examples. Two demonstrate items from the Num tab of the Math menu, and the third shows the sine function on the (SIN) key. As always, the best way to get a feel for this new skill is to work through the examples on your own calculator, although if you're in a hurry, you can skim these and then skip straight to the list of functions in section 2.4.2.

Let's first play with the lcm(function, which as you might expect calculates the lowest common multiple of two numbers.

FINDING THE LOWEST COMMON MULTIPLE OF TWO NUMBERS

As you may have learned in math class, the lowest common multiple (LCM) of two numbers a and b is the smallest number that is both a multiple of a and a multiple of b. Because it's mathematically simple to find such a number but may be time consuming, it's a great thing to use your calculator for. You could work through each multiple of a (a, $2a$, $3a$, $4a$, …) and manually test if each multiple was also a multiple of b until you found the LCM, or you can just let your calculator do it. Figure 2.16 shows three screenshots from this process.

Because the LCM is calculated from two numbers, it stands to reason that the lcm(function takes two arguments. You'll find the lcm(function, paste it to the home-screen, type the two arguments, and then calculate the result. First, press (MATH). As you might have noticed, most of the general-purpose functions you'll use are in the Math menu, whereas specialized functions are in menus such as Matrix, Stats, and Vars. Press (▶) once to move to the Num tab (notice how it changes to white text on a black background); then move the cursor down to 8:lcm(and press (ENTER) to paste it. Alternatively, you can press (8).

Now you need to type the two arguments. Enter your first number, such as 13, type a comma with (,), and then enter the second number, such as 37. As you can see, I'm assuming that you're getting more comfortable with your calculator and that I don't have to tell you to press (1)(3) to type the number 13. After your second number, press (,) to close the lcm(function.

Press (ENTER), and read off the result—481 is indeed the LCM of 13 and 37, as figure 2.16 shows, because 13*37=481. The LCM of a and b is not always $a \times b$—for example, when a = 4, b = 2, and their LCM is 4—but in the case of the previous example, the

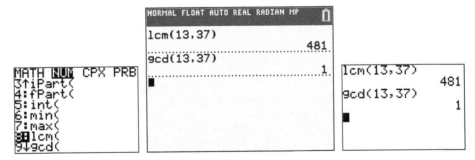

Figure 2.16 Finding the LCM and greatest common divisor (GCD) of two numbers. The Num tab of the Math menu (accessed by pressing (MATH) and then the right-arrow key once) contains the lcm(and gcd(functions. Press (ENTER) on lcm(and then type the two numbers with a comma in between to find the LCM. You also need to close the opening parenthesis and then press (ENTER). The middle screenshot shows computing the LCM and GCD of two numbers on a TI-84 Plus C Silver Edition, and the right screenshot shows the same thing on a TI-83 Plus or TI-84 Plus.

LCM of *a* and *b* is indeed *a* × *b*. Feel free to try some other pairs of numbers: you can press (2nd) (ENTER) to get the equation back and then use (DEL) and the Insert mode to change the arguments, as sections 2.3.2 and 2.3.3 taught you.

Want to get the greatest common divisor of the two numbers, instead? Select the gcd(function from the Num tab of the Math menu and use that instead. The right screenshot in figure 2.16 shows that your calculator knows 1 is the GCD of 13 and 37.

Another useful function in the Num menu is round(. Let's work with that next.

ROUNDING A NUMBER

round(is an unusual function in that it can take either one or two arguments. The one-argument version is more useful when you're programming TI-BASIC on your calculator than for math, so you shouldn't worry about it too much for now (check out the first line on the right side in figure 2.17). We'll use the two-argument version: round(*number, decimal places*), which rounds *number* to *decimal places*. If you add the decimal places argument, you must specify between zero and nine decimal places; anything else will make the calculator produce an ERR:DOMAIN error.

If you went through the LCM example, this one should be easy. Go to the Math menu, move to the Num tab, and choose 2:round(. If you don't know how to do any of that, review the previous example. Once you paste round(to the homescreen, add the two arguments. First type the number that you want to round, then a comma, and then how many decimal places you want to round the number to. If you round to zero decimal places, you'll round to the nearest integer (like 9.876 to 10, as figure 2.17 shows). If you round to one decimal place, you'll get one decimal place.

How about tossing some trigonometry into the mix? Let's take a look at how you can calculate the sine of an angle in radians or in degrees with the sin(function.

FINDING THE SINE OF A NUMBER

It shouldn't be a surprise that your calculator is good at trigonometry, considering the (SIN), (COS), and (TAN) keys prominently centered on its keypad. These are among the few functions you don't need to go into a menu to find. You press one of those keys, add the number (or expression) for the angle to take the sine, cosine, or tangent of, and then add a closing parenthesis. Let's try with sin(.

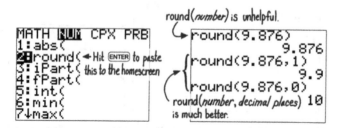

Figure 2.17 Using the round(command from the Num tab of the Math menu to round a number. round(number) doesn't do much, but you can add a second argument that tells the calculator how many decimal places to round to. If you ask for zero decimal places, it rounds to the nearest integer.

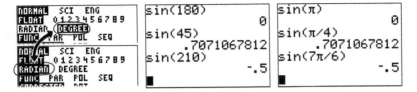

Figure 2.18 Calculating the sine of various angles. The center screenshot uses angles in degrees, and the right screenshot uses angles in radians. The left screenshot shows how to use the Mode menu, accessed with the MODE key, to switch between Degree and Radian modes. On different calculators, your Mode menu may look different, but the Radian/Degree choice will still be there.

You can take the sine of angles in degrees, as in the center in figure 2.18, or you can work with angles in radians, as on the right in figure 2.18. If you put the number by itself, the calculator has no way to guess whether you're dealing with degree or radian angles. The way it decides is a setting in the Mode menu, which section 2.5 will discuss in depth. For now, press MODE and look for the line that says RADIAN DEGREE. Whichever word is in white text on a black background is the current mode. In Radian mode, all angles are assumed to be radians, whereas in Degree mode, all angles are assumed to be degrees. You can also explicitly tell the calculator if you're entering a radian or degree angle, regardless of the mode, but this is something you won't need to deal with until chapter 6.

Switch into the mode of your choice in the Mode menu by using the arrow keys to move the cursor over RADIAN or DEGREE and pressing ENTER. Leave the Mode menu by pressing 2nd MODE (quit), and then try the sin(function. You can try with degree angles like 180, 45, and 210 or their radian equivalents, π, $\pi/4$, and $7\pi/6$ (or any other angles that catch your fancy). You can also try the cosine (COS) and tangent (TAN) functions if you want.

Although you've now seen quite a few functions in action, you've barely scratched the surface of all the functions your calculator has available for you to use. The coming chapters will cover most of these, so for now let's move on to a list of the major menus and what functions you can find in each.

2.4.2   A guide to finding functions

As you use this book, you'll learn about more menus in which you can find useful functions. For example, when you learn about lists and matrices, you'll learn about the List Operations, List Math, and Matrix Math menus and the many functions those menus contain. If you want to find a specific function, though, you might have flipped straight to this section, so I'll do my best to help.

Examine table 2.3, and you're likely to find the menu you need. For each menu, you press the relevant access key(s); you may need to switch menu tabs with the ◀ and ▶ keys or scroll up and down with ▼ and ▲ to find what you're looking for.

Table 2.3   Where to find many of your calculator's useful functions (commands)

Menu	Access key(s)	Functions	Covered in...
(None)	[SIN] [COS] [TAN]	sin(, cos(, tan(, sin⁻¹(, cos⁻¹(, tan⁻¹(	Section 6.2
Math	[MATH]	fMin(, fMax(, nDeriv(, fnInt(, Σ(, logBASE(	Chapter 3 (fMin/ fMax), section 6.4 (logBASE), chapter 7 (calculus functions)
Num (numbers)	[MATH]	abs(, round(, iPart(, fPart(, int(, min(, max(, lcm(, gcd(, remainder(	Chapter 2
Cpx (complex numbers)	[MATH]	conj(, real(, imag(, angle(, abs(	Section 6.1
Prb (probability)	[MATH]	rand, randInt(, randNorm(, randBin(	Section 9.4
Angle	[2nd] [APPS]	R▶Pr(, R▶Pθ(, P▶Rx(, P▶Ry(	Section 5.2
Draw	[2nd] [PRGM]	ClrDraw, Line(, Horizontal, Vertical, Tangent, DrawF, Shade(, DrawInv, Circle(, Text(	Section 5.4
Statistics	[STAT]	SortA(, SortD(, many more	Chapter 8
List Operations	[2nd] [STAT]	SortA(, SortD(, dim(, Fill(, seq(, cumSum(, ΔList(, Select(, augment(, List▶matr(, Matr▶list(	Section 4.2
List Math	[2nd] [STAT]	min(, max(, mean(, median(, sum(, prod(, stdDev(, variance(	Section 4.2
Matrix Math	[2nd] [x⁻¹]	det(, dim(, Fill(, identity(, randM, augment(, many more	Section 4.3

MATHPRINT SHORTCUT MENUS You can get to the five functions abs(, Σ(, nDeriv(, fnInt(, and logBASE(on all MathPrint calculators by pressing [ALPHA] [WINDOW], the F2 key combination. If you have a TI-84 Plus C Silver Edition, you'll find the probability tools nPr, nCr, and ! in the same menu.

This chapter is the crash course to regular math and algebra on your calculator, before we get into graphing, lists, matrices, calculus, probability, and all that fancy stuff, so I must explicitly tell you about a few functions that you won't see anywhere else in this book. Table 2.4 lists each of these functions, along with their arguments and what menu on your calculator they can be found in. Each is important enough to merit a mention here but won't fit into any of the later subjects we discuss.

Table 2.4 **Important math functions that you won't see in other chapters**

Function	Arguments	Description
`abs(`	`abs(number)`	Calculates the absolute value of the number in question. On MathPrint calculators, this appears as absolute value bars instead of a function: $\lvert 3.1 \rvert$.
`round(`	`round(number, decimal places)`	Rounds the given number to the specified number of decimal places (see section 2.4.1). You can specify zero to nine decimal places.
`iPart(`	`iPart(number)`	Returns just the integer part of a number: $iPart(3.1) = 3$, $iPart(3.9) = 3$, and $iPart(^-3.9) = ^-3$.
`fPart(`	`fpart(number)`	Returns just the part of a number after the decimal point: $fPart(3.1) = 0.1$, $fPart(3.9) = 0.9$, and $fPart(^-3.9) = -0.9$.
`int(`	`int(number)`	Rounds a number down to the nearest integer. For positive numbers, this is the same as `iPart`. But it rounds in the opposite direction for negative numbers: $int(3.9) = 3$, but $int(^-3.9) = 4$ and $int(^-3.1) = 4$.
`min(`	`min(a,b)`	Returns whichever of a or b is smaller.
`max(`	`max(a,b)`	Returns whichever of a or b is larger.
`lcm(`	`lcm(a,b)`	Calculates the LCM of a and b.
`gcd(`	`gcd(a,b)`	Calculates the GCD of a and b.
`remainder(`	`remainder(a,b)`	Calculates the remainder when a is divided by b. Only MathPrint calculators have this function.

Except for `remainder(`, all these are available on your calculator regardless of which operating system version you're using.

With a roadmap to your calculator's menus under your belt, we can move on to the last two topics in this chapter: changing modes and solving algebraic equations with unknowns. You already got a taste of setting modes with Degree and Radian modes in section 2.4.1; now you'll learn about all the other items in the Mode menu and what they do.

2.5 *Setting modes*

You got your first introduction to modes in section 2.4.1, where you learned the difference between Radian and Degree modes. When you went to investigate what mode your calculator was using for that example, you probably saw that the Mode menu was full of all kinds of options. In this section, I'll tell you what each one is used for. Luckily, it's not nearly as overwhelming as it might first appear.

Modes in a jiffy

Modes are settings that control how your calculator graphs, calculates, and does math. You change modes by pressing (MODE), using the arrow keys to move the cursor to the mode you want to set, and pressing (ENTER). Modes that are set appear in white text on a black background. You can only choose one of the items in each row, so, for example, you can't set both Normal and Scientific (Sci) modes at the same time.

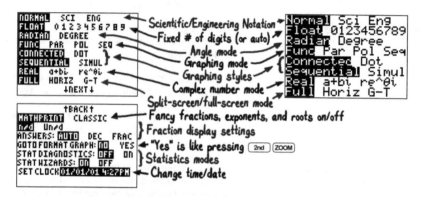

Figure 2.19 Various possible Mode menus, plus what each row is for. The left screenshots are from the two-page MathPrint mode menu on a newer TI-84 Plus, whereas the right screenshot is from a TI-83 Plus without MathPrint. Both let you change the Radian and Degree modes, Complex Number mode, and graph settings. The TI-84 Plus menu also lets you set MathPrint settings and change the calculator's time and date.

Figure 2.19 shows two possible forms the Mode menu might take. The two screenshots on the left side are from a TI-84 Plus running OS 2.55MP, and the one on the right is from a TI-83 Plus running OS 1.19. There's also a version of the right screenshot that only adds the ability to set the time and date, which is used on TI-84 Plus and TI-84 Plus Silver Edition calculators with OS 2.43 or lower.

To get started, press (MODE) and take a look. All the options that are currently selected are set in white text on a black background, whereas all the other options that are in black text on a white background are options you can choose. Depending on what OS version you have (remember that you can check with (2nd) (+) (1)), you may have some or all the following options in the Mode menu. You can select any mode.

TI-84 Plus C Silver Edition Mode menu

The Mode menu on the color-screen TI-84 Plus C Silver Edition is a lot like the Mode menu on the TI-84 Plus Silver Edition. It has almost all the same options, except that the larger screen means they all fit on one page. Section 12.1.1 talks about the few new options in its Mode menu, but almost everything here applies to the TI-84 Plus C Silver Edition.

```
NORMAL FLOAT AUTO REAL RADIAN MP        ▯
MATHPRINT  CLASSIC
NORMAL  SCI  ENG
FLOAT  0 1 2 3 4 5 6 7 8 9
RADIAN  DEGREE
FUNCTION  PARAMETRIC  POLAR  SEQ
THICK  DOT-THICK  THIN  DOT-THIN
SEQUENTIAL  SIMUL
REAL   a+bi  re^(θi)
FULL  HORIZONTAL  GRAPH-TABLE
FRACTION TYPE: n/d  Un/d
ANSWERS: AUTO  DEC  FRAC-APPROX
GO TO 2ND FORMAT GRAPH: NO  YES
STAT DIAGNOSTICS: OFF  ON
STAT WIZARDS: ON  OFF
SET CLOCK  02/23/13 2:24AM
```

**Mode menu on the TI-84 Plus
C Silver Edition**

NUMERIC OPTIONS

These options control what the numbers the calculator displays and uses look like, including answers on the homescreen and how the calculator interprets angles. All of these are available on every TI-83 Plus and TI-84 Plus calculator.

- *Normal/Scientific/Engineering*—These modes control when answers are expressed in exponent form and when they're shown in normal form. The left side in figure 2.20 shows the differences among the three modes. In Normal mode, the calculator only switches to exponent notation when the number is too big or too small to show normally. Scientific (Sci) and Engineering (Eng) modes both use exponents all the time, although Scientific always shows a single digit before the decimal point, whereas Engineering shows one to three digits before the decimal point and keeps the exponent as a multiple of 3.

- *Float/0123456789*—These modes select how many digits are shown after the decimal point. Ordinarily, Float mode is the best, because it shows precisely as many digits of precision as the number has. In any of the other modes 0–9, called Fix modes, the calculator always displays exactly that number of digits. The right side in figure 2.20 shows the difference between Float and Fix 2.

- *Radian/Degree*—These modes control how the calculator interprets numbers that are angles, especially for trigonometry functions like sin(and cos(.

- *Real/a+bi/re^θi*—These modes change the way the calculator handles complex numbers. In Real mode, it produces ERR:NONREAL ANS for any complex answers.

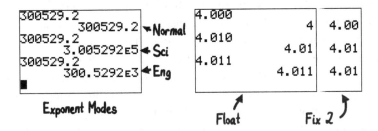

Figure 2.20 The different exponent display modes (left), and an example of Float/Fix modes (right)

a+b*i* mode is also known as Complex mode, and re^θ*i* mode is Polar Complex mode. In both of the latter modes, complex numbers are displayed.

GRAPHING OPTIONS

The following modes show how to change the type of graphing currently being done, as well as how graphs look:

- *Function/Parametric/Polar/Sequential*—These modes switch the graphing mode. The "regular" type of graphing, where you define a Y= equation, is Function (or Rectangular) mode. The other options are Parametric (Par), Polar (Pol), and Sequential (Seq) modes. Rectangular graphing is covered in chapter 3, and the other types are discussed in chapter 5.

- *Connected/Dot*—Your calculator uses a graphing method designed to be both fast and accurate. In Dot mode, the calculator plots one *y* dot for every *x* value (or the equivalent for other modes). In Connected mode, it connects all the dots to make a curve.

- *Sequential/Simultaneous*—These modes control how multiple graphed functions are drawn, but they don't change the result you see when the calculator finishes. Sequential mode means the calculator graphs multiple functions one after the other, whereas Simultaneous (Simul) mode means it graphs them all at the same time. There's no speed benefit either way.

- *Full/Horizontal/G-T*—There are full-screen and split-screen modes. In Full mode, graphs and the homescreen each take the entire screen when they're active. In Horizontal (Horiz) mode, the top half of the screen displays the graph, and the bottom half of the screen displays any other active feature, like the homescreen and Y= editor. In G-T (Graph-Table) mode, the left half of the screen is the graph, and the right half is the table, which shows pairs of *x* and *y* coordinates.

MATHPRINT OPTIONS

These options are only available if you have a calculator with a MathPrint operating system (like 2.53MP or 2.55MP). Section 1.3 explains more about MathPrint.

- *MathPrint/Classic*—These modes turn MathPrint mode on (MathPrint) or off (Classic). This book covers both options, so you should choose whichever you prefer to work with (or whatever your teacher instructs you to use).

- *n/d/Un/d*—When the calculator needs to display an answer as a fraction, choose whether it uses proper/improper (n/d) or mixed (Un/d) fractions.

- *Answers: Auto Dec Frac*—In Auto mode, the calculator only outputs fractions if you entered fractions with the n/d or Un/d template in the Math Num menu. Dec mode makes it always display decimal answers, and Frac mode forces it to try to convert the answer to a fraction whenever possible.

- *Goto Format Graph*—This is just like pressing ⟨2nd⟩ ⟨ZOOM⟩—it opens the Graph Format menu.

- *Stat Diagnostics*—This mode displays or hides the fitness (r and r^2) of statistical regression functions fitted to data.
- *Stats Wizard*—This mode adds "wizards" to help you use statistical functions.

The final option, present on all TI-84 Plus-family calculators, lets you change the calculator's stored time and date and set its time and date display formats.

MATHPRINT, STATISTICS, AND G-T   If you choose the G-T split-screen mode from the Mode menu on a MathPrint calculator, and you enable a statistical plot (discussed in chapter 8), your data lists will be shown in the table next to the plot.

That's pretty much all you need to know at this point. For the lesson you've learned thus far, only the first two numeric options, Normal/Sci/Eng and Fix/012345789, are relevant. The remaining options will become important as you go through the coming chapters. Speaking of the upcoming chapters, including soon-to-be-introduced graphing skills, we have only a final set of skills left for this chapter's material: solving equations with your calculator.

2.6   Solving equations and checking your answers

"Solving equations?" you might be thinking to yourself. "Isn't that what we've been doing all along?" Actually, you technically have been using your calculator to simplify expressions, such as combining numbers with arithmetic operations, square roots, trigonometric functions, and the rest. In this section, you'll learn to solve equations, such as taking $3x - 40 = 8$ and finding that $x = 16$. You'll also learn to test equations, to find out if two different expressions are equal.

Your calculator can't simplify symbolic equations: it has no idea that `4(5X+X)*X` can simplify to `24X²`. But given a value for X, it can substitute the value into `4(5X+X)*X` to get an answer that's essentially X plugged into `24X²`. Because it's fundamentally a tiny computer, it can also try to find a value for an unknown variable by trying hundreds of different possibilities per second until it finds one that works. In the first part of this section, you'll learn to use that tool. In the latter half, you'll learn to ask the calculator to check whether equalities and inequalities like `4/√(2)<1.5` are true or false.

Even though your calculator can't manipulate symbolic equations, it can still help you solve simple algebraic equations. Let's look at two examples that will teach you how.

2.6.1   Using the Equation Solver tool

The Equation Solver, or Solver, is an often-overlooked tool hiding at the bottom of the Math menu, used to solve algebraic equations with one unknown variable. In this section, we'll work through an example of the Solver on the TI-83 Plus and most TI-84 Plus calculators. If you have a TI-84 Plus C Silver Edition, you might want to flip ahead to section 12.1.4 instead, because its Solver works a bit differently.

The Solver tool will make more sense if we go through an actual example, so let's start with a simple equation that has only one answer: $3x - 8 = 40$. You can probably see that you can solve it by hand by first adding 8 to both sides to get $3x = 48$ and then dividing both sides by 3 to get $x = 16$. You'll almost always need to be able to solve both easy and hard equations by hand, but the Solver is helpful for double-checking your answers. Let's enter the $3x - 8 = 40$ equation into the Solver. First get into the tool from the Math menu: you access it by pressing (MATH), scrolling down to B:Solver…, and pressing (ENTER).

Equation Solver in a nutshell

To use the Solver to find the solution(s) to an equation with one unknown variable, follow these steps:

1. Find the Solver at the bottom of the Math menu.
2. Rearrange your equation to get 0 on one side and enter it. Use X as the unknown variable, even if it's a different variable in the original.
3. Press (ENTER), enter a guess next to X= (optional), and press (ALPHA) (ENTER).
4. If you get an error, try a different guess; if you still get an error, then the equation may have no solution.
5. If you get an answer and the equation has more than one answer, enter a different guess and see if the Solver converges to a different answer.

The Equation Solver on the TI-84 Plus C Silver Edition is a bit different. Section 12.1.4 demonstrates how to use it.

But wait! It already says eqn:0= (or if it doesn't, press (CLEAR) to clear the old equation)! Yup: you must rearrange any equation you solve with this tool to have 0 on one side. For our simple example of $3x - 8 = 40$, you can subtract 40 from both sides to get $3x - 48 = 0$ or, flipped around, $0 = 3x - 48$. Remember that your calculator understands implicit multiplication, so you can type 3X instead of 3*X. One thing might be new: how do you type the variable X? You have two options:

- You can press (XTθn), which types X as long as you're in Function (Func) mode (see the "Graphing options" subsection of section 2.5).
- You can type (ALPHA) (STO▸), because X is the green letter above (STO▸).

Therefore, type (3) (XTθn) (−) (4) (8) and press (ENTER). You won't get an answer just yet, as figure 2.21 shows. You instead arrive at a screen with three options: X=, bound=, and left-rt=. The X= line is where the calculator displays the answer it finds. If you put a value there, the calculator starts guessing from that value. You'd want to do this if your equation has more than one answer, to help guide it to which of the equation's answers you want it to find.

In general, you won't have to touch the bound={…} option, which tells the calculator the range the answer must be in. If you changed it to {0,10}, for example, the calculator would only look for answers between and including 0 and 10. left-rt= is something the calculator fills in when it finds an answer, and it indicates how close it

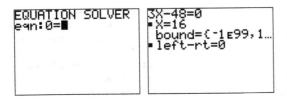

Figure 2.21 Using the Equation Solver to discover that $x = 16$ satisfies the equation $3x - 8 = 40$. Notice that you must rearrange the equation to get 0 by itself on one side, in this case by subtracting 40 from each side.

was able to get to a good answer. If this number is 0, then the calculator found an answer that works perfectly.

Anyway, you can leave everything as it is without changing any of these options, and press ALPHA ENTER (Solve) to ask the calculator for a solution. It will think for a second and then display X=16 and left-rt=0. You can tell when it has found an answer, because it puts a little black square next to the lines it just filled in.

SOLVING A QUADRATIC EQUATION

Let's try another example equation, this one a second-order polynomial: $x^2 - 4x + 2 = 0$. It already has 0 on one side, which is a good start. If you know how to use the Quadratic Formula, you might be able to find out that this equation has two answers, namely $2 + \sqrt{2}$ and $2 - \sqrt{2}$. But if you don't, or if you want to check the results of the quadratic equation, your calculator can rush to your rescue.

Re-enter the Solver from the Math menu. If you're at the screen with bound= and left-rt=, press (▲) until you get back to the eqn= screen, as on the left side in figure 2.21. This time, enter X²-4X+2, remembering that the squared symbol is (x²) and that you can type X either of two ways. Press ENTER and then ALPHA ENTER, and wait for the calculator to think. It will produce one of the two answers for x shown in figure 2.22.

How do you get the other answer? If you got the left answer, 3.414, then type in something like 0 or ⁻5 for x, which will make the calculator start searching for answers at that number and work its way upward to the actual solution of 0.586. If that's the one you got, then type in something like 5 or even 10, and it will work its way down to 3.414. After you type in the new "hint" x value, remember to press ALPHA ENTER.

It's important that you can see for yourself without the calculator's help how many answers there are to a given equation, because the calculator can't work it out for itself. Thus, this feature is most useful for checking your answers when you've already worked an equation through by hand. It can even fail to find an answer, in which case it may produce an error such as ERR:NO SIGN CHNG or ERR:TOL NOT MET. For such errors, you're back to working out the equation by yourself on paper.

There's a final trick that I want to show you for checking equations, which will let you determine if the two sides of an equation are equal and, if not, which side is larger.

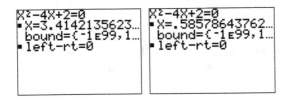

Figure 2.22 Using the Solver to find the two solutions to a second-degree polynomial, something you could also do by hand with the quadratic equation. The Solver can help you double-check your results.

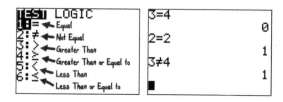

Figure 2.23 The Test menu and a few simple tests. A result of 0 means false or incorrect, whereas 1 means true or correct. 3=4 is false (0) because 3 does not equal 4. 2=2 is true (1) because 2 does equal 2. 3≠4 is true (1) because it is true to claim that 3 and 4 are not equal.

2.6.2 *Boolean algebra with the Test/Logic menu*

You might have initially been confused at your calculator's missing = key and the fact that you instead press (ENTER) to get a result. In this section, you'll learn where the = symbol is hiding, how to store numbers into variables like X, and how to use those skills to check equations. Let's go through a series of three steps to build up what you need to know to check equations.

TESTING ASSERTIONS

Step 1 is testing equality to see whether an assertion is true or false. A simple assertion might be 3 = 4. You know this is false or incorrect, because 3 is certainly not equal to 4. Any number is only equal to itself. In calculator terms, "false" is represented by 0 and "true" by 1. You can test the assertion 3=4 on your calculator by typing it on your calculator's homescreen; the = sign is in the Test menu, found under (2nd) (MATH). In fact, the equal sign, not-equal sign, and the four types of inequality symbols are also there, as figure 2.23 shows.

When you test out 3=4 on the homescreen, you get 0, or false. If you try something that should be true, 2=2, you get 1, or true, just as you should. If you try 3≠4, you get 1 (true), because it is correct to claim that 3 is not equal to 4. You can use more complex expressions instead of just numbers: 2*4=8 is true (1), whereas 2*(4-1)=10-5 is false. You can also try inequalities: 2>1 is true, whereas ⁻10≥0 is false. You can combine inequalities and complex expressions, like 2*(4-1)<10-3 (which would be true, because it simplifies to 6<7).

STORING TO AND USING VARIABLES

Step 2 is to be able to store values into variables. Variables are named containers that you can put things in. The letter variables A–Z plus θ (the Greek letter theta) can all hold a single number. To store a number into a variable, you use the → (store) symbol. When you store a number into a variable, it stays there in that variable until you store a different number into it (or erase your calculator's memory). The X and Y variables are also changed by the calculator when it draws graphs.

Anyway, you store a number to a variable by typing the number to store, then the → symbol with the (STO▸) key, and then the name of the variable to store into, such as X, A, or M. Figure 2.24 demonstrates storing 100 into X; you can replicate this by typing (1)(0)(0)(STO▸)(XTθn) or (1)(0)(0)(STO▸)(ALPHA)(STO▸), because either (XTθn) or (ALPHA)(STO▸) types X. Once you press (ENTER), you have stored 100 into X, and you can use the letter X wherever you might want to use 100, such as to calculate 3X=3*100=300 or X-99=100-99=1.

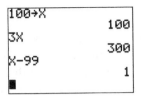

Figure 2.24 Storing 100 to the X variable and then using X in expressions: 3X is 3*100, which is 300, whereas X-99 is 100-99, which equals 1.

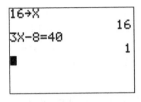

Figure 2.25 Testing if X=16 satisfies the equation 3X-8=40. The response 1 from the calculator (meaning true) means that X=16 is a solution (actually, the only solution) to 3X-8=40.

TESTING EQUATIONS WITH VARIABLES

Step 3 is to put steps 1 and 2 together to store a test value to a variable and then try out an equation. In section 2.6.1, we solved $3x - 8 = 40$ and discovered that $x = 16$ was the answer. Want to make sure that's the case? Store 16→X and then test if 3X-8=40. Figure 2.25 shows how that might look on your calculator; you should be able to try it yourself without any help with what you now know. Lo and behold, the calculator responds 1 (true), meaning that $3x - 8$ does indeed equal 40 when $x = 16$.

There was also that second-degree equation we played with, X²-4X+2=0. We got two answers, 2+√2 and 2-√2, which are roughly 3.414 and 0.586, respectively. You can test these two answers and make sure they both work in the equation. First, store 2+√(2)→X and press (ENTER) to make it stick. Next, type in X²-4X+2=0 and press (ENTER); remember that the = symbol is in the Test menu. Figure 2.26 shows what this looks like on a MathPrint calculator; the only difference on a non-MathPrint calculator is that the square root looks slightly less fancy and includes parentheses around the 2. It's true! Now try the other possible solution, 2-√2, which also returns a 1 (true). You can also try some numbers that aren't solutions; try storing other numbers to X and testing them in the equation.

You can test equality, nonequality, and inequality with this technique. Between testing equations and the Solver, you have quite a few tools at your disposal for solving and double-checking solutions to equations. Combined with everything else you've learned in this chapter, you already know most of what you need to use your calculator as an effective and powerful math tool.

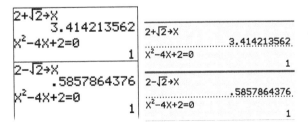

Figure 2.26 Testing the two solutions to X²-4X+2=0: 2+√2 and 2-√2. These screenshots are both from MathPrint calculators; the display doesn't look much different on a non-MathPrint calculator. The left is from a TI-84 Plus, the right from a TI-84 Plus C Silver Edition.

2.7 *Summary*

You've gotten started using your TI-83 Plus or TI-84 Plus graphing calculator for math, from turning on the calculator to performing arithmetic, using functions, and changing modes to solving equations. We started with background details about the calculator, such as changing the batteries, turning it on, and clearing the memory. We then jumped immediately into doing math through quite a few examples, and you learned how to use the calculator's keypad to find functions and edit calculations. Next, you discovered what functions and arguments are and how to use them, and I introduced where in the coming chapters you'll learn about those functions. Finally, you explored changing your calculator's mode settings, and we investigated solving equations and testing out possible solutions.

Throughout the rest of this book, we'll look at more specialized tools, from graphing to statistics to calculus to probability. To use each of those tools properly, you'll have to use what you learned in this chapter; I might be tempted to say that this is the most important chapter in the book, and if you read through only a single chapter in full, it should be this one. Follow me into the next chapter, where we'll look at the graphing part of your graphing calculator.

Basic graphing 3

This chapter covers
- How to graph functions and solve problems with graphs on your calculator
- Finding minima, maxima, values, intercepts, zeroes, and more
- Zooming, panning, and adjusting graph styles
- Using Table to examine graphed functions

Your graphing calculator's most noticeable difference from a regular calculator is the large LCD screen. Whereas a simple calculator only needs to display numbers, your graphing calculator needs its big screen to display graphs. Its graphing features are a big deal, and in this chapter you'll learn all about using them.

A graph is a curve or line drawn from a mathematical function, sketched over a coordinate plane. What does all that mean? Say you want to graph a function, as if you were your calculator. You start with a two-dimensional (2D) plane, like a piece of paper that stretches out to infinity in all four directions. You take a mathematical function, such as $y = x^2$. You plug every possible x value into the equation, get out a y value, and plot (draw) those (x,y) points on the plane. If you plot enough of them, you'll have so many little dots that it looks like one continuous line. This is essentially what your calculator does when you graph.

In this chapter, you'll learn how to create graphs both complex and simple. We'll try a few examples to show you how the graphs you draw can relate to real problems. You'll learn how to find the minima and maxima of functions, their values at certain points, and where they intersect with other functions. I'll show you how to scroll and pan around a graph and how to use the table view to see a list of (x,y) coordinates. By the end of the chapter, you'll be comfortable with graphing functions on the rectangular (Cartesian) plane and using the tools your calculator provides to explore those graphs. You'll need some of the skills you learned in chapter 2, such as moving around menus and typing equations, so if you skipped that chapter, now would be a good time to go back and read it.

Let me sneak in a quick note on the color-screen TI-84 Plus C Silver Edition. If you get a chance to read chapter 12, you'll see that the TI-84 Plus C Silver Edition's graphing features are what sets it apart the most from the earlier TI-83 Plus and TI-84 Plus-family calculators. Its screen means it can show more detail in graphed functions and differentiate functions with colors. Nevertheless, all the examples in this chapter are designed to apply to the entire TI-83 Plus and TI-84 Plus family, the TI-84 Plus C Silver Edition included. When there are important differences, you'll find extra calculator-specific screenshots and sidebars.

Let's jump straight into the basic steps of graphing to get you started; then we'll step back and look at each of the requisite skills and calculator features in more depth.

3.1 Getting started with graphing

Graphing on your calculator can be as simple or as complex as you want. At its simplest, you enter an equation and press one button to graph it. At its most complex, you can move left and right along a graphed line, zoom in and out, find out how multiple graphed functions interact, and calculate exact (x,y) values along the graph. In this section, we'll work at the "simple" end of the spectrum.

Graphing in a nutshell

We'll graph a simple $y = f(x)$ function, such as $y = x^2 + 1$, in four easy steps:

1. Press (MODE) and make sure FUNC (or FUNCTION, on a TI-84 Plus C Silver Edition) is white text on a black background. If not, move the cursor over FUNC and press (ENTER).
2. Press (Y=) to get to the menu where you enter equations to graph. Use the arrow keys and (CLEAR) to remove any equations already entered.
3. Type your own equation next to $Y_1=$ (use X for the independent variable x in equations, where X is the (XTθn) key), and press (GRAPH).
4. Use the functions in the Zoom menu to zoom in and out, and press (TRACE) followed by the (◄) and (►) keys to scroll left and right along the graph.

Let's assume that you want to graph the function $y = x^2 + 1$ on your calculator. The first thing you need to do is make sure your calculator is in Function mode. In this mode, you enter functions in the form $y = f(x)$, where y is the dependent variable and x is the

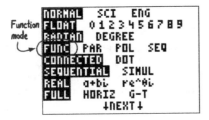

Figure 3.1 The Mode menu, where you can change the graphing mode among Function, Parametric, Polar, and Sequential. If FUNC isn't highlighted, use the arrow keys to move the cursor over the word and press (ENTER). It doesn't matter what all the other modes are; you don't need to make your Mode menu match this screenshot.

independent variable. Your calculator has three other types of graphs it can draw: polar, parametric, and sequential graphs; chapter 5 will teach you all about those. For now, though, we'll stick with Function mode, so you should make sure your calculator is indeed in that mode. Press the (MODE) key, and make sure the word FUNC is white text on a black background, as shown in figure 3.1.

Next, you need to enter the equation that you want to graph. Press (Y=) to get to the Y= menu, where you can enter between 1 and 10 equations to graph. You can also work with statistics plots from here, but that's a subject for chapter 8, so make sure Plot1, Plot2, and Plot3 at the top of the screen are all black text on a white background (disabled). If any is enabled (white text in a black box), move the cursor up to it and press (ENTER) to turn it off. If there are any equations already entered in the Y= menu, use the arrow keys to move to them, and press (CLEAR) at each one to erase it.

INVALID DIM If you ever get an ERR:INVALID DIM message when you try to graph, then one of the statistics plots has been accidentally turned on. Press (Y=), move the cursor to whichever of Plot1, Plot2, and Plot3 is white text on a black background, and press (ENTER) to turn it off.

Type in your equation. From reading chapter 2, you should know how to type on your calculator and enter equations, but if you don't, you should go back and review those skills. For this crash-course in graphing, we're trying the equation $Y_1 = X^2 + 1$; remember that you can type X with the (XTθn) key when you're in Function mode. If you type it properly, the result will look something like figure 3.2.

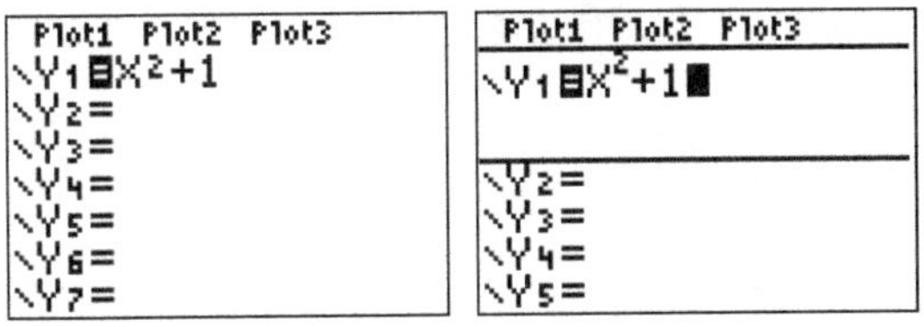

Figure 3.2 Entering the equation $y = x^2 + 1$ to graph without MathPrint (left) and with MathPrint (right). For more discussion of what MathPrint is and how to turn it on and off, see section 1.3. Notice that Plot1, Plot2, and Plot3 are black text on a white background, indicating that statistical plots are disabled. Make sure they're also disabled on your calculator for now (move the cursor over any that are black on white and press (ENTER) to disable them).

Changing line colors on the TI-84 Plus C Silver Edition

As outlined in more detail in section 12.1, the color-screen TI-84 Plus C Silver Edition lets you specify one of 15 possible colors for each graphed function. To change line colors, go to the Y= menu, and use the arrow keys over the rectangle of color at the far left next to any equation. Press (ENTER) to open the Graph Style dialog, where you can change the line color and style.

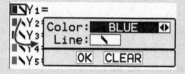

Opening the Graph Style dialog, where you can control the line color and style of a graphed function

There's not much you need to do in the Y= editor other than type in the equation you want to graph, so you can now press (GRAPH) and check out the result. You should see a parabola that opens upward, somewhat like the one in figure 3.3. If you don't, then you might need to reset the graph window. Press (ZOOM), and choose 6:ZStandard (zoom standard); you should now see what figure 3.3 shows.

At this point, you could do any of many things to explore this $y = x^2 + 1$ graph:

- You could press (TRACE) and then use the arrow keys to scroll left and right along the graphed curve.
- You could explore the Table tool by pressing (2nd) (GRAPH).
- You could zoom in and out with the Zoom menu, accessible via the (ZOOM) key.
- You could turn the axes, grid, and other graph decorations on and off in the Format menu, from (2nd) (ZOOM).
- You could add more functions to graph at the same time in the Y= menu.

You'll learn about all these and much more in the coming sections. We'll build on the graphing skills you learned here, exploring some specific word problems so

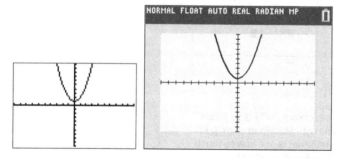

Figure 3.3 At left, the equation $y = x^2 + 1$**, graphed on a TI-83 Plus or TI-84 Plus graphing calculator. If you don't see exactly this, you might need to use zoom standard (ZStandard in the Zoom menu) or adjust whether the axes are displayed (by pressing (2nd) (ZOOM) to open the Format menu). The TI-84 Plus C Silver Edition version is shown at right.**

that you can get a better feel for how math problems can be solved and visualized with graphs.

Let's move on to those examples; keep the skills you just learned in your mind as we go. In particular, remember how to erase and add functions in the Y= menu and how to view them with GRAPH.

3.2　*Visualizing solutions and examining graphs*

Graphing on your calculator can fall anywhere on the difficulty spectrum from very easy to very challenging, depending on which features you want to exercise. In section 3.1, you graphed a simple parabola; in this section, in the midst of the examples we'll work with, you'll learn to find the minima and maxima (the plurals of *minimum* and *maximum*) of functions, the values of functions at specific points, and more.

In the first example you'll work with models by throwing a ball straight up into the air. Physics has a set of equations that describe this so-called *projectile motion*, which can work in either one dimension (like throwing a ball straight up in the air) or two dimensions (like firing a cannonball over a battlefield). We'll look at the one-dimensional (1D) version, and you'll graph the height of the ball versus the time since you threw it. I'll show you how to use the graph to figure out the maximum height the ball reaches, how long it takes to fall to the ground, and more.

The second example will show you how to graph a problem where two trains leave stations far apart at the same time and travel toward each other. When you graph each train's distance from its starting point versus how long it has been traveling, you'll see exactly where they meet. I'll explain the Intersect function and how to use it.

I'll get you started graphing the first example, and then I'll explain the rudiments of the physics behind it and how you can use the graph.

3.2.1　*A ball is thrown: maximum and minimum of a function*

As I'll explain shortly, you can represent the position of a ball thrown straight up into the air as an equation. For this particular example, we'll assume that you're throwing the ball up into the air at 20 meters per second (m/s), that you're standing at ground level at $y = 0$, and that gravity is 9.8 m/s^2, the average for Earth. If any of these terms or units don't make sense, I recommend you check out your favorite physics textbook or website or bug your physics teacher. If you don't know or care about the physics, you can skip the section titled "What the physics?"; the graphing skills taught are still valuable.

I HAVE NO AXES! Not to worry: press (2nd) (ZOOM) to get to the Format menu, move your cursor over AxesOn, and press (ENTER).

The equation we'll be using is

Y$_1$=20X+.5*$^-$9.8*X^2

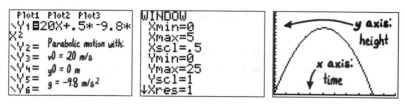

Figure 3.4   Graphing a parabola with the projectile motion equations. On the left, entering the equation $y = y_0 + v_0t + 0.5at^2$, using X to represent time (*t*), $y_0 = 0$ (the ground), and $v_0 = 20$ m/s (thrown upward). The acceleration due to gravity is the standard for Earth, 9.8 m/s². In the center screenshot, adjusting the window to fit the parabola well. On the right, the graphed parabola, peaking around $y = 21$ meters and falling back to the ground around $x =$ time = 4.1 seconds.

Enter this on your calculator, clearing out any old equations you might have there. Remember that the negative symbol is the (–) key, not to be confused with the subtraction key. Also, .5 is just a shorter way to type 0.5. When you type out this equation, it should look like the left side of figure 3.4. Don't forget that if you're on a MathPrint calculator, it might look slightly different. Typed in the equation? Press GRAPH.

But wait, what happened? You probably see a graph that doesn't make any sense and doesn't look like the right side of figure 3.4 at all. The problem is that the calculator's default window, the *x* and *y* values of the edges of the screen, don't work for this problem. To change the window, press WINDOW, where you'll see options like the ones in the center of figure 3.4. Section 3.3 will review how to change the window and what the various options are for; for now, make sure your window matches what figure 3.4 shows. Now press GRAPH again.

Voila! You should have quite the nice-looking graph now, with time represented on the *x* axis and height on the *y* axis. You throw the ball from $y = 0$ and time $x = 0$, the lower-left corner of the screen, and it goes up as time ticks forward, reaches a maximum height, and then begins to fall back down. Near the right edge of the screen, it finally hits the ground. Let me briefly explain what you're looking at, and then I'll show you how to find out some interesting facts about this graph.

WHAT THE PHYSICS?

Projectile motion, or parabolic motion, can be described in one of several ways. First, you need at least one equation for each dimension: one for movement in the *x* direction (horizontally) and one for movement in the *y* direction (vertically). In this case, you only care about vertical motion, because you're throwing the ball straight up.

Next, we have several issues to deal with in this one dimension. We have the initial velocity, which is how hard the thrower tossed the ball. I'm sure you can imagine throwing a ball up in the air: you know it will slow down and stop at some peak height and then fall back toward the ground. The force making it slow down and come back down is gravity, which imparts a constant acceleration of 9.8 m/s² on the ball. In other words, for every second that the ball is in the air, gravity makes it go 9.8 m/s faster toward the ground:

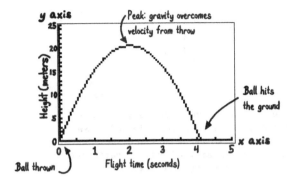

Figure 3.5 **A closer look at the graphed flight of the ball, showing it reaching its peak just after $x = 2$ seconds at a peak height around $y = 21$ meters and then hitting the ground just after $x = 4$ seconds**

- If you throw the ball up in the air at exactly 9.8 m/s, then gravity will make it reach its peak exactly one second later, because it will have slowed it down to 0 m/s upward. It will then begin to fall.
- If you throw it up in the air at exactly 19.6 m/s, then it will reach its peak after 2 seconds. Because in the example you're throwing the ball up at 20 m/s, you know it will reach its peak after slightly over 2 seconds. Check out figure 3.5 for graphical proof.

So what's the actual equation? It needs to involve the initial velocity of the ball, the force of gravity, and the current time. We also add the initial height, just in case you're on top of a cliff when you throw the ball. Normally, we use t for time, but because your calculator graphs using X and Y, we'll use x for time:

$$y = y_0 + v_0 x + 0.5 a x^2$$

This equation generates the current height of the ball (y) at any time (x) in seconds after the ball was thrown. y_0 is the initial height, v_0 is the initial velocity (speed), and a is the acceleration due to gravity. Because we're starting at $y_0 = 0$ and $v_0 = 20$, and gravity is always $a = -9.8$, we end up with exactly the equation I had you enter and graph:

$Y_1=20X+.5*^-9.8*X^2$

PICKING THE WINDOW
Remember how in the center of figure 3.4 I showed you window values to type in? These essentially tell the calculator what part of the graph you want to see by defining the x coordinates of the left and right sides of the screen and the y coordinates of the top and bottom of the screen. I told you to set Xmin and Ymin to 0, Xmax to 5, and Ymax to 25. These turn out to work well, but where did I pull them from?

In your own graphing adventures, you'll need to deal with the challenge of picking a good window to examine a graph. You want to make sure it's wide and tall enough to see the whole area of the graphed function that you're interested in, but not so large that the graph is tiny. I followed three steps to choose my window, which you can do too:

1 A good place to start is often the "standard" window, which you can get by choosing 6:ZStandard from the Zoom menu. This sets Xmin = –10 (the left side of the

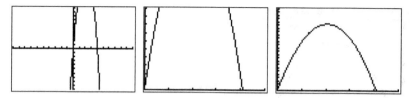

Figure 3.6 Adjusting the zoom for the tossed ball graph. First, use ZStandard, which sets Xmin and Ymin to –10 and Xmax and Ymax to 10. In the middle, we realize that we only care about positive time ($x \geq 0$) and height that is above the ground (Y $\geq$ 0), so we set Xmin = Ymin = 0 and Xmax = 5. Finally, we get the top of the graph onto the screen in the right figure by setting Ymax = 25.

screen), Xmax = 10 (right), Ymin = –10 (bottom), and Ymax = 10 (top). As you can see from the left side of figure 3.6, this is way too wide and not tall enough.

2   We only care about positive x values (time after $x = 0$) and positive y values (ball position above, not under, the ground!). Also, it looks like the curve crosses the x value at about $x = 4$ (each tick is 1), so let's try Xmin = 0, Ymin = 0, Xmax = 5, and Ymax = 10. This gives us the center of figure 3.6, which is closer but still imperfect.

3   Let's get the top of the graph on the screen. I tried Ymax = 15, which wasn't enough, and then Ymax = 25, which was enough. We end up with Xmin = 0 and Ymin = 0, Xmax = 5, and Ymax = 25. You can also adjust Xscl and Yscl, which control the spacing between ticks on the x and y axes, respectively.

Now that you can see where I got the equation you graphed and how to make sure you can fit a whole graph on the screen, let me show you how to use your calculator's tools to figure out the peak height of the ball and when it hits the ground.

THE PEAK: FINDING A MAXIMUM

Your calculator can find what is called a *local maximum*: the highest y value of a graph in some interval, plus the x value where that maximum y occurs. It can also find the *local minimum*, the lowest y value of a graph in some interval, but that's not important for this thrown-ball problem. For the maximum, you'll delve for the first time into the Calculate menu, used to calculate interesting information about graphs.

Finding a maximum, minimum, or zero of a graphed function

1   Graph the function, and then press ⎡ 2nd ⎤ ⎡TRACE⎤ and choose 2:zero, 3:minimum, or 4:maximum.

2   If you have more than one function graphed, use the ⎡▲⎤ and ⎡▼⎤ keys to choose the function to examine.

3   Use the ⎡◄⎤ and ⎡►⎤ keys to move the cursor along the graphed function to select left and right bounds on the region where the zero, minimum, or maximum lies. Press ⎡ENTER⎤ when you get the cursor to the correct location.

(continued)

4 After you select the left and right bounds, the calculator asks you to guess where the zero, minimum, or maximum is. It's not important that you be very accurate with the guess unless the function is complex, but it will help your calculator find the zero, minimum, or maximum faster. If you choose a guess outside the bounds you picked, you'll get an error, ERR:BOUND.

5 When you press ENTER after making your guess, your calculator will think for a bit and spit out the *x* and *y* coordinates of the point.

First, make sure you have the equation for this thrown-ball problem entered and graphed, looking something like figure 3.5 or the right side of figure 3.6. Press GRAPH if you're not already staring at the graph. Now, press 2nd TRACE to get to the Calculate menu, as the word Calc above the TRACE key suggests. You'll see seven options, as figure 3.7 shows. Not surprisingly, you want to scroll down to 4:maximum and press ENTER.

```
CALCULATE
1:value
2:zero
3:minimum
4:maximum
5:intersect
6:dy/dx
7:∫f(x)dx
```

Figure 3.7 The Calculate menu, which gives you tools to use for examining graphed functions

Once you choose 4:maximum, you'll return to the graph screen; the calculator will ask you first for a left bound and then for a right bound. You need to help the calculator understand the interval in which you want it to find the maximum. That's why the tool is for finding *local* maxima: if the graph has several peaks, you can find the exact location of each one by telling the calculator only to search near each one. For this example, set the left bound just to the left of the peak and the right bound a bit to the right of the peak.

Use the ◀ and ▶ keys to move the cursor along the graph, and when you find a good spot, press ENTER. After you set both the left and right cursors, as in figure 3.8, your calculator will ask you for a guess. This guess is a point where it can start searching for the maximum, so try to pick a point near the peak of the graph, as on the right side of figure 3.8.

After you give it those three points—the left bound, right bound, and guess—your calculator will think for a second and generate the answer. It will give you the *x* and *y* coordinates of the maximum *y* value in the given range, just as figure 3.9 shows. For this particular example, figure 3.9 shows a maximum of *y* = 20.4, the maximum height

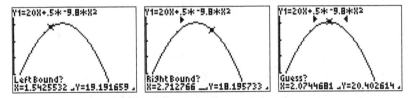

Figure 3.8 Calculating a function's maximum by selecting a left bound, a right bound, and then a guess between those bounds. After you select all three points, your calculator will find the maximum value within the left and right bounds.

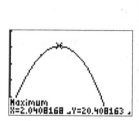

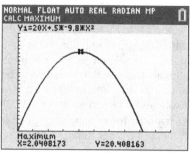

Figure 3.9   The result of your calculator finding the maximum height a ball thrown straight up in the air at 20 m/s reaches. It gets to a height of 20.4 meters before starting to fall again and takes 2.04 seconds to reach that peak.

in meters the ball reaches, at $x = 2.04$, the time in seconds after being thrown that it reaches this height.

The other interesting thing to know about this graph is how long it takes the ball to hit the ground after it's thrown. Your calculator can easily calculate that too.

FLIGHT TIME: FINDING A ZERO

Just as your calculator can find the maximum value of a graphed function within some interval, it can also find the exact x value at which a function crosses the x axis. That is, it finds a coordinate (x,y) where $y = 0$ within user-specified bounds, if it can. This point is called a *zero* of the function, and it can be useful for a variety of purposes. You could, for example, graph a quadratic equation and use the zeroes function to find the roots of the quadratic equation. Here, you'll use the function to find when the ball hits the ground and name the time (x) when the ball reaches height $y = 0$.

The steps for finding a zero are nearly identical to the steps for finding a maximum value; a few snapshots from the process are shown in figure 3.10. Choose 2:zero from the Calculate menu (2nd TRACE), choose left and right bounds around the zero, and guess its approximate location. You might need to move the cursor to a location where the graph goes off the top or bottom of the screen, but that's okay. After you enter your bounds and guess, the calculator will find the zero, as shown on the right in figure 3.10. For more detailed steps, you can also refer to the "Finding a maximum, minimum, or zero of a graphed function" sidebar.

For this function, the calculator finds a zero $(y = 0)$ at time $= x = 4.08$ seconds. As you might expect if you've taken physics, the ball took the same amount of time (2.04 seconds) to reach its peak as it did to fall back down to where it was thrown from

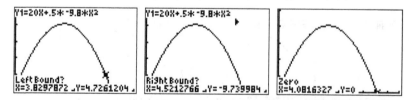

Figure 3.10   Calculating a zero (x-axis intercept) of a function. On the left and in the center, choosing the left and right bounds on the search interval. You'll then also have to provide a guess, and as shown on the right, the calculator finds the zero.

(4.08 – 2.04 = 2.04 seconds). If you solved the original equation $y = 20x + 0.5 \times -9.8 \times x^2$ as if it was a quadratic equation with $y = 0$, namely $-4.9x^2 + 20x + 0 = 0$, you would have gotten the solutions $x = 0$ and $x = 4.08$.

This physics example has shown you how to examine a graph of height versus time for a ball thrown straight up in the air. You learned about calculating a maximum and a zero of a graph, plus the closely related skill of finding a minimum. Let's now look at one of the classic types of word problems, two trains going in opposite directions, and how it can teach finding intersections and specific values of functions and how to trace along a function.

3.2.2 Two trains: intersection of two functions

"Two trains are traveling in opposite directions...." It's probably a phrase you have heard many times in math or physics class, so you might know the basic concept of the problem. In this case, we have two trains separated by 100 miles, racing toward each other. The steam locomotive chugs along at 45 miles per hour (mph), while the Santa Fe diesel engine keeps up a swift 75-mph pace, as you can see in figure 3.11. How long will they travel until they meet? How far will each train have traveled by the time they reach each other?

This well-known problem can be solved with some straightforward algebra. The most important fact toward solving it is that $d=rt$ (distance = rate × time). For example:

10 mph × 1 hour = 10 miles
45 mph × 3 hours = 135 miles

Here, the two trains are leaving at the same time, so they will travel the same amount of time (call it x) before they meet. The distance that the steam train travels in x hours, call it d_{slow}, is $45 \times x$ or just $45x$; and the distance the diesel travels in x hours, call it d_{fast}, is $75 \times x$ or $75x$. You know that because the trains start out 100 miles apart, when they meet, they will have traveled a total of 100 miles. This means $d_{slow} + d_{fast} = 100$ miles, or in other words

$75x + 45x = 100$
$120x = 100$
$x = 100/120 = 5/6 = 0.833$ hours

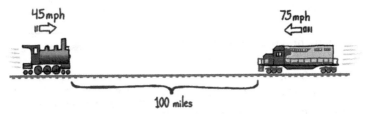

Figure 3.11 Two trains travel in opposite directions, one going 45 mph, and the other going 75 mph. They start out 100 miles apart. How long does it take them to meet, and how far has each one traveled?

```
Plot1  Plot2  Plot3        WINDOW
\Y1■45X                    Xmin=0
\Y2■100-75X                Xmax=2
\Y3=                       Xscl=.25
\Y4=                       Ymin=0
\Y5=                       Ymax=100
\Y6=                       Yscl=10
\Y7=                      ↓Xres=1
```

Figure 3.12   **Entering the equations for the slow and fast trains' positions as a function of time (left), and adjusting the window so that the entire area of interest is visible at once (right)**

Long story short, the trains will meet in 0.833 hour, or 50 minutes after they start moving. At that point, the steam engine will have traveled 45 × (5/6) = 37.5 miles, and the diesel locomotive will have gone 100 − 37.5 = 62.5 miles. But to figure this out, you had to do a bit of algebra. What if the equations for the trains' movement were not straight lines but included acceleration and stops at stations? In that case, you might want a graphical method of finding where the trains met. Your calculator has you covered.

Let's start by graphing the two equations for distance versus time. Put time on the x axis (so x = time in hours) and distance on the y axis (so y = distance in miles). You can use the equation rate × time = distance, or y = rate × x. Based on the fact that the slow train moves forward from 0 and the fast train moves in the opposite direction from 100 miles, you can enter two equations on your calculator:

```
Y₁=45X
Y₂=100-75X
```

The second equation is Y₂=100-75X because the faster train starts at a distance of 100 miles and moves toward 0 miles; its elapsed distance ($75x$ miles) must be subtracted from its starting point (100 miles). You can enter these in the Y= menu as in figure 3.12, and you'll also need to adjust the window, as shown in the same figure. This will make the y axis run from 0 to 100 (miles) with ticks every 10 miles and the x axis go from 0 to 2 (hours) with ticks every 0.25 hour.

As in the thrown-ball example, you could experiment to find a good window for this graph, using some educated guessing to help. You know that you need at least y = 0 through y = 100, because the trains will meet somewhere in between. With those clues, you just need to set Xmin = 0 and increase Xmax until the intersection point is visible, which the equations said was at exactly 50 minutes (0.83 hour). The resulting graph looks like figure 3.13.

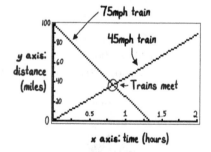

Figure 3.13   **Graphing the location of two trains versus time, and figuring out where they meet**

You could figure out when each train reaches the opposite end of the line 100 miles from its starting point from the graph, but the interesting bit is the point where the two lines intersect. Remember, each line represents where each train was at every moment in time after it began its journey. Where the two lines intersect, the two trains reached the same point along the rails (distance) at the exact same time, passing each other to continue their journeys.

A MEETING OF TRAINS: INTERSECTION

Your calculator can determine the (x,y) point where two functions intersect. The sidebar "Finding the intersection of two functions" discusses the steps in a nutshell; let's go through them explicitly for this train graph.

Finding the intersection of two functions

1　Choose 5:intersect from the Calculate menu (〔2nd〕〔TRACE〕).
2　Select the two graphed functions whose intersection you want to find. You can use the 〔▲〕 and 〔▼〕 keys to move between functions and press 〔ENTER〕 to make your selection final.
3　Your calculator asks you to guess the approximate intersection point; then press 〔▼〕.
4　If the two functions intersect near the guess, you'll get the (x,y) coordinates of the point of intersection.

First, make sure you have the two functions graphed and the window set to something sane, so that the point of intersection is visible onscreen. Revisit the Calculate menu by pressing 〔2nd〕〔TRACE〕; then choose 5:intersect. Your calculator needs three pieces of information from you: the two functions for which you want to find the intersection point and a rough guess of where the point is (in case there's more than one such point). Use the 〔▲〕 and 〔▼〕 keys to switch between functions, and choose Y_1 for the first curve and Y_2 for the second curve. For the guess, move the cursor toward the point of intersection, as in figure 3.14, and press 〔ENTER〕.

Your calculator will determine that the two functions intersect at $x = 0.833$ hour, or 50 minutes, and $y = 37.5$ miles (from where the slower train started). This is exactly what you calculated with algebra! You'll see something like figure 3.15 on your screen, minus my annotations.

We need to discuss two more tools that you might find useful; we'll save the last two items in the Calculate menu for the calculus discussion in chapter 7.

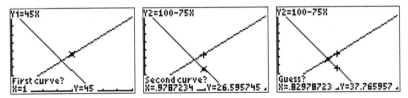

Figure 3.14　Finding the intersection of two graphed functions. First you must choose the two lines to use; you can switch between lines using the 〔▲〕 and 〔▼〕 keys. Then you guess the approximate intersection and press 〔ENTER〕. As you can see in figure 3.15, your calculator finds the exact intersection.

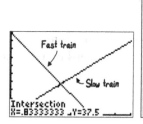

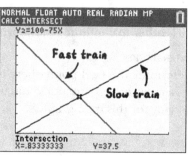

Figure 3.15 The result of calculating the intersection of two functions: a single (x,y) point of intersection

EXACT GRAPH VALUES

The first option in the Calculate menu is 1:value. If you choose this option, you get a prompt X=, asking you to enter some arbitrary *x* value. You must choose an *x* value that is on the screen (such as 0.5 for the example), and the calculator will show you the exact *y* value for that *x* value, as in figure 3.16. You can even use the ▲ and ▼ keys to switch between functions to see the value of every function at that *x* coordinate.

TRACING ALONG A FUNCTION

In a similar vein, you can trace along functions to get an idea of their (x,y) values along their length. Tap the (TRACE) key (no (2nd) this time!) to enter Trace mode, which lets you move a cursor directly along graphed functions, displaying the *x* and *y* values as you go. You use the ◀ and ▶ keys to move left and right along a function or use the ▲ and ▼ keys to switch between functions.

Tracing is good for getting a general sense of functions' values and to find approximate coordinates. You scroll left and right along the functions one pixel at a time, and your calculator shows you the *x* and *y* coordinates of each point along the function. Figure 3.17 shows what you might see if you were tracing along one of two graphed parabolas. If you want to see more accurate numbers, you can zoom in or use the value function in the Calculate menu.

You've now worked through two full examples where you solved real-life problems with your calculator's graphing features. You learned how to graph multiple functions at once, to find minima and maxima, and to find where two graphs intersect. I showed you how to calculate zeroes and specific values on a graph and how to use the trace function to examine graphed curves. Now that you're becoming a pro at examining graphed values, let's look in more depth at changing how graphs look.

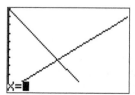

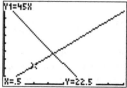

Figure 3.16 Calculating an exact value; here, the *y* value at *x* = 0.5 for the slow train. You must choose an onscreen point, so *x* = 0.5 works here, but *x* = –10 would not.

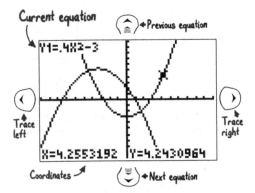

Current equation

Previous equation

Y1=.4X²−3

Trace left

Trace right

X=4.2553192 Y=4.2430964

Coordinates

Next equation

Figure 3.17   Using the trace function to examine $Y_1=.4X^2-3$ and $Y_2=-.3X^2+2-2X$, along with the keys you use to control the trace tool

3.3   *Manipulating graphs*

Throughout the examples we've been discussing, I've occasionally referred to the graph window, the set of numbers that defines what portion of the graph is visible. I taught you one of the Zoom commands, ZStandard. I mentioned in passing how to turn the axes on if they have gotten turned off. In this section, you'll learn all about panning around the graph, zooming in and out, and adjusting how graphs appear.

At the beginning of the chapter, I told you to think of the graph as an infinite plane, a sheet extending forever horizontally and vertically. What you see on the screen when you graph a function is a small rectangular window looking onto that infinite plane. Zooming out makes you see a bigger rectangle, whereas zooming in focuses on a smaller area. We'll start with how you can pan (move) the graph around and how to zoom. We'll then move on to the graph format options that control whether the axes, grid, and other graph decorations are displayed. The section will finish with changing graph styles to draw bolder lines and to shade areas of the graph.

Let's start with viewing different parts of the graph by zooming, panning, and adjusting the window.

3.3.1   *Viewing different parts of the graph*

It stands to reason that with the infinite variety of functions you might want to graph on your calculator, you'll want to focus on different areas of each graph. *X* and *y* coordinates can be literally any number, and any graphing tool worth its salt must be able to show you any region of the graph at a moment's notice.

Your calculator has three broad classes of features to let you change which part of a graph you're examining. First, it lets you pan (move) left or right along a graph, following it to examine how its *y* values change as the *x* coordinates increase or decrease. Second, it lets you zoom in, zoom out, or zoom to one of several predefined settings. Finally, you can manually set the window, which determines the *x* and *y* coordinates of the screen's edges. In this section, I'll show you how to work with each of these tools.

Let's start with panning the graph left and right, the easiest but most limited of the three ways you can change which part of a graph you're looking at.

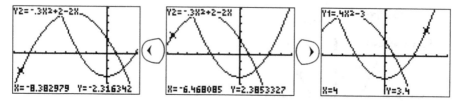

Figure 3.18 Panning left and right along a graph. If you use the trace tool to move left and right along a graph and you get to the edge of the screen, the calculator will scroll one-quarter of a screen in that direction.

Figure 3.19 The many facets of the Zoom menu

PANNING THE GRAPH

While you're tracing a function using the trace tool ((TRACE)), you might reach the edge of the screen and want to know what happens to the graph beyond that edge. Luckily, your calculator can help you out: go off the left or right edges of the screen with the trace tool, and the graph automatically scrolls a fraction of a screen left or right. Figure 3.18 shows what this looks like.

You can't arbitrarily scroll up or down, but if your trace cursor goes off the top or bottom edge of the screen, you can use a feature TI calls Quick Zoom. Press (ENTER), and the graph is recentered with your trace cursor in the center.

ZOOMING THE GRAPH

Zooming sets the window (the coordinates of the screen's edges) to specific values. There are the obvious ones, zooming in and out, but there are also many more options, shown in figure 3.19. You can choose any of these options from the Zoom menu, accessed with the (ZOOM) key.

There are a lot of options here (17, in fact, or 10 on non-MathPrint calculators!), but they're all pretty straightforward. I'll tell you about the most important ones first, the ones that you'll likely use most often:

- Zoom In, Zoom Out—When you choose either of these options, the calculator puts a cursor on the graph screen so that you can choose where the zoom in or out is centered. The new window after the zoom will be centered on that point.

- ZStandard—Sets the window back to the calculator's default, $Xmin = Ymin = -10$ and $Xmax = Ymax = 10$.

- ZSquare—Because your calculator's screen is a rectangle, the ZStandard window makes graphs not be properly proportioned. A circle, for example, is graphed as an ellipse that's wider than it is tall. ZSquare expands the Xmin and

Xmax values of the current window to make circles circular and graphs properly proportioned.

- ZDecimal—Sets the window so that every pixel you move horizontally or vertically is an increase or decrease of exactly 0.1. In standard zoom, coordinates are much messier.

You probably won't have an opportunity to use the other options quite as often, but it's still a good idea to know what they're for. Keep in mind that if you're not using a MathPrint operating system, some of these options will be missing:

- ZBox—Zooms the window to a specific rectangle. Your calculator will ask you to choose the top-left corner of the window first and then the bottom-right. As always, use the arrow keys and (ENTER) to choose the locations of the corners.
- ZTrig—Sets Xmin to just above -2π, Xmax to just under 2π, Ymin to -4, and Ymax to 4. It also sets the Xscl to $\pi/2$, so the ticks on the x axis are separated by $\pi/2$.
- ZInteger—Sets the window so that when you move the cursor around by one pixel in any direction, the x or y coordinate increases or decreases by exactly 1.
- ZoomStat—Adjusts the window to fit any currently displayed statistics plots (see chapter 8). If you don't have any stats plots enabled, then this doesn't do anything.
- ZoomFit—Adjusts the window to fit interesting areas of the entered equations onscreen. I find that it isn't that reliable.
- ZQuadrant1—Sets the bottom-left corner of the screen to Xmin = 0, Ymin = 0, and adjusts Xmax and Ymax so that you change x or y by 0.1 when you move the cursor around.
- ZFrac—There are six possible ZFrac options, from ZFrac1/2 to ZFrac1/10. Each changes the window so that you change the x or y coordinate by that particular fraction when you move the cursor around. For example, ZFrac1/4 changes Xmin to $-47/4$, Xmax to $47/4$, Ymin to $-31/4$, and Ymax to $31/4$. Every time you move the cursor, X or Y changes by $1/4$.

What if panning left and right doesn't help, and none of the zoom options does exactly what you want? As a last resort, you can manually set the edges of the window.

SETTING THE WINDOW

The tool that gives you the most control over what part of a graph you examine is the Window menu. At the same time, it takes the most work to master as a result of the control it gives your over the window. You set the coordinates of the left, right, top, and bottom edges of the screen, as well as the spacing of the ticks on the x and y axes. Figure 3.20 shows how the window options correspond to how the graph screen is displayed on any of the black-and-white calculators. The color-screen equivalent for the TI-84 Plus C Silver Edition is shown in figure 3.21.

You access the Window menu by pressing (WINDOW). Depending on whether you have a MathPrint calculator, you're presented with either seven or eight options. Refer to figure 3.20 or 3.21, and check out what each of the Window options is for:

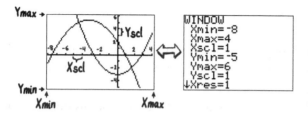

Figure 3.20 **How the numbers in the Window menu relate to how the graph ends up looking on the TI-83 Plus and TI-84 Plus. Figure 3.21 shows the same equivalence on the TI-84 Plus C Silver Edition.**

- Xmin—Sets the x value that corresponds to the left edge of the screen.
- Xmax—Sets the x value that corresponds to the right edge of the screen.
- Xscl—Sets the x spacing between the ticks on the x axis.
- Ymin—Sets the y value that corresponds to the bottom edge of the screen.
- Ymax—Sets the y value that corresponds to the top edge of the screen.
- Yscl—Sets the y spacing between the ticks on the y axis.
- Xres—Very complicated graphs may take a long time to render. You can change this to a number higher than 1 to speed it up, but you'll get much less accurate graphs. It's a good idea to leave this as 1.

- Δx—This option is only available in the Window menu on MathPrint calculators. On other calculators, you can find it via (VARS) (1). If you set Xmin and then this option (which controls the horizontal spacing between pixels), the calculator automatically sets Xmax.
- TraceStep—This option is only available on the TI-84 Plus C Silver Edition. It controls how far the trace cursor (activated with the (TRACE) key) moves when you press the arrow keys.

If you need a pair of good examples of how the window settings can be used, look back to the two problems we worked through in section 3.2.

We've been talking about viewing different parts of the graphs, but your calculator has more tools to help you change how graphs look. Did you know that you can turn the axes on and off, superimpose a grid on the graph screen, and more? You'll learn how to control these options and others in the next section.

3.3.2 *Modifying graph format settings*

Your calculator can display graphs in a variety of useful ways to help you understand graphed functions more easily. You've probably been working with your calculator's

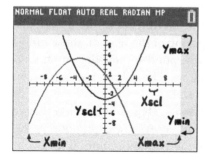

Figure 3.21 **The window settings from the Window menu shown in figure 3.20, as they affect the graph screen on a TI-84 Plus C Silver Edition. As you can see, the settings are exactly the same, albeit on a higher-resolution color screen.**

Figure 3.22 The Format menu, holding the six graph-formatting options. Each row is an option, so you must choose between having the axes on or off, the grid on or off, and graph coordinates in rectangular or polar form. For the expanded TI-84 Plus C Silver Edition version of this menu, take a look at the sidebar "Graph Format options on the TI-84 Plus C Silver Edition" or flip to section 12.2.2

defaults so far, which include things such as axes turned on and (*x,y*) coordinates visible when you trace along a function. But to let you adjust your graphs' appearances to what works for you, your calculator has a menu that can control how the graph screen looks.

All these options are available in the Format (or Graph Format) menu, which you access with [2nd] [ZOOM]. You'll see 6 lines of options (10 on the TI-84 Plus C Silver Edition), which should look something like figure 3.22. All the options that are white text on a black background are currently selected, just like with the Mode menu, and the ones in black text are available if you want to switch to them.

Changing graph Format options

To change a formatting option, go to the Format menu by pressing [2nd] [ZOOM]. The options in white text on a black background are currently selected. You can select options by moving the flashing cursor over them and pressing [ENTER]. To see the results of a new option, revisit the graph by pressing [GRAPH].

The items in the left column are your calculator's defaults: when you start from factory settings, the axes are turned on, the grid is off, coordinates are on, and so on. But what does all that mean? I'll take you through five of the options, leaving the RectGC/PolarGC option for chapter 5. Just set it to RectGC for now, and forget about it. The first choice we want to look at is CoordOn/CoordOff. This particular option changes what happens when you trace along a graphed function or move the cursor around the graph screen, as you can see from figure 3.23. With CoordOn, you see the current *x* and *y* coordinates of the cursor at the bottom of the screen, whereas with CoordOff, they disappear. As you might realize, you'll usually want to leave this as CoordOn.

Next is the GridOff/GridOn option. The grid is a grid (surprise!) of dots displayed over the graph screen, with dots spaced out to match the ticks on the *x* and *y* axes. Look at the right side of figure 3.24, and you'll see exactly what I mean. The

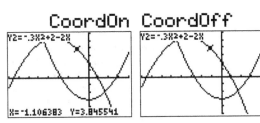

Figure 3.23 The CoordOn/CoordOff options control whether you see the (*x,y*) coordinates while tracing along a graph. In most cases you'll want to leave the coordinates on.

grid can make it much easier to figure out the coordinates of points on a graphed function, but some people find that it makes the graph screen too cluttered or confusing. It's up to you to choose. Try graphing a function with the grid on and off, and check out the difference! On the TI-84 Plus C Silver Edition, you can set the grid to dots or lines.

Next is AxesOff/AxesOn, which you might use a little more frequently than some of the other options. Oddly enough, this option lets you choose whether the *x* and *y* axes are on or off, as figure 3.25 illustrates. There's not much more to say about that!

The fourth option is LabelOff/LabelOn, which controls whether the *x* and *y* axes are labeled with little x and y letters or not. Assuming that most people know which axis is the *x* axis and which one is the *y* axis, TI turns this option off by default on your calculator; but if you want your graphs to look a little fancier, as in figure 3.26, you can turn the labels on. As you can see from the same figure, your calculator doesn't always choose to put those labels in locations that make sense.

The fifth and final option we'll discuss is ExprOn/ExprOff, which controls whether the equation (or expression) for a traced function is displayed. For the sake of clarity, you probably usually want to leave this as ExprOn, as you can see from figure 3.27. If the expression is covering an area of the graph that you want to see, you can temporarily choose ExprOff and later switch back to ExprOn.

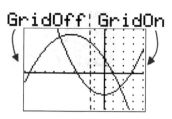

Figure 3.24 The difference between GridOff **and** GridOn. **With the grid on, dots are placed at the intersection of integer *x* and *y* coordinates.**

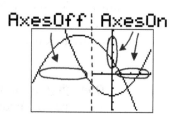

Figure 3.25 The effect of turning the axes on or off. On the left, the *x* and *y* axes aren't visible with AxesOff; **on the right, both axes are visible.**

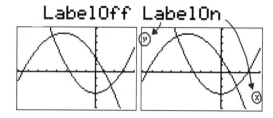

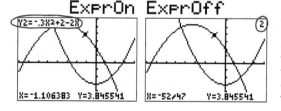

Figure 3.26 A graph displayed with LabelOff **(left) versus** LabelOn **(right). With** LabelOn, **the *x* and *y* axes are labeled, although as you can see, the labels are sometimes placed far from their proper locations.**

Figure 3.27 **ExprOn **and ExprOff **control whether the equation for the current curve is displayed when you use the trace tool. If you turn off the Expr (expression), then the calculator displays the number corresponding to the equation you're tracing, in this case** Y_2.

Graph Format options on the TI-84 Plus C Silver Edition

The Format menu on the color-screen TI-84 Plus C Silver Edition has a few new options. Section 12.2.2 discusses them in detail, but here are the most important ones:

- `GridOff`/`GridDot`/`GridLine` let you put a grid of lines or dots behind functions so that you can easily figure out coordinates of points on the line. The `Grid-Color` option lets you adjust the color of those lines or dots.
- Instead of turning the `Axes` option on or off, you can now set `Axes` to `Off` or any of 15 colors.
- You can set the color of the border around the graph with `BorderColor` and choose an `Image` (photo) to put behind your functions with `Background`.

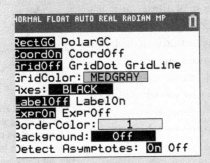

The new look of the Format menu on the TI-84 Plus C Silver Edition

As you've progressed through this section, you've been learning a myriad of tools to control how graphs look and which pieces you're examining. You now know how to zoom and set the window to select a region of a graph and how to control the options that define how the graph screen looks. There's one final set of options. These control how the graphed lines themselves look.

3.3.3 Graph styles, shading, and inequalities

In every example I've shown you so far, a graphed function is drawn as a single, thin, continuous black curve or line on top of a canvas that's blank except for a pair of axes. Your calculator lets you change how these lines look, from making them bolder to shading above or below lines. I'll first show you how to change these options and list what they do, and then I'll briefly show you the results of trying the bold and shade settings.

You change the graph styles from the Y= menu. Every Y= function has what looks like a backslash before it, so you see \Y₁=, \Y₂=, and so on down the screen. Rather than actually being a slash, it's a symbol meaning that the graphed Y_1 and Y_2 lines will be thin black lines. You can change this! After you enter an equation, move the cursor to the left until the \ is flashing. You can scroll through a variety of graph style options by pressing (ENTER); here's what each of the options means:

- ╲Y1—The normal style, as a thin line.
- ╲Y1—A thicker line, but otherwise similar to the normal style.

- ◥Y₁—The area above the line is shaded.
- ◣Y₁—The area below the line is shaded.
- ⊸0Y₁—While the function is graphed, an animated circle traces out the function, leaving behind the normal graph line.
- 0Y₁—Similar to the animated drawing, but only the circle appears; no line is left behind.
- ∴Y₁—An unconnected line, composed of dots.

The TI-84 Plus C Silver Edition has an eighth option. Instead of a dotted line composed of small dots (the last option shown previously), you can choose a dotted line of large dots.

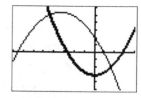

It's pretty straightforward to test each of these, and it's hard to take screenshots of some of them. For example, if I try to show a screenshot of the animated mode, it will just look like a circle. But three of the options appear well in screenshots and are useful in normal math usage. First, there's the bold graph style, which you can see in action in figure 3.28. It's a bit easier to see than the thinner style.

Figure 3.28 The bold graph style applied to one of two graphed parabolas, with the other left thin for the sake of comparison

There are also the graph shading options, which make the calculator shade the graph screen above or below a graphed line. Figure 3.29 shows what that looks like, shading above or below one of two graphed parabolas.

Now you know how to change graph styles, modify graph formatting options, and adjust which area of a graph is visible. You learned how to pan left and right along a graph, use the many zoom options that your graphing calculator offers, and manually change the window settings. These skills built on your experience earlier in the chapter with solving problems using graphs, to give you more control over graphing. The final graph-related tool I want to show you in this chapter gives you one more way to examine the values that make up a graphed function.

3.4   *Using the Table*

Throughout this chapter, you've been looking at graphing as a visual tool: a way to get a picture of what a function looks like. You've used tools like the value feature in the Calculate menu to find the value of a function at a specific point, but even that was still on top of the graph. Your calculator gives you a way to view a list of (x,y) values that make up a function without the graph screen, a tool called the Table.

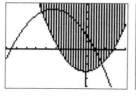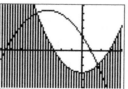

Figure 3.29 Shading above and below a graphed function, with the other expression left as a single unshaded line

As I talk about the Table tool, it would be good if we had a real example to make the explanation clearer. Let's return to the example of the two trains, first introduced in section 3.2.2. The graph for this looked like figure 3.30, and the equations for the slow and the fast trains were

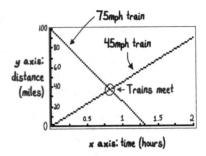

Y₁=45X
Y₂=100−75X

Figure 3.30   The graph of the slow and fast trains for the example in section 3.2.2, as previously shown in figure 3.13

If you don't still have those two equations entered in your calculator, now might be a good time to put them back so that you can follow along as I introduce the Table tool. Don't forget to modify the window to make the graph easier to see. I'll first show you how to access the Table tool and modify the values that are displayed; then I'll show you the two split-screen modes that your calculator includes to let you view the graph and other tools simultaneously.

The first thing you need to know is how to get to the Table tool and control what it shows.

3.4.1   Examining graph values

If you're in a hurry, jump straight to the sidebar titled "The three-step guide to the Table tool." Otherwise, let's get started by examining the default table and playing with settings. First, press (2nd) (GRAPH) (table) to access the Table tool. You'll see a three-column menu. If you entered the preceding Y₁ and Y₂ equations for the train problem, the table will look like the left side of figure 3.31. The left column is X values (X is the independent variable), and the middle and left columns are Y values for Y₁ and Y₂. By default, the first row in the table is X = 0, and X increases by 1 for each subsequent row.

The three-step guide to the Table tool

1 To access the Table tool, press (2nd) (GRAPH). The arrow keys scroll up and down, as well as left and right if you have more than two equations entered.
2 To change the Table settings, go to the Table Setup menu by pressing (2nd) (WINDOW). The Indpnt option controls whether X values are automatically filled in according to TblStart and ΔTbl or if you manually type in each X value you want to appear in the table.
3 If you set the Depend option in the Table Setup menu to Ask, then you have to press (ENTER) in the Y₁, Y₂, ... columns to make values appear (which is as confusing as it sounds, perhaps good for guessing and checking?).

X	Y₁	Y₂
0	0	100
1	45	25
2	90	-50
3	135	-125
4	180	-200
5	225	-275
6	270	-350

Press + for ΔTbl

TABLE SETUP
TblStart=0
ΔTbl=1/6
Indpnt: **Auto** Ask
Depend: **Auto** Ask

X	Y₁	Y₂
0	0	100
.16667	7.5	87.5
.33333	15	75
.5	22.5	62.5
.66667	30	50
.83333	37.5	37.5
1	45	25

Press + for ΔTbl

Figure 3.31   Displaying and modifying the Table. At left, the default Table tool view, with TblStart (the first X value) equal to 0 and ΔTbl (the difference between successive X values) equal to 1. In the center, the Table Setup menu, where I changed the ΔTbl to 1/6 to display the positions of the two trains from section 3.2.2's example in 10-minute intervals.

Unfortunately, although this is informative and makes sense given the speeds of the trains, the values are spaced too far apart for this problem. Because X is the time in hours, you can see that the slow train for Y₁ is 45 miles farther along at each hour, which makes sense given that it's traveling at 45 mph. Similarly, the faster train under Y₂ moves 75 mph in the opposite direction, just as you'd expect. To adjust the spacing of values, you can visit the Table Setup menu.

Press 2nd WINDOW to access Table Setup. See the sidebar "The three-step guide to the Table tool" for an explanation of the Indpnt and Depend options; we'll focus on TblStart and ΔTbl (pronounced "delta table"). TblStart is the value in the first row of the table, and it's usually the first value you want to examine. In this case, it makes sense to keep this at 0, because there's no sense in looking at time values less than X = 0. ΔTbl is the amount to add to each X value to get the next one, and because 1 hour was too much, you could try 10 minutes. An hour has 60 minutes, so 10 minutes is 10/60 hours = 1/6 hour; as shown in the center of figure 3.31, you enter 1/6, and press 2nd GRAPH again to return to the table.

Now you have something more helpful to look at, as shown on the right in figure 3.31. The first row is at 0 minutes, the next at 10 minutes (0.167 = 1/6 hour), the next at 20 minutes, and so on. You can see the whole first hour of travel there, including when the two trains intersect at 50 minutes = 5/6 or 0.833 hour. If you use the ▲ and ▼ keys, you can see more rows of the table above and below where you started. If you're graphing more than two equations at the same time, you can also scroll left and right to see the other equations. The Table view on the TI-84 Plus C Silver Edition is just like the earlier calculators', except that the bigger screen lets it fit more rows and columns at once.

If you want to compare the graph and the table, you might have to keep flipping back and forth between the two. What if you don't want to?

3.4.2   *G-T and Horiz split screen*

You don't have to flip back and forth between the graph and the table: you can view them both at the same time using a split-screen mode called G-T. There's also a second split-screen mode called Horiz, which lets you view the graph screen and the homescreen at the same time. Both are designed to let you keep the graph in view while you use other tools.

First, G-T mode puts the graph and the table on the screen at the same time. The graph goes on the left and the table on the right, just as in figure 3.32. If you press (GRAPH), the graph will become active, and you can still use all the normal graph tools, but the table will also remain visible on the right side. If you instead press (2nd) (GRAPH), you can scroll through the table while keeping an eye on the graph. If you want to switch your own calculator to this mode, press (MODE) and choose the G-T option by highlighting it and pressing (ENTER).

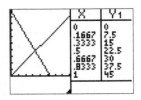

Figure 3.32 The G-T split-screen mode, which shows both the graph and the table at the same time

SPLIT-SCREEN MODES ON THE TI-84 PLUS C SILVER EDITION Because more text can fit on the TI-84 Plus C Silver Edition's higher-resolution screen, G-T mode is spelled out as Graph-Table, and Horiz mode is spelled out as Horizontal.

The other split-screen mode is called Horiz, which splits the screen horizontally. The top half of the screen is the graph, and the bottom of the screen is a four-line home-screen. You can see this in action in figure 3.33, including a line where I tried checking the value of Y_2 at $X = 5/6$. This can be useful for performing calculations while look-ing at the graphed functions, although it has fewer applica-tions than the G-T view. To get to the Horiz mode, press (MODE) and choose the Horiz option by highlighting it and pressing (ENTER).

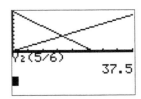

Figure 3.33 Horiz split-screen mode, with the graph at the top and the homescreen at the bottom

GRAPH FUNCTIONS ON THE HOMESCREEN Want to use Y= graph functions on the homescreen as in figure 3.33? You can find them in the Y-Vars tab of the Vars menu, under 1:Function. On MathPrint calculators, you can press (ALPHA) (TRACE) (F4) instead. You can put an x value in parentheses after the function name to compute the value of the function at that point.

If you want to leave either of the split-screen modes and return to the normal view, return to the Mode menu and choose the FULL option by highlighting it and press-ing (ENTER).

With the split-screen options and information about the Table tool under your belt, we're at the conclusion of this introduction to graphing. Hang onto your seat for chapter 4, the last chapter of part 1, which will introduce matrices, lists, and variables; and stay tuned for chapter 5, which will teach you more advanced graphing skills.

3.5 Summary

In this chapter, you got a complete primer about graphing. You started from the basics of entering an equation and graphing it in rectangular, or Cartesian, mode. I then showed you two full examples in depth: one where you graphed the height of a ball as it was thrown into the air, the other following the paths of two trains headed in opposite directions. Through those examples, you learned to find intersections of functions, maxima and minima, zeroes, and the value of functions at specific points. The next section taught you to manipulate graphs, from changing which part of a function is visible on the screen to how the axes are displayed to how to bold and shade graphed functions. We concluded with a look at the Table tool and your calculator's split-screen options. You should now have a good sense of using your calculator as a graphing tool.

In chapter 5, you'll learn about polar, parametric, and sequence graphing, three other modes your calculator offers other than the rectangular mode covered in this chapter. You'll also learn about drawing on top of graphs and saving graphs as pictures. Before we get to that material, though, let's discuss variables, matrices, and lists in chapter 4, the capstone of part 1.

Variables, matrices, and lists

This chapter covers

- Defining and using scalar (real), vector (list), and matrix variables
- Performing computations on one-dimensional (1D) lists of numbers
- Working with two-dimensional (2D) matrices of numbers

In chapter 1, you saw how to solve the Quadratic Formula when you're given values for *a*, *b*, and *c*. In that example, which took up the whole of section 1.1.2, you saw how numbers could be temporarily stored in variables A, B, and C on your calculator. In chapter 2, you saw another special variable called Ans. In each case, those variables were containers where numbers could be stored and later used. In fact, a variable on your calculator is almost exactly like a variable in algebra class.

If you can store and reuse single numbers, why not store and reuse groups of numbers all at once? Perhaps there's a way to put a set of related numbers in a single container and then be able to use them individually or all at the same time. Because I'm suggesting it, the answer is of course that there is: something called a *list*. You can have lists that are similar to the numbers on your calculator, in that you use them temporarily in an equation but don't save them. Just as 3.41 is a number,

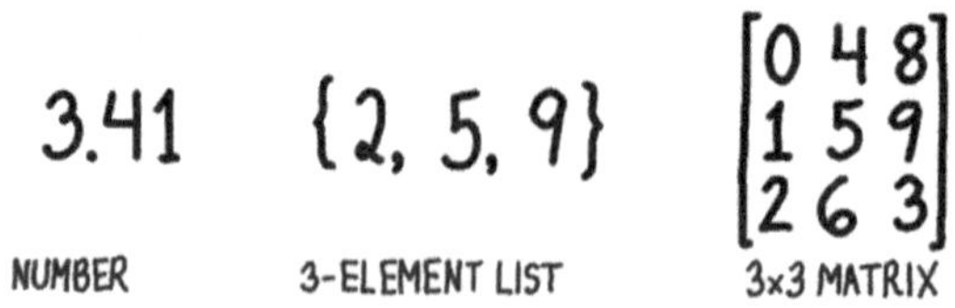

$$3.41 \qquad \{2, 5, 9\} \qquad \begin{bmatrix} 0 & 4 & 8 \\ 1 & 5 & 9 \\ 2 & 6 & 3 \end{bmatrix}$$

NUMBER   3-ELEMENT LIST   3×3 MATRIX

Figure 4.1   A single number, a three-element list of three numbers, and a 3 x 3 matrix holding nine numbers

{2, 5, 9} is a list of three numbers, as figure 4.1 shows. You can also store lists into list variables to save them for later use, just as you can save numbers into variables to save them for later. Lists have a wide variety of uses, although you'll probably run across them most frequently in probability and statistics.

If you wanted to get ambitious, you could consider taking that 1D list of numbers and expanding it into two dimensions, creating a grid of numbers. These 2D grids of numbers are called *matrices*, and they show up in all sorts of math. As I've mentioned in previous chapters, it's beyond the scope of this book to teach you the nitty-gritty of the math behind lists and matrices, but you'll get a complete introduction to the skills necessary to use lists and matrices on your calculator.

This chapter will start with a look at what variables are, why you need them, and how you use them. It will show you examples of variables being used to plug values into well-known types of equations like the Pythagorean Theorem and a third-degree polynomial. We'll then move on to lists. You'll first learn how to work with lists of numbers on your calculator; then I'll show you list variables, where you can store lists for future use. The final third of the chapter will cover matrices, including how you type them on your calculator, how to manipulate them, and how to store them.

Before you get too far into this chapter, and in case you're a bit confused by it, be aware that many of the topics covered in this chapter aren't things you'll be working with in everyday math. Variables are important, especially if you're manipulating a lot of numbers on your calculator, but they're more for saving time and making math easier. Lists and matrices are vital for storing lots of numbers together, and they're indispensible for some math classes, but you wouldn't necessarily run across them in general calculator usage. For the list and matrix sections in particular, remember that this book is a companion to your favorite math textbook and teachers rather than a replacement, so be sure you have a good foundation on what sets (lists) and matrices are before you dive in. With that said, the topics in this chapter are fun, and your calculator makes them easy.

By the end of this chapter, you'll be well versed in typing and using numbers, lists, and matrices. You'll know how to store numbers into variables, lists into list variables, and matrices into matrix variables. Let's get started with the simplest case, numeric variables, which each hold a single number.

4.1   *What are variables? Why do I need them?*

Chapter 1's Quadratic Formula solver showed you how to enter an equation with letter variables and then change the numbers stored into those letter variables to change

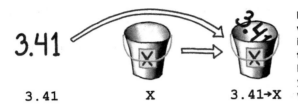

Figure 4.2 A number on the left, an empty variable in the middle. Storing the number into the variable at right. Storing a number to a variable will replace whatever was in it before, if anything. When you use a variable, you copy out the number inside, but a copy will remain inside so you can use it again.

the result of the equation. The letters were A, B, and C, corresponding to the variables *a*, *b*, and *c* that are always used in the Quadratic Formula. By now you certainly know that if you type an equation made up of numbers on your calculator, like 2+3.2*5, your calculator knows that 2, 3.2, and 5 are numbers and performs the requested multiplication and division.

But what about variables? If you give your calculator the equation 2+5X, it's clear to you as a human that there are still three numbers, namely 2, 5, and X. As a human, you would know to ask for a value of X, so that you could multiply X by 5 and then add 2 to the result. Your calculator thinks of X as a container, a bucket if you will, into which it can place a number to retrieve later. Look at figure 4.2 for elaboration on this concept.

Variables start out as empty buckets that could contain a number but don't. If you use an empty variable, your calculator pretends it holds zero. When you use a variable in an equation, it's exactly like you're using the number inside the variable. Your calculator substitutes the value in the variable into the equation and then uses it to finish computing the answer. Check out the sidebar "A variable primer" for how to store values into variables and how to type variables in equations. The letter variables available to you are A through Z and θ, so you have 27 variables to work with.

A variable primer

Variables are buckets with names you can store numbers in and later get numbers out of. Using variables is easy:

- You store values into variables using the [STO▸] key, with the value to store typed before the → symbol and the name of the variable typed after. For example:

  3.75→M

- To use a value stored in a variable, just use that letter in an equation where you might otherwise use a number.
- To type the variable's letters, press [ALPHA] and then the key that has the letter you want in green. The M variable is [ALPHA] [÷], for example.

The best way to learn any new concept is to work through examples of the skill in action, and variables are no exception. Let's try three examples together. We'll start easy, with a polynomial that uses a single variable, *x*. The second example you'll work on using three variables, representing the length, width, and height of a box, to calculate the volume of that box. In the third and final example, you'll test the Pythagorean

Theorem, solving for the missing number in a Pythagorean triple and then checking that the three numbers you get in fact form a valid triple.

Let's start with a relatively simple third-degree polynomial, an equation involving the variable x with four terms.

4.1.1 Plugging x into a polynomial

Polynomials are the sums of coefficients times variables raised to a power. What a mouthful! How about some examples? $x^2 + 1$ is a polynomial. $5x - 4$ is a polynomial too. So are $-4x^2 + x - 4$, $3x^3 + 2x^2 + x$, and $7x^4 - 3x^3 - 11x^2 + 13x + 1$. Every polynomial is a sum of one or more terms, with a few restrictions on what can be in the terms. For more information, refer to your favorite math book or teacher. For this example, we'll be working with this polynomial:

$$x^3 + 6x^2 - 6x - 1$$

This is a third-degree polynomial, because the largest power that x is raised to is 3 and x is the only variable in the polynomial. It has four terms, which means it has four coefficients. If you've browsed through chapter 3, you might know that you can find the roots (values of x that make the polynomial equal 0) by graphing this equation and looking for the zeroes. But your goal for this example is not necessarily to find the zeroes but to be able to plug any x value into the equation and find out what it returns.

You'll be working in the homescreen area of the calculator, just as you were in chapter 2. It's on the homescreen that you store values to variables and use those variables in equations. You can also use variables in graphed equations and programs exactly the same way you use them on the homescreen, but I won't cover that here. Anyway, you should start by putting a value in the X variable. As detailed in the sidebar "A variable primer," you need to type the value to store, then press (STO►) to type the → symbol, and then type the name of the variable to store the value. Try storing 3 to X like this:

3→X

The left side of figure 4.3 shows what this will look like.

The right side of the homescreen shows 3, to confirm that 3 has been stored into X. Now you can use X anywhere you might have otherwise wanted to plug in the value 3. Let's use that value in an equation. You can type it on your calculator like this:

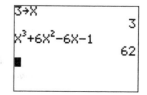

X^3+6X²−6X−1 or X³+6X²−6X−1

You should know how to type this on your calculator; the only possible exception might be the cubed (^{3}) symbol, which is in the Math menu. If you don't want to use that, you can just type (∧) (3). Need help with exponents? Look back

Figure 4.3 Using the variable X to test different values in a third-degree polynomial. The screenshot shows a value of X = 3 substituted into the polynomial.

at section 2.2.3. Anyway, when you press (ENTER), you should get 62 as a result, as in figure 4.3. If you figure out the value of $x^3 + 6x^2 - 6x - 1$ by hand, plugging in 3 everywhere you see x, then you'll get the same value, 62.

The whole point of using variables this way is to let you try different values without having to retype the equation. Let's try the same thing with X equal to 1. Type 1→X and press (ENTER), and your calculator will confirm that 1 has been stored into X. Now, you'll want to test the equation with the new X value, but surely it would be annoying to have to type the equation over again. Luckily, you can recall an old equation or expression that you entered, as you learned in chapter 2. Press (2nd) (ENTER) to scroll backward through your history, or, if you're using a calculator with MathPrint enabled, press (▲) until you find the equation you want and then press (ENTER). Once you have X³+6X²-6X-1 back on the current line, running it to get a value for the equation with X equal to 1 is as simple as pressing (ENTER). Depending on whether you're using a MathPrint calculator, you'll see something like one of the sides of figure 4.4, but the bottom line is that the answer will be 0.

You could keep doing this as much as you want, storing values to X and then recalling the polynomial to see its value for that given X. If you worked through chapter 3, you might be thinking to yourself, "Why can't I just enter this as a Y= equation and use the value feature in the Calculate menu?" You'd be correct. For an equation that has only a single independent variable (like X in this polynomial), you could enter the equation as a Y= equation with whatever variable was in the equation as X. You could trace along the graphed function to examine values or go to the Calculate menu and choose the value tool.

But what if you have more than one variable? You can't graph an equation that has multiple independent variables on your TI-83 Plus or TI-84 Plus. Trying to graph something like 4P+3.3S-1.8T, your calculator would throw up its proverbial hands. Luckily, you can work with equations with multiple variables on the homescreen just as easily as you can an equation with a single variable.

4.1.2 Finding the volume of a box

A simple equation that uses three variables calculates the volume of a box. Given the length, width, and height of a box, you multiply the three variables together, and you get the volume of the box. If you represent the three dimensions of the box as l, w, and h, respectively, then the volume of the box is $l*w*h$. It should come as no great surprise that you can use the variables L, W, and H to store the dimensions of the box and then use the equation L*W*H or even just LWH to calculate the volume of the box on your calculator.

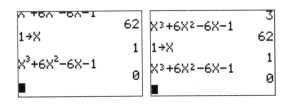

Figure 4.4 Testing the same polynomial, with a value of X = 1 instead of the original X = 3. The left screenshot shows the result with MathPrint enabled, and the right screenshot has MathPrint disabled. The differences are minor.

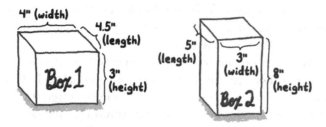

Figure 4.5   The two boxes we'll examine in this problem. As you'll calculate, Box 1 has a volume of 54 cubic inches, and Box 2 has a volume of 120 cubic inches. If these boxes look familiar, it's because you learned how to find the volume of a box (without variables) in chapter 1.

You'll first store the three dimensions of the box to variables and then execute the equation to get the volume of the box defined by those dimensions. Check out figure 4.5, which shows the two boxes we'll be testing this on, the first 4.5 x 4 x 3 inches and the second 5 x 3 x 8 inches.

You'll first have to store the length, width, and height of the box you'll be analyzing. You've seen the technique of storing to multiple variables on the same line in the Quadratic Formula solver in chapter 1, but it's helpful enough to be worth repeating. If you put any sort of calculations on the same line, separated by colons, your calculator will calculate all of them. But it will only display the result of the last calculation, so for regular math, it has limited usefulness. One particularly good use is for storing to multiple variables on the same line. Why? So that you can use (2nd) (ENTER) to go back and adjust all the variables on a single line instead of having to scroll back to three different items in your history.

First, set L equal to 4.5, W equal to 4, and H equal to 3, to match the dimensions of Box 1 in figure 4.5. As in the previous example, use the (STO▸) key to type the arrow that separates numbers and the variable they're being put into. The colon is (2nd) (·), as you can confirm by looking at the blue or orange text above the (·) key. As always, press (ENTER) at the end of each completed line to run it. The first two lines on the left side of figure 4.6 show what you should see after you store values to L, W, and H.

For this example, performing the actual calculation is the easy part: type LWH to request that the calculator (implicitly) multiply L, W, and H, and press (ENTER). If nothing goes wrong, you'll get 54, as shown on the right side of figure 4.6. Although it's unlikely that your calculator would make a mistake, you can double-check the result

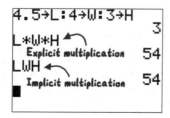

Figure 4.6   Multiplying three variables to get the volume of a box. The length times the width times the height of the box yields its total volume. A 4.5 x 4 x 3–inch box has a volume of 54 cubic inches, as the calculator reveals. Notice that your calculator can understand both implicit and explicit multiplication.

by multiplying 4.5 by 4 in your head (which is 9 x 2, which is 18) and then multiplying that by 3 (yielding $3 \times 18 = 3 \times 10 + 3 \times 8 = 30 + 24 = 54$) to get 54.

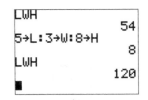

For Box 2 from figure 4.5, enter the new values for the length, width, and height. The easiest way to do this is to press 2nd ENTER twice, to get to the previous line that stored the dimensions, and then edit the numbers on the line. Remember, DEL deletes letters and symbols from the middle of a line, and 2nd DEL switches you from Overwrite mode to Insert mode. When you've finished setting L to 5, W

Figure 4.7 Finding the volume of Box 2. This 5 x 3 x 8–inch box has a volume of 120 cubic inches.

to 3, and H to 8, calculate LWH again. You'll get a volume of 120 cubic inches, as shown in figure 4.7.

So you can use variables with equations involving one unknown and equations using many unknowns. You can apply these same skills to more complex equations, such as polynomials. The final example in this section will show you one such polynomial in the form of the Pythagorean Theorem. You'll discover how to use variables to find the third number in a Pythagorean triple with the other two known, and then check that the resulting three numbers are valid solutions to the Pythagorean Theorem.

4.1.3 Testing the Pythagorean Theorem

The Pythagorean Theorem is a well-known theorem and formula concerning the lengths of the legs of a right triangle. A right triangle is a special kind of triangle where one of the three angles between the sides is a right angle, that is, 90°. The two sides that form the right angle are labeled *a* and *b*, and the third side, called the hypotenuse, is labeled *c*. If you take each letter to be a variable holding the length of the respective side, then the Pythagorean Theorem says that for *any* right triangle, $a^2 + b^2 = c^2$.

In other words, if you square the lengths of the sides that form the right angle, the sum of those two numbers is equal to the square of the length of the hypotenuse. One of the important side effects of the Pythagorean Theorem is that if you know a triangle is a right triangle, and you know the lengths of two of the legs, you can calculate the length of the third leg without measuring. Lost yet? Take a gander at figure 4.8; maybe it will help.

For this particular example, we'll be dealing with the Pythagorean triple where $a = 5$, $b = 12$, and $c = 13$, sometimes also written {5, 12, 13}. A *Pythagorean triple* is a set of three numbers that make the Pythagorean formula $a^2 + b^2 = c^2$ true when you plug them in. In

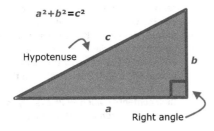

Figure 4.8 A right triangle, with the two legs that form the right angle labeled *a* and *b* and the hypotenuse labeled *c*. When you sum the squares of the lengths of *a* and *b*, you get the square of the length of *c*, codified in the Pythagorean Theorem. Cool result: you can calculate the length of *a*, *b*, or *c* if you know the lengths of the other two.

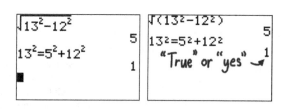

Figure 4.9   Using numbers (not variables) to first solve for the missing number in a Pythagorean triple and then making sure the three numbers (5, 12, and 13) in fact create a Pythagorean triple, where $a^2 + b^2 = c^2$. From the last section of chapter 2, the results of a comparison (the equals sign) can be either 1 (true/yes) or 0 (false/no). These two screenshots show the same thing, except that the left side uses MathPrint and the right side does not.

this example, we'll use 12 and 13 plus the fact that they're part of a Pythagorean triple to derive the third number in the triple, 5. We'll then use the equality testing method you learned at the end of chapter 2 to make sure $a^2 + b^2 = c^2$ is true for these values.

   And we'll perform these steps twice, so that you can see why using variables here is relevant. First, take the square root of $13^2 - 12^2$, as shown on the top line of figure 4.9. Don't forget that the squared symbol is the ⌨ x^2 key, the square root symbol is ⌨ 2nd ⌨ x^2, and that this equation will be slightly different depending on whether your calculator has MathPrint enabled.

   You should get an answer of 5, the third number in the triple. The equation I had you enter is just $a^2 + b^2 = c^2$, rearranged to put a by itself on one side, and with $b = 12$ and $c = 13$ substituted in. You can check that 5, 12, and 13 are a proper Pythagorean triple by typing in $13^2 = 5^2 + 12^2$ and pressing ⌨ ENTER. As chapter 2 demonstrated, the equal symbol is used to check if two expressions are equal on your calculator. You can find it in the Test menu under ⌨ 2nd ⌨ MATH. Your calculator should generate 1, its way of saying "Yes, those two things are in fact equal." You can now be confident that your calculator agrees that {5, 12, 13} is a Pythagorean triple.

   But if you want to test a lot of different potential triples, you'll have to keep typing those squared symbols and that equal sign over and over. Why don't we just use variables A, B, and C, because the Pythagorean Theorem is written in terms of variables a, b, and c anyway? That's exactly what we'll do. First, we'll store 5 to A, 12 to B, and 13 to C and then perform the same two calculations but using variables instead of numbers.

   Store the requisite values to A, B, and C, as you've been doing all along. I recommend storing them all on a single line, using colons to separate the store operations, but it's up to you. The top-left of figure 4.10 shows how I did it.

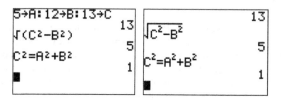

Figure 4.10   Using variables for the same tests as in figure 4.9. Here, we store a, b, and c to the variables A, B, and C and then find the missing number in the triple and check the validity of the triple, just as in figure 4.9. The left and right sides show the same thing, but because the MathPrint version on the right uses taller lines, the line where A, B, and C get their contents (which looks exactly the same) have already scrolled off the top.

Next, type the same square root expression, this time using C and B, making the expression $\sqrt{(C^2-B^2)}$. Figure 4.10 shows this with and without MathPrint. You'll still get 5, because you're basically doing the same math as before, just using the variables to hold the numbers you used directly earlier. This verifies that using the Pythagorean Theorem and two of the three numbers in a Pythagorean triple, you can derive the third one. Finally, let's take the three numbers in the triple and test that they can be properly slotted into the Pythagorean Theorem. A few paragraphs ago, you tested $13^2=12^2+5^2$ and found that the calculator returned 1 (yes/true). Because you have A = 5, B = 12, and C = 13, you can easily substitute the variables for the numbers and instead test $C^2=A^2+B^2$.

Type in the equation, press (ENTER), and predictably enough, your calculator will generate 1, indicating that A^2+B^2 is indeed equal to C^2. From here, you could test other potential Pythagorean triples by storing a new A, B, and C and running $C^2=A^2+B^2$ again. You could, for example, test the sets of {A, B, C} values {3, 4, 5}, {4, 6, 9}, and {20, 21, 29} to see which of those are valid Pythagorean triples.

There are lots of other reasons you might want to store sets of related numbers together, besides the three numbers of a Pythagorean triple. Your calculator has a great way to store up to 999 numbers together in a single container, called a list. Let me give you the tour.

4.2 Using sequences of numbers: lists

Your calculator can manipulate sets of numbers together, just as it can manipulate single numbers by themselves. Just as you can add a number to another number, you can add a number to every one of a set of other numbers. You can find the maximum, minimum, sum, and mean of a list of numbers. And just as you can store numbers into variables for later recall, you can store lists into list variables. If you think of a variable as a bucket that you put a number into, then a list is a series of numbers, and a list variable is a set of buckets nailed to a plank. When you put a list into a list variable, you put each of the numbers in the list into one of the buckets that make up the list variable. Figure 4.11 is what you might imagine a list variable looking like.

In this section, I'll teach you what a list is and how to create and use lists. I'll also show you how to work with list variables. You'll see lists again when you reach chapter 8, so if you finish this material and need to know more about using lists for statistics, flip to chapter 8.

The first thing you need to do is learn list-related terminology and how to create and manipulate lists. Let's start there. First, let's be absolutely clear on the terminology. We'll be dealing with lists, list variables, and list elements:

Figure 4.11 A list variable, which you can visualize as a series of buckets nailed to a plank. This is a three-element list variable, which can hold a three-element list consisting of three numbers. Each of the numbers goes in a bucket. You can use the whole list (L_1) at once, or you can use one of the list elements by itself (the middle bucket is $L_1(2)$, for example).

- A *list* is a collection of many numbers, stored together as a group. Lists are represented by a set of numbers, separated by commas and enclosed in curly braces. Here are some examples of lists: {1}, {4,‾6,5}, and {8,8,8,5.451,‾103.5}. Your calculator's lists can each have up to 999 elements (numbers) inside.
- A *list variable* is a semipermanent place to put a list on your calculator. You'll most often deal with list variables L_1 through L_6, which can be typed with (2nd) (1) through (2nd) (6). There are also so-called *custom list variables*, which can have any name you want with one to five letters.
- A *list element* is one of the numbers that makes up a list. The first number in a list is the first element, the second number is the second element, and so on. If a list has a *dimension* of 5, it means it holds five numbers.

When you perform operations that result in lists, your calculator outputs a list instead of a single number. Sometimes the list is too wide to fit on the screen, so you can use the left- and right-arrow keys to scroll through it. Let's give typing short and long lists a quick try.

4.2.1   *Typing lists*

Type the two-element list {3,4} on your homescreen. First, the opening curly brace { is (2nd) (( ). The 3 and 4 are obvious, and the comma is the (,) key. You don't type a space between the comma and the next number. End the list with the closing curly brace, (2nd) ( )). When you press (ENTER), your calculator will respond with exactly the list you entered, because you didn't ask it to perform any calculation with the list. Figure 4.12 shows what this will look like. Now let's try a list that's too long to fit on one line. Try typing {1,1,2,3,5,8,13,21,34} and pressing (ENTER). Figure 4.12 shows what you'll see.

Your calculator uses symbols to alert you that part of the list answer is offscreen. If you're using a MathPrint calculator, these are small arrows, like ◀ and ▶. On non-MathPrint calculators, these are ellipses, like .... You can scroll left and right with the (◀) and (▶) keys to explore the list, although once you start typing on the new line, you won't be able to scroll any more.

Remember the Ans variable from chapter 2? Ans is a special variable that is automatically filled with the number returned as the last answer to a calculation and displayed on the right side of the screen, without you explicitly storing values to it. We

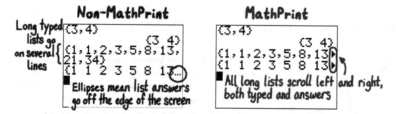

Figure 4.12   Typing short and long lists on your graphing calculator's homescreen, without MathPrint (left) and with MathPrint (right)

only looked at how Ans holds single numbers, but it can hold lists (and matrices and other data types) as well. If the answer to any calculation on the homescreen is a list rather than a single number, Ans will instantly (and temporarily) become a list variable, until a new calculation puts a different answer into it. And because you can automatically store lists into Ans, why not store lists into long-term list variables?

4.2.2 *Storing lists into list variables*

Because I've been mentioning it for over a page, it's no surprise that you can indeed store lists into list variables. We'll just worry about L_1 through L_6, the six standard lists, for now. Keep in mind for future reference that you can create your own lists with custom names. Storing lists into list variables is a lot like storing numbers into numeric variables, as you can see from the handy sidebar titled "Storing and using list variables." As the sidebar notes, anywhere you can use a list, you can use a list variable instead, just as you can use a numeric variable anywhere you might want to use a number.

Storing and using list variables

List variables hold lists containing up to 999 numbers. The most commonly used lists for general math are L_1 through L_6, typed with (2nd)(1) through (2nd)(6):

- To store a list to a list variable, type the list, press (STO▶), and then type the name of the variable to store the list to. For example:

  $\{1,4,9,16\} \rightarrow L_5$

- List variables aren't the same as regular variables that each store a single number. You can't store a list in the A, M, or X variable. You can have lists in Ans, but you'll need to store Ans to a list (like Ans→L_2) to keep it.
- You can use a list variable anywhere you might otherwise use a list, just as you can use a numeric variable anywhere you might use a number. Your calculator substitutes in the list what the list variable contains.
- To use a single number from a list (an element), the syntax is list(*index*), where *index* is the element number to pluck out. See section 4.2.3 for an example.
- To remove all the elements in a list variable, use the ClrList command from (STAT)(4). It can take one or more list variables as arguments, such ClrList L_4 or ClrList L_1, L_3, L_5.

For example, to store a three-element list containing 1, 5, and –43 to list L_1, you type the list, press (STO▶), and then type L_1 with (2nd)(1). You'll see something like the top line of figure 4.13.

You can check the value of L_1 by putting it on a line by itself and pressing (ENTER), as in the second line of figure 4.13. You get the same result as if you had typed out the complete list $\{1,5,-43\}$ instead of just L_1. You can then use L_1 in equations. I'll show you some of the operations you can perform on lists in section 4.3, but for now, I'll just tell you that 2*L_1 returns a new list where each element is twice the corresponding element of L_1. Try it out, as in the third line of figure 4.13.

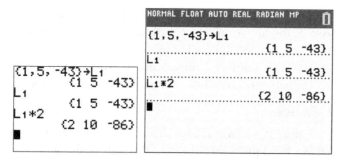

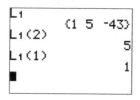

Figure 4.13   Storing a three-element list into list variable L_1, returning L_1 by itself, and returning $2*L_1$. In section 4.3, you'll see how to perform operations like $2*L_1$. The right side shows what this set of operations looks like on the TI-84 Plus C Silver Edition, and the left side covers all the earlier calculator models.

Suppose you wanted to pull out a single element of a list as a number, rather than returning the entire list. That's possible too.

4.2.3   Isolating a single list element

Every element of a list has an index, a number describing where it is in the list. The first element has index 1, the second index 2, the third index 3, and so on. To fetch a single element of a list, you put the index of the desired element in parentheses after the list name. To get the second element of L_1, you type $L_1(2)$; the third element is $L_1(3)$; and so on. Figure 4.14 shows an example you can try for yourself. You might still have L_1 set from the previous example; if not, store at least two values to L_1 before you try the example in figure 4.14.

> **ERR: DIM**   If you try to get from a list an element that doesn't exist, you'll get an error. For example, if you have a three-element list, you can't get the fourth element: there is none. You also can't get elements 0, –1, 1.5, or –1.5. All indices (indexes) must be between 1 and the number of elements in the list.

Because you can use any list element the same way you'd use a number or a variable, you can, for example, use lists to store sets of numbers that you want to try in an equation. Here's a form of the Pythagorean triple test where L_1 holds $\{a, b, c\}$:

$$L_1(1)^2+L_1(2)^2=L_1(3)^2$$

To make things even more interesting, you could use a variable for the index, such as $L_4(X)$ instead of $L_4(10)$, after storing $10 \to X$.

Figure 4.14   Pulling out single values from list variable L_1. Putting 2 in parentheses after the list name makes the calculator pull out the second element of the list as a number, as if you had used a variable like C or T. A 1 in parentheses extracts the first element, a 4 the fourth element, and so on.

Now you know how to type lists, how to put lists into list variables, how to use list variables, and how to fetch individual elements out of list variables. You don't know the sorts of math you can do with whole lists, which is the order of business we'll now discuss. There are three classes of list math operations that your calculator can perform, so I'll show you each of the three along with some examples to help make the new skills more concrete.

4.3 List operations and functions

You now know what lists are, but you don't know much of what you can do to manipulate them. You know you can add, subtract, multiply, and divide numbers. You know you can square and square root numbers, take the sine and cosine, and figure out which of two numbers is higher. What about lists?

Lists are a different animal. You can do three main things with lists:

- *List-wise operations*—You use a whole list or two whole lists for the operation. For example, you can sum a list or find the maximum value in an entire list. You can also add two complete lists together, as long as they have the same dimension (size), which adds the corresponding elements of the lists together.
- *Element-wise operations*—You apply the same operation to each element of a list. For example, you can add 2 to every element of a list, or divide each by 6.8, or negate every element.
- *Single-element operations*—You pull out one value and use it like a number. These aren't really list operations, because they're exactly the same as the math you did in chapter 2. I won't discuss this further, other than the explanation at the end of section 4.2.3.

I'm going to first show you an overview of all the list-wise operations you can do with your calculator. I'll then move on to the element-wise operations. Although there are a fair number of commands and operations you can do with lists on a graphing calculator, each is fairly straightforward, so you'll quickly get the hang of it.

Let's begin with list-wise operations, which include any list math that uses one list as a whole or two lists together.

4.3.1 List-wise algebra operations

You can perform a variety of list-wise algebra operations with two lists on your calculator. All these operations work with two lists of the same length and apply an algebraic operation to corresponding elements of the two lists. Look at figure 4.15 for a few examples of what I'm talking about.

In figure 4.15, you can see addition, subtraction, exponentiation, multiplication, and division between two two-element lists. Adding two lists together produces a single new list, the elements of which are the sums of the corresponding elements of the two original lists. Similarly, multiplying two lists together produces a new list in which the elements are the products of corresponding elements of the original list. If you're

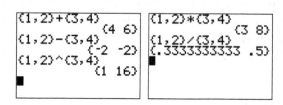

Figure 4.15 Performing list-wise algebraic operations, from adding and subtracting two lists, to raising the elements of one list to the power of another list, to multiplying and dividing lists. Notice that for each of these five operations, the operation (addition, subtraction, exponentiation, multiplication, or division) is applied to corresponding elements of the two lists.

still a bit confused, look at figure 4.16, which shows how two three-element lists are multiplied together.

There's not too much else to say about list-wise algebraic operations, except perhaps that you can use a list variable anywhere you might otherwise use a list. For example, if list variable L_1 contains a three-element list, you can calculate

$L_1*\{5,3,2\}$

instead of

$\{1,2,4\}*\{5,3,2\}$

If L_1 didn't contain a three-element list, though, you'd get a DIM MISMATCH error.

ERR: DIM MISMATCH   If you try to perform algebraic list-wise operations with two lists of different sizes, your calculator will produce this error message. You can only calculate list-wise operations between two lists with the same dimensions (size). For example, you can add two four-element lists together, but you can't add a four-element list to a five-element list.

EXAMPLE: ADDING TWO LISTS

Say you have four classes one afternoon, and you want to know when each class will end. You have two four-element lists, $\{1,0.5,1,1.5\}$ and $\{1,2,3,5\}$. The first list represents how long each of the four classes will take (in hours), and the second holds the starting hour of each class. You can use algebraic list operations on your calculator to find the end time of each class by adding its duration to its start time.

Type $\{1,2,3,5\}+\{1,0.5,1,1.5\}$ on your calculator, and press ⎯ENTER⎯. Because this is list-wise math, the calculator will add the corresponding start time and duration of each class together, resulting in a four-element list that holds the end time of each class. Figure 4.17 shows that the result of this addition is $\{2,2.5,4,6.5\}$. Because these values are in hours, you know that your first class will end at 2 pm, the second at 2:30 pm, the third at 4 pm, and the fourth at 6:30 pm.

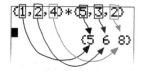

Figure 4.16 Multiplying the lists $\{1,2,4\}$ and $\{5,3,2\}$. Each term of the output is the product of the corresponding elements of the original lists. The first element is 1 × 5 = 5, the second is 2 × 3 = 6, and the third is 4 × 2 = 8.

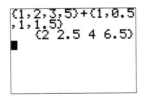

Figure 4.17 Adding two lists together to figure out what times your four classes on an afternoon will end. The first list contains the starting times of each class (1 pm, 2 pm, 3 pm, and 5 pm), and the second list holds the duration of each class in hours.

Your calculator can manipulate two lists together with ease. Besides simple algebraic operations, your calculator has a host of functions for mathematical functions involving one or two whole lists. I'll show you all those in the next section.

4.3.2 List-wise math functions

Your calculator has a set of functions that pertain to list-wise math, all of which can be found in the Ops and Math tabs of the List menu. Recall from chapter 2 that a function is something like gcd(, round(, or max(. To access this menu, press 2nd STAT. The first tab, Names, shows all the lists that are currently on your calculator. This will come in handy if you're not sure which variables you've defined. You want to look at the Ops and Math tabs, however. Figure 4.18 shows what you'll find under those tabs.

Look at table 4.1 to see what the various commands in the Ops tab of the List menu do. As you can see, some can operate on either lists or list variables and some only on list variables. I haven't explained every item in the menu, because there are a few that you won't use in everyday math.

The items in the Math tab of the List menu are much easier to use. Each one takes a list of any length, with the exception of stdDev(and variance(, which both need lists at least two elements long:

- The min(and max(functions find the smallest and largest elements of the input list, respectively.
- The mean(and median(functions return the average and median of the input list.
- The sum(and product(functions add or multiply all the elements of the input list together and return the result.
- The stdDev(and variance(functions, which both take a list of two or more elements, return the standard deviation and variance of the input list, respectively.

```
NAMES OPS MATH
1:SortA(
2:SortD(
3:dim(
4:Fill(
5:seq(
6:cumSum(
7↓▸List(
8:Select(
9:augment(
0:List▸matr(
A:Matr▸list(
B:L
```

```
NAMES OPS MATH
1:min(
2:max(
3:mean(
4:median(
5:sum(
6:prod(
7↓stdDev(
8:variance(
```

Figure 4.18 The Ops and Math tabs of the List menu, accessed with 2nd STAT. The Ops menu contains functions that sort lists, create lists based on formulae, join lists together, and convert between lists and matrices. The Math menu calculates list statistics and will be reviewed in section 8.2.

Table 4.1   Some list-wise operations in the List Ops menu

Function	Description	Example(s)
SortA (SortD (	Sorts a list variable's elements into ascending (A) or descending (D) order. Only works on list variables, and stores the resulting list back to the variable on its own.	SortA(L_1) <div align="right">Done</div>SortD(L_3) <div align="right">Done</div>
dim (	Gets the length (dimension) of a list or resizes a list. If you make a list smaller, items get chopped off; if you make it bigger, the new elements are filled with zeroes.	$\{1,2,3\}$→L_2 <div align="right">$\{1,2,3\}$</div>dim(L_2) <div align="right">3</div>4→dim(L_2) <div align="right">4</div>L_2 <div align="right">$\{1,2,3,0\}$</div>
Fill (	Sets every element of a list variable to a given number. The number comes first and then the name of the list variable. The list must already have at least one element; otherwise, you'll get an ERR: INVALID DIM error.	Fill($8,L_2$) <div align="right">Done</div>L_2 <div align="right">$\{8,8,8,8\}$</div>
cumSum (	Returns a list holding the cumulative sum of a list. The first element is the first element of the list by itself. The second element is the sum of the first two elements of the original list, the third element is the sum of the first three elements, and so on.	cumSum($\{1,1,1\}$) <div align="right">$\{1,2,3\}$</div>cumSum($\{4,^-4,0\}$) <div align="right">$\{4,0,0\}$</div>
ΔList (	Generates a list in which each element is the difference between adjacent elements in the input list.	ΔList($\{2,4,6\}$) <div align="right">$\{2,2\}$</div>
augment (	Concatenates (join) two lists together. The function returns the new larger list; you can store it to a list variable if you need to save it.	augment($\{1,2\},\{8,9\}$) <div align="right">$\{1,2,8,9\}$</div>

Look at figure 4.19 for four examples of these functions in action.

EXAMPLE: CALCULATE 10 MULTIPLES OF 17

One of the most complex list functions on your calculator is the seq(function, which I didn't discuss in table 4.1. I'll show it to you here to repair that omission. The seq(, or sequence function, takes an equation with one independent variable (like 17X or 5A-A^2+3 or 1+X), calculates its value at evenly spaced values of the variable, and returns the result as a list. It's a lot like the table view I showed you in chapter 3,

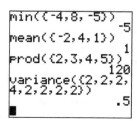

Figure 4.19   A composite screenshot of four of the functions under the List Math menu in action. The min (function picks out the smallest number in the input list, mean (takes the average, and prod (multiplies the elements of the list together. Variance (finds the statistical variance of the elements in the list.

 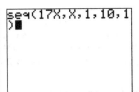

Figure 4.20 The MathPrint wizard used for creating sequences (left) and typing out the sequence by hand on non-MathPrint calculators (right). The seq(function produces a list by plugging values between *start* and *end* into the *variable* in the *expression*, adding *step* to the variable for each subsequent value. The results are placed into a list.

except that the output is a list instead of a table. The seq(function is sufficiently complex that it's easier to explain with an example: let's use it to calculate the first 10 multiples of 17.

Start at a blank homescreen line, press (2nd) (STAT) (▶) to go to the Ops tab of the List menu, and choose 5:seq(. Depending on whether you have MathPrint enabled, you'll either see a "wizard" that looks like the left side of figure 4.20 or just the seq(token pasted to the homescreen. Fill in an equation of 17X, variable X, start = 1, end = 10, and step = 1. This means seq(will create a sequence of values for 17X where X starts at 1, ends at 10, and increments by 1 for each subsequent list element. If you type it out by hand, the proper syntax is seq(*equation*, *variable*, *start*, *end*, *step*), as on the right in figure 4.20.

Once you press (ENTER), your calculator will generate the requested sequence, as in figure 4.21. As you can see, the first element is 17X where X = 1, the next is 17X where X = 2, and so on. These, therefore, are the first 10 multiples of 17. Remember, you can use the (◀) and (▶) keys to scroll left and right along this long result list.

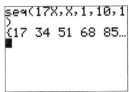

Figure 4.21 Using the seq(command to generate the first 10 multiples of 17 on the homescreen, as explained in the example in the text

I mentioned one final type of trick you can do with lists: element-wise operations. Those can be handy for quickly modifying all the elements of a list, so let's take a look.

4.3.3 Element-wise list operations

Element-wise operations are surprisingly similar to the list-wise algebraic operations you saw earlier. Instead of involving two lists of the same size, however, they require a list of any size and a single number. Element-wise operations apply the operation to every item in the list. For example, the operation 3*{1,2,3} multiplies every element of the list by 3 to produce {3,6,9}. The operation {10,15,20}-10 would produce {0,5,10}.

Why would you want this? Because you can easily change every element of a list without either entering a new list or using a list-wise operation with a long repetitive list. You can perform element-wise operations with addition, subtraction, multiplication, division, and exponentiation, just like list-wise algebraic operations. Figure 4.22 illustrates a few of these operations in action.

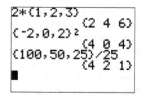

```
2*{1,2,3}
           {2 4 6}
{-2,0,2}²
           {4 0 4}
{100,50,25}/25
           {4 2 1}
■
```

Figure 4.22   Some element-wise operations in action. Multiplying each of the elements of a list by 2 on the top line, squaring each element of a list on the second line, and dividing every element of a list by 25 on the third line.

EXAMPLE: SUBTRACTING A LIST FROM ITS OWN SQUARES

Say you have the list $\{1,2,3,4,5\}$, and you want to square the list and then subtract the original list from those squares. You could use Ans, you could type out the list twice, or you could use a list variable. You'll need to first apply the element-wise exponentiation operation to square each element of the list and then use list-wise subtraction to subtract the original list.

Let's try the Ans method on the left side of figure 4.23, although the center and right of figure 4.23 show the other two methods I mentioned:

1 Type $\{1,2,3,4,5\}$, and press (ENTER). As you've seen in chapter 2 and earlier in this chapter, this will make the special Ans variable a list containing $\{1,2,3,4,5\}$.

2 Now you can square Ans and subtract Ans from that value, because until you press (ENTER) on a new calculation, Ans will still hold the five-element list you typed. The complete expression is Ans²–Ans (where Ans is (2nd) ((-))), as shown on the left in figure 4.23.

3 Press (ENTER), and the calculator will square the list, internally producing $\{1,4,9,16,25\}$ (which it won't show, because it doesn't show you intermediate steps in calculations). It will then subtract $\{1,2,3,4,5\}$ and display the final result: {0,2,6,12,20}.

You've now seen many ways you can use and manipulate lists. You learned how to create lists, store lists into list variables, and get them out again. You learned how to extract individual list elements, what functions are available to manipulate lists, and how to perform list-wise and element-wise algebraic operations on lists. Chapter 8 will give you a much richer introduction to the practical applications of lists for statistics, although you're sure to find many other reasons you'd need sets of numbers stored together.

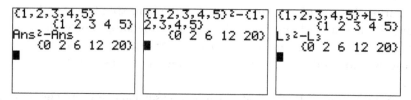

Figure 4.23   Three different, equally valid ways to subtract a list from its own squares. In each case, you start with the list $\{1,2,3,4,5\}$, use element-wise math to square the individual elements, and use list-wise algebra to subtract the original list's elements. On the left, putting the original list in Ans. In the center, typing out the original list twice so you can do the whole calculation in one line. On the right, storing to a permanent list variable instead of using Ans.

Now that you know how to work with single numbers and long strings of numbers, I want to show you 2D grids of numbers, called *arrays* or *matrices*. Your calculator can store and manipulate matrices, as well as perform all the matrix math operations that your textbooks will teach you how to do by hand. You can even use a matrix to solve a system of equations!

4.4   *Exploring 2D matrices*

If lists are 1D sets of related numbers, then matrices are 2D sets of numbers. Matrices on your calculator can be anywhere from 1 row by 1 column (called a 1 x 1 matrix) to 99 rows by 99 columns (called a 99 x 99 matrix), although the calculator's memory is too small to fit a full 99 x 99 matrix. A 10 x 2 matrix has 10 rows and 2 columns. Each cell in the matrix, at the intersection of a row and a column, holds a number, just as each element in a list holds a number. A 10 x 2 matrix contains 20 numbers. Figure 4.24 shows a 4 x 6 matrix that contains 24 elements.

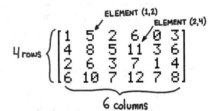

Figure 4.24   A 4 x 6 matrix with four rows and six columns. Individual elements are named by their row and column, so element (2,4) is on the second row, at the fourth column.

In this section, you'll learn to do for matrices what the preceding section taught you for lists. You learned to create lists, store list variables, and then do math with lists. Here, you'll learn to create matrices, store to and use matrix variables, and perform matrix math on your calculator. I'll show you the two ways to create matrices, one on the homescreen and the other in your calculator's matrix variable editor.

Matrices in a nutshell

A matrix is a rectangular array (2D grid) of numbers. On your calculator, a matrix has 1–99 rows and 1–99 columns:

- You type a matrix on the homescreen by enclosing the whole thing in a pair of square braces. Inside those braces, you put the rows, starting from the top and going toward the bottom. Each row starts with a [, continues with all the numbers in that row separated by columns, and ends with a]. For example, a 2 x 3 matrix might be [[1,2,3][4,5,6]].
- You can type the braces with (2nd) (x) and (2nd) (−).
- Just as you can store lists into list variables, you can store matrices into matrix variables. Your calculator has 10 matrix variables, [A] through [J], found in the Names tab of the Matrix menu ((2nd) (x⁻¹)). You *cannot* type out the names manually with the three characters [, A, and]; instead, you must paste them from the Matrix menu.
- To access the element at row M, column N of matrix [A], enter [A](M,N). For example, to access the element at row 2, column 3, type [A](2,3). You can even do this with a matrix in Ans: Ans(2,3).

Figure 4.25   Create a new matrix, without MathPrint (left) and with MathPrint (center and right). In both cases, we've created a two-row, three-column matrix containing six elements. On the TI-84 Plus C Silver Edition, the MTRX shortcut menu in the center is rearranged but contains the same options.

4.4.1   *Typing matrices on the homescreen*

You can type matrices on your calculator's homescreen regardless of whether you have MathPrint enabled. The difference is that with MathPrint, you get a more user-friendly grid into which you can enter your matrix elements, although this grid only allows matrices up to six rows by six columns to be entered. For larger matrices, and on non-MathPrint calculators, you need to enter matrices manually.

To enter a matrix manually, you type [to indicate the start of the matrix, then the matrix's rows one by one from top to bottom, and then] to indicate the end of the matrix. Each row looks like a list: it's a series of one or more numbers separated by commas. But instead of curly braces like { and }, each row starts with a [and ends with a]. A one-element matrix containing just a 2 would be [[2]]. A two-row, three-element matrix would have two rows, each containing three numbers separated by commas and enclosed in square braces, together enclosed in another set of square braces. The left side of figure 4.25 demonstrates entering a 2 x 3 matrix and shows how a non-MathPrint calculator displays the result.

The middle and right sides of figure 4.25 show how you can enter small matrices more easily on a MathPrint calculator. Press (ALPHA) (ZOOM) (that is, F3) to access the MATRX (matrix) tab of the special MathPrint homescreen window. Select how many rows and columns your matrix has, as in the center screenshot in figure 4.25, and then move the cursor down to OK and press (ENTER). You'll then be able to enter a value in each element of your matrix.

If you create a matrix or calculate a matrix answer and want to save it for later use, you'll need to put it into a matrix variable.

4.4.2   *Creating and using matrix variables*

Just as your calculator has list variables, it also has matrix variables. It has 10 variables into which you can store any matrices you want, as long as your calculator has enough memory to fit them. The matrix variables are named [A] through [J], as discussed in the sidebar "Matrices in a nutshell." You can store matrices to matrix variables using the (STO▸) key, and you can use a matrix variable in an equation where you might otherwise use a matrix. If you get a matrix as the result of a calculation, you can store it to

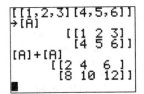

Figure 4.26 Storing a matrix to the [A] matrix variable and then using that matrix in a mathematical expression. Notice that adding a matrix to another matrix (in this case, itself) adds corresponding elements, just like adding two lists together! You'll learn more about that soon.

a variable by using the trusty Ans variable, which automatically becomes a matrix when the answer to the last calculation was a matrix.

TYPING MATRIX VARIABLE NAMES   You can't type matrix variable names like [, B,] for the [B] matrix variable. You must instead select the variable name from the Names tab of the Matrix menu ((2nd) (x⁻¹)) to paste it to the home-screen. On the earlier TI-82 or TI-83 (non-Plus) calculators, there's a dedicated [MATRX] key.

Look at figure 4.26 for an example of storing a matrix to a list and then using that matrix by adding it to itself. Notice that matrix variables are similar to lists in this respect, differing only in that matrices are two-dimensional and lists are one-dimensional.

There's one final way to type out a matrix, which combines the lessons on creating matrices and storing matrix variables. Your calculator has a matrix editor that stores the matrix you type directly into a matrix variable.

4.4.3   *Typing matrices in the matrix editor*

All calculators, MathPrint or not, have a matrix editor, although you can only use it for editing stored matrix variables [A] through [J]. To access it, you go to the third tab (Edit) of the Matrix menu, accessed via (2nd) (x⁻¹). As you can see in figure 4.27, the Edit tab displays each of the matrix variables available on your calculator, plus the current dimensions of the matrix variable, if it exists. If there are no dimensions shown, the variable hasn't been created yet.

Choose any of the 10 variable names in the Edit tab to enter the matrix editor, as illustrated in figure 4.28. At the top, you can edit the number of rows and columns in the matrix.

Figure 4.27   The Edit tab of the Matrix menu. Choose any variable and press (ENTER) to enter the matrix editor, as shown in figure 4.28.

MATRIX SIZE LIMITS   Although matrices can be up to 99 × 99 elements, your calculator cannot fit a 99 * 99 = 9801–element matrix in its memory. A single 49 × 49 matrix will fill the memory of the TI-84 Plus C Silver Edition, whereas a single 51 × 51 matrix is the largest that will fit on the other TI-83 Plus and TI-84 Plus calculators. You can have many smaller matrices, and you can have matrices that are 4 × 99 or 99 × 20, for example.

In the middle, the contents of the matrix are shown. You can move the cursor over any element and press (ENTER) to edit that element's value. Type in the new value, which

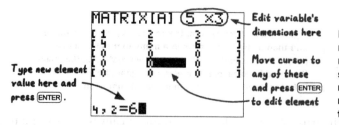

Figure 4.28 The heart of the matrix editor. You edit the matrix dimensions at the top, scroll around the contents of the matrix in the middle, and type new matrix element values at the bottom.

appears at the bottom of the screen, and press ENTER again to store the value into the matrix element. When you're satisfied with the matrix, you can press 2nd MODE to return to the homescreen.

You can then use the matrix variable you just created or edited like any other matrix or matrix variable. Let's move swiftly on to look at the matrix math operations available on your calculator so that you can see how your calculator can manipulate matrices.

4.5   *Matrix operations and functions*

Matrix math can be a confusing beast, especially when you see it for the first time in math class. For example, the order of the matrices matters when you multiply two matrices together; reverse them, and you get a different answer. And while you multiply a number by 1 to get the same number back, you need to multiply a matrix by an identity matrix filled with a pattern of 1s and 0s to get the same matrix back.

Your calculator can perform matrix addition, subtraction, and multiplication, all of which operate on whole matrices. I'll show you these matrix-wise algebraic operations first, all of which resemble the list-wise algebraic operations that you saw in section 4.3.1. I'll also briefly discuss element-wise operations, which are more limited for matrices than for lists. There is an assorted handful of operations that modify or produce a single matrix, which I'll show you as single-matrix operations. Finally, your calculator contains a set of row-wise operations that can be useful but are too niche to deserve a lot of space here.

For the most part, the matrix operations your calculator can perform look and behave exactly as they do in your textbook and when you do them by hand. Your calculator can be great for checking your hand-calculated matrix math or, when you get into higher math or engineering, for saving you the tedium of doing matrix math manually and potentially making mistakes. To that end, let's start with matrix-wise algebraic operations.

4.5.1   *Matrix-wise algebraic operations*

Your calculator can perform four matrix-wise algebraic operations: addition, subtraction, multiplication, and division. Addition and subtraction are like their list-wise counterparts—they add or subtract the corresponding elements of two matrices and must be performed on two matrices with equal dimensions. Multiplication and division are a bit different, as your favorite math textbook can explain thoroughly. Let's

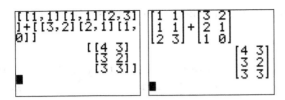

Figure 4.29 Adding two matrices without MathPrint (left) and with MathPrint (right). The result is the same in both cases, but it's easier to see the shape and contents of the original matrices on the right.

start with addition and subtraction; then I'll explain the requirements for matrix multiplication and division.

Matrix addition and subtraction are performed between corresponding elements. The input matrices must be the same size: they must have matching column counts and row counts. You can add two 4 x 2 matrices together, but you can't add a 4 x 2 matrix to a 3 x 2 matrix. The result is a matrix that's the same size as the input matrices but in which the elements are the sum of the corresponding elements of the inputs. Figure 4.29 shows an example of matrix addition with and without MathPrint-style matrices.

Matrix multiplication and division aren't like multiplying and dividing numbers or even lists. It's beyond the scope of this book to explain the mechanics behind matrix multiplication, but instead of two equal-size matrices, it requires that the number of rows in the second matrix to be multiplied is equal to the number of columns in the first matrix to be multiplied. If the first matrix is m x n, meaning that it contains m rows and n columns, then the second matrix must be n x p, having n rows and p columns. Check out figure 4.30 for an example of multiplying a 3 x 2 matrix by a 2 x 1 matrix, yielding a 3 x 1 result.

> **ERR: DIM MISMATCH** If you try to perform matrix multiplication with incompatible matrices, your calculator will produce an error. The number of columns in the first matrix must always equal the number of rows in the second matrix when you perform multiplication.

Matrix division is even more complex. When you perform matrix division, your calculator *inverts* the second matrix (not to be confused with *transposing* it); then it multiplies the first matrix by this inverse matrix. To make things worse, only square matrices (with an equal number of rows and columns) can be inverted, and not all square matrices are invertible.

To multiply or divide matrices, just stick a * or / between the two matrices, as in figure 4.30. You can combine several matrix-wise algebraic operations together into a single equation, although with matrices, the order of the operands is important. Lest we

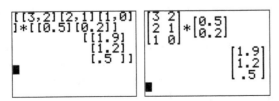

Figure 4.30 Multiplying a 3 x 2 matrix by a 2 x 1 matrix, yielding a 3 x 1 matrix by the rules of matrix multiplication. The left side shows the process on a non-MathPrint calculator, the right side a MathPrint calculator doing the same operation.

get too far into the side of matrix math that most often confuses beginners, let's look at element-wise operations.

ELEMENT-WISE OPERATIONS

In section 4.3.2, you learned that adding a number to a list adds that value to each element of the list and returns the resulting list. Multiplying a list by a number multiplies each element of the list by that number and produces the resulting list. Unfortunately, of the many element-wise operations available for lists, only multiplication by a number is available for matrices, which multiplies each element of the matrix by that number. Figure 4.31 demonstrates that operation. You can't add, subtract, or divide a number from a matrix.

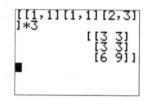

Figure 4.31 Multiplying a matrix by a number, the only sort of element-wise operation between matrices and numbers that your calculator can perform

If you try to add, subtract, or divide a number from a matrix, you'll receive an ERR: DATA TYPE. You can also raise a matrix to an integer power, but this is equivalent to multiplying a matrix by itself. If you calculate $[A]^2$, you're calculating $[A] * [A]$, and $[A]^3$ is $[A] * [A] * [A]$. Because of the rules of matrix multiplication, to multiply a matrix by itself, it must be square.

Other than matrix-wise operations between two matrices and element-wise multiplication between a matrix and a number, your calculator can perform a variety of operations on single matrices. Some of these are math operations, and others are functions.

4.5.2 *Single-matrix operations*

Your calculator can manipulate single matrices to perform common matrix tasks. The most important operations among these are taking the determinant of a matrix, determining the transpose and inverse of matrices, and producing an identity matrix. The determinant and identity matrix are calculated using functions from the Matrix Math menu, the second tab under (2nd) (x^{-1}). The transpose is a symbol found in the Matrix Math menu, and the inverse of a matrix is taken using the inverse key, (x^{-1}).

The mechanics of each of these four operations are simple:

- To take the *determinant* of a matrix, use the det(function, found under 1:det(in the Matrix Math menu. The det(function takes one argument: the matrix of which you want to take the determinant. You can put either a matrix variable or a matrix inside the parentheses. For example:

```
det([C])
det([[1,1][-4,5]])
```

- To produce an *identity matrix*, use the identity(function, available in the Matrix Math menu as 5:identity(. Because identity matrices are always square, but can be any square size from 1 x 1 up to 99 x 99, the identity(function takes one argument. That argument is the number of rows and columns to put in the identity matrix, so identity(1) creates a 1 x 1 identity matrix, identity(3) creates a 3 x 3 identity matrix, and so on.

- To get the *transpose* of a matrix, use the ^T symbol, which you place after a matrix like an exponent. You can find it under 2:^T in the Matrix Math menu. For example, [C]^T produces the transpose of the matrix stored in the [C] matrix variable.
- To *invert* an invertible matrix, use the ⁻¹ symbol with the (x⁻¹) key. Like the transpose symbol, you place it after a matrix like an exponent, so [[1,4][2,3]]⁻¹ will invert the given 2 x 2 matrix.

Figure 4.32 shows calculating the determinant of a 3 x 3 matrix, generating a 5 x 5 identity matrix, and calculating the inverse and transpose of a 2 x 2 matrix. There are a few other important functions in the Matrix Math menu that you may find handy in a few limited situations, which I'll briefly explain in case you ever do need them.

USE YOUR RESOURCES Your teachers and textbooks are there to help you. Matrix operations aren't easy, and it's tough to remember all the rules for matrix multiplication and inverses, calculating determinants, and similar tasks. It will take practicing and frequently checking your reference materials to master these topics.

ROW-WISE OPERATIONS AND OTHER FUNCTIONS

The Math tab of the Matrix menu contains 15 different functions and tools that you can use to create and manipulate matrices, as shown in figure 4.33. I've picked out a few of the most potentially useful ones that you might run across to describe in a bit more detail. Keep in mind that these functions are listed in table 4.2 for reference, so if you find yourself stuck trying to do something esoteric with a matrix at some point later in your math career, take a look to see if this table has anything to help you.

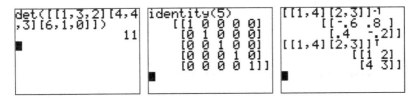

Figure 4.32 **From left to right, calculating the determinant of a 3 x 3 matrix, creating a 5 x 5 identity matrix, and producing the inverse and transpose of the same 2 x 2 matrix**

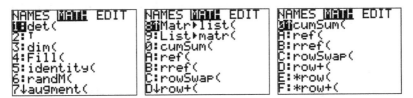

Figure 4.33 **The 15 items in the Math tab of the Matrix menu, accessible via (2nd) (x⁻¹). Note that the right screenshot contains only two extra functions.**

Table 4.2 The most useful functions in the Matrix Math menu that you haven't yet seen

Function	Description	Example(s)

Matr▶list	Stores column(s) of a matrix to one or more lists. If you specify a matrix and one list, the first column will be extracted. If you specify a matrix and three lists, the first three columns will be extracted, and so on.	`[[1,1,1] [2,⁻5,4]]`
		　　　　　`[[1,1,1]`
		　　　　　`[2,⁻5,4]]`
		`Matr▶list(Ans,L₁,L₂,L₃)`
		　　　　　　　`Done`
		`L₂`
		　　　　　　　`{1,⁻5}`

List▶matr	Creates a matrix variable out of one or more lists, each of which will form one column of the resulting matrix variable. The lists must all have the same length.	`List▶matr({1,6},`
		`{2,8},[C])`
		　　　　　　　`Done`
		`[C]`
		　　　　　　　`[[1,2]`
		　　　　　　　`[6,8]]`

ref(
rref(
	Converts a matrix into row-echelon format or reduced row-echelon format. This is useful for solving a system of equations with a matrix.	`rref([[2,1,10] [0,`
		`1,5]])`
		　　　　　`[[0 1 2.5]`
		　　　　　`[0 1 5]]`

rowSwap(	Swaps two rows of a matrix. Because it can operate on matrices or matrix variables, it returns the result instead of storing it back to a matrix variable.	`rowSwap([B],1,3)`

row+(
*row(
*row+(
	These three commands, plus rowSwap(, are used internally by the calculator when performing the ref(and rref(commands. row+(adds one row to another, *row(multiplies all the elements in a row by a number, and *row(performs the two operations together.	`row+(`
		`*row(`
		`*row+(`

Solving a system of equations with a matrix

A handy matrix trick lets you solve a system of equations with *m* equations and *n* unknowns using an m x n+1 matrix. Arrange each equation so that the coefficients to the unknown variables appear in order, with all the unknowns on the left of the equals sign and the constants on the right. Fill the coefficients into a matrix, and then use the rref(function to put the matrix in reduced row-echelon form (a process called Gaussian elimination). If the system is solvable, each row of the matrix will give you the value of one of the unknowns.

Solve: $2x+y=10$
$x-3y=19$

$$\begin{bmatrix} 2 & 1 & 10 \\ 1 & -3 & 19 \end{bmatrix} \Rightarrow_{rref(} \begin{bmatrix} 1 & 0 & 7 \\ 0 & 1 & -4 \end{bmatrix} \Rightarrow \begin{array}{l} x=7 \\ y=-4 \end{array}$$

Solving a system of two equations with two unknowns using a matrix and the rref(function

In this section, you saw examples of the many matrix operations that your calculator can apply to manipulate matrices, and together with section 4.4, you know just about all the skills you need to effectively use matrices on your calculator.

4.6   *Summary*

Throughout this chapter, you've learned about the many ways your calculator can store and manipulate groups of numbers. We started with single numbers stored in your calculator as variables, and you worked through three examples of variables in real-world use. I then showed you sets of numbers grouped together as lists and those lists stored into memory as list variables. You learned how your calculator lets you manipulate lists and perform list calculations, including list-wise operations that operate on whole lists, element-wise operations that manipulate individual elements, and list functions your calculator provides for statistics and more.

In the matrix sections, you learned about the 2D sets of numbers called matrices, which can be stored for later use as matrix variables. I taught you about creating matrices on the homescreen and editing matrix variables in the matrix editor. I took you through the matrix algebra tools available on your calculator, which follow standard matrix math rules, and introduced some of the many matrix-related functions the Matrix Math menu offers.

Having reached the conclusion of the first part of this book, you now have a complete set of skills for normal calculator use. You know how to do math with your calculator, how to graph functions and examine the resulting graphs, and how to work with lists and matrices. As we move into the second part of this book, you'll begin to learn more specialized skills, most if not all of which will become important at some point in your educational career. I understand if you choose to use the remainder of this book as a reference guide when you reach each of the corresponding subjects in school, but if you have the time, I urge you to work through the coming chapters, especially the examples, one by one. You're sure to learn lots more about the power and features of your graphing calculator and have fun doing it. We'll be starting with expanding your graphing skills. Your calculator can graph in Function, Polar, Parametric, and Sequence modes, but you've seen only Function mode so far. Chapter 5 will show you the other three modes, plus drawing on and saving graphs.

Part 2

Precalculus and calculus

Part 1 of this book taught you general-purpose calculator skills: doing arithmetic, graphing functions, and working with variables, lists, and matrices. Part 2 will start you on a journey into more specialized skills, beginning with precalculus and calculus. In the three chapters in this part, you'll learn three new types of graphing, as well as how you can draw and sketch over graphs. You'll learn to work with imaginary and complex numbers, trigonometric function, limits, and logarithms. You'll compute integrals and derivatives, and you'll discover the capabilities and limitations of your TI-83 Plus/TI-84 Plus's calculus tools.

Chapter 5 starts with three new graphing modes: Parametric, Polar, and Sequence. We'll look at a few examples of each graphing mode in action, from the practical to the pretty. You'll explore recursion, the Fibonacci series, Lissajous curves, and more. This chapter will also show you how to draw on the graphscreen, either to annotate graphs, to draw diagrams, or just to doodle. You'll see more precalculus tools in chapter 6. Working with real, complex, and imaginary numbers is presented first; you'll then learn how to use trigonometric functions and examine the unit circle. Although your calculator doesn't have a specific tool to find limits, I'll show you how you can do so anyway. Chapter 6 concludes with logarithms and exponential functions.

Chapter 7 concludes this part with the calculus features of your graphing calculator. It shows you how to find numerical derivatives, how to compute the slope of a curve at a point, and how the first and second derivative can be used to find extrema and points of inflection of functions. You'll also learn to compute numeric integrals, most often used to find the area under a curve.

Expanding
your graphing skills

This chapter covers

- Working with Parametric, Polar, and Sequence graphing modes
- Drawing diagrams and annotating graphs
- Saving and restoring graph snapshots and graph settings

Graphing is one of the key features of your graphing calculator; chapter 3 pointed out that it's so important that it's half of the device's name. In that chapter, we worked with normal Cartesian graphing, where you visualize equations like $y = x^2 + 1$. In this chapter, you'll see many of the advanced graphing features your calculator includes, such as new graphing modes and annotating graphs with drawings.

Why would you want to graph in other schemes than Cartesian graphing, anyway? The short answer is that there are many functions and graphs that you can't represent in the form $y = f(x)$, which defines the vertical position (y) of each point in the graph by passing its horizontal position (x) through a function. Figure 5.1 shows the four different types of graph coordinate systems that your calculator can work with.

Whereas chapter 3 taught you rectangular or Cartesian graphing, this chapter will introduce the other three modes in figure 5.1. We'll first go through Parametric

Graph Coordinate Systems

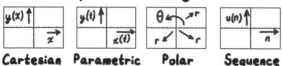

Cartesian   Parametric   Polar   Sequence

Figure 5.1   The four types of graph coordinate systems your calculator knows. At far left, Cartesian (or rectangular) coordinates, where *x* is the independent variable and *y(x)* is the dependent variable. Parametric mode at center-left makes both *x* and *y* dependent on a third independent variable, *t*, which lets you graph functions that can't be expressed as Cartesian functions in the form *y(x)*. At center-right, polar coordinates, where the radius *r* is dependent on the independent variable θ (angle). Finally, sequence graphing is for normal or recursive functions applied to independent *n* values.

(PAR) mode, including some of the types of graphs it makes possible. Next, I'll show you Polar (POL) mode, touching on the graph variables used for polar graphing and examples of polar functions. The third and most esoteric type of graph you'll learn is Sequence (SEQ) mode. With all four of the graphing modes your calculator supports under your belt, we'll move on to drawing.

You can annotate any kind of graph with lines, points, text, and sketches, as you'll learn in the latter half of this chapter. You can save annotated graphs to later recall. Many enterprising (and bored) students have even used the drawing tools to doodle or draw diagrams on their calculators. If you have a bunch of graphed equations that you need to use later, you can save and recall those too, as I'll show you.

GRAPH STYLES ON THE TI-84 PLUS C SILVER EDITION   In chapter 3, you learned to set the color and line style of rectangular (Function mode) graphs. The same skills apply to parametric, polar, and sequence graphs. You can change graphs' lines to any of 7 different styles and 15 different colors.

Let's get started with Parametric mode, which is the closest of the three new graphing modes to the rectangular graphing you're now familiar with.

5.1   *Parametric mode*

You've learned all about graphing functions that map *x* values to *y* values, such as $Y_1=2+X$ or $Y_2=\sin(3X/5)$. One of the most noticeable shortcomings is that you can have only one *y* value for every *x* value. Imagine a parabola, like the one in the left screenshot in figure 5.2. If you were to draw a vertical line through any *x* value, you'd hit only one point on the graph, whereas a horizontal line might hit zero, one, or two points on the graph. Rectangular mode can only create graphs like those in the left screenshot, where any vertical line crosses a graphed function at one or zero points.

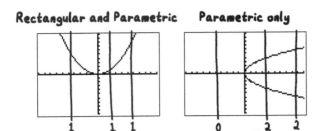

Vertical line crosses the function in how many places?

Figure 5.2 The power of parametric graphing. Rectangular graphing can map only one *y* value to each *x* value, meaning that any vertical line will cross a graphed function in exactly one place (or zero, if there is a discontinuity). Parametric mode can graph anything Rectangular mode can, but it can also draw graphs with multiple (or zero) *y* values for each *x*. The sideways parabola on the right side is one such example.

The right side of figure 5.2 shows an example of what Parametric mode can do with ease, although Rectangular mode can't manage it. The graph shown is essentially the equation X=(Y/2)², which is the Y=(X/2)² graph shown on the left turned on its side. Parametric mode is only one of two ways to graph equations of the form $x = f(y)$, in addition to being able to graph circles, functions that trace over themselves many times, and much more.

Parametric graphing in a nutshell
- To switch to Parametric mode, press (MODE), move the cursor to PAR, and press (ENTER).
- When you go to the Y= menu, you'll see pairs of functions you can enter, such as X_{1T} and Y_{1T}. You must enter equations in pairs.
- When you press the (XTθn) key in PAR, it will type a T instead of an X, because T is the independent variable for parametric graphing.
- As in normal (Function/Rectangular) mode, in Polar mode the Zoom menu options discussed in section 3.3.1 can be used to adjust what you see in the graph.
- To adjust the range and granularity of T values plugged into the parametric functions, use the Window menu.

You can see that parametric graphing is powerful, but how exactly can it do what it does? What gives it its power? Your favorite math book or teacher can give you more details, but the essentials are that every point in a parametric graph is defined by two functions, not just one. In rectangular graphing, as shown on the left in figure 5.3, you take each *x* value and plug it into a single function (written as $y = f(x)$), and the *y* value pops out. By definition, each *x* value can have only a single *y* value, because a function can't give two different *y* values when the same *x* value is plugged in.

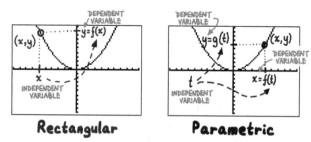

Figure 5.3   The mechanical differences between rectangular and parametric graphing. With rectangular graphing, every y value is generated by passing a corresponding x value through the function to be graphed. Parametric graphing is much more powerful because graphed functions can pass through the same x coordinates, y coordinates, and even (x,y) point multiple times.

Parametric graphing, by contrast, defines every point on the graph by *two* functions; call them $x = f(t)$ and $y = g(t)$. By making both x and y depend on t but not on each other, you can express many more graphs. You can have graphs with multiple x values for the same y, multiple y values for the same x, and even graphs that intersect with themselves or trace over themselves.

If you have time for a longer introduction than the "Parametric graphing in a nutshell" sidebar, let me lead you through two parametric graphing examples. The first will show you how to graph a circle and then modify the T values plugged in to draw a semicircle. The second exercise will demonstrate graphing a Lissajous curve ("*LEASE-a-ju*"), a fancy family of graphs that can only be drawn in Parametric mode.

5.1.1   *Parametric example: graphing a circle*

Graphing a circle is a challenge in Function mode but surprisingly easy in Parametric mode. It's so easy because if you have an angle (call it t, for example) and a radius (call it r), then the (x,y) position of the point r units from $(0,0)$ at angle t is simply

$$x = r\cos(t)$$
$$y = r\sin(t)$$

Because parametric graphs work perfectly with equations for x and y that are both in terms of a third independent variable t, you could use this to draw a circle. If you pick a constant radius, say $r = 6$, and plug in every possible t (angle) value, you'll get points forming a circle around the origin $(0,0)$.

You can apply this almost exactly as written to graphing a circle in Parametric mode on your graphing calculator. Enter $X_{1T}=6\cos(T)$ and $Y_{1T}=6\sin(T)$, after making sure you set your calculator to Parametric mode (see the "Parametric graphing in a nutshell" sidebar). The equations should look like the left screenshot in figure 5.4. Remember, (XTθn) types T when you're in Parametric mode. Press (GRAPH), and your calculator should draw a circle, as illustrated on the right in figure 5.4.

 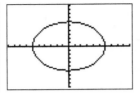

Figure 5.4 **Graphing a circle of radius 6 in Parametric mode. On the left, entering the X and Y equations that define the circle, as described in the text; on the right, the results of graphing these equations.**

My circle isn't round. Figure 5.4 shows a circle that looks more like an ellipse. As mentioned in chapter 3, your calculator's default zoom sets Xmin and Ymin to −10 and Xmax and Ymax to 10. But because the screen is wider than it is tall, this makes circles look stretched horizontally. You can fix this (for any Zoom setting!) by pressing (ZOOM) and choosing 5:ZSquare.

If anything looks wrong, and the graph doesn't look like the right side of figure 5.4, press (ZOOM). Choose the trusty 6:ZStandard option that even in Parametric mode resets graph settings to sane defaults. In Parametric mode, ZStandard sets the same graph edges as in Rectangular mode, namely Xmin = −10, Xmax = 10, Ymin = −10, and Ymax = 10. It does something else—it sets Tmin, Tmax, and Tstep (found under (WINDOW)):

- To graph a pair of functions like X₁T and Y₁T, your calculator plugs T values between Tmin and Tmax into the pair of functions. By default, Tmin = 0 and Tmax = 2π.
- Your calculator can't plug in *every* value of T between Tmin and Tmax, because there are infinitely many. The Tstep value tells the calculator how much to add to T each time it plugs in a new value. By default, Tstep is π/24.

You can adjust the Tmin, Tstep, and Tmax values to change how a parametric graph looks. I'll show you how changing Tmax can turn the circle you graphed into a semicircle.

GRAPHING A PARTIAL CIRCLE

You may recall from trigonometry or geometry that a circle is 2π radians (or 360°) around. Because by default Tmin = 0 and Tmax = 2π, your calculator plugs all the values necessary into your X₁T=6cos(T) and Y₁T=6sin(T) equations to draw a full circle of radius 6. If a full circle is 2π, it stands to reason that half of a circle is just π. Press (WINDOW), move the cursor down to Tmax=, and change the value to π (which you can type with (2nd) (^)). The left screenshot in figure 5.5 shows what you'll see. Press (ENTER) to set the value, and the screen will transform into what you see in the center in figure 5.5.

Press (GRAPH) to graph the result: a semicircle that should match the right side in figure 5.5. Your calculator plugs in T values from T = 0 to T = π, and you get the first half of the circle. You can change Tmin to π and Tmax to 2π if you want the other half of the circle. You can also try making Tstep smaller and larger. Notice that if you make it larger, the circle gets rougher, because your calculator is plugging in fewer T values. Make it smaller, and the circle gets smoother but also takes longer to graph. If you set it low enough, you might even be able to draw polygons!

We can revisit parabolic or projectile motion from chapter 3 with parametric graphing, this time throwing a ball in two dimensions.

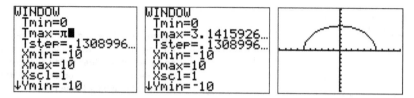

Figure 5.5   Modify the Window settings to graph a semicircle instead of a circle. Press WINDOW **to access the menu shown at left and center, where you can modify Tmin, Tmax, or Tstep. Once you store your changes and press** GRAPH**, you'll see the modified graph, such as the semicircle at right.**

5.1.2   *Parametric example: throwing a baseball*

In section 3.2.1, we used Rectangular graphing mode to look at what would happen when you threw a ball into the air. You graphed time on the x axis and the height of the ball on the y axis, and observed the height of the ball from the time you threw it straight upward until it fell back to the ground. If you didn't throw the ball straight up but instead lobbed it across a field, the problem would get more complicated. Luckily, because Parametric mode lets you graph x and y as a function of t, you can use it to easily graph the path of a thrown baseball. This example will show you how.

Chapter 3 taught you that the equation for the height of a thrown ball looks like this:

$$y = y_0 + v_0 x + 0.5 a x^2$$

In this equation, a is the acceleration due to gravity (-9.8 meters/second^2), y_0 is the initial height of the ball when thrown, v_0 is how fast it was going (in meters/second) when you threw it, x is time, and y is the height of the ball at time x (in seconds). If you switch to the more intuitive variable t for time, you can use x for the horizontal position at time t and make x_0 represent the starting horizontal position of the ball. If you threw a ball across a field with an initial velocity v_0, here's what the two equations describing its motion would look like:

$$x = x_0 + v_{0x} t$$
$$y = y_0 + v_{0y} t + 0.5 a t^2$$

GRAPHING A BASEBALL'S PATH

You can use these equations to graph the path of a thrown baseball over time. A professional baseball player might be able to throw a ball at 90 miles per hour, or about 40m/s. Let's say he throws it at a 10° angle to the ground, as shown in figure 5.6. Physics and trigonometry tell us that the x-component and y-component of that initial velocity, shown in figure 5.6, are

$$v_{0x} = v_0 \cos(10°) = 40*0.985 = 39.39 \text{ m/s}$$
$$v_{0y} = v_0 \sin(10°) = 40*0.174 = 6.95 \text{ m/s}$$

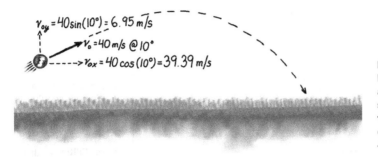

Figure 5.6 Throwing a baseball at a 10-degree angle to the ground and seeing how to calculate the *x*- and *y*-components of the initial velocity of 40 m/s

The math to calculate these components is shown at left in figure 5.7, along with the equations you'll soon enter.

You can create a pair of parametric equations describing the motion of the baseball in figure 5.6 by plugging v_{0x} and v_{0y} for this ball into the equations for x and y and substituting x_0, y_0, and a as well. You may recall that acceleration due to gravity, called either g or a, is –9.8 m/s² (negative because it's acceleration downward). To make things easy, let's assume that the ball starts at horizontal position $x_0 = 0$ meters, and that if the person throwing the baseball is about 2 meters tall, the ball's height when he releases it is $y_0 = 1.8$m:

$$x = x_0 + v_{0x}t = 0 + 39.39t = 39.39t$$
$$y = y_0 + v_{0y}t + 0.5at^2 = 1.8 + 6.95t - 4.9t^2$$

Enter these equations as X_{1T} and Y_{1T}. Press (Y=), and if there are any equations already entered, clear them or disable them. If you don't see pairs of parametric equation prompts, as at center in figure 5.7, go to the Mode menu and make sure you're in Polar mode.

DEGREE SYMBOL?   Figure 5.7 shows the degree symbol. If you want to use
`sin(` and `cos(` without specifying an angle mode in the Mode menu, you can
put the ° (degree) or ^{r} (radian) symbol after a number to specify whether it's
a degree or radian angle. Both symbols are in the Angle menu ((2nd) (APPS)).

You also need to choose a window. Because the ball starts at $x_0 = 0$, Xmin=0 seems like a good choice; and because the ball can't go below the ground, Ymin=0 is also logical. You can find the maximum y (height) the ball will reach graphically or by taking the

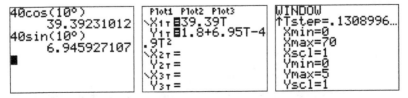

Figure 5.7   Calculating the *x*- and *y*-components of the baseball's initial velocity (left). Entering the equations for the motion of the ball for a parametric plot (center), and a good window to see the function (right).

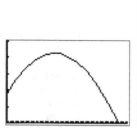

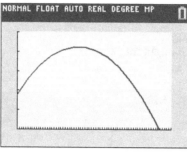

Figure 5.8 Graphing the motion of a ball in two dimensions versus time, on a TI-83 Plus or TI-84 Plus (left), or on a TI-84 Plus C Silver Edition (right)

derivative of the expression for *y*. Try adjusting Ymax until you get the graph to fit well, or take the derivative and find the roots. As a hint, Ymax=5 works well. You can also plug in 0 for *y* to figure out when the ball will hit the ground, which will tell you a good Xmax. Alternatively, you can guess and check. You'll probably end up with Xmax=70 or so, as shown at the right in figure 5.7.

Your resulting graph should look like one of the screenshots in figure 5.8. Because the ball started moving with rightward and upward velocity, it curves upward before beginning to fall again. Remember that you're now graphing as if you were standing in the bleachers, watching the ball's movement. You can figure out where the ball was at each instant by tracing over the graph. Press (TRACE), and observe the T, X, and Y values shown. Unfortunately, the calculator can't find maxima, minima, or zeroes in Parametric mode, so you'll have to use the Table or calculus to figure out when the baseball reaches the peak of its curve or when it hits the ground.

Let's look at a third and final parametric graphing example: a fancy family of curves called Lissajous curves.

5.1.3   *Parametric example: a Lissajous curve*

A Lissajous curve, also called a Bowditch curve, is a family of parametric functions created with sine and cosine. Figure 5.9 shows an example of a Lissajous curve drawn on a graphing calculator. You can test it yourself by plugging in the two equations shown on the left in figure 5.9, resulting in the graph shown on the right. As always, press (ZOOM) and choose 6:ZStandard if you don't get the same graph.

To give you a bit of background, a Lissajous curve is any of a family of parametric curves of the form

$$x(t) = a \sin(ct + d)$$
$$y(t) = b \sin(et)$$

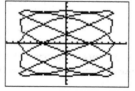

Figure 5.9 Graphing a Lissajous curve in Parametric mode. The left screenshot shows the equations to enter, and the right shows the result.

In these equations, *a*, *b*, *c*, *d*, and *e* are constant numbers, not variables. In the example I just showed you, we picked $a = b = 8$, $c = 5$, $d = 0$, and $e = 3$. You should try fiddling with these variables to get different curves in the family, some of which are unique.

The keen eye might also notice that circles are technically in the Lissajous curve family! If you let $c = e = 1$, $d = \pi/2$, and $a = b$, you'll get a circle of radius *a*. You can also graph an ellipse by keeping $c = e = 1$ and $d = \pi/2$ but making *a* and *b* unequal. The semi-minor radius (the distance from the middle of the ellipse to the top or bottom) will be equal to *a*, and the semi-major radius (the distance from the middle of the ellipse to the left or right side) will be equal to *b*.

IMPROVING PARAMETRIC RESOLUTION

Want to make that curve look smoother? You can apply a lesson I taught you in the parametric circle example: make `Tstep` smaller. Try changing `Tstep` to $\pi/48$ by pressing (WINDOW), changing `Tstep`, and then pressing (GRAPH). The curve should appear much smoother, as in figure 5.10, although it will take longer to render.

Parametric mode is a powerful change of pace, great for expressing functions that are impossible in Rectangular mode. We'll now move on to Polar mode, which offers some secrets of its own.

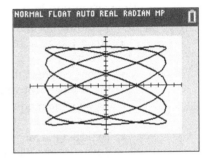

Figure 5.10 A Lissajous curve graphed on a TI-84 Plus C Silver Edition with `Tstep=π/48`

5.2   *Graphing polar functions*

Polar mode shares some attributes of both function and parametric graphing. As in Function mode, single equations map an independent variable to a dependent variable. Like Parametric mode, Polar mode gives you a way to express graphs that would be impossible in Rectangular mode and that overlap themselves.

In Polar mode, the independent variable is θ (the Greek letter theta, which represents an angle). By default, θ ranges from 0 to 2π. The dependent variable is r or radius, a distance from the origin at angle θ. There are six polar equations, numbered r_1 through r_6. Once you switch your calculator into Polar mode, as explained in the "Polar graphing in a nutshell" sidebar, the Y= and Window menus will change to reflect the new variables and equations.

To get you accustomed to polar graphing, let's start with an example of the easiest graph you can draw in Polar mode: a circle. Ironically, it's one of the hardest things to do in Rectangular mode, requiring two equations and careful tweaking of the Δx variable. Polar mode plugs in θ values from 0 to 2π to any equation you enter, gets a radius, and plots a point a distance *r* from the origin in the θ direction. If you enter a constant number like 4.2 or 8 for a polar equation, then your calculator will draw a circle of that radius. Let's try $r_1 = 7$.

The first thing you need to do is make sure your calculator is in Polar mode. Go to the Mode menu, move the cursor to POL, and press (ENTER). You should see what the left

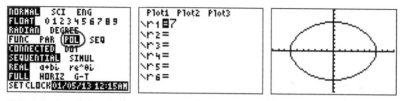

Figure 5.11 Setting Polar mode and graphing your first polar equation. The left shows switching to POL in the Mode menu. The center screenshot displays a simple equation to graph, and the right is the resulting circle.

Polar graphing in a nutshell

- To switch to Polar mode, press (MODE), move the cursor to POL, and press (ENTER).
- When you go to the Y= menu, you see six single functions you can enter, from r_1 to r_6.
- When you press the (XTθn) key in POL, it types a θ instead of an X, because θ is the independent variable for polar graphing.
- As with Parametric and Function (Rectangular) modes, the Zoom menu options discussed in section 3.3.1 can be used to adjust what you see in the graph.
- To adjust the range and granularity of θ values plugged in to the parametric functions, use the Window menu.

screenshot in figure 5.11 shows. Now press (Y=), enter $r_1=7$ to match the center screenshot in figure 5.11, and press (GRAPH) to see the result. You'll see what the right screenshot in figure 5.11 shows: a circle of radius 7 centered on the origin. Remember, as we've discussed before, it looks like an ellipse even though it's a circle because your screen isn't square.

If you wanted to fix the confusing shape of the circle, you could press (ZOOM) and choose the 5:ZSquare option. In fact, for the other two examples I'm going to show you in this section, I recommend that you use the ZSquare setting. Because polar graphing inherently deals with circular things, it's particularly helpful to be able to see polar graphs in proper proportions.

Converting between polar and rectangular coordinates

Although this section teaches you to graph polar equations, you might also want to convert between polar (r, θ) and rectangular (x, y) coordinates. If you want to change whether the graphscreen shows polar or rectangular coordinates when you use the Trace feature, you can switch between RectGC and PolarGC in the Graph Format ((2nd) (ZOOM)) menu.

If you have numerical (r, θ) or (x, y) coordinates, you can convert them to the opposite form on the homescreen using four functions from the Angle menu. All will heed your current Radian/Degree setting in the Mode menu. Press (2nd) (APPS) and use one of these:

(continued)

- R▶Pr(x, y)—Computes r for the polar coordinate form (r, θ) of the rectangular coordinates (x, y)
- R▶Pθ(x, y)—Computes θ for the polar coordinate form (r, θ) of the rectangular coordinates (x, y)
- P▶Rx(r, θ)—Computes x for the rectangular coordinate form (x, y) of the polar coordinates (r, θ)
- P▶Ry(r, θ)—Computes y for the rectangular coordinate form (x, y) of the polar coordinates (r, θ)

To help you get a feel for your calculator's polar graphing features, I want to take you through two examples. The first will show you how to graph a spiral, and the second will introduce a graph called a polar rose. Let's begin with a spiral, a surprisingly easy shape to graph in Polar mode.

5.2.1 *Polar example: a spiral*

Graphing a spiral might seem rather impossible at first, but Polar mode makes it simple. If you start with a circle, which has a constant radius, then to make a spiral, you can break the circle and pull one end into the center. A first attempt at a spiral might be $r_1=\theta$, so that when $\theta = 0$, $r = 0$; when $\theta = \pi$, $r = \pi$; and when $\theta = 2\pi$, $r = 2\pi$. In other words, as θ increases, the radius r increases as well.

The initial $r_1=\theta$ spiral gets very far from the origin very quickly. You can make it a tighter spiral by dividing θ by a constant, say π, giving you $r_1=\theta/\pi$. The left screenshot in figure 5.12 shows entering this equation, and the right screenshot illustrates what happens when you press the (GRAPH) key (note that this screenshot was taken with ZStandard rather than ZSquare).

That's not much of a spiral! How can you make it continue? Remember that by default θ goes from 0 to π, so you get only one revolution of the spiral around the origin. To create more of the spiral, you need to make θmax larger. First, press (WINDOW) and change θmax to 6π. This will give you three revolutions of the spiral, which should look much more interesting. To make the spiral look even better, switch to a square window: press (ZOOM) and select the 5:ZSquare option, if you didn't already have a square window. Now tap (GRAPH) once more, and you should see the attractive graph in figure 5.13.

You can reverse the direction of the spiral by setting $r_1=-\theta/\pi$ instead. You can make the spiral tighter or looser by adjusting the scaling factor (here $1/\pi$). You can modify θmin, θstep, and θmax to see more or less spiral or to make your calculator graph a smoother spiral. I encourage you to experiment and see what you can do with the graph.

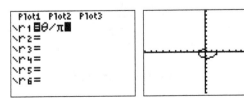

Figure 5.12 An initial attempt at drawing a spiral. With the default graph settings, you get only one section of the spiral from $\theta = 0$ to $\theta = 2\pi$.

Let's examine another polar exercise: a family of graphs that creates shapes called polar roses.

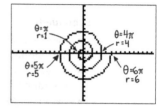

5.2.2   *Polar example: polar rose*

The *polar rose* is a family of graphs that, as you might guess from the name, are drawn in Polar mode and look like roses. Specifically, they're centered on the origin and have a number of petals. For the sake of this discussion, the general equation for a polar rose is $r(\theta) = a \sin(b\theta)$. The a term controls the size of the rose and is roughly equivalent to a radius from the middle of the rose to the tip of any petal. The b term controls how many petals the rose has:

Figure 5.13   Your final spiral, from $\theta = 0$ to $\theta = 6\pi$. Notice the annotated points on the graph, showing the (θ, r) coordinates at several points along the spiral.

- If b is even, any rose graphed from $r(\theta) = a \sin(b\theta)$ has $2b$ petals: if $b = 2$, it has 4 petals, and if $b = 5$, it has 10 petals.
- If b is odd, the rose has b petals: if $b = 3$, it has 3 petals, and if $b = 7$, it has 7 petals.

I'll explain how you can graph polar roses, but it's up to you to decide how many petals you want. A few of the possible roses with even numbers of petals are shown in figure 5.14.

First, pick your number of petals. Use the preceding rules about odd and even values of b to decide what value b needs to have. I recommend a radius of $a = 8$, but you're welcome to choose any radius you want. For the following discussion, I'll assume values of $a = 8$ and $b = 4$. Here's how you graph the $r(\theta) = 8\sin(4\theta)$ rose:

1. Make sure you're in Polar mode. If necessary, choose `ZStandard` and then `ZSquare` from the Zoom menu to set the edges of the graph to good values.
2. Press `Y=`, clear out any existing equations, and enter `r₁=8sin(4θ)`. The easiest way to type the θ variable is to press the `XTθn` key, as long as you're in Polar mode.
3. Press `GRAPH`, and your rose will appear.

As in previous exercises, I encourage you to play around with different graph settings and values for the rose equation, if you have time. Tweak a and b to see how the rose changes, and try varying θstep to make the rose petals smoother or rougher.

Now you've worked with two new graphing modes in this chapter, and you know how to use three of the four modes your calculator offers. The fourth and final mode, Sequence, is the least used but still powerful and handy.

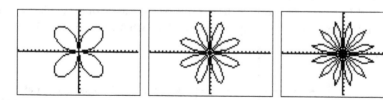

Figure 5.14   Three sample polar roses, all of which have $a = 8$. From left to right, $b = 2$, $b = 4$, and $b = 6$.

5.3   *Graphing sequences*

Sequences are special types of equations that produce successive terms, rather than a continuous set of values. Each term of a sequence is a number, and it may or may not depend on previous values in the sequence. Here are two simple sequence examples:

- A simple sequence where terms did not depend on the values of previous terms would be the set of positive even numbers, {2, 4, 6, 8, 10, 12,...}. If you want to name terms of the sequence, you can call the first one u_1, the second one u_2, and so on. The nth term is u_n, so the equation for this sequence is $u_n = 2n$: for example, $u_1 = 2$ and $u_3 = 6$.
- A simple sequence where terms depend on the values of previous terms would be a sequence where each term is the sum of the previous two terms. This is a special sequence called a Fibonacci sequence, and it starts {1, 1, 2, 3, 5, 8, 13, 21,...}. In this section, I'll demonstrate graphing the Fibonacci sequence on your calculator.

As in the previous discussions of new graph modes, the "Sequence graphing in a nutshell" sidebar tells you everything you need to know to quickly get started graphing sequences. If you have time to explore two exercises with me, I'll show you how to graph and examine two sequences. The first will be the sequence $u_n = n^2$, where each term is the square of its index. The second sequence is the Fibonacci sequence, a classic and fun example.

Sequence graphing in a nutshell

- To switch to Sequence mode, press (MODE), move the cursor to SEQ, and press (ENTER).
- When you go to the Y= menu, you'll see one setting (nMin) and three pairs of items. u(n), v(n), and w(n) are the sequences to be graphed, and u(nMin), v(nMin), and w(nMin) are lists of initial values, necessary for recursive sequences.
- When you press the (XTθn) key in SEQ, it types an n instead of an X, because n is the independent variable for sequence graphing.
- To type recursive functions, you might need to type u(n−1), u(n−2), v(n−1), and similar expressions. The sequence equation letters u, v, and w can be typed with (2nd) (7), (2nd) (8), and (2nd) (9), respectively.
- As for every other mode, the Zoom menu options discussed in section 3.3.1 can be used to adjust what you see in the graph. ZoomFit is particularly useful for sequences.
- The Window menu for Sequence mode has a lot of options. nMin and nMax control the range of n values that are plugged into the sequences. There's no such thing as nStep, because n always increases by 1. There are also settings for the coordinates of the edges of the screen, as in every graphing mode.
- The PlotStart and PlotStep options in the Window menu control which values of the sequences are shown on the graph. This won't change the values that are calculated, though, which are controlled by nMin and nMax.

RECURSIVE A recursive sequence is one where, to find the value of the sequence term u_n, you need to calculate other terms in the sequence as well. *Recursive* means that to calculate those other terms, you need to find still more terms, and the chain continues. The Fibonacci sequence we'll examine in section 5.3.2 is a popular series or sequence for teaching recursion.

Let's start with the easier of our two exercises, the sequence of squares. This will give you a good introduction on how to enter sequences and graph them, as well as how you can use the handy Table tool to see successive values of sequences.

5.3.1 Sequence example: a sequence of squares

Sequences can range from the simple and easily understood to the very complex. We'll start near the easy end, with a sequence containing the squares of the positive integers. Its equation is $u_n = n^2$, so $u_1 = 1$, $u_2 = 4$, $u_3 = 9$, $u_4 = 16$, and so on. It's particularly simple, as far as sequences go, in that you can calculate any term without knowing any other term. To calculate u_9, you plug 9 into $u_n = n^2$ to get $u_9 = 81$.

Start by switching your calculator into Sequence mode, as described in the "Sequence graphing in a nutshell" sidebar. Next, head to the Y= screen, and enter the u(n) equation for this sequence:

u(n)=n^2

Remember, the (XTθn) key types the independent sequence variable n for you. As you can see in figure 5.15, on the left, you should leave u(nMin) blank for now, because it's only used for a recursive equation. You might also remember from chapter 3 that the three dots next to u(n) mean that you're graphing this sequence as disconnected dots instead of a line.

When you press (GRAPH), you'll see the results in the center in figure 5.15. Of course, if you don't have the ZStandard window set, things might look different, but choosing 6:ZStandard under the Zoom menu will swiftly fix that. Because this window is only big enough to show three of the points in this series, you might want to adjust the window. Intuition would tell you that you need to see more of the graph above the current window, so you should increase Ymax. The right graph in figure 5.15 exemplifies the window changed to Ymin = 0 and Ymax = 100.

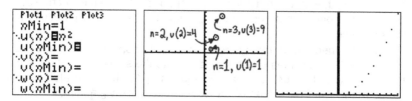

Figure 5.15 Graphing a sequence of squares. On the left, entering the u(n) equation. No u(nMin) is necessary, because the equation isn't recursive. The center is the result with a ZStandard window, and the right is the result with Ymin adjusted to 0 and Ymax changed to 100.

USING ZOOMFIT WITH SEQUENCES

The "Sequence graphing in a nutshell" sidebar said that ZoomFit is handy for sequences, so let's give that a try. Whether or not you already adjusted the window doesn't matter; go to the Zoom menu and choose 0:ZoomFit, the tenth item in the list. Your calculator will look at the values of nMin and nMax, plus the values of the sequence at the $u(n)$, $v(n)$, and/or $w(n)$, and tailor a good window to the sequence(s) you've graphed.

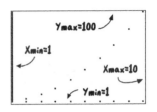

Figure 5.16 Using ZoomFit in the Zoom menu to automatically pick a good window to see part of a sequence

Try it for this sequence: $u(n) = n^2$. With the graph entered, choose ZoomFit from the Zoom menu, and you'll immediately see the result, which should look like figure 5.16. If nMax is set to a large value, this might take a bit longer. The calculator decided to set Xmin = nMin = 1, Xmax = nMax = 10, Ymin = $u(1)$ = 1, and Ymax = $u(10)$ = 100. This does a good job of showing all the relevant terms in the sequence between $n = 1$ and $n = 10$.

EXAMINING SEQUENCE TERMS: TRACING AND THE TABLE TOOL

It's great to visualize sequences on the graphscreen, but often you also want to know exact numerical values of each term. As it often does, your calculator has your needs covered. There are several ways you can get values, but two are particularly fast and easy:

- *Use the Trace feature*—Enter one or more sequences in the Y= menu, graph them, then press (TRACE). Use (◄) and (►) to move between sequence terms; the (▼) and (▲) keys switch between different sequences, if you entered more than one. Chapter 3 explains more about using Y=.
- *Use the Table tool*—In section 3.4, you learned how to use the Table tool to see function (rectangular) graph values. The Table tool works for all four graphing modes and is useful for sequences. Graph one or more sequences, and then press (2nd) (GRAPH). Figure 5.17 shows what the Table tool looks like for the sequence of squares you experimented with in this section. Because the TI-84 Plus C Silver Edition has a larger screen, you may want to switch to the Graph-Table split-screen mode from the Mode menu and then view the table, as illustrated on the right of figure 5.17.

Remember that if you want to change where the table starts or the spacing between values in the table, you can adjust TblStart and ∆Tbl from the TblSetup menu, accessed with (2nd) (WINDOW).

The sequence of squares I showed you in this section was a relatively easy (and nonrecursive) sequence. You'd be missing an important piece of your sequence graphing knowledge if you didn't also go through a recursion exercise.

5.3.2 *Sequence example: the Fibonacci series*

There are endless examples of recursive functions that are useful in programming, science, and engineering, but the Fibonacci series is a classic and easy-to-understand example. The Fibonacci series was invented by a 13th-century Italian mathematician

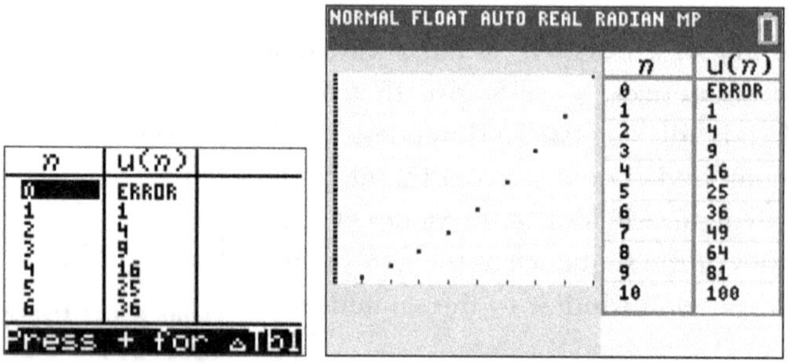

Figure 5.17   Checking sequence values with the Table tool. After graphing a sequence, press ⟨2nd⟩ ⟨GRAPH⟩ to view the table. As with normal graphing, you can modify Table tool settings from the TblSetup (⟨2nd⟩ ⟨WINDOW⟩) menu. If you use a TI-84 Plus C Silver Edition and switch to the Graph-Table mode from the Mode menu, you'll see the results on the right side instead.

named Leonardo Fibonacci. It's a sequence where the first two terms are 1, and every subsequent term is the sum of the two terms right before it. The base cases (see the "More on recursion" sidebar) of the Fibonacci sequence are $u_1 = 1$ and $u_2 = 1$, and the recursive definition is $u_n = u_{n-1} + u_{n-2}$:

- $u_3 = u_2 + u_1 = 1 + 1 = 2$
- $u_4 = u_3 + u_2 = 2 + 1 = 3$
- $u_5 = u_4 + u_3 = 3 + 2 = 5$
- $u_{10} = u_9 + u_8 = ?$ We can't tell without calculating u_9 and u_8, which requires u_7 and u_6.

In testing the Fibonacci sequence on your calculator, you'll learn how to enter the expression for a recursive series, including teaching your calculator the base case(s). We'll explore how changing the base cases changes every other term in the series. I'll also reiterate the lessons about using ZoomFit to see the graphed function better and the Table tool to get exact values.

More on recursion

- Every recursive series has a definition of the *recursive function.* $u_n = u_{n-1} + n$ is a definition that looks back at preceding terms. $u_n = u_{n+1} - n$ is a less-used type of definition that looks forward at following terms.
- Recursion *recursively* calculates values backward (or forward). Because we'd never get values if a recursive function recursed indefinitely, recursive functions need at least one *base case.* When the recursion reaches the base case, it can stop. For example, $u_1 = 1$ would be a useful base case for $u_n = u_{n-1} + n$.

GRAPHING THE FIBONACCI SERIES

Just to enter the Fibonacci series in your calculator's Y= menu, you need to learn two new things. First, you need to learn how to refer to other terms in a series while you're writing a recursive function definition as u(n). Second, you need to know how to tell your calculator the base cases for the recursive series.

The first problem is defining the function for the recursive series. You already know that each term is u(n), and your calculator plugs in values for n. What if you want to refer to the previous term, which in math notation is u_{n-1}? Use u(n-1), typed with 2nd 7 (XTθn – 1). As the "Sequence graphing in a nutshell" sidebar explains, 2nd 7 is the u equation, XTθn is the n variable in Parametric mode, and the rest is stuff you've seen before. If you want to refer to the term before that, use u(n-2), and so on. For the Fibonacci example, enter u(n)=u(n-1)+u(n-2), as shown on the left in figure 5.18.

> **FORWARD REFERENCES** On your calculator, you can't refer to terms after the current term in a sequence, such as u_{n+1} via u(n+1). This is invalid syntax. If you try, you'll get an ERR:DOMAIN error. You can only refer to terms before the current term.

Next, you need to enter the base cases:

- If you have one base case, you can enter it as a single number next to u(*n*Min) (and v(*n*Min) and w(*n*Min), if you have two or three sequences). For example, you could enter u(*n*Min)=5.
- If you have more than one base case, which happens when you have a recursive function that refers to the u_{n-2} term or further back, you need to enter the base cases as a list. For two base cases, you might enter {4,2}; for three, {4,2,1}.

For our Fibonacci exercise, we have two base cases: enter the list {1,1} for u(*n*Min), because those are the first two terms in the Fibonacci sequence. The curly braces are 2nd (and 2nd), as chapter 4 explained.

You have entered u(n) and u(*n*Min), so you're ready to graph the Fibonacci series by pressing GRAPH. In all likelihood, the graph won't look quite right. An easy fix is the ZoomFit tool we looked at in the first sequence example. Press ZOOM, and choose 0:ZoomFit. Much better! Now you should see the plot shown on the right in figure 5.18.

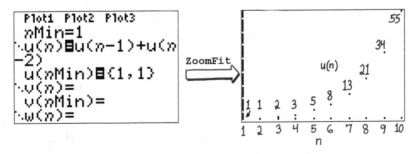

Figure 5.18 Graphing the first 10 terms of the Fibonacci series on your calculator in Sequence mode. The left shows entering the recursive function and the base cases. The right is the graph after you adjust the window with ZoomFit.

VIEWING FIBONACCI SERIES VALUES

You could trace along that graph, but an easier way to examine the values of the series is to look at the table. Switch into Table mode with 2nd GRAPH, and you'll see values of the Fibonacci sequence side-by-side with their indices (n), as figure 5.19 illustrates. You can use the arrow keys to scroll up and down, and you'll soon discover that you can't go to indices before $n = 1$, because there are no terms in the Fibonacci series before $u_1 = 1$. You can have negative indices in sequences on your calculator; the lowest possible n value is whatever nMin is set to. If you want to scroll way down (or way up) the table, you should press 2nd WINDOW and adjust the TblStart variable.

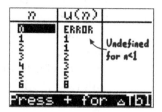

Figure 5.19 Viewing the table of indices and values for the recursive Fibonacci sequence

You've learned just about everything you need to know to use Sequence graphing mode effectively on your calculator to explore recursive and nonrecursive series. In fact, between this chapter and chapter 3, you know all four graphing modes that your calculator offers: Function, Parametric, Polar, and Sequence modes. But did you know you can draw on top of graphs and save those annotated graphs for later? Drawing and saving graphs and graph settings are the subject of the remainder of this chapter.

5.4   *Drawing on graphs*

Graphing calculators are wonderful math tools. In a few seconds you can go from staring at an equation in a textbook to exploring a graph of the function, without having to tediously draw out the graph by hand. Say you find an interesting point in such a graph. You want to circle the point, add some text next to it to explain what it is, and save the graph to show to your teacher later. At this point, you'll probably end up trying to sketch the graph on a page in a notebook and annotate it by hand. After you read this section, though, you'll know how to draw those annotations directly on the graph. By the end of section 5.5, you'll also have learned how to save the annotated graph in your calculator's memory.

Your calculator includes a host of drawing tools, including 10 ways to draw lines, circles, text, and even pieces of functions, and 6 ways to draw points. You can draw directly on the graphscreen, or you can run drawing functions as homescreen functions. In this section, I'll show you how to draw on top of graphs. You'll learn to use these functions directly on the graph and which ones can also be used on the homescreen. I'll also show you the three graphing tools that are related to graphed functions: DrawInv, DrawF, and Shade(. By the time you get to the end of this section, you'll be well versed in drawing on your calculator. And because I'm nothing if not a realist, I know that many of you will end up using these tools to sketch drawings of your own. I did it too back in the day.

Let's start with drawing functions like Horizontal, Line(, and Text(used on the graphscreen and homescreen.

5.4.1 Graphscreen drawing tools

No matter what you're trying to draw on your calculator, from graph annotation to geometry diagrams to doodles, your calculator has a full complement of tools to help you. The best way to learn to use the drawing tools is to play around with them, so I'm going to cover the high level of using the tools in general and let you experiment for yourself. To guide you, I've created tables 5.1 and 5.2 (later in this section) explaining each of the tools.

With few exceptions, most drawing tools can be used one of two ways:

- Go to the graphscreen by pressing (GRAPH). Optionally, you can graph equation(s) first. From the graphscreen, press (2nd) (PRGM) to get to the Draw menu, pick a tool, and use it. Continue until you're happy with your creation.
- Go to the homescreen and enter drawing commands as functions, like round(and gcd(and all their friends. This requires memorizing the *arguments* to each function, the values you put in parentheses after the function names. Chapter 2 explained how to use functions on the homescreen.

I'll start you with drawing by example, namely graphing a parabola and annotating that graph. We'll then touch briefly on homescreen drawing commands and conclude this section with a table of the drawing tools you'll use most frequently. If you have a TI-84 Plus C Silver Edition, you may also want to refer to section 12.3, which discusses the differences between drawing on the older and newer calculators.

USING DRAWING TOOLS ON THE GRAPHSCREEN: ANNOTATING A PARABOLA

The easiest way to draw on your calculator is to use its drawing tools directly on the graphscreen. You can draw lines, circles, text, points, and more. To select any drawing tool, start on the graphscreen, press (2nd) (PRGM) to access the Draw menu, and pick the tool you want. The Draw menu has three tabs—DRAW, POINTS, and STO—as you can see from figure 5.20. You'll learn about the STO tab in section 5.5. On the TI-84 Plus C Silver Edition, there's a fourth tab called Background, but you won't need to use that unless you're writing a program.

When you pick a drawing tool from the Draw menu, that tool will remain active until you pick another one. You can draw multiple lines, circles, strings of text, and more without needing to keep reselecting the same tool from the Draw menu. You'll use that technique in this section's example: annotating a parabola.

Start with a parabola by switching to Function mode (by accessing the Mode menu), entering $Y_1 = 5 - (X-2)^2$ in the Y= menu, and pressing (GRAPH). Doesn't look like figure 5.21? No problem; go to the Zoom menu, and choose 6:ZStandard. You can

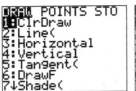
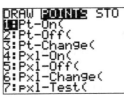

Figure 5.20   The DRAW and POINTS tabs of the Draw menu, containing general tools (left) and point-drawing tools (right). The STO tab contains ways to save and restore graph settings and pictures, as you'll see in section 5.5.

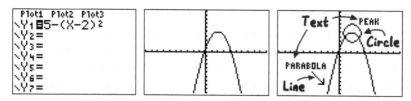

Figure 5.21   Graphing a parabola and annotating it. PEAK and PARABOLA are drawn with the Text tool, the circle is a Circle, and the arrow is three Lines. The left side shows the equation, and the middle shows the graph before being annotated.

always turn the axes on and off and modify other graph format options using the ⟨2nd⟩ ⟨ZOOM⟩ keys.

Now let's try some annotations:

1   Try circling the peak. From the graph, press ⟨2nd⟩ ⟨PRGM⟩ to open the Draw menu, and scroll down to 9:Circle(. Move the cursor over the peak, press ⟨ENTER⟩ to set the circle's center, and then move the cursor to a point where you want the edge of the circle to be and press ⟨ENTER⟩ again. A circle!

2   Write out PEAK, as in figure 5.21. Go to 0:Text(in the Draw menu, and then use the arrow keys to move the cursor. Place it at the top-left corner of where you want the word PEAK to appear, and type PEAK. Remember that to type a string of letters, you press ⟨2nd⟩ ⟨ALPHA⟩ to engage Alpha-Lock, and then press the keys that have the letters you want printed over them.

3   You can type PARABOLA without returning to the Draw menu. Move the cursor to a new position with the arrow keys, and type PARABOLA.

4   Create the arrow pointing to the parabola in figure 5.21. Go to the Draw menu, and select the 2:Line(tool. For each line, move the cursor to the first endpoint, press ⟨ENTER⟩, move the cursor to the second endpoint, and press ⟨ENTER⟩ again. The tool you select stays active until you select another tool, so you don't need to return to the Draw menu before each new line. The arrow in figure 5.21 is three lines.

While you were drawing, you might have been frustrated that the coordinates at the bottom of the screen were getting in your way. If you don't mind them while you're drawing, but you want them to go away when you finish drawing, press ⟨CLEAR⟩. Don't worry; it won't clear the screen. At worst, you might accidentally quit to the home-screen, at which point you need only press ⟨GRAPH⟩ to return to the drawing. If you don't want coordinates to show at all while you draw, select CoordOff from the Graph Format menu, ⟨2nd⟩ ⟨ZOOM⟩. If you're on a TI-84 Plus C Silver Edition, you could press ⟨GRAPH⟩ in the middle of drawing any shape to access the Style menu, as indicated by the onscreen Style button above the ⟨GRAPH⟩ key.

CLEARING THE GRAPHSCREEN: CLRDRAW

The 1:ClrDraw command from the Draw tab of the Draw menu clears the entire graphscreen. If you have the axes or grid enabled, it redraws them as well and then rerenders any functions you've graphed. Press ⟨GRAPH⟩, and then go to the Draw menu with ⟨2nd⟩ ⟨PRGM⟩, and choose 1:ClrDraw. If you're on the homescreen, you can enter ClrDraw as a command on a line by itself and press ⟨ENTER⟩.

Be aware that zooming a graph, panning left or right, changing the window, or changing or removing an existing graphed function will also erase the graphscreen. Adding a new function will *not* erase annotations you've drawn, as long as you don't change existing functions.

SKETCHING ON A BLANK SCREEN   Want a blank screen for your doodles, diagrams, and sketches? Turn off the axes and grid by making sure AxesOff and GridOff are selected in the Graph Format menu, under ⟨2nd⟩ ⟨ZOOM⟩. Don't forget how to turn them on again if you need to graph, but remember that graphing and modifying Graph Format options will erase anything you've already drawn!

5.4.2 *Using drawing tools on the homescreen*

It's easy to use your calculator's drawing tools on the graphscreen, but sometimes you need more precision than you can get by using the tools directly on the graphscreen. Or perhaps you need to draw lines or circles that are partially offscreen. In this case, you'll want to use the drawing tools from the homescreen.

Let's go through an exercise, because that's the easiest way to learn anything. You'll draw a circle, a horizontal line, and a vertical line from the homescreen. Here are the steps:

1   Remove any equations from the Y= menu. You can also turn off the axes with AxesOff from the Format menu (⟨2nd⟩ ⟨ZOOM⟩) if you want. You may want to use ZStandard and then ZSquare from the Zoom menu to make your results match my screenshots.

2   Use ClrDraw from the Draw menu to start with a blank graphscreen.

3   From the homescreen, issue the commands Circle(2,4,10) to draw a circle centered at (2,4) of radius 10; you can see the command in figure 5.22 or figure 5.23. If you're using a TI-84 Plus C Silver Edition, use the command Circle(2,4,10,RED); you can find RED under ⟨VARS⟩ ⟨▶⟩ ⟨▶⟩.

4   Use the Horizontal ⁻6 and Vertical ⁻8 options to draw two lines tangent to the circle. You should see something that matches the right side in figure 5.22 or figure 5.23. If you have a TI-84 Plus C Silver Edition, try Vertical ⁻8,GREEN instead of Vertical ⁻8.

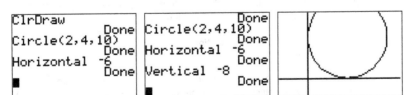

Figure 5.22   Using drawing commands from the homescreen to draw a circle, a horizontal line, and a vertical line. For this example, I turned off the axes with AxesOff and used ZStandard and ZSquare to set up the window.

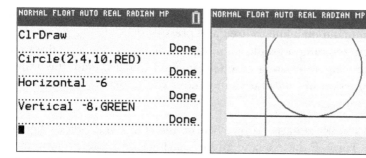

Figure 5.23 **The same set of drawing commands as figure 5.22 on the TI-84 Plus C Silver Edition. I used colors in two of the commands, found in the Color tab of the Vars menu.**

For the full list of drawing commands, look at tables 5.1 and 5.2. Table 5.1 contains most of the interesting commands from the Draw menu, and table 5.2 lists the commands from the Points tab.

Table 5.1 **Drawing functions in the Draw tab of the Draw menu. You must first go to the graphscreen, press** (2nd) (PRGM) **and select the function you want, and then use it. You can also go to the homescreen instead to use many of these functions. If you have a TI-84 Plus C Silver Edition, you should instead refer to table 12.2 in section 12.3.**

Command	What it does	Homescreen syntax
Line(	Draws a line between two points. On the graphscreen, move the cursor to the first point, press (ENTER); move it to the second point, and press (ENTER) again.	Line(<x_1>,<y_1>,<x_2>,<y_2>) Example: Line(⁻1,0,8.2,8)
Horizontal	Draws a horizontal line across the whole screen. Move the line to where you want it, and press (ENTER) to make it permanent.	Horizontal <y coordinate> Example: Horizontal 1.5
Vertical	Draws a vertical line down the whole screen. Move the line to where you want it, and press (ENTER) to make it permanent.	Vertical <x coordinate> Example: Vertical ⁻4
Tangent(	Draws a line tangent to a given function at a given x point. Always assumes that functions are rectangular (FUNC) functions, even if the calculator isn't in Function mode. On the graphscreen, you select the function and then the point.	Tangent(<func>,<x coord>) Example: Tangent(3X²,1.25)
Circle(	Draws a circle with a center and radius. On the graphscreen, select the center, press (ENTER), and then choose a point on the edge of the circle.	Circle(, <center y>,<radius>) Example: Circle(2,⁻1,4)

Table 5.1   Drawing functions in the Draw tab of the Draw menu. You must first go to the graphscreen, press 2nd PRGM **and select the function you want, and then use it. You can also go to the homescreen instead to use many of these functions. If you have a TI-84 Plus C Silver Edition, you should instead refer to table 12.2 in section 12.3.** *(continued)*

Command	What it does	Homescreen syntax
Text(	Writes out text. Move the cursor where you want the top-left corner of the text to be, and start typing (no need to press ENTER). Remember to press ALPHA if you want to type letters. For entering Text(on the homescreen, row and column are pixels from the top-left of the screen, which is row 0, column 0. The bottom-right is row 62, column 94.	Text(<row>,<column>, "STRING") Example: Text(57,1,"GRAPH TITLE")
Pen	Somewhat like drawing with an Etch-a-Sketch. Move the cursor to where you want to start, press ENTER to put the "pen" down, and move the "pen" to draw a black line behind it. You can press ENTER to lift the "pen" and move it to a new spot to draw again.	(You can't use the Pen as a homescreen command.)

Table 5.2   Point and pixel commands, all in the Points tab of the Draw menu

Command	What it does	Homescreen syntax
Pt-On(Pt-Off(Pt-Change(	Once you enable this tool, you can freely move the cursor around the graphscreen. Every time you press ENTER, it will turn the point on (to black), turn it off (to white), or change it. From the homescreen, this command uses (x,y) coordinates. If you omit <type>, it draws a single dot. You can enter 2 for type for a square and 3 for a cross.	Pt-On(<x>,<y>,[<type>]) Pt-Off(<x>,<y>,[<type>]) Pt-Change(<x>,<y>,[<type>]) Example: Pt-On(5,1.2)
Pxl-On(Pxl-Off(Pxl-Change(	Can't be drawn on the graphscreen; only for use as a homescreen function. Like Text(, takes pixel coordinates. Row and column are pixels from the top-left of the screen, which is row 0, column 0. The bottom-right is row 62, column 94.	Pxl-On(<row>,<column>) Pxl-Off(<row>,<column>) Pxl-Change(<row>,<column>) Example: Pxl-Off(30,52)

There are three more drawing commands that we haven't discussed yet in the Draw tab of the Draw menu, all of which work with graphed equations. You'll learn how to use those before we move on to the final topic of the chapter, saving and restoring pictures and graph settings.

5.4.3   *Drawing graphlike functions: DrawInv, DrawF, and Shade*

Three of the tools in the Draw menu (2nd PRGM) take functions as arguments and draw something based on equations. All three work only in Function mode or act as if the calculator is in Function mode regardless of the current settings. These three functions are as follows:

- DrawInv—Draws the inverse of a Y= rectangular equation. Useful for drawing X= equations (see the "Graphing X= equations" sidebar for more information). This function takes one argument: the equation to graph the inverse of. For example: DrawInv X^2+3.
- DrawF—Graphs a function, just as if you had entered it in the Y= menu. This function works only with rectangular/function (Y=) equations, even if the graphing mode is set to one of the other modes. Like DrawInv, it takes a single argument: an equation to graph. For example, DrawF $\sqrt{}$(X) would be equivalent to setting Y$_1$=$\sqrt{}$(X).
- Shade—Draws a solid or hashed shade between two functions (or y coordinates). It takes at least two arguments: the two functions (or y coordinates) bounding the shaded area. For example, Shade(X^2,10) shades the area between $y = x^2$ and $y = 10$ in solid black. You can also choose minimum and maximum x coordinates on the shaded area, so Shade(X^2,10,0,2) only shades between $x = 0$ and $x = 2$.

> **Graphing X= equations**
> Many graphing-calculator users struggle to find a way to graph equations of the form $x = f(y)$, such as $x = y^2$ or $x = 1 + 5\sin(y)$. If you're looking for a way to graph X= equations, there are *two* possible methods:
>
> - DrawInv—If your calculator is already in Function (Rectangular) graphing mode, use the DrawInv command from the Draw menu. DrawInv takes one argument: the function to graph, with Ys replaced by Xs. In other words, DrawInv X^2 draws the equation $x = y^2$.
> - *Parametric mode*—Take your $x = f(y)$ equation, such as X=1+5sin(Y), and replace the Ys with Ts. Enter your equation as x$_{1T}$, such as X$_{1T}$=1+5sin(T), and set Y$_{1T}$=T. You'll also need to adjust Tmin to Ymin and Tmax to Ymax.

Except for DrawInv's use as a way to graph X= equations, you probably won't find yourself using these three tools that often. Nevertheless, for the sake of completeness, I'd like to show you a brief exercise that uses all three of these drawing tools. You'll use DrawF and DrawInv to graph Y=3sin(X) and X=3sin(Y) and then shade between Y=3sin(X) and Y=3sin(X)-3 using the Shade(command.

To set up, press MODE and change your calculator to Function mode, if it's not already in it. Turn on the axes from the Graph Format menu (2nd ZOOM) if they're not already on, and select 6:ZStandard from the Zoom menu. Finally, if you still have anything on the graphscreen, clear any entered equations from the Y= menu,

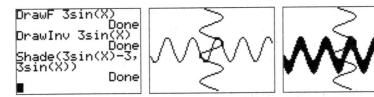

Figure 5.24 Using the DrawF, DrawInv, and Shade(commands. The left shows the three commands to enter, the center shows the effect of just DrawF and DrawInv, and the right is the result after the Shade(command.

and, if necessary, select 1:ClrDraw from the Draw menu ((2nd) (PRGM)). Next, follow these steps:

1 Select 6:DrawF from the Draw menu, and add 3sin(X) as an argument. You'll end up with DrawF 3sin(X), as in figure 5.24. Press (ENTER) to execute the command.

2 Choose 8:DrawInv from the Draw menu, and add 3sin(X) again, to get Draw-Inv 3sin(X). This graphs $x = 3\sin(y)$; from the DrawF and DrawInv commands, you'll get the screenshot in the center of figure 5.24.

3 Use the Shade(command from the Draw menu to shade between $y = 3\sin(x) - 3$ and $y = 3\sin(x)$ with Shade(3sin(X)-3,3sin(X)). Press (ENTER), and when the calculator finishes drawing, you'll see something that resembles the right side of figure 5.24.

As with all the other drawing tools, and in fact nearly every skill you've learned so far, I encourage you to experiment with these three new drawing features to see how they can help you with your academic work and your own drawings. But what if you want to save the results of your drawing efforts? In the next section, you'll learn to store snapshots of the graphscreen and restore them, as well as save and restore graph settings for later use.

5.5 Saving graph settings and pictures

The final skills of this chapter are among the easiest of the new graphing and drawing skills, and thus I saved them until the end to relax your brain after the rigors of graphing and drawing. In addition, there's no point saving pictures of the graphscreen and your graph settings if you have neither graphs nor pictures. In a nutshell, this section will show you how to take a snapshot (or picture or screenshot, if you prefer) of the graphscreen and save it into your calculator's memory. You can later restore one of those pictures to return the graphscreen to how it looked when you took the picture, regardless of any new graphs, drawings, mode changes, and format changes that you made in the meantime. This section will also explain graph databases (GDBs), a way to store all currently graphed equations plus your Graph Format settings and graph window into memory. You can then later restore a GDB to return your graphs and settings to the way they were when you stored the GDB.

Saving and recalling pictures (pics) is useful whenever you've made an annotated graph or a drawing that you want to store for later. Pictures are the first topic we'll examine. The second is saving and recalling GDBs, which is handy when you have your graphed functions and graph format settings exactly as you want them and want to be able to later switch back to those settings.

Let's get right to it with a look at your calculator's picture variables and features.

5.5.1 Saving and recalling picture variables

Just as your calculator has numerical variables for storing numbers, list variables for storing lists, and matrix variables for storing matrices, it has a set of 10 picture variables for storing pictures or snapshots of the graphscreen. Named `Pic1` through `Pic9` plus `Pic0`, each is a location in your calculator's memory, and each can store a full image of the graphscreen.

> **WHY NOT PIC0 THROUGH PIC9?**   In section 5.5.1, I refer to "`Pic1` through `Pic9` plus `Pic0`" instead of just saying "`Pic0` through `Pic9`." This isn't an error or an attempt to confuse you. Because your calculator thinks of `Pic0` as `Pic10`, it's the last of the 10 picture variables, after `Pic9`.

The `StorePic` and `RecallPic` commands, which respectively store and recall picture variables, can be found in the STO tab of the Draw menu. To access this menu, shown in figure 5.25, press ⌈2nd⌉ ⌈PRGM⌉ ⌈▶⌉ ⌈▶⌉. Once you choose `StorePic` or `RecallPic`, the command is pasted to the homescreen. Add a 1, 2, 3, …, 9, or 0 after either `StorePic` or `RecallPic` to save or open that picture number.

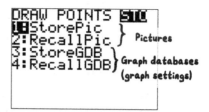

Figure 5.25   The STO tab of the Draw menu, from which you can save and recall both pictures and graph settings (GDBs)

> **PICTURE CAVEATS**   If you `StorePic` a picture that already exists, your calculator will overwrite the old picture without warning you. If you try to `RecallPic` a picture that doesn't exist, your calculator will show an `ERR:UNDEFINED` message.

If you want to see a list of which picture variables you have on your calculator, you can press ⌈2nd⌉ ⌈+⌉ to access the Memory menu, then choose `2:Mem Mgmt/Del…`, and choose `8:Pic…`. You'll see a list of any picture variables on your calculator, and you can archive, unarchive, and delete pictures from here. Press ⌈DEL⌉ next to any picture to delete it, which saves memory (RAM). If you archive a picture by pressing ⌈ENTER⌉ next to it, which adds an asterisk (*), then it won't take up RAM and will survive a RAM clear. But you can't `StorePic` or `RecallPic` that variable until you unarchive it by returning to the Memory menu and pressing ⌈ENTER⌉ next to it again.

To demonstrate saving and recalling pictures, I drew a sketch on the graphscreen, as shown on the left in figure 5.26. Next, I cleared the graphscreen with `ClrDraw` and then recalled the picture that I saved, as shown in the center in figure 5.26. When I pressed ⌈GRAPH⌉, the sketch I had drawn was restored.

Figure 5.26 Demonstrating how `StorePic` and `RecallPic` let you save a snapshot of graphs, annotations, or drawings on the graphscreen. Here, I store the DNA doodle I drew, clear the screen (erasing the doodle), and then use `RecallPic` to restore the sketch.

What if you want to save not the exact contents of the graphscreen but the equations that you have currently graphed, plus the window and format settings? Then you should use a GDB.

5.5.2 *Saving and recalling graph databases*

A graph database, or GDB, is a somewhat different animal than a picture variable. There are 10 of them, `GDB1` through `GDB9` plus `GDB0`, and they're located in your calculator's memory. But instead of holding an exact snapshot of the pixels on the graphscreen, GDBs hold all the following:

- Any equations you have entered in the Y= menu, for all four modes.
- The current graph mode.
- The Graph Format settings from the Format menu, including whether the axes, the grid, and coordinates are on or off.
- The window variables, including `Xmin`, `Xmax`, `Ymin`, `Ymax`, and any other values in (WINDOW).
- On the TI-84 Plus C Silver Edition, it also saves the colors of each graphed equation, the axes color, the grid color, and the color of the border around the graph. It does *not* save the background picture or color.

Saving and recalling GDBs use the `StoreGDB` and `RecallGDB` functions from the STO tab of the Draw menu, as shown in figure 5.25. You follow `StoreGDB` and `RecallGDB` with a number from 0 to 9, exactly as with `StorePic` and `RecallPic`. I showed you how to list the picture variables on your calculator and archive and delete them from the Memory menu. You can list, delete, and archive the GDB variables nearly the exact same way: press (2nd) (+) to access the Memory menu, then choose 2:Mem Mgmt/Del…, and choose 9:GDB….

Figure 5.27 shows an example of storing a GDB, messing with Graph Format settings and graphed equations, and then recalling the original GDB. By recalling `GDB4`, the initial set of functions and settings from the left in figure 5.22 is restored, undoing the changes I made to the graph format and the window settings.

And now we've reached the end of what you need to know for advanced usage of your calculator's drawing and graphing features! From here on, we'll focus on advanced

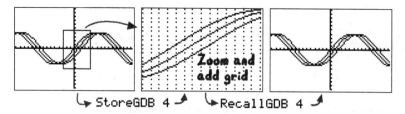

Figure 5.27   **Starting with the graph on the left, the `StoreGDB 4` command stores the graphed equations and graph settings to graph database `GDB4`. After I turn the axes off and the grid on and change the window settings, the graph changes to what you see in the center. The `RecallGDB 4` command restores it to the right view, just as it was when the `StoreGDB 4` command was issued.**

math features, although some of the discussion, such as statistics, will include use of plots and graphs on the graphscreen.

5.6   *Summary*

In this chapter, you learned advanced skills for graphing and drawing. We started with the three graphing modes that chapter 3 didn't explore: Parametric mode, Polar mode, and Sequence mode. You learned how Parametric mode lets you express and graph functions that would be impossible in Function or Rectangular mode. You explored examples of polar functions, from circles and spirals to rose-shaped graphs. We worked through sequence graphing exercises of a recursive series like the Fibonacci series and a nonrecursive series like the squares of the positive integers.

In the latter half of the chapter, I showed you the many drawing and annotation tools that your calculator offers. From ways to mark up graphed equations to shade functions and graph X= equations, there's not much you can't draw on your calculator's graphscreen. You even learned how you can use the graphscreen as a creative canvas for freehand sketches and diagrams. We concluded with a look at the tools for storing and recalling pictures, which store the pixel-by-pixel contents of the graphscreen; and GDBs, which hold the currently graphed equations and graph settings.

As we move forward into the rest of part 2 of this book, you'll be graduating to the realm of precalculus and calculus. Chapter 6 focuses on precalculus features of your graphing calculator that you haven't explored yet. You'll look at complex numbers, the nitty-gritty of trigonometry, limits, and logarithms. Onward!

Precalculus
and your calculator

This chapter covers

- Working with complex numbers on your calculator
- Using trigonometric functions and modes
- Calculating limits on your calculator
- Understanding logarithms and bases

Precalculus encompasses a set of important math skills, both on their own and as a foundation on which to build your calculus education. Precalculus is generally taught after algebra, and it includes topics like polar graphing, sets and series, real and complex numbers, trigonometry, and exponents and logarithms. In chapter 4, you learned about lists and their uses for holding sets. In chapter 5, you explored polar and sequence graphing. This chapter will fill in the rest of the precalculus skills your calculator can help you with.

We'll start with imaginary and complex numbers. In the first five chapters of this book, you dealt only with real numbers. Now you'll be able to represent numbers that include $\sqrt{(-1)}$, called *imaginary numbers*. When a number has both a real and an imaginary part, it's called a *complex number*. You'll learn to type and manipulate complex numbers, and you'll see an example of calculating imaginary roots from the Quadratic Formula. You'll move on to your calculator and trigonometry, focusing on using the trigonometric functions your calculator provides. In the midst of the lesson, you'll also learn about the unit circle and inverse trigonometric functions.

The latter two topics in this chapter are limits and logarithmic functions. Although your calculator can't determine the exact values of limits on its own, you can use graphing and the Table tool to approximate limits without calculus. You'll learn this skill through a complete example. Finally, you'll meet the logarithmic and exponential functions built in to your calculator, and you'll see the inverse nature of exponents and logarithms in action.

Let's jump right into this chapter's set of precalculus skills with imaginary, complex, and real numbers.

6.1   *Imaginary and complex numbers*

Throughout this book, you have (and will continue) to deal with all kinds of numbers. These numbers are everything from integers like 0 and 100, to decimals like –3.1 and 539,658.0001, to rational and irrational numbers like 2/3 and π. All these numbers are part of the set of numbers called *real numbers*. There's another set of numbers called *imaginary numbers*, and they all involve the square root of –1.

"But that's impossible!" you say. "When I learned about square roots, I was taught that you can't take the square root of negative numbers." And if you're dealing with only real numbers, no, you can't. But when you know how to use imaginary numbers, square roots of negative numbers are possible. Everything is based on the definition of a constant called i, equal to $\sqrt{(-1)}$. You can figure out the square roots of other negative numbers based on i:

$$\sqrt{(-4)} = \sqrt{(-1)} \times \sqrt{(4)} = 2\sqrt{(-1)} = 2i$$
$$\sqrt{(-7)} = \sqrt{(-1)} \times \sqrt{(7)} = i\sqrt{(7)} \approx 2.646i$$

Your calculator can easily work with imaginary numbers, plus the set containing real and imaginary numbers used together, called *complex numbers*.

6.1.1   *Complex number functions and symbols*

As you can see from the sidebar "Complex and imaginary numbers on the TI-83 Plus/ TI-84 Plus," there are three main skills for using complex numbers on your graphing calculator. You need to know how your calculator's mode settings affect complex math, how to type i, and what functions your calculator includes for complex numbers. In this section, you'll learn each of these in order.

Your calculator has a mode that controls how it deals with complex numbers. If you try to take the square root of a negative number in Real mode, your calculator will flash an ERR:NONREAL ANS message. If you press (MODE) and switch to *a+bi* mode, your calculator will return imaginary or complex answers when you take the square root of a negative number.

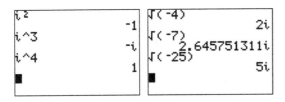

Figure 6.1 Testing powers of the imaginary constant *i* (left) and calculating square roots of negative numbers in *a+bi* mode (right). All three of the calculations on the right would produce ERR:NONREAL ANS if run in Real mode instead of *a+bi* mode.

Complex and imaginary numbers on the TI-83 Plus/TI-84 Plus

The quick-and-easy use of complex and imaginary numbers on your graphing calculator centers on three skills:

- *Changing between a+bi mode and Real mode*—You can use the imaginary symbol *i* in both modes. But you must be in *a+bi* mode to take the square root of negative numbers. You can change modes in the Mode menu.
- *Typing √(-1)*—Your calculator has a way to type the *i* symbol that represents √(-1): (2nd) (·) (*i*).
- *Using complex number–related functions*—All the functions your calculator provides for manipulating complex numbers are in the CPX tab of the Math menu (CMPLX on the TI-84 Plus C Silver Edition). Five of the commands are particularly useful: conj(, real(, imag(, angle(, and abs(. Table 6.1 explains these functions and provides examples of each one in use.

To type the imaginary symbol *i*, you press (2nd) (·). By hand, you could figure out that because $i = \sqrt{(-1)}$, so then $i^2 = \sqrt{(-1)}^2 = -1$, $i^3 = \sqrt{(-1)}^3 = -1 * i = -i$, and $i^4 = \sqrt{(-1)}^4 = -1 \times -1 = 1$. Your calculator can calculate i^2, i^3, and i^4 for you as well. Give it a try by typing i^2, i^3, and i^4 on the homescreen. You should see the results shown in figure 6.1, which confirm what manual calculations of the same values reveal. You can also see a simple imaginary number test, taking the square root of –25, –4, and –7. Remember, you can use *i* no matter what mode your calculator is in, but you can't take the square root of negative numbers in Real mode: you must switch to *a+bi* mode instead. The screenshot on the right in figure 6.1 was taken in *a+bi* mode.

The third skill you need for complex and imaginary numbers is familiarity with the complex number functions your calculator offers. All five functions can be found in the CPX tab of the Math menu: (MATH) (▶) (▶). The menu looks like figure 6.2; as you can see, it has seven items, the first five of which are functions. Table 6.1 shows what each of those functions is for and how to use it.

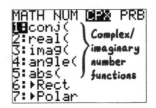

Figure 6.2 The five functions in the CPX tab of the Math menu for working with complex, real, and imaginary numbers. Table 6.1 explains how you use each one.

COMPLEX VARIABLES Just as you can put real numbers in real variables A–Z and θ, you can put complex and imaginary numbers in the same variables. Use the same → ((STO▶)) symbol to store Ans or a literal complex number into a variable, and then use that variable anywhere you might otherwise need to type a complex number.

Table 6.1 Commands to work with real, complex, and imaginary numbers, all of which can be found in the CPX tab of the Math menu. The first three are particularly important.

Command	What it does	Example usage
conj(	Takes a complex number, negates the imaginary part only, and returns the result.	conj(5+2i) 5-2i
real(	Returns only the real part of a complex number (including 0 if there is no real part).	real(5+2i) 5
imag(	Returns only the imaginary part of a complex number without the *i* (including 0 if there is no imaginary part).	imag(5+2i) 2
angle(	Finds the angle of a complex number represented in the complex plane (which is outside the scope of this book). Depends on the current angle mode (Radian or Degree).	angle(5+2i) .3805063771
abs(	Calculates the magnitude of a complex number. Given a complex number c, this is equivalent to $\sqrt{(\text{real}(c)^2 + \text{imag}(c)^2)}$ This is the exact same abs(command used to get the absolute value of positive and negative real numbers.	abs(5+2i) 5.385164807

You've seen all the basic skills you need for working with complex numbers; let's go through a complete example that uses these new skills. In chapter 1 and again in section 2.6.1, you learned about solving quadratic equations on your calculator, but there were roots you couldn't find. Complex numbers are the solution to the missing roots.

6.1.2 *Complex roots with the Quadratic Formula*

Remember from chapters 1 and 2 that the Quadratic Formula is used to find values of x that satisfy a quadratic equation $ax^2 + bx + c = 0$, where a, b, and c are constants. The Quadratic Formula is $x = (-b \pm \sqrt{(b^2 - 4ac)})/(2a)$, and it yields two unique or identical values for x. Unfortunately, for some values of a, b, and c, both of the roots are complex or imaginary. You'll see how this is possible and what to do about it.

First, you can do some detective work to figure out how you can possibly get complex or imaginary x values from the Quadratic Formula. First, assume that a, b, and c are all real numbers. This leaves the square root of a negative number to be the only way to get an imaginary value, and the Quadratic Formula has a square root: $\sqrt{(b^2 - 4ac)}$. For this to yield an imaginary value, $b^2 - 4ac < 0$, which means that $b^2 < 4ac$. In other words, whenever b^2 is larger than $4ac$, the Quadratic Formula will yield complex roots. Also, because the value of $b^2 - 4ac$ is the same for a pair of roots, either both roots are complex or neither is, not just one.

Let's come up with values for a, b, and c that will force our roots to be complex and then let our trusty graphing calculators figure out the result. We want to make sure $b^2 - 4ac < 0$, and we should try to make it a perfect square as well; $b^2 - 4ac = -4$ would be

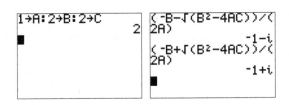

Figure 6.3 Using *a+bi* mode to let your calculator calculate complex and imaginary roots of a quadratic equation using the Quadratic Formula. As you can see, instead of throwing an ERR:NONREAL ANS error because the number inside the radical (square root symbol) is negative, the calculator figures out the proper roots.

nice, because $\sqrt{(-4)} = 2i$. If we set $a = 1$, $b = 2$, and $c = 2$, then $b^2 = 4$, $4ac = 8$, and $\sqrt{(b^2 - 4ac)} = 2i$. Let's give this a try:

1 Switch to *a+bi* mode, if you're not already in it. Press (MODE), move the cursor to a+b*i*, and press (ENTER). Quit back to the homescreen.

2 Store the values on your calculator's homescreen, 1→A, 2→B, and 2→C. The left screenshot in figure 6.3 shows how to do this. Remember, the (STO►) key types the → symbol.

3 Enter (⁻B-√(B²-4AC))/(2A) and (⁻B+√(B²-4AC))/(2A) to calculate the two roots. Remember that if you're on a MathPrint calculator, the square roots will look different from the screenshot in figure 6.3.

Regardless of whether you're using MathPrint, you'll get roots of $-1 - i$ and $-1 + i$. These are straightforward (and correct) answers, especially compared to the unhelpful NONREAL ANS error you'd get if your calculator wasn't in *a+bi* mode.

You can type imaginary and complex numbers on your calculator; you know the difference between real, complex, and imaginary numbers and variables; and you can use the five complex-number functions your calculator provides. This chapter teaches you four major precalculus skills, and you already have the first one under your belt. The second and most complicated of the four is trigonometry.

6.2 *Experimenting with trigonometry*

In my experience, students often find trigonometry to be particularly intimidating. Between unusual functions like sine, cosine, and tangent and new symbols like π and θ, trigonometry, or trig, can seem daunting. As most students soon learn, it's not as bad as it seems, and your calculator is a great tool for making trigonometry even easier. In this section, we'll start with the trig functions your calculator offers and how to use them. You'll see sine, cosine, tangent, and their friends cosecant, secant, and cotangent. We'll then move on to a specific example of using trigonometry on your graphing calculator: exploring the unit circle and the Pythagorean Theorem and how they fit into trig.

As always, you should have a rough understanding of trig basics before you attack this section, but I'm confident you'll pick up extra math hints in this section that may help trig seem clearer. Let's start with the basics: the trig functions your calculator offers and how to use them.

6.2.1   *Trig functions*

In chapters 3 and 5, you saw a few examples of trig functions used in graphs. At that point we glossed over the details of what sine, cosine, and tangent are, other than functions that take a single number as an argument and produce another number as a result. The argument to each trig function is an angle, and the output is the magnitude of that function at the given angle. Because we're dealing with angles, your calculator's angle mode (Radian or Degree) matters for trigonometric functions.

A quick guide to trig functions

The sine, cosine, and tangent functions are available directly from the keypad, without going into any menus. You type `sin(`, `cos(`, and `tan(` with ⎣ SIN ⎦, ⎣ COS ⎦, and ⎣ TAN ⎦, respectively, and then add a number or expression and a closing parenthesis (⎣) ⎦). You can use trig functions on the homescreen, in graphed equations, in programs, and anywhere else you can use numbers and variables.

For secant, cosecant, and cotangent, you must use `sin(`, `cos(`, and `tan(`. Recall the definitions from your math class:

- $\sec(x) = 1/\cos(x)$
- $\csc(x) = 1/\sin(x)$
- $\cot(x) = 1/\tan(x)$

The results of `sin(`, `cos(`, and `tan(` depend on whether you're in Radian or Degree mode. $\sin(90) = 1$ if you're in Degree mode, but $\sin(90) = 0.894$ in Radian mode. You can change the angle mode by pressing ⎣MODE⎦, moving the cursor over RADIAN or DEGREE, and pressing ⎣ENTER⎦. To check the current mode, press ⎣MODE⎦ and see if RADIAN or DEGREE is highlighted.

First, there are the three most-used trig functions: *sine, cosine,* and *tangent.* On your calculator, these are the functions `sin(`, `cos(`, and `tan(`, respectively. The sidebar "A quick guide to trig functions" explains how to type these: use the handy ⎣ SIN ⎦, ⎣ COS ⎦, and ⎣ TAN ⎦ keys on your calculator's keypad. You can then add an expression and a closing parenthesis, giving you something like `sin(1)`, `cos(π+X)`, or `tan(0.1*X²)`. You can use the trig functions on the homescreen, in graphed equations (as you've seen in chapters 3 and 5), or just about anywhere you can enter expressions on your calculator.

There are three other less-used but still important trig functions: *cosecant, secant,* and *cotangent.* Your calculator doesn't have specific functions for these, but their definitions make it easy to calculate them on your TI-83 Plus or TI-84 Plus anyway:

- *Cosecant,* or csc, is equal to 1/sine. Therefore, to calculate cosecant of $\pi/2$ on your calculator, type `1/sin(π/2)`.
- *Secant,* or sec, is equal to 1/cosine. Therefore, to calculate the secant of 90 on your calculator, type `1/cos(90)`.
- *Cotangent,* or cot, is equal to 1/tangent. To calculate the cotangent of 0.5, type `1/tan(0.5)`.

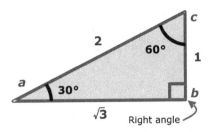

Figure 6.4 A classic 30°–60°–90° triangle, where angle *a* = 30°, *b* = 90°, and *c* = 60°. The acronym **SOHCAHTOA** tells you how to calculate the sine, cosine, and tangent of *a*, *b*, or *c*. The example in the text looks at angle *a*.

Let's give sine, cosine, and tangent a try with a triangle, using something you might know: SOHCAHTOA.

TESTING TRIG FUNCTIONS WITH **SOHCAHTOA**

You've probably seen the acronym SOHCAHTOA before. It stands for "Sine: Opposite over Hypotenuse; Cosine: Adjacent over Hypotenuse; Tangent: Opposite over Adjacent." In other words, if you have a triangle and you know the angle of each corner, you can find the sine, cosine, and tangent of any of the angles. Take a gander at figure 6.4, which shows the triangle we'll use in this example. It's a right triangle because angle *b* = 90°, and it has side lengths 1, √3, and 2. If you want to check this triangle with the Pythagorean Theorem, you'll find that $1^2 + \sqrt{3}^2 = 1 + 3 = 4$, which does indeed equal 2^2.

Let's look more closely at angle *a*, the 30° angle shown in figure 6.4. From SOHCAHTOA, you can find the sin(*a*), cos(*a*), and tan(*a*). You'll compare the answers that SOHCAHTOA provides with the results from your graphing calculator's `sin(`, `cos(`, and `tan(` functions. Before you can start, though, you need to make sure your calculator is in Degree mode, because this example works with triangle angles expressed in degrees. From the homescreen, press the (MODE) key to access the Mode menu, as shown in figure 6.5. Move the flashing cursor over the word DEGREE, and press (ENTER). It will turn into white text on a black background to indicate that it's enabled, as illustrated in figure 6.5. Don't forget that if you have a TI-83 Plus or a TI-84 Plus without MathPrint, or if you're using a TI-84 Plus C Silver Edition, this menu may look slightly different.

Next, let's try some trigonometry. SOHCAHTOA tells us that sine is opposite over hypotenuse. From figure 6.4, the side opposite angle *a* has length 1, and the hypotenuse

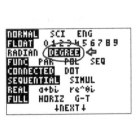
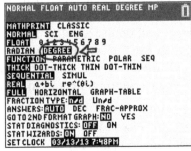

Figure 6.5 Setting Degree mode. For the SOHCAHTOA example in the text, you'll want to set your calculator to Degree mode from the Mode menu. Don't forget to set it back to Radian mode if you need that for a class.

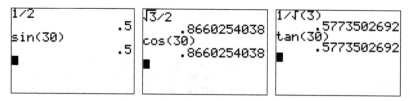

Figure 6.6 Using SOHCAHTOA to test your calculator's answers for sine, cosine, and tangent based on the triangle in figure 6.4. Notice that the center (cosine) screenshot illustrates a square root with MathPrint enabled, whereas the right screenshot shows a square root without MathPrint.

has length 2. Even though you don't need to, by plugging 1/2 into your calculator, you find that sin(a) is equal to precisely 0.5. Let's see if sin(30) agrees; it should! Because you already put your calculator in Degree mode, there's no need to be extra specific and add a degree symbol (°). Type in sin(30), and press ENTER: lo and behold, the same number. The left screenshot in figure 6.6 shows this rather simple process on your calculator's homescreen.

You can repeat the same process with cos(. Cosine is adjacent over hypotenuse, and from figure 6.4, adjacent/hypotenuse is √(3)/2. Type this into your calculator as in the middle of figure 6.6, and you get roughly 0.866. Try cos(30), and you get the same answer. The square root symbol in the cosine screenshot is a MathPrint radical; chapter 2 explained the details of typing square roots under MathPrint.

How about the final of the thee functions, tan(? Tangent is opposite over adjacent, which for this triangle is $1/\sqrt{3}$. Type in 1/√(3) and press ENTER, and your calculator returns around 0.5774. Likewise, when you try tan(30), you get exactly the same value! Figure 6.6 shows the tan(results. Trigonometry on your calculator therefore works nicely, and so does SOHCAHTOA.

If you wanted to be really ambitious, you could also get values for the secant, cosecant, and cotangent of 30° using the definitions of each plus SOHCAHTOA and compare those to your calculator's values. You could also try looking at the triangle's 60° angle.

INVERSE TRIG FUNCTIONS

Sometimes you want to work the other way around: instead of finding the sine, cosine, or tangent of an angle, you want to start with the output of a trig function and work backward to the angle that created it. In other words, you know that sin(x) = 0.4, but you don't know what x is. The inverse trig functions are written as sin⁻¹(, cos⁻¹(, and tan⁻¹(and do exactly that. If you know the sine of something is 0.4 (say, sin(x) = 0.4), then sin⁻¹(0.4) will show you exactly what that x is. Likewise, if you know tan(h) = −0.5, then tan⁻¹(⁻0.5) will tell you what h is.

You can type the three inverse trig functions like this:

- sin⁻1(: [2nd] [SIN] (inverse sine)
- cos⁻1(: [2nd] [COS] (inverse cosine)
- tan⁻1(: [2nd] [TAN] (inverse tangent)

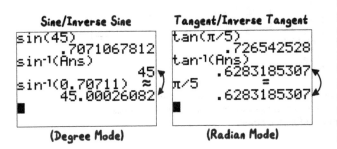

Sine/Inverse Sine Tangent/Inverse Tangent

(Degree Mode) (Radian Mode)

Figure 6.7 Testing sine with inverse sine in Degree mode (left) and tangent alongside inverse tangent in Radian mode (right). Notice that because Ans holds the full precision of the sin(result, sin⁻¹(is able to return exactly 45°. sin⁻¹(0.70711) is a shade above 45°, but you can recognize that the difference is just a precision problem.

Figure 6.7 demonstrates the correctness of the inverse trig functions with a few examples. Don't forget that mode matters! If your calculator is in Degree mode, the inverse trig functions return angles in degrees; in Radian mode, the functions return angles in radians.

Now you know all the trig functions your calculator has, from sin(, cos(, and tan(, to the inverse trigonometric functions, and the tricks to construct cosecant, secant, and cotangent. You also saw a handful of examples, the most complete being a right triangle, proving the correctness of SOHCAHTOA. I want to show you a final complete example, connecting the unit circle with trigonometry. Your calculator is particularly handy for this, because you can use graphing and drawing tools to visualize how trig functions work.

6.2.2 *Trigonometry and the unit circle*

The *unit circle* is a circle of radius 1, centered at the origin, (0,0). It's special in that if you draw any radius from the center to a point on the edge, that line can be used to calculate trigonometric function values. The (x,y) coordinates of the point on the edge of the circle are equal to $(\cos(\theta), \sin(\theta))$, where θ is the angle the line makes relative to the positive x axis. In this example, you'll see how and why that works, and you'll use this technique to determine the sine and cosine of $\pi/4$.

You should start by graphing a unit circle. We'll be using Polar mode for this exercise, because Polar mode works well with graphing circles. Go to (MODE) and select POL. We'll also be using radian angles, so choose Radian mode. Next, go to (WINDOW). We want the unit circle to be nice and big, so set Xmin=⁻1, Xmax=1, Ymin=⁻1, and Ymax=1. Remember that because the screen is wider than it is tall, this will give an elliptical shape for a circle, so we want to Zoom Square. Press (ZOOM), and choose 5:ZSquare. If you double-check the Window settings, they should now match the center in figure 6.8.

Now enter r₁=1 as your equation to graph, and press (GRAPH). If everything is set up properly, you'll see a good-looking circle, as demonstrated on the right in figure 6.8. If the axes are missing or other Graph Format settings are weird, check the Graph Format menu in (2nd) (ZOOM). You might also need to adjust Xscl and Yscl to 1 to change where the ticks appear on the axes. If everything looks good, you can draw a radius and turn it into a triangle.

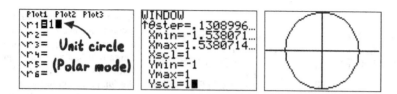

Figure 6.8   Drawing a unit circle. First, enter Polar mode and add `r=1` as an equation. Then, set `Xmin=Ymin=-1`, `Xmax=Ymax=1`, and use the `ZSquare` tool. Finally, you see the graph of a nice circle.

There are two ways you can draw a radius on the unit circle and turn it into a triangle. Freehand, you can start on the graph screen, press 2nd PRGM to get to the Draw menu, select the 2:Line tool, and draw out the radius by hand. With the cursor at (0,0), you could press ENTER to start the line, drag it out to the edge of the circle, and press ENTER to finalize it. You could then draw a second line down (or up, depending on what point on the circle you picked) to the *x* axis. This would be the more "realistic" way to do things, because you wouldn't be relying on already having a `sin(` and `cos(` function available to you.

You can try that if you want, but I'll show you the details of a second method. Switch to the homescreen if you're not already there (press CLEAR or 2nd MODE from the graphscreen), and type the two lines of commands shown on the left in figure 6.9:

```
Line(0,0,cos(π/4),sin(π/4))
Line(cos(π/4),0,cos(π/4),sin(π/4))
```

> **MISSING CLOSING PARENTHESES**   The keen-eyed observer will notice I left off the final closing parentheses in figure 6.9; your calculator is forgiving about such things. If you leave off parentheses, brackets, or curly braces at the very end of a line, it won't complain, although I don't recommend doing that as a regular practice.

`Line(` is in the Draw menu, accessed from 2nd PRGM, Ans is 2nd (-), and you already know how to type the rest of it from practice. You can type the second line as is, or you could be clever and optimize it:

```
cos(π/4):Line(Ans,0,Ans,sin(π/4))
```

This version puts `cos(π/4)` by itself to store it to Ans, so when the next command begins (commands on the same line are separated by colons, as you saw in chapters 1 and 2), you can use Ans instead of typing `cos(π/4)` twice. If you're confused by this trick, stick with the commands shown in figure 6.9.

You'll get the lines shown in the center and right screenshots in figure 6.9. If you don't, go back to the Mode menu and make sure you selected Radian mode. These lines define a triangle with one angle of π/4, or 45°: this is a 45°–45°–90° triangle. Start pressing the arrow keys, and a cursor will appear. If you don't see x and y coordinates at the bottom of the screen, you need to select `CoordOn` from the 2nd ZOOM menu. Move the cursor over to where the right angle in the triangle appears, and

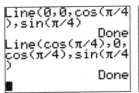 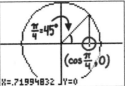 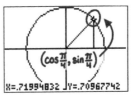

Figure 6.9 Adding a triangle on top of the unit circle, for an angle of π/4 radians or 45°. The left screenshot shows the commands that draw the diagonal and vertical lines. The center and right screenshots are moving the graph cursor (circled) around the screen with the arrow keys and examining (x,y) coordinates.

you'll see that the (*x,y*) coordinates are about (0.72,0). Move the cursor up to the end of the radius (the hypotenuse of the triangle), and you'll get coordinates that are about (0.72,0.71).

We know from SOHCAHTOA that the sine of the angle closest to the origin, with the angle measuring π/4, is opposite over hypotenuse. The height of the vertical leg is about 0.71, as you just measured, and the hypotenuse is exactly 1, because the circle has radius 1, and thus we can estimate that sin(π/4) is about 0.71. For cosine, equal to adjacent over hypotenuse, we get cos(π/4), which is equal to about 0.72. To double-check our results, we can switch back to the home-screen and calculate sin(π/4) and cos(π/4) directly. Lo and behold, as figure 6.10 demonstrates, we get equal values of 0.7071. These are extremely close to the 0.71 and 0.72 values that we determined by visual inspection of the graphed unit circle.

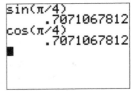

Figure 6.10 Sine and cosine values for π/4 radians or 45° that match the triangle drawn over the unit circle

As you can see, the unit circle is a handy tool for calculating sine and cosine values by hand, assuming you can accurately measure angles. Alternately, if you have inverse sine and cosine functions available to you (perhaps from your handy graphing calculator), you can use the coordinates of a point on the edge of the circle to calculate the angle formed by a line from the origin to that point.

With hopefully a firm handle on trigonometry and your calculator, we'll move on to another popular precalculus skill: understanding and finding limits. As with every skill we've looked at so far, your calculator can help make this easier.

6.3 *Understanding limits*

Imagine that you, an enterprising math student, are working with the equation in figure 6.11: $y = 12(\sqrt{(x^2 + 4)} - 2)/x^2$. You try plugging in various values of *x* to try to understand more about the shape of this function. You try *x* = 5, *x* = 3, and *x* = 2. You try *x* = 1 as well; the findings are shown on the left in figure 6.11 to help us follow along.

When you get to *x* = 0, though, you hit an unexpected snag. You end up with 12 times 0/0, and being an astute mathematician, you know that 0/0 is an undefined value! To help understand your confusion, you write your calculations for *x* = 0

$$y(x) = 12 \frac{\sqrt{x^2+4}-2}{x^2}$$

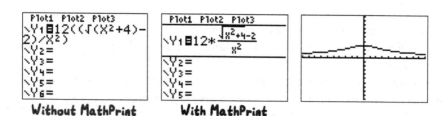

SOLUTION WHERE $x=1$	SOLUTION WHERE $x=0$
$y(1) = 12\dfrac{\sqrt{1^2+4}-2}{1^2} = 12\dfrac{\sqrt{5}-2}{1} \approx 2.833$	$y(0) = 12\dfrac{\sqrt{0^2+4}-2}{0^2} = 12\dfrac{0}{0} = \text{???}$

Figure 6.11 The equation that will prove troublesome in this section, along with two attempts to evaluate it at specific values of *x*. At *x* = 1, you get a reasonable answer; at *x* = 0, something goes wrong.

Without MathPrint   With MathPrint

Figure 6.12 The initial graph of the function (right), along with its equation in the Y= menu with (center) and without (right) MathPrint. It looks like the graph is continuous, but if you plug X=0 in to the equation, you'll see that Y₁(0) is the undefined value 0/0.

(shown on the right in figure 6.11). Baffled but determined to get to the bottom of this mystery, you turn to your trusty graphing calculator. You plug in the equation you've been working with as an equation to graph, which you can see in figure 6.12. Depending on whether you have MathPrint enabled, that equation might look like either the left or center screenshot. Satisfied that you have the equation correct, you press GRAPH and examine the result.

But the graph you get, shown on the right in figure 6.12, just deepens the mystery. That looks like a smooth enough graph, with no crazy peaks or vertical asymptotes. So whence therein lies the rub? as Shakespeare might say. Having read chapter 3 of this book, you know that your calculator's Table tool might offer some answers, and so you press (2nd) GRAPH. Finally, something that makes sense: your calculator agrees that the value of Y₁ at X=0 is ERROR, as the screenshot in figure 6.13 confirms.

You talk to your math teacher, who explains that you have stumbled on a point where the graph isn't defined. But you can use a *limit* to get infinitely close to that point without actually touching it and use some mathematical tricks to find the value of this equation as *x* approaches 0. Your teacher explains that once you get to calculus, you'll know how to use a method called L'Hôpital's Rule

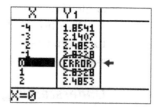

Figure 6.13 The calculator's Table tool confirms that there's no value for the function Y₁ at exactly X=0. That's why you need to use a limit; your calculator can help you empirically determine that limit's value.

to simplify this equation, but for now, you can use your calculator's Table tool to get more detail.

Start by writing the expression for the limit:

$$y(0) = \lim_{x \to 0} 12\,\frac{\sqrt{x^2+4}-2}{x^2}$$

This is a two-sided limit, meaning you can approach $x = 0$ from $x > 0$ or $x < 0$ and get the same answer for the limit. As your math teacher may have mentioned, some limits can be approached from only one side. At any rate, to examine values closer to $x = 0$, you can change the ΔTbl value, the difference between X values for successive rows of the table. The left screenshot in figure 6.14 shows how to adjust ΔTbl to 0.1 and TblStart to -0.5.

Now you can see that at both $x = -0.1$ and $x = 0.1$, y is 2.9981, which is nearly 3. If you go back to [2nd] [WINDOW] and adjust ΔTbl to 0.01, you'll see that the y values at $x = -0.01$ and $x = 0.01$ are even closer to 3. Therefore, you can safely conclude that the limit of this function as $x \to 0$ is 3. You can follow this method to find any limits, by examining values of the function in question very close to the *discontinuity*, the point where the graph isn't defined.

You should be careful, though, because your calculator is still just a computer, and due to the way it calculates very small numbers, the y values closer than 0.0001 to the discontinuity may be increasingly inaccurate. For this particular example, x values around 0.000001 start collapsing to 0 instead of getting close to 3, which isn't helpful. Make sure you look at a range of values before you make a decision as to the value of

 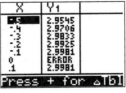

Figure 6.14 You can repeatedly zoom in on the table to see the values of the function near X=0.

the limit. It's also important to look at the graph to get a ballpark for the limit; you can see from figure 6.14 that the limit is probably about 3.

Checking your limits with L'Hôpital's Rule

L'Hôpital's Rule is a method in calculus used for determining limits. If both the numerator and denominator of a fractional function are 0 or ∞ at the x value for the limit, then you can repeatedly take the derivative of the numerator and denominator separately until one of them is no longer 0 or infinity.

The math is far too tedious to write out for this example, but applying L'Hôpital's Rule twice yields $y(0) = \lim x \to 0$ of $24/(x^2 + 4)^{3/2}$, $4^{3/2} = 8$, and $24/8 = 3$, so the limit is indeed 3.

Another important topic in precalculus involves logarithms and exponents. Your calculator contains a variety of functions and constants to help you manipulate logarithms, the last topic I'll cover in this chapter.

6.4   *Exponents and logarithms*

You're probably familiar with raising a number to a power or an exponent. If you square a number, raising it to the second power, you multiply two of itself together: $4^2 = 4 \times 4 = 16$. Raise it to the fourth power, and you're effectively multiplying four copies of it together: $3^4 = 3 \times 3 \times 3 \times 3 = 81$. In this section, we'll talk about two special types of exponents. We'll also discuss logarithms, which are the reverse operation to exponentiation. Just as dividing by 4 "undoes" multiplying by 4, and subtracting 10.4 reverses adding 10.4, a logarithm undoes raising a number by a power.

Let's start with raising 10 to a power and the base-10 logarithm. From everyday math, you're well accustomed to math involving powers of 10. Multiplying a number larger than 1 by 10 invariably adds another digit to the left of the decimal place, and dividing the same number by 10 removes a digit to the left of the decimal place. Because powers of 10 are equivalent to multiplying 10 together a certain number of times, something like 10^5 is equal to 100,000, or 10 with five zeroes. $10^{5.2}$ is also six digits, as you can see from figure 6.15.

Logarithms are the inverse function to exponents. In mathematical terms, if $b^x = y$, then $\log_b(y)$ (which you read as "log base b of y") is equal to x. Put another way, $10^{\log x} = x$, and $\log(10^x) = x$. Notice that omitting the base next to the logarithm makes it default to $b = 10$; when you calculate a logarithm on your calculator with the ⌞LOG⌟ key, it

$10^5 = 10*10*10*10*10$
  $= 1\underbrace{00000}$
     1 WITH 5 ZEROES

$10^{5.2} = 10*10*10*10*10*10^{0.2}$
   $= 1\underbrace{58489}.319...$
     NUMBER WITH 5 MORE DIGITS

$\log_{10}(100000) = 5$

$\log_{10}(158489.32) = 5.2$

Figure 6.15   Demonstrating powers of 10 (left) and base-10 logarithms (right). On your calculator, the ⌞LOG⌟ key, which types log (, calculates log base-10.

assumes that you're looking for a base-10 logarithm. Because I've broached the subject, here's how you find powers and logarithms of 10 on your calculator:

- *10^x*—To raise 10 to a given power, a shortcut is (**2nd**)(**LOG**). This types $_{10}$^ (; add the power to raise it to 10, and finish with a closing parenthesis.
- *log(*—For the inverse operation, taking a base-10 logarithm, use the (**LOG**) key by itself. This types the log(function, after which you should put the number to calculate a logarithm of and a closing parenthesis.
- *Normal exponents*—You learned all about these in chapter 2. Type the number to raise, the (**∧**) key, and then the number to raise it to. You can also use variables and more complex expressions instead of simple numbers for each part.

Although base-10 is popular for powers and logarithms in intermediate math, higher math and engineering often focus on powers and logarithms of an irrational number called *e*. *e* is equal to 2.71828…, an infinitely long decimal, just as another irrational constant, π, is equal to 3.14159…. *e* is sometimes called Euler's ("*Ol-ler's*") number and is equal to the sum of an infinite but converging series. Among other things, it turns up in real-world equations for compound interest and gambling probabilities. Your calculator can raise *e* to powers and take a base-*e* logarithm, called the natural log:

- *e^x*—To raise *e* to a given power, type (**2nd**)(**LN**), which inserts the e^ (symbol. As with raising 10 to a power, type the power and then a closing parenthesis.
- *ln(*—Just as the (**LOG**) key types the base-10 logarithm function, log(, the (**LN**) (natural logarithm) types the base-*e* logarithm, ln(. Follow ln(with the number or expression to calculate the natural log, and end with a closing parenthesis.

Logarithms of base *b*

Until the MathPrint operating systems arrived, TI-83 Plus and TI-84 Plus calculators could only calculate logarithms of base-10 and base-e. MathPrint adds a new function at the bottom of the Math tab of the Math menu called logBASE(. To use it, press (**MATH**) and select A:logBASE(. If it's not there, then you aren't running a MathPrint operating system. logBASE(takes two arguments: the number to calculate the logarithm of, and the base. For example, you can calculate the base-2 log of 256: logBASE(256,2) = 8, because $2^8 = 256$. Also, logBASE(100,8) ≈ 2.214, because $8^{2.214}$ ≈ 100.

If you have MathPrint enabled, then your calculator offers a MathPrint template for a logarithm of base *b*. You fill in the base *b* first as a subscript and then the number to take the logarithm of, as shown in the figure.

$\log_8(100)$

  2.21461873

$\log_2(256)$

  8.

$\log_{\blacksquare}(\blacksquare)$

Demonstrating the MathPrint template for logarithms of base *b*. Although this screenshot is from a TI-84 Plus C Silver Edition, the skill applies to the entire TI-84 Plus family.

Let's quickly work through an example just to cement these new skills, even though there's not much in the way of nuances to these commands. Say that you want to calculate the natural log of 20. You type ln(20) on the homescreen, as shown in figure 6.16. You just learned that ln(is the (LN) key, and the (2) (0) ()) that types the 20) is from chapter 2. As figure 6.16 illustrates, you'll get just under 3. You can double-check this result by calculating e^{Ans} or $e^{2.9957}$: type e^(Ans) via (2nd) (LN) (2nd) ((-)) ()), and press (ENTER). As the last line of figure 6.16 demonstrates, you get your original 20 back out.

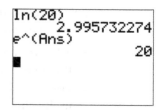

Figure 6.16 Calculating the natural log of 20 with the ln(function and then checking the answer with the e^(function. Because ln(and e^(are mutually inverse functions, ln(e^(X))=X.

Bonus skill: summations

The first MathPrint operating system for the TI-84 Plus family of calculators (as introduced in chapter 1) added a way to calculate summations on the graphing calculators. If you have a MathPrint operating system but MathPrint is disabled, then you use the 0:summation Σ(, found in the first tab of the Math menu, like this:

Σ(*expression*,*variable*,*lower value*,*upper value*)

For example, you can compute Σ(1/X², X, 1, 10) for the summation of $1/x^2$ from $x = 1$ to $x = 10$. If you enable MathPrint, then you'll get a MathPrint template for the summation operation, shown here. You can also access the summation template from the FUNC tab of the MathPrint shortcut menus, via (ALPHA) (WINDOW).

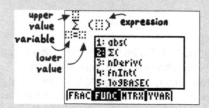

The MathPrint template for summation on the TI-84 Plus family of graphing calculators. You can access the summation template from the Math menu or from the FUNC shortcut menu, via (ALPHA) (WINDOW).

You've reached the end of this selection of precalculus skills, so it's time to move on to some calculus. Keep in mind that many of the other things you've explored in chapters 3–5, especially the different types of graphing, may also be part of your precalculus curriculum.

6.5   *Summary*

In this chapter, you rounded out the precalculus skills you collected in previous chapters with four new solid sets of skills. You learned how to use your calculator to manipulate real, imaginary, and complex numbers and to work with trigonometric functions. You discovered how to use graphs and the Table tool to find the values of limits, an important alternative to the more complex methods you'll learn in your calculus class.

Finally, I introduced you to the logarithmic and exponential functions your calculator provides, using base-10, base-e, and, for MathPrint users, arbitrary bases.

Because you now know just about everything your calculator can do to help you with precalculus, it should come as no great surprise that calculus is next. You'll learn about your calculator's tools for integration, differentiation, and everything in between in the next chapter.

Calculus on the
TI-83 Plus/TI-84 Plus

This chapter covers

- Calculating numerical derivatives and integrals on your calculator
- Applying derivatives to find the slope, extrema, and inflection points of curves
- Using integrals to find the area under graphed curves

Calculus is a far-reaching subject, used throughout science, engineering, and many other fields. It was first developed by mathematicians Newton and Liebniz in the 17th century. Liebniz invented the integral notation that we use to this day, and he also built some of the first mechanical calculators. Newton used his work on calculus as a foundation for much of his well-known contributions to physics.

Calculus is related to the study of extremely small values, and the two best-known skills from basic calculus are *integration* and *differentiation*. If you imagine a graphed function, integration is used to find the area underneath that function by dividing the area into tinier and tinier rectangles. Differentiation (the process of calculating a derivative) finds the slope of a line tangent to a function by moving two points defining the line infinitely close to each other.

In algebra, you learned the difference between variables and numbers. A variable like m or x can take any specific value, like 7 or –1398.4, but on its own a variable represents a space where a number will be placed. *Symbolic calculus* is like algebra in that you can find the derivative of $2x^3 + x$ with respect to x, which happens to be $6x^2 + 1$, without plugging a value into x. Your calculator can't perform symbolic calculus operations like finding indefinite integrals or symbolic derivatives (although the TI-89, TI-92, and TI-Nspire CAS calculators can). What your calculator can do is *numerical calculus*.

Numerical calculus is used to find the derivative of a function at a specific point, or the definite integral of a function. Numerical calculus is what you perform when you find the slope of a line tangent to some function or the area under a curve between two x values. What does this mean for your classes? You can use your calculator to check your answers for symbolic integrals and derivatives by plugging in values for x (or whatever the independent variable is). You can calculate numerical integrals and derivatives for physics and other science courses. But you can't use your calculator to perform general, indeterminate, or symbolic calculus.

In this chapter, you'll learn how to use TI-83 Plus/TI-84 Plus calculus tools. You'll first learn how to calculate derivatives at a point and how you can find the line tangent to a curve. Next, we'll explore how you can graph the first and second derivatives of a function and apply the result to finding the extrema and inflection points of a function. Finally, you'll find out how to calculate integrals on the homescreen and graphscreen, and we'll work through an example applying this to finding the area under a curve.

You'll be happy to hear that finding the derivative of a function and applying that skill to calculate the slope of a line at a point is easy with a graphing calculator. Let's start there.

7.1   *Derivatives and slope*

Differentiation, or calculating a derivative, is the inverse operation to integration: the derivative of the integral of a function is the function itself. Practically, the first derivative of a function tells you the slope of the original function at any point. If you take the derivative of the derivative, called the *second derivative*, then you can easily find the *inflection points*: the points where the function changes from concave up to concave down. Your calculator can't do symbolic differentiation any more than it can do symbolic integration, but it has tools to calculate numerical derivatives. In this section, I'll show you how to find the slope of any point on a function on the graphscreen or the homescreen. In the next section, I'll show you how even without knowing the equation for the function's derivative, your calculator can graph the first and second derivatives.

Derivatives in a nutshell

As with integrals, your calculator can find the value of a derivative on the graphscreen or on the homescreen. As with integrals, you can only find the numerical derivative of a function at a specific point, not the equation for the symbolic derivative. But section 7.2 will show you how to graph the derivative function without knowing the exact equation. Following are the two ways to calculate a derivative at a point:

- *On the graphscreen*—Graph an equation, and then go to the Calculate menu (2nd TRACE) and choose 6:dy/dx. You'll be asked to pick a function only if you have more than one equation graphed. Next, move the cursor left or right to choose the point where you want to calculate the derivative; you can also start typing an *x* coordinate. Press ENTER to get the result.
- *On the homescreen*—Use the nDeriv(function from the Math menu. You specify the function (either directly or as a variable from VARS   ▶   1) as the first argument, the letter of the independent variable as the second argument, and the point at which to find the derivative as the third argument:

```
nDeriv(equation,X,x-coordinate)
```

7.1.1   *Calculating derivatives on the graphscreen*

I'll teach you to work with the derivative of a function at a point via an example. For consistency, we'll use the equation $y = (0.4x)^3 - 2x + 3$. On your calculator, this becomes

```
Y₁=(.4X)^3-2X+3
```

(Of course, it doesn't have to be Y₁, but it's neater to use the first equation first.) Make sure your calculator is in Function mode if you changed to a different graphing mode; then go ahead and type this equation into the Y= menu. When you press GRAPH, you should see something like the graph in figure 7.1; if not, try turning the axes on from 2nd   ZOOM and resetting to the standard window with the 6:ZStandard option in ZOOM.

Once you're satisfied with the graph, you can jump right to calculating the derivative of the equation at a point. The graphscreen differentiation tool, labeled dy/dx, is found in the same menu as the graphscreen integration tool. Press 2nd   TRACE to access the Calculate menu, and choose 6:dy/dx, as shown on the left in figure 7.1. Because you have only one function graphed, the first (and only) thing the calculator asks for is the point where you want to calculate the derivative. If you had more than one function graphed at the same time, the calculator would ask you to pick which equation to differentiate before asking for the point.

To choose a point, you can move the cursor left or right along the graphed function using the arrow keys, shown in the center of figure 7.1. If you know the precise *x* coordinate, you can also type it in using the number keys, as you could while finding the area under a curve. If you're using a TI-84 Plus C Silver Edition, the process of choosing a point and the resulting slope display will match figure 7.2. When you're satisfied with the point you've chosen, press ENTER, and your calculator will find the

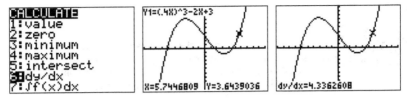

Figure 7.1 **Finding the slope of a function at a point. Here we find that the slope of $y = (0.4x)^3 - 2 + 3$ at $x = 5.745$ is about 4.34.**

derivative of the function at that point. You can see that I picked $x = 5.745$ in figure 7.1 and 5.758 in figure 7.2, but you can choose any point you want. My TI-84 Plus calculator displayed dy/dx=4.336..., the slope of $y = (0.4x)^3 - 2x + 3$ at $x = 5.745$, as you can see in figure 7.1. My TI-84 Plus C Silver Edition found that dy/dx=4.364 at x=5.758, illustrated in figure 7.2.

It's not easy to check the result of the differentiation operation without knowing the symbolic derivative, so I'll tell you that dy/dx $= 0.192x^2 - 2$ in this case. Plug in $x = 5.745$, and you get dy/dx $= 0.192(5.745)^2 - 2 \approx 6.336 - 2 = 4.336$. It's a match!

7.1.2 *Calculating derivatives on the homescreen*

You can also calculate this numerical derivative on the homescreen, as illustrated in figure 7.3. The key is to use the nDeriv(function from the Math menu.

To give this a try, quit from the graphscreen to the homescreen. Starting on a blank line, press (MATH) and choose 8:nDeriv(. The nDeriv(function takes three arguments: the function to differentiation, the letter of the independent variable (usually X for us), and the point at which to find the derivative. For the function, you can either type the equation directly (as in the second line of figure 7.3) or use one of the Y_n variables from (VARS) (▶) (1) (as in the first line of figure 7.3).

As you can see from figure 7.3, either option gets you almost exactly the same result as finding the derivative on the graphscreen; the only difference is from using

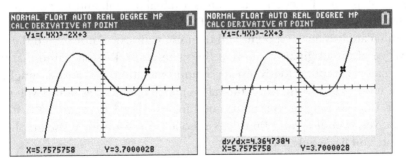

Figure 7.2 **Computing the slope of a function at a point on a TI-84 Plus C Silver Edition. The only reason the slope doesn't exactly match the results from a TI-83 Plus or TI-84 Plus in figure 7.1 is that the *x* value I chose wasn't precisely the same: 5.758 instead of 5.745.**

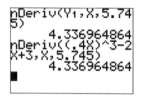

Figure 7.3   Calculating the derivative of a function at a point on the homescreen, using Y_1 or a typed-out function. Remember that your calculator can find only numerical derivatives, not symbolic derivatives.

the point $x = 5.745$ instead of the full $x = 5.744689$ that I got from moving the cursor along the function on the graphscreen.

The MathPrint derivative template

On MathPrint operating systems on TI-84 Plus-family calculators, you can use a derivative template that looks like what you might see in your favorite math textbook. It takes the same arguments as the `nDeriv(` command: the equation of which you're taking a derivative, what variable you're differentiating with respect to, and the value at which to differentiate.

The figure here shows an example of a MathPrint derivative in action (top) and the unpopulated template (bottom). I used X for the variable of differentiation here, but you could use any other variable. If you have a MathPrint operating system and Math-Print is enabled, you can access the MathPrint derivative template from `8:nDeriv(` in the Math menu or via the FUNC MathPrint shortcut menu, (ALPHA) (WINDOW).

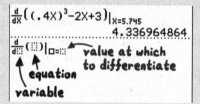

Using the MathPrint derivative template. With a function and value filled in (top) and before being filled in (bottom). Although this is a TI-84 Plus C Silver Edition screenshot, the template looks very similar on the other TI-84 Plus family calculators.

Finding the slope of a function at a point is a valuable tool, and it can be especially helpful for checking symbolic derivatives. If you find the symbolic derivative by hand, you can calculate its value at a point and then use your calculator to find the numerical derivative of the original function at the same point. Keep in mind that because your calculator computes derivatives via approximation, its answer might differ slightly from the precise solution. If the values match up for a few points, you probably got it right. But you can use your trusty graphing calculator to graph the first and second derivatives, even if it can't find the symbolic expression for those graphs. In the next section, you'll see how it's done.

7.2   *Finding minima, maxima, and inflection points*

It can be counterintuitive to hear that your TI-83 Plus or TI-84 Plus can find the derivative of a function and a point, and that it can even graph the derivative across many points, but it doesn't know the equation for the derivative. When you calculate a derivative by hand, you apply a variety of rules to it, such as that d/dx (the derivative with respect to x) of $ax^n = anx^{n-1}$. Your calculator could be programmed to find symbolic derivatives the same way, but it takes a lot of software for it to know all the different rules for symbolic differentiation and to apply them the correct way. Therefore, it can only perform numerical differentiation at a point.

But if it can find the numerical derivative at one point, it can find it at a point nearby and at a third point close to that one. String together a hundred points or so, and it can connect the dots to graph the equation of the derivative. If you put the nDeriv(function in a Y= equation and graph it, that's exactly what your calculator can do. We'll use that trick to graph the first and second derivatives of our favorite $y = (0.4x)^3 - 2x + 3$ in this section.

FIRST DERIVATIVE The first derivative of a function tells you the slope of a function. Anywhere that the first derivative crosses the x axis, the slope changes between negative and positive, so that point is either a local maximum or a local minimum of the original function.

The syntax for using nDeriv(in a Y= function is the same as using it on the home-screen. The only difference is that instead of specifying a number for the point where you want to differentiate, you use the variable X. This means for every point along the graph, you want the y value to be the derivative of the original function at that point. I'll ask you to type the nDeriv(of Y_1 as function Y_2 and the nDeriv(of Y_2 as function Y_3; these equations are also shown on the top-left in figure 7.4:

```
Y₁=(.4X)^3-2X+3
Y₂=nDeriv(Y₁,X,X)
Y₃=nDeriv(Y₂,X,X)
```

If you have a MathPrint calculator, you might want to use the MathPrint nDeriv(template under (ALPHA) (WINDOW). Refer to the sidebar "The MathPrint derivative template" for information on using this. Notice from figure 7.4 that I set the original function to be bold. To do this, move the cursor over the \ to the left of Y_1, and press (ENTER) once.

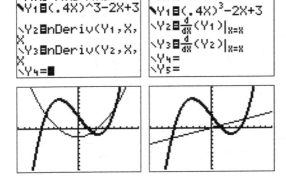

Figure 7.4 Plotting the first and second derivatives of a function. The top row shows how to do it without MathPrint (top left) or with MathPrint (top right). Bottom left is the first derivative, and bottom right is the second derivative. You can find the local extrema (minima and maxima) and the inflection points of the curve from these graphs.

You can see the first derivative with the original function at lower-left in figure 7.4 and the second derivative at lower-right. You'll get all three functions on a single graph; I separated them so that you can see them more clearly. As you can see, the first derivative crosses the *x* axis twice, so there are two extrema (minima or maxima) in the original function. Because the second derivative crosses the *x* axis once, there's also one inflection point.

> **SECOND DERIVATIVE**   The second derivative of a function tells you the slope of the slope of a function. In other words, anywhere the slope of the function changes between increasing and decreasing, the second derivative will be zero. These points are called *inflection points*.

Here's how you can use the 2:zero tool from the Calculate menu to find the extrema and inflection point of Y_1 from the first and second derivatives:

1 Go to the graph, press `2nd` `TRACE` to get to the Calculate menu, and choose 2:zero. You learned to use this tool in chapter 3; you select the function you want, left and right bounds on the area to search inside for a zero, and a guess where the zero is.

2 Choose Y_2 for the function, around –4.5 as the left bound, and about –2 as the right bound. The guess should be around –3.4. Your calculator will find a zero in Y_2 at about $x = -3.227$: you can see that Y_1 has a maximum at this point. The left side of figure 7.5 also shows this result.

3 Use the zero tool again on Y_2, this time for the minimum. Your left bound should be about 1.7, your right bound at 4.5 or so, and your guess near 3.4. Your calculator finds a zero in the first derivative at $x = 3.227$, and you can see that the Y_1 function has a local minimum there. Figure 7.5 demonstrates this in the center screenshot.

4 Use the zero tool on Y_3 to find the inflection point. Because the local minimum and maximum were equally far from $x = 0$, you can probably guess that the inflection point is at $x = 0$, but let's double-check. Choose Y_3 as your function for the zero tool, and move to a left bound below $x = 0$. Notice how slow it is to move the cursor along Y_3: your calculator needs to do a lot of thinking to

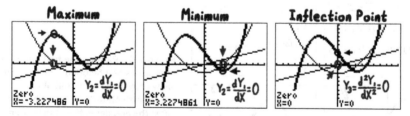

Figure 7.5   Finding the local maximum, local minimum, and inflection point of a function on your calculator. You find the zeroes of the first derivative to find the minimum and maximum and find the zero of the second derivative to find the inflection point.

calculate these *y* values. Choose a right bound above $x = 0$ and a guess right around 0. You'll see, as also shown at right in figure 7.5, that the inflection point is at precisely $x = 0$.

You can use this same process to find the extrema and inflection points for any function. Graph the function, then graph the `nDeriv(` of the function to get its first derivative, and finally graph the `nDeriv(` of the first derivative to get the second derivative. Because of technical limitations of your calculator, you can't graph the third or higher-order derivatives. Use the `zero` tool from the Calculate menu to find the zeroes of the first derivative, which tells you where the minimum and maximum points on the original function are. Use the `zero` tool on the second derivative to find any inflection points (there may be none).

You can find integrals with your calculator nearly as easily as you can compute derivates.

7.3   Integrals and area under a curve

Integrals are a fairly abstract concept, but they can be made much more concrete by using them to calculate the area under a curve. As you know, you can calculate the area of a rectangle by multiplying its width by its height. You could try to divide the area under a curve into a series of small rectangles, and you'd see that the sum of the areas of the rectangles would be close to the area under the curve. If you made the rectangles narrower and narrower, you'd get closer and closer to the exact area, a technique known as a *Riemann sum*. Figure 7.6 shows an example of a "middle" Riemann sum, so called because the middle of each rectangle touches the curve. The reason it's only an approximation is the triangles missing between the curve and the rectangles or the extra bits of the rectangles above the curve. The narrower the rectangles, the smaller these errors become.

Because your calculator can't calculate the symbolic integral of a function, as I explained, it performs a Riemann sum. In general, this can be quite accurate, as you'll see in this section's example. As always, if you're in a hurry, you can skip straight to the "TI-83 Plus/TI-84 Plus integrals in 60 seconds" sidebar. If you have time to stick around and play with an example, you'll find the area under $y = (0.4x)^3 - 2x + 3$, review graphing skills, and learn to use your graphing calculator's integral tool along the way. You'll see that you can calculate integrals visually on the graphscreen, selecting the left and right bounds for the definite integral using the arrow keys. I'll also

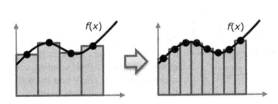

Figure 7.6   You can approximate a numerical integral by hand, without knowing calculus. The area under a curve is roughly equal to the sum of a set of rectangles filling the area under the function; the narrower the rectangles, the more accurate the approximation. Because your calculator can't do symbolic calculus, this is exactly how it calculates integrals.

show you how to perform the same steps on the homescreen to get a value you can use in other calculations.

TI-83 Plus/TI-84 Plus integrals in 60 seconds

Your calculator can calculate numerical integrals on the graphscreen or homescreen:

- To calculate an integral on the graphscreen, type a function in the Y= menu and then press (GRAPH). If you're satisfied with the graph, press (2nd) (TRACE) to access the Calculate menu, and choose 7:∫f(x)dx. You'll be asked to pick the equation only if you have more than one equation graphed. You can then move the cursor to select the left and right bounds of the integral or use the number keys to type the x coordinates. Press (ENTER) after selecting each bound. After you pick both edges of the definite integral, the area will be shaded and the value displayed (see figure 7.10, later in this section).
- To calculate the same integral on the homescreen, press (CLEAR) or (2nd) (MODE) to return to the homescreen after you graph the equation in question. Press (MATH), and choose 9:fnInt(from the first tab of the Math menu. You'll need to enter the equation, the independent variable, the x value of the left bound, and the x value of the right bound. For example, fnInt(Y₁,X,⁻5,0) (Y₁ is in (VARS) (▶) (1)) in figure 7.12 shows more; here are the arguments to fnInt(in a nutshell:

```
fnInt(equation,X,lower bound,upper bound)
```

7.3.1   Computing integrals on the graphscreen

For the example, you'll be working with $y = (0.4x)^3 - 2x + 3$. Make sure your calculator is in Function (Rectangular) graphing mode. If you're not sure, press (MODE) and make sure FUNC is highlighted. You'll first want to enter an equation to graph; you usually want to graph a function to find the area underneath it. Go to (Y=) and enter the equation; here, type

```
Y₁=(.4X)^3-2X+3
```

Press (GRAPH) to see how it looks; it should resemble figure 7.7. If not, you might want to choose ZStandard from the Zoom menu to make sure you're using the default window. You may also need to adjust the graph formatting settings, such as whether the axes are displayed, accessible from (2nd) (ZOOM).

If you're satisfied with the graph, you can now find the area under it using a definite integral. Starting from the graphscreen, press (2nd) (TRACE) to open the Calculate menu, shown in figure 7.8. In chapter 3, you learned about using the first five options

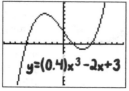

Figure 7.7   Graphing $y = (0.4x)^3 - 2x + 3$ **on your calculator in Rectangular (FUNC) mode, with the default window settings and the axes on. You'll find the area under this curve from** $x = -5$ **to** $x = 0$.

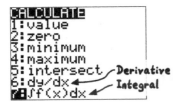

Figure 7.8 The Calculate menu, which you saw in chapter 3. Besides letting you find zeroes, maxima, and minima of functions, it can also calculate derivatives and integrals.

from this menu, including 2:zero, 3:minimum, and 4:maximum. This time, select 7:∫f(x)dx, which you may know means "the integral of $f(x)$ with respect to x." If you have more than one function graphed, it will ask you to choose the function to use by pressing the ▼ and ▲ keys to flip through the functions and (ENTER) to finalize your selection.

Your calculator will prompt you for the left and right bounds for the definite integral. You can use the ◀ and ▶ keys to move the cursor along the function; or, if you want to select an exact x value, start typing the number. For this example, the left bound is –5, so press (-) (5), as shown on the left in figure 7.9; then press (ENTER). The right bound is 0: type 0 and press (ENTER) again, as shown in the center in figure 7.9.

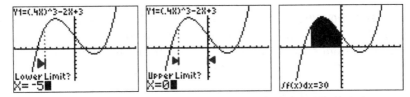

Figure 7.9 Graphically determining the area under a curve on your calculator. After selecting ∫f(x)dx from the Calculate menu, you choose a left bound and a right bound, and the calculator shades the area under the curve within those bounds and figures out the area.

After thinking for a second, the calculator will shade the area and display the answer, shown on the right in figure 7.9. If you have a TI-84 Plus C Silver Edition, choosing the bounds will look like the left side of figure 7.10, and the result will resemble the right side of figure 7.10, but the steps and resulting value are the same.

Here, the value of the integral is exactly 30. Want to double-check? We can perform a rough approximation of the Riemann method by hand; we'll do the left Riemann method, which means the top left of each rectangle (as in figure 7.6) touches the function. I've zoomed in on the function in figure 7.11 and drawn out the rectangles. To find the y values of each point, we can use the handy Table, found by pressing (2nd) (GRAPH) and scrolling up to –5. The Table view for this particular function, $Y_1=(.4X)^3-2X+3$, is shown on the right in figure 7.11.

For this left Riemann sum, we have five rectangles, all one unit wide, so to get the area of each rectangle, we multiply the heights from figure 7.11 by 1. The sum is $5 \times 1 + 6.904 \times 1 + 7.272 \times 1 + 6.488 \times 1 + 4.936 \times 1$. We stop at –1 because that final term represents the rectangle between $x = -1$ and $x = 0$. Add up all those terms, and we get

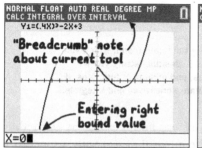
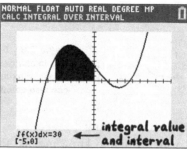

Figure 7.10   The same integral operation on the graphscreen of a TI-84 Plus C Silver Edition. The steps to compute the integral are exactly the same. The new details are an extra hint about what you're currently doing (in the status bar, shown at left) and the addition of the lower and upper bounds of the interval displayed (at right).

30.6. Pretty close! As you know, the inaccuracy is from the missing white triangle between $x = -5$ and $x = -4$ and the extra shaded triangles above the function between $x = -3$ and $x = 0$.

> **AREA BETWEEN TWO CURVES**   Your calculator can only find the area between a curve and the x axis. To find the area between two curves, subtract the area beneath the bottom curve from the area beneath the top curve. This works even if one or both curves are below the x axis.

7.3.2   *Computing integrals on the homescreen*

If you need to get the value of an integral fast, or want to tweak the bounds without staring at the graph all day, you can calculate integrals on the homescreen. You can either type your equation in the Y= menu, or you can type the equation directly on the homescreen. Either way, you'll use the fnInt(command from the Math tab of the Math menu, as shown in figure 7.12. From the homescreen, go to the Math menu and select that command to paste it back to the homescreen.

If you're following along with this section's example, you can put Y_1 as an argument to fnInt(to represent the equation typed in Y_1 in the Y= menu. You can find the list of all the Y= equations by pressing (VARS), moving (▶) to the Y-Vars tab, and choosing 1:Function.... If you want to enter an equation directly, type it as the first argument to fnInt(. The second argument is the letter of the independent variable, the third argument is the lower (left) bound, and the fourth argument to

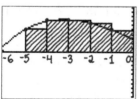
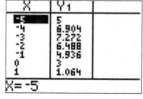

Figure 7.11   Computing a left Riemann sum by hand to double-check the integral value that the calculator generated. You can use the (x,y) pairs in the Table view to approximate the area under a curve.

 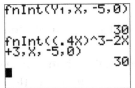

Figure 7.12 **Calculating an integral from the homescreen. You select** fnInt(**from the Math menu and then enter the equation, independent variable, and minimum and maximum values for the region.**

fnInt(is the upper (right) bound. If you're thoroughly confused, try one (or both) of these two:

```
fnInt(Y1,X,-5,0)
fnInt((.4X)^3-2X+3,X,-5,0)
```

The right side in figure 7.12 shows the result of either using Y_1 or directly typing out the equation. As you can see, if you wanted to change the bounds, you could press 2nd ENTER to edit the last entry (a skill you learned in chapter 2) and type over the -5 or the 0. You could even edit the equation without going to the Y= menu if you used the second form.

The MathPrint integral template

On MathPrint operating systems on TI-84 Plus-family calculators, you can use an integral template that looks like what you might see in your favorite math textbook. It takes the same arguments as the fnInt(command: the equation of which you're taking an integral, what variable you're integrating with respect to, and the upper and lower bounds of the definite integral.

The figure shows an example of a MathPrint integral in action (top) and the unpopulated template (bottom). I used the X for the variable of integration here, but you could use any other variable. If you have a MathPrint operating system and MathPrint is enabled, you can access the MathPrint integral template from 9:fnInt(in the Math menu or via the FUNC MathPrint shortcut menu, ALPHA WINDOW.

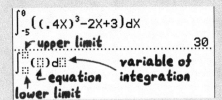

Using the MathPrint integral template. With a function and limits filled in (top) and before being filled in (bottom). Although this is a TI-84 Plus C Silver Edition screenshot, the template looks very similar on the other TI-84 Plus family calculators.

And that's nearly everything you need to know about calculating integrals on your calculator! It's simple; the most complicated part is remembering the arguments to the fnInt(function. If you're content with avoiding homescreen integrals and are willing to calculate all your integrals on the graphscreen, you won't even need to memorize how to use the fnInt(function.

As you can see, your calculator is handy for calculating numerical calculus solutions and letting you check your symbolic calculus results.

7.4   *Summary*

In this chapter, you learned about the (limited) tools your TI-83 Plus or TI-84 Plus includes to help you with calculus. We worked on finding the slope of a function at any point by calculating its numerical derivative at that point. I showed you how you can graph the whole derivative as a function, plus the derivative of that derivative (the second derivative), without knowing the actual equations for the derivatives. With those first and second derivatives, you can find the extrema and inflection points of the original function. You can find definite integrals, most often used to calculate the area under a curve. With the numerical integrals and derivatives of a function, you can also check your work in finding symbolic integrals and derivatives by hand. By plugging in values to your symbolic integrals and derivatives, you can see if you get the same values your calculator finds, which will give you a good indication as to whether you have the correct symbolic equations.

You've now reached the end of the precalculus and calculus skills you need to know to use your calculator as an effective math tool. It's always handy to go back, review, and try out each of the new skills you've learned with new equations and new problems, so if you have the time, I certainly recommend you do so. It's the best way to cement the new skills in your head. We'll now move on to statistics, probability, and finance, starting with a look at the many tools your graphing calculator has for manipulating and visualizing statistics.

Part 3

Statistics, probability, and finance

Part 3 of this book comprises three chapters: two cover the related topics of statistics and probability, and a third teaches you how to solve financial problems. The probability and statistics material will show you how to plot sets of collected data, fit functions to that data, work with probability distribution functions, generate random numbers, and much more. In the finance chapter, you'll learn about your calculator's TVM solver, which can help you work with interest, loans, and mortgages.

Statistics can be a confusing subject for students, and your graphing calculator is particularly well equipped to help you understand it. Chapter 8 shows you how to enter sets of data into your calculator as lists and then compute properties of that data or plot it in any of several different forms. You'll see how to create histograms, scatter plots, box plots, and more. The chapter concludes with performing regression, or fitting functions to your data to help you understand it better.

Chapter 9 teaches the related topic of probability. We'll work with probability distribution functions (PDFs) and cumulative distribution functions (CDFs), including computing probabilities and plotting the functions. You'll see how you can solve combinatorics problems and generate several types of random numbers. The final chapter of this part, chapter 10, covers the Time-Value of Money (TVM) solver that your graphing calculator includes for solving financial problems. It lets you calculate the initial or final value of an investment, payment, interest rates, and more. The chapter is filled with examples relevant to any finance class or the real world.

Calculating
and plotting statistics

Statistics is the study of data sets. The purpose of statistics is to take large amounts of data and organize, summarize, and visualize it to make it easier to interpret (as in figure 8.1). For example, you can measure the heights of 800 students, but until you figure out the average height and graph how many people are each height, those 800 samples are just a mass of numbers. Because statistics deals with calculating and graphing sets of numbers, it makes sense that a graphing calculator would be particularly handy for statistics. In this chapter, you'll learn all about your calculator's statistics tools.

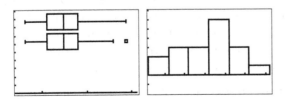

Figure 8.1   A taste of visualizing statistics on your calculator. On the left, a box-and-whisker plot (top) and a modified box-and-whisker plot (bottom) of finishing times from a 1-mile race. On the right, a histogram of SAT scores from one class.

The key to statistics is having easy ways to work with a lot of data. Data can be numbers, pairs or collections of numbers, or even words. You could calculate statistics over the ages of your friends, their favorite colors, or the relationship between how many hours a week you study for each class and your test grades for those classes. As you might expect, your calculator can only compute statistics over numbers, and it needs a way to store sets of numbers together. As you learned back in chapter 4, those sets of numbers are called lists. If you skipped chapter 4, or if it has been a while since you read it, you might want to refresh your memory with a quick skim over section 4.2 and possibly 4.3. If you think you're reasonably familiar with typing and using lists, then read on.

We'll start with a statistics-oriented refresher on the idea of lists, including how you put data in lists and how you use lists for one- and two-variable statistics. I'll show you the List Editor, which will make typing and reviewing statistical data much easier. We'll move on to summarizing statistical data by finding the average, median, maximum, minimum, and quartiles of data. Statistics can be dry without the graphical portion, so you'll learn how to plot data sets on the graphscreen with Stat Plots and then how to fit equations to data sets. By the time you finish this chapter, you'll know almost everything that your calculator can do to help you understand and visualize sets of statistical data.

Make sure you either remember how to use lists or recently reviewed sections 4.2 and 4.3, because this chapter will deal heavily with entering values into lists and then using those lists. Let's start with how you can get data onto your calculator, a very important first step if you want to compute statistics on that data.

8.1   *Working with data lists*

In statistics, you work with samples, which can be one number, two or several numbers, or numbers and other information. For example, the age of each of your classmates is a set of samples, each of which is a single number. If you recorded the number of rabbits in a colony every month, then each sample would be a pair of numbers: the months since you started measuring and the number of rabbits. All this data gets stored in lists on your calculator. The data isn't going to magically appear, so in this section, you'll learn how to get data into lists.

Lists are containers that can hold one or more numbers, called *elements* of the list. Your calculator can hold any number of lists, limited only by how much free memory it has. Section 4.2 mentioned the different types of available lists:

- The six built-in lists, L_1 through L_6, can be typed via $\boxed{\text{2nd}}$ $\boxed{1}$ through $\boxed{\text{2nd}}$ $\boxed{6}$.
- You can create your own custom lists, with names between one and five characters long. The list names can contain letters and numbers, but they must start with a letter. You type a custom list name with the small ∟ from $\boxed{\text{2nd}}$ $\boxed{\text{STAT}}$ $\boxed{\blacktriangleright}$ $\boxed{\blacktriangle}$. Valid custom list names include ∟A, ∟MINE, ∟DATA, and ∟SAT14.

In section 4.2, you saw that you can store data into lists on the homescreen. For example, this line would put four numbers into list L_1, making it a four-element list:

{4.2,5,6,7.4}→L₁

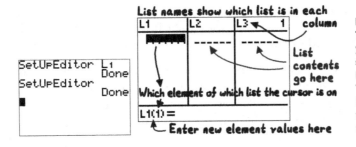

Figure 8.2 The List Editor. The left screenshot shows how you can reset the List Editor to show only list L_1 (top) or show lists L_1 through L_6 (bottom). The right screenshot shows the List Editor in its default form, with the first three of the lists visible, each in its own column.

You can use all four numbers the list contains together, or you can access and change the individual elements in the list. But it can be tedious to enter long lists in this format on the homescreen. To make typing lists easier, your calculator contains a List Editor. You can see what it looks like on the right in figure 8.2; it might remind you of the Table tool you learned to use in chapter 3.

A brief guide to the List Editor

As its name suggests, the List Editor is used for editing lists of numbers. Here's how you use it:

- You can reset the List Editor by running the `SetUpEditor` command on the homescreen. It will start with lists L_1 through L_6 shown, each in its own column.
- Access the List Editor via (STAT) (1), the 1:Edit... option.
- Move the cursor to a blank space (indicated by a set of 6 underscores: _____), type a number, and press (ENTER) to append a new element to the end of a list. To edit the value of an existing element, move the cursor over a number, type a new number, and press (ENTER).
- To delete an element from a list, move the cursor over the element and press (DEL).
- Move the cursor over one of the list names above a column and press (DEL) to remove that list from the List Editor. This doesn't delete the list from your calculator.
- To show a new list in the List Editor, move the cursor to a blank column header, type the name of the list (or paste it from the List menu, via (2nd) (STAT)), and press (ENTER).

If you've never used the List Editor before, then it's probably already set up properly. But just to make sure, this would be a perfect time to learn about the `SetUpEditor` command. Found at the bottom of the Stat menu (via (STAT)), the `SetUpEditor` command can be used on its own, or it can take arguments. Run on a line of the homescreen by itself (as seen on the second line on the left in figure 8.2), `SetUpEditor` gives the List Editor six columns, filled with L_1 through L_6. You can use the List Editor to edit any of those lists, delete elements, or add elements on the end.

WHAT LISTS DO I HAVE? You can see a list of all the lists you have on your calculator with the List menu, accessed via (2nd) (STAT). If you choose any of the lists here, the name is pasted to wherever you were when you entered the menu.

You can also give the SetUpEditor command the names of the lists you want to appear. These can be lists like L_1 and L_4 or custom-named lists like ∟AGES and ∟TIMES. The first line on the left in figure 8.2 shows running the SetUpEditor command with one list argument; run this way, L_1 will be in the first column of the List Editor, and the other columns will be blank. Say that you want L_3 and ∟DATA to both appear in the List Editor. There are three ways you could do this:

- Run the command SetUpEditor L_3, ∟DATA. If either of the lists doesn't already exist, the SetUpEditor command creates it. This command looks like the first line on the left in figure 8.3.
- Run the command SetUpEditor L_3, DATA. You can leave off the ∟ before custom list names, and the SetUpEditor command won't complain. This command is like the second line on the left in figure 8.3.
- Enter the List Editor via (STAT) (1), where you can modify the lists shown. The sidebar "A brief guide to the List Editor" explains how you can hide lists from the List Editor and show new ones instead. The center screenshot in figure 8.3 shows this procedure in progress.

Everything is less confusing with an example, so let's try using the List Editor to enter the heights of a group of seven students into a list. We'll use this list in section 8.2, where you'll learn to calculate the maximum, minimum, and average height, among many other properties of the data. To start this example, you'll want to set up the List Editor with its default settings. For this, you can run the SetUpEditor command on the homescreen, as you saw in figures 8.2 and 8.3. Don't give the SetUpEditor command any arguments; as a reminder, it's the fifth item in the Stat menu.

MY LISTS ARE FILLED WITH NUMBERS! Want to quickly clear all the elements out of a list? From the homescreen, press (STAT) and choose 4:ClrList. Add the name of the list you want to clear, be it a standard list like L_6 or a custom list like ∟MINE3. Press (ENTER), and the list's contents will be wiped clean.

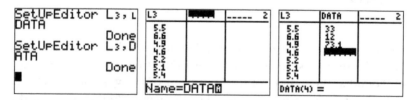

Figure 8.3   Setting up the List Editor to show two lists, L_3 and ∟DATA. As discussed, there are three ways to do this, two ways via the SetUpEditor command (left) and one by editing the headers over the columns in the List Editor (center). The right screenshot shows the result. Of course, if you try this, you might have different data in your lists or entirely empty lists.

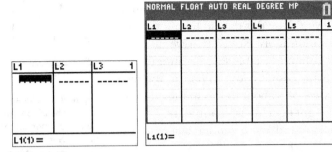

Figure 8.4   The empty List Editor, set to its defaults with the SetUpEditor command and with the existing lists cleared of data. You can now start typing in numbers to fill the lists shown. The right side shows the List Editor on the TI-84 Plus C Silver Edition; the left side covers all the other TI-83 Plus and TI-84 Plus-family graphing calculators.

If you proceed to the List Editor via (STAT) (1), you'll see L_1, L_2, and L_3 in the three visible columns. Scroll left and right, and you'll discover that L_4, L_5, and L_6 are there as well. If you have a TI-84 Plus C Silver Edition, you'll see L_1 through L_5, because the screen is wider; you can scroll right to find L_1. You'll be entering data into list L_1, so if there are any numbers already filling L_1, you'll need to remove them. The slow and easy way is to move the cursor over each number and press the (DEL) key. If you'd rather clear the whole list in one fell swoop, read the callout "My lists are filled with numbers!" When you finish, the List Editor should look like figure 8.4. Don't worry if there are any numbers left in L_2 and L_3; you won't be using those yet, and now you know how to clear them if you so desire.

Next you'll enter data. Table 8.1 shows the data you'll be typing: the heights of seven students. As you can see, they're in inches; apologies to our metric-using friends who would prefer heights in centimeters. Because this is a short list, you can find the minimum height (55 inches) and maximum height (74 inches) by staring at it, and you could calculate the average pretty easily. With a much longer list, that wouldn't be feasible, which is where your calculator comes in to save the day. Anyway, type the heights in inches into the List Editor in list L_1.

Table 8.1   The heights of seven students. You'll enter the heights into a list in this section and calculate properties of this data in section 8.2.

Name	Height (inches)
Student 1	62
Student 2	60
Student 3	62
Student 4	55
Student 5	64
Student 6	74
Student 7	62

When you finish, you'll see results that resemble figure 8.5. We won't do anything with these values in this section, but in sections 8.2.1 and 8.2.2 you'll use this data to try out your calculator's data-summarization tools. Notice that we didn't do anything with the first column of table 8.1, because the students' (anonymized) names don't count as part of the data. Because this is statistics, we care about trends in the entire set of heights, not which height matches which student.

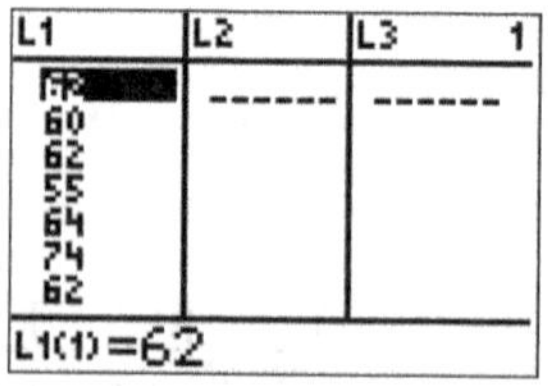

L1	L2	L3	1
52	------	------	
60			
62			
55			
64			
74			
62			
L1(1)=62			

Figure 8.5   The seven student heights from table 8.1 typed into the List Editor. Notice that the line at the bottom of the screen, where you enter list values, shows both the index (1) and value (62) of the list element under the cursor.

Now that all the background about getting data onto your calculator is out of the way, we can proceed to using that data. Before you can do fancy plotting and graphing of data, you should know how to calculate properties of data, from the simple like minimum, maximum, and average, to the more complex like median, standard deviation, and variance.

8.2   Calculating properties of data

The most important task in statistics is making sense of a jumble of data. Instead of caring about individual values in your data set, you care about the story that the data as a whole tells. Statisticians and mathematicians have devised a variety of ways to meaningfully summarize data sets, and in this section, you'll see your calculator's version of those tools. As always, this is a calculator guide rather than a math book, so I hope you'll refer to your favorite math reference if you're confused about the details of calculating and using the sample deviation, population deviation, variance, and other such details. Of course, I'll do my best to help you along as we go.

In this section, you'll learn two ways to summarize data and two data types to summarize. First, you'll learn to apply commands like `min(`, `mean(`, and `stdDev(` to individual lists. Section 4.3.2 covered some of the same functions; here you'll see them again in a statistics-specific light. Second, you'll learn about the `1-Var Stats` and `2-Var Stats` commands and how they can find all the same properties of a single independent list or two related lists of data. By the end of this section, you'll be comfortable entering data sets into your calculator and figuring out all the important statistical properties of the data.

Summarizing statistical data

This section teaches you three ways to summarize one or two sets of related data:

- To get individual properties of a single list, use six helpful functions from the List Math menu: `min(`, `max(`, `mean(`, `median(`, `stdDev(`, and `variance(`. Each takes a single argument: the list to evaluate, such as `mean(L₃)`. The List Math menu can be accessed via (2nd) (STAT) (▶) (▶).
- You can see these same properties and more calculated automatically for a single list with the `1-Var Stats` tool. Go to (STAT) (▶) and choose `1:1-Var Stats`.

(continued)

> Without MathPrint, add the name of the list to summarize and press (ENTER). With MathPrint, type the name of the list next to `List:`, move the cursor down to `Calculate`, and press (ENTER).
>
> - The 2-Var Stats tool does the same thing for two related lists. This command is `2:2-Var Stats` in the Stat Calculate menu, reached via (STAT) (▶). It takes two arguments: for example, `2-Var Stats L₁,L₂`.
>
> Sections 8.2.1 and 8.2.2 elaborate on what all the different statistical properties mean.

We'll begin with the commands to manually calculate each of the properties, so that you understand where they all come from.

8.2.1 Summarizing data

Your TI-83 Plus or TI-84 Plus can calculate six important measures on a list of data, properties that help you understand the set of values as a whole. Three of them pick specific values out of the list:

- The *minimum*, the lowest value in the list
- The *median*, the middle value in the list when sorted from smallest to largest
- The *maximum*, the highest value in the list

Three of them are calculated from all the values in the set examined together:

- The *mean*, or average, which like the median is a way to calculate the "center" of the group of values. It's found by dividing the sum of all the values by the number of values.
- The *variance* (represented by the square of the Greek letter sigma, or σ^2) is a way of calculating how far all the values in the list are from the average. The formula is somewhat complex and beyond the scope of this book, but the more spread out the values are, the larger the variance.
- The *standard deviation* (represented by σ) also measures the spread of the values and is calculated by taking the square root of the variance.

Each of these six properties is calculated with a command that takes the list of values as an argument. All six commands are found in the Math tab of the List menu, accessed via (2nd) (STAT) (▶) (▶). If you want to test each of the six commands, I recommend that you start with the seven-value list shown in table 8.1, because that's the data from which the six properties in figure 8.6 were calculated. If you're not sure how to get those seven heights into a list, you should review the second half of section 8.1.

Assuming that you have all seven elements in list L_1, you can try out the six relevant commands in the List Math menu, with results as shown in figure 8.6:

- `min(L₁)=55`—Uses the `1:min(` command from the List Math menu. Student 4 is the shortest, at 55 inches.
- `max(L₁)=74`—The `2:max(` command shows that Student 6 is the tallest, at 74 inches.

Figure 8.6   Six important properties of a single list of data. The mean is the average, the median is the middle number (or average of the two middle numbers) when the elements are sorted, and the standard deviation and variance are measures of how clustered or spread out the data items are.

- mean(L₁)≈62.7—The 3:mean(command sums the seven values (439) and divides by the number of values ($439/7 \approx 62.7$).
- median(L₁)=62—The 4:median(command sorts the seven elements in increasing order and picks the middle one. The sorted list is {55,60,62,62,62,64,74}, so the median is 62.
- stdDev(L₁)≈5.74—The mean and median are close, and two of the seven values (55 and 74 inches) are farther from the five values clustered around 60 inches. Technically, this standard deviation (from the 7:stdDev(command) means that 68% of the data points are between (62.7 – 5.74) and (62.7 + 5.74), the mean ± the standard deviation.
- variance(L₁)≈32.9—The variance isn't used as often as the standard deviation, but it's the square of the standard deviation. The command is 8:variance(from the List Math menu.

If you need just one of those properties, it's fast to go to the List Math menu, paste the relevant command, and add the name of the list you want to examine. If you need to know the minimum, maximum, and standard deviation all at once, you're better off using the 1-Var Stats tool. If you want to look at two related lists at once, the 2-Var Stats tool is perfect.

8.2.2   *1-Var Stats and 2-Var Stats*

Knowing that you often want to see all the different statistical properties of a data set at once, your graphing calculator's designers created the 1-Var Stats and 2-Var Stats tools. As you might guess from the names, 1-Var Stats is for a single independent list of values, such as the seven students' heights that we've been working with. 2-Var Stats is for two related lists, such as the height and weight of each student or the distance a bunch of cars drive in a day and how much gas each of those cars burns over those distances.

As always, these skills are best taught with examples. If you need the 30-second version, flip back to the sidebar titled "Summarizing statistical data." If you have time to learn through some examples, read on. We'll start with 1-Var Stats, using our trusty data set of seven students' heights.

CALCULATING 1-VAR STATS ON A SET OF HEIGHTS

In section 8.1, you entered the heights of seven students into your calculator in list L₁. You used this list of heights in the previous section, where you learned to summarize data with the individual functions min(, mean(, and more; you'll use it again in this section. You should start by making sure L₁ is intact, holding the data in table 8.1. You

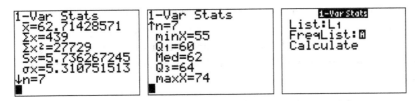

Figure 8.7 The results of the 1-Var Stats command calculated over the seven heights from table 8.1. On non-MathPrint calculators, you enter the 1-Var Stats command on the homescreen, followed by the name of the list in question. On MathPrint calculators, you use the 1-Var Stats Wizard shown on the right.

can check using the List Editor (which you learned to use in section 8.1) or by displaying L_1 on the homescreen by pressing (2nd) (1) (ENTER).

If L_1 contains the seven numbers it should, then you're ready to use the 1-Var Stats tool, a very easy step. The only complication is that with many statistics-related tools, the steps are slightly different depending on whether you have MathPrint enabled:

- Without MathPrint, select the 1:1-Var Stats command from the Stat Calc menu, the first option in (STAT) (▶). This pastes 1-Var Stats to the homescreen, after which you add the list you want to evaluate. For this example, type L_1 to make the full command 1-Var Stats L_1.
- With MathPrint, there are Stats Wizards that make the process slightly easier. When you choose 1-Var Stats from the Stat Calc menu ((STAT) (▶)), you're brought to the 1-Var Stats Wizard, which looks like the right screenshot in figure 8.7. Type the list (here L_1) next to the List: prompt. Leave FreqList blank, move the cursor to Calculate, and press (ENTER).

In either case, you'll see a screen that you can scroll up and down, which shows you the various pieces of data from the left and center screenshots in figure 8.7. Here's what each of those items means:

- $\bar{x}$ represents the mean or average of the items in the list.
- Σx and Σx^2 are, respectively, the sum of all elements and the sum of the squares of all the elements.
- Sx is the *sample* standard deviation. This means that if these seven heights are samples from a total class of 800 students, you should use Sx as the standard deviation.
- σx is the *population* standard deviation. You should use this as the standard deviation only if the data in the list is *all* the data: for example, if you want to examine statistics in the group of 800 students and you have all 800 heights.
- n is the number of samples, or the number of elements in the list.
- minX, Q1, Med, Q3, and maxX are together called the *five-number summary* of the data. The range is maxX–minX, the difference between the smallest and largest numbers in the set. Med is the median, and Q1 and Q3 are the first and third quartile, respectively. Your favorite math teacher or textbook can explain more about quartiles; all the data points less than Q1 – 1.5 × (Q3 – Q1) or greater than Q3 + 1.5 × (Q3 – Q1) are called *outliers*.

As you can see, your calculator can tell you a lot about the data. As you might expect, the more data you have, the more useful this is, because it gets harder and harder to calculate all these properties by hand. In fact, the task gets twice as hard if you have two lists of related data instead of a single independent list; your calculator can help there too.

CALCULATING 2-VAR STATS ON CAR EFFICIENCIES

You haven't seen any two-variable statistics in this chapter yet, but from here on, they'll be a vital component of our discussion. Much of statistics involves trying to find the relationship between two potentially correlated data sets. For example, it's obvious that if you measure the miles each of eight cars travels versus how much gas each of those cars burns over that distance, the two data sets are related by how efficient each car is. It's not as obvious if being taller is correlated with being richer, though, or if there's no relationship between the two.

Although this section won't teach you how to evaluate the relationship between two possibly related data sets, it will show you how you can calculate all the properties the 1-Var Stats tool computed for one list over two lists at once. Sections 8.3 and 8.4 will show you how to use your calculator's statistical visualization tools to try to find the relationship between two lists of data.

The tool for this section is unsurprisingly the 2-Var Stats command. To use it, we'll start with another table of data, table 8.2. Whereas table 8.1 contained only one column of useful data, the heights of the students, this table holds two useful and correlated data sets. You'll put the miles each car traveled in one day in your first list, L_1, and the gallons of gas each car used in your second list, L_2. Notice that it's important that you match corresponding pieces of data to corresponding list elements. The second car in table 8.2 traveled 240 miles and used 8.9 gallons of gas, so $L_1(2)$ (the second element of list L_1) must contain 240, and $L_2(2)$ must contain 8.9. If you mix up the order of the data samples, the tools in sections 8.3 and 8.4 won't work properly.

Table 8.2   Miles traveled versus gallons of gas used for eight different cars. This data could be used to estimate the efficiency of each car in miles per gallon (MPG).

Miles traveled	Gallons of gas used
150	5.2
240	8.9
200	6.7
175	3.8
120	2.7
295	8.0
220	6.3
195	5.7

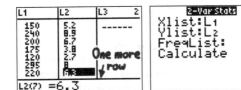 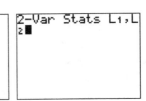

Figure 8.8 Setting up to calculate two-variable statistics on fuel efficiency. Here, we've entered the miles traveled as L_1 and the gallons used by each respective car in L_2. The center screenshot is the 2-Var Stats Wizard on MathPrint calculators, and the right shows the arguments to the 2-Var Stats command on non-MathPrint calculators.

Go ahead and enter the data from table 8.2 into lists L_1 and L_2. It's probably easiest to use the List Editor, as shown on the left in figure 8.8. Because the List Editor can fit only seven list elements vertically, you'll have to scroll down to see the eighth element of each list. When you've finished entering the data, and you've double-checked that it all matches table 8.2, quit from the List Editor to the homescreen via (2nd) (MODE) and get ready to enter the 2-Var Stats tool.

The 2-Var Stats tool is extremely similar to the 1-Var Stats tool. It's in the same menu, Stat Calculate, accessed by pressing (STAT) (▶). If you select 2:2-Var Stats, your next step depends on whether you're on a MathPrint calculator. If you see something like the center screenshot in figure 8.8, you're indeed using a MathPrint Stats Wizard. Type L_1 next to Xlist and L_2 next to Ylist. Move the cursor down to Calculate, and press (ENTER). If you're on a non-MathPrint calculator, the 2-Var Stats command is pasted to the homescreen, so add L_1, L_2 afterward, as shown on the right in figure 8.8, and press (ENTER).

In either case, you'll get the list of results shown in figure 8.9. Most of this is familiar from the 1-Var Stats output; the only difference is that you now have x properties and y properties, with x corresponding to the first list you entered (here, L_1) and y corresponding to the second list (here, L_2). It omits the median and Q1/Q3 quartile information but also shows an extra property, Σxy, the sum of the products of respective elements of L_1 and L_2. In other words, $\Sigma xy = L_1(1) * L_2(1) + L_1(2) * L_2(2) + \ldots$

As with the 1-Var Stats output, these properties can be useful for understanding the whole picture created by a large data set, instead of trying to summarize it in your

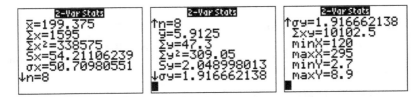

Figure 8.9 The results of the 2-Var Stats tool. The mean, sum, sum-squared, mean, standard deviations, and number of samples are displayed for the x list (L_1) and y list (L_2). The dot product and minimum and maximum values in each list are also shown.

Scatter plot

XYLine plot

Histogram

Modified box plot

Box plot

Normal plot

Figure 8.10   The icons for the six types of statistical plots your calculator can draw. The left column is from the calculators in the TI-83 Plus and TI-84 Plus family with black-and-white screens; the right column shows the similar icons from the TI-84 Plus C Silver Edition.

head by examining the values one by one. They say that a picture is worth a thousand words, but for us, a picture is worth a thousand statistical properties. The next section shows you how to take all those numerical data samples and plot them on the graphscreen. Once you see your data summarized as a graph, getting a grasp on the story the data is telling becomes much easier.

8.3   *Statistical plots*

Numbers are great for many things. They are exact and precise, and they convey exactly what they mean. When we have as many numbers as statistics deals with, however, it can be unwieldy and even uninformative to try to examine statistics purely as numbers. Therefore, it's helpful to plot statistics as graphs. Your calculator offers six different ways to plot data on the graphscreen, and in this section, you'll learn about all six of them. Some are well suited to single lists of data, such as the heights of a group of students or the salaries of different professions. Others are better for two related lists of data, such as the number of rabbits in a colony versus the number of years the colony has existed. Figure 8.10 shows the symbols used for each of the six types of statistical plots.

We'll start with *Scatter* and *XYLine* plots, two closely related ways to display two correlated data sets. For the example, you'll work with the population of a rabbit colony over time. Next, you'll learn about the *Histogram* plot, used to group values together to show how a lot of single data points are spread out. *Box* plots and *Modified Box* plots are a way of graphically displaying the five-numbers summary of a single list of data: the minimum, maximum, mean, first quartile (Q1), and third quartile (Q3). Finally, the rarely used *Normal* plot is a way of graphically checking how closely a data set fits to a normal (Gaussian) distribution.

Stat Plots menu in a nutshell

These steps are nearly the same for all six Stat Plots menu types. Section 8.3.1 contains the most detailed guide to creating a statistical plot (Stat Plot), so if you get stuck, try skimming it.

1 Put the data to be plotted in one or two lists. Any built-in or custom list will do. Scatter and XYLine plots take two lists; Histogram, Box, Modified Box, and Normal plots all take a single list.

(continued)

2 Go to the Stat Plot menu via (2nd) (Y=), turn on one of the Stat Plots, and choose which plot style/type you're using. Also select the one or two lists holding the data. In most cases, you can ignore the Freq: option or set it to 1.

3 View the plot via (GRAPH). It's often helpful to automatically adjust the window settings by using the ZoomStat option in the Zoom menu.

4 Turn off Stat Plots when you've finished with statistics and want to return to normal graphing. Otherwise, you may get an ERR:INVALID DIM error when you try to graph.

It's important to note that creating each of these six different Stat Plots types entails similar steps. The first explanation, for Scatter and XYLine, contains the most detail. If you're looking at one of the later types and are confused about some detail, try flipping back to the Scatter, XYLine, and Histogram sections. Without further ado, let's start with the Scatter and XYLine plots, which let you plot the corresponding elements of two lists as (x,y) points.

ERR:INVALID DIM Don't forget to turn off all Stat Plots before you try to do normal graphing! If you forget, you may get an ERR:INVALID DIM error if you accidentally delete one of your lists without disabling the corresponding Stat Plot.

8.3.1 *Using Scatter and XYLine*

In many cases, two related lists containing pairs of data points can be plotted to help understand the data. Back in chapter 1, in the example in section 1.5, I told you about a scenario where a car was driving at a steady speed on a highway; a team of volunteers with stopwatches and GPS devices measured how long it took for the car to go different distances. By plotting the distance for each measurement as the y coordinate and the time for each measurement as the x coordinate of a point, you ended up with five points that were nearly in a straight line. Drawing a line roughly going through all the points told you how fast the car was going (the slope of the line) and let you estimate how long it would take for the car to go any distance.

That's exactly the point of the Scatter and XYLine plots, both of which you'll learn about in this section. Both types of plots take two lists of equal length and plot the corresponding elements of the two lists as (x,y) points. You can modify how the points look, and if you choose XYLine instead of Scatter, the only difference is that line segments are drawn between adjacent points. As has proven effective through the rest of this book, I'd like to teach you this plotting skill via an example: the population of a colony of rabbits over time. You discover a field where a family of rabbits has moved in, and you return once a year to count the rabbits. The observations are listed in table 8.3.

As in section 8.2, the first thing you'll need to do to use this data on your calculator is to get it into lists. Because L_1 and L_2 are the first two built-in lists, we'll use them for the sake of simplicity. Use the List Editor to get the number of years elapsed into L_1 and the number of rabbits you counted into L_2. If you need to flip back to section 8.1

Table 8.3   Observed population of a colony of rabbits over time. This data can be placed into two lists and plotted using either a Scatter or XYLine plot.

Years elapsed	Number of rabbits
1	4
2	17
3	67
4	254
5	1,053
6	4,195

and review how to use the List Editor to create and edit lists, take your time. I'll wait. Once you've finished, make sure your years elapsed (L₁) and rabbits counted (L₂) lists match figure 8.11.

OK, back up to speed, or didn't need to check? Now you need to enable a Stat Plot in Scatter mode. Press (2nd) (Y=), which brings up the main Stat Plots menu, as shown on the left in figure 8.12. Make sure Plot2 and Plot3 are set to Off; if either of them is On, move the cursor to it, press (ENTER), move the cursor to Off in the new menu you reach, and press (ENTER) again. Return to the main Stat Plots menu and press (ENTER) on Plot1 to change the Plot1 settings. You want your settings to match the screenshot on the right in figure 8.12: Plot1…On, set to the first little icon (the Scatter icon), with Xlist:L₁ and Ylist:L₂. You can change Mark: to be whatever you want; that's the type of point your calculator will use to mark each data point. If you're satisfied that you have the settings correct, press (GRAPH).

STAT PLOTS MENU ON THE TI-84 PLUS C SILVER EDITION   On the TI-84 Plus C Silver Edition, you have the option to change the color of the line and/or points, and you also have one extra option for the Mark. Section 12.4.2 gives more detail about the new options.

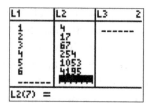

Figure 8.11   Years elapsed (L₁) and rabbits counted (L₂) lists in the List Editor. You'll plot this data on the graphscreen in this section. That's a lot of rabbits!

Figure 8.12   Setting up the first Stat Plot to be On, in Scatter mode, with Xlist:L₁ and Ylist:L₂. The left screenshot shows the main Stat Plots menu; choose any of the Stat Plots to proceed to the menu on the right.

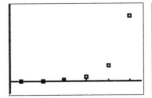 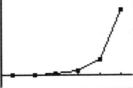

Figure 8.13 The population of a colony of rabbits (*y* axis) versus the number of years since you started counting them (*x* axis), plotted as Stat Plots. On the left is the Scatter plot; on the right is the XYLine plot.

But wait, where's the plot? Perhaps you're experienced enough with the graphscreen to realize that you need to adjust the window settings, but if not, don't worry; now you know. Press the (ZOOM) key, and choose `9:ZoomStat`. This option tries to automatically fit the Stat Plot to the data shown, so that all the points are onscreen. Once you choose this, you should see a plot that looks like the left side of figure 8.13. All six points are onscreen, and you can see that the population grows more and more every year. In section 8.4, you'll learn to figure out exactly how much it grows between years.

If you'd rather see those six points joined by lines using the XYLine style, go back to the Stat Plots menu, under (2nd) (Y=); press (ENTER) to edit `Plot1`; and change the plot type to the second icon, the one that looks like a solid jagged line. Press (GRAPH) again (the window will stay set properly), and you'll see the version illustrated on the right in figure 8.13. Your teacher may point out that it's not always correct to put those lines over the Scatter plot, because they imply that there is intermediate data that might not be known.

LINES OVER MY STAT PLOT   If you have extra lines and curves beyond the ones shown in figure 8.13, most likely you forgot to disable any graphed functions. Press (Y=), move the cursor over each equal sign (█) that is white on black, and press (ENTER). The equal sign will turn to black text on a white background, indicating that the function is disabled. You can repeat the process to enable those functions again later.

See if you can come up with other pairs of lists you can plot with these two Stat Plots options. Any two correlated data sets would do: for example, money spent on a house in a certain town versus the size of the house, or the number of cylinders in a certain car's engine versus how many horsepower the engine is. Try to come up with similar data sets you could plot. Keep in mind that comparing dissimilar data items won't necessarily form a coherent line. To prove this to yourself, plot the data in table 8.2, and you'll see that the different fuel efficiencies of various cars mentioned produce a more scattershot graph.

Stat Plots and data side by side

On any TI-84 Plus-family calculator, regardless of whether you're running a MathPrint operating system, you can view statistical data in the Table tool side by side with a Stat Plot of that data. Plot data normally using a Stat Plot, and then go to the Mode menu and choose the `G-T` (or `GRAPH-TABLE`) option. When you press either (GRAPH) or

(continued)

TRACE), you'll see the Stat Plot and the Table side by side, but the Table will contain your list(s) instead of X and Y values.

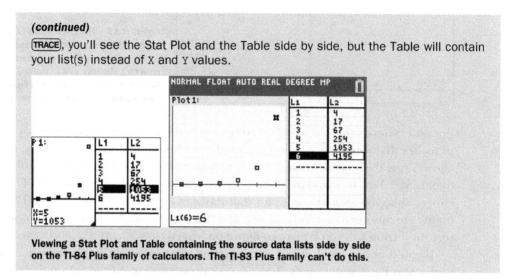

Viewing a Stat Plot and Table containing the source data lists side by side on the TI-84 Plus family of calculators. The TI-83 Plus family can't do this.

But what if you wanted to plot the fuel efficiencies of those cars in a more useful way, or you wanted to visualize the ages of a group of Olympic athletes? A Histogram plot would help you there, so let's examine that option next.

8.3.2   Plotting a histogram

A Histogram plot is a one-variable plot where you take a large data set and sort all the points into a few bins. For example, consider recording what time you got up in the morning every day for a year. You'd have 365 samples, but to make sense of them, it wouldn't be helpful to graph every possible time. You might wake up at the exact same time only a few times a year. Instead, you could group all your wake-up times into 15-minute bins: 9:00 am to 9:15 am could be the first bin (or bucket, or category), and 9:15 am to 9:30 am would be the next. You would count the number of samples in each bin and then graph the bins on the *x* axis and the number of items in each bin on the *y* axis.

If this sounds abstract, look at figure 8.14, where you see a histogram of the ages of a group of Olympic athletes. You can also look back at the sample on the right in figure 8.1. As you can see from table 8.4, plotting all these individual ages as an XYLine or Scatter plot wouldn't be very meaningful. With the ages on the *x* axis, the *y* axis could only be the number of athletes with each age, which can only be 0, 1, or 2 in this case. With a histogram, you get a much better idea of the central peak around 25 years old, sloping off in both directions.

Table 8.4   The ages of 18 imaginary Olympic athletes. You can enter these into your calculator in a single 18-element list: try ∟AGES.

22	23	42	26	18	27
25	24	25	19	26	26
25	21	31	18	27	25

The instructions for creating a Histogram plot are similar to the steps for an XYLine or Scatter plot, so we'll go through this quickly:

1   Enter the list of ages from table 8.4 into an 18-element list, either ∟AGES or L_1. We'll use ∟AGES, which you can type via (2nd) (STAT) (▶) (▲) (ENTER) (for the ∟) and (2nd) (ALPHA) (MATH) (TAN) (SIN) (∧) (for the AGES). The List Editor would be perfect for this (see section 8.1); you could also enter the list like this:

   {22,23,42,26,18,27,25,24,25,19,26,26,25,21,31,18,27,25}→∟AGES

2   Go to the Stat Plots menu via (2nd) (Y=), press (ENTER) to modify Plot1, and set it to On. Use the Histogram plot type (the bar graph–looking icon on the right of the top row), type ∟AGES (or L_1, if that's where you put the ages) for Xlist, and leave Freq at 1.

3   Press (ZOOM), and choose 9:ZoomStat. The plot will appear.

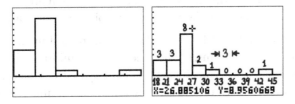

Figure 8.14   A histogram of theoretical Olympic athlete ages plotted with the default ZoomStat (left). Manually adjusting the bin width to 3 from 4.8 (right) generates a more meaningful histogram.

The left side of figure 8.14 shows what you'll see. It shows the data well, with the ages clustered between 19 and 31 years old and an outlier at 42. But suppose you want more bins (boxes), which you would have to do by making each bin narrower. There didn't seem to be any option for this when you defined the Stat Plot, so what's the solution?

If you press (WINDOW), you'll see that Xscl is set to 4.8, meaning each bin is 4.8 years wide. That's not helpful at all; let's try 3 years instead. Set Xscl to 3; then press (GRAPH) again. You'll see the type of histogram on the right side in figure 8.3. Try moving the cursor around with the arrow keys to examine the values at the edges of each bin (X) and the height of each bar (Y). The moral of the story: ZoomStat is a great way to set up a default zoom that shows all your data, but carefully adjust the bin width via Xscl, plus Xmin and Xmax, if you want to fine-tune the result.

ADJUST HISTOGRAM BIN WIDTH   Change the Xscl value in the (WINDOW) menu to modify the width of each bin. Bins that are too wide or too narrow defeat the purpose of a histogram.

The next plot type to examine is actually two closely related styles, the Box plot and the Modified Box plot. Both are ways of examining the range and interquartile range of a single data set.

8.3.3   Understanding Box plots

A Box plot is a way to graphically examine the *five-number summary* of a data set, a term for the minimum, first quartile, median, third quartile, and maximum. In section 8.2, you learned how to calculate the one-variable stats for a data set, which include these five values. You discovered that these five numbers are found by sorting a set of data samples in increasing order and then picking out five values:

1   The minimum is the first (lowest) value in the sorted list.

2   The maximum is the last (highest) value in the list.

3   The median is the middle value in the list by *place*, not by pure value. In other words, if you have a seven-number list, the fourth element of the sorted list is the median. The median is sometimes also called the second quartile (Q2). If the list has an even number of elements, the median is the average (mean) of the middle two values.

4   The first quartile (Q1) is the value halfway between the median and the minimum in the sorted list, again by place instead of value.

5   The third quartile (Q3) is the value halfway between the median and the maximum in the sorted list, once again halfway between by place rather than value.

Consider the sorted list {1,1,2,3,6,8,10,20,21}. Here, the minimum and maximum are 1 and 21, respectively. The list has nine items, so the median is the middle value, 6. Q1 is halfway between 1 and 6 in the list, specifically 3. Q3 is halfway between 6 and 21, so it's 10. Your calculator can find all five numbers easily and quickly, and it can plot those numbers in an easy-to-understand form.

For this example, we'll use the nine average annual salaries listed in table 8.5. As you can see, most of these salaries are between about $80,000 and $110,000 per year, with a single outlier. The Box plot will give us a graphical view of how these salaries are distributed. The Modified Box plot will add information about whether there are *outliers*, a few values that are much different than the rest of the samples. We'll plot a regular Box plot and a Modified Box plot at the same time:

Table 8.5   Average annual salaries of nine different jobs for college graduates. Notice that there is one outlier, fast food cook, which will become important for the Modified Box plot.

Occupation	Average annual salary
Computer scientist	$103,160
Architect	$79,300
Electrical engineer	$89,200
Physicist	$112,090
Fast food cook	$18,720
Veterinarian	$91,250
Economist	$100,270
Real estate broker	$83,830
Art director	$95,500

1 Enter the nine numbers from table 8.5 into a list, either in the List Editor or on the homescreen. For simplicity, I used L₁, but you can use any built-in or custom list. As in the previous Stat Plots examples, flip back to section 8.1 if you need help with the List Editor.

2 Press (2nd) (Y=) to get to the Stat Plots menu. Press (ENTER) to edit Plot1's properties; they should match figure 8.15. Pick the Box plot icon (the middle icon in the second row), set Xlist to L₁ (if that's what you're using for the data), and be sure to set the plot to On.

3 Press (2nd) (Y=) again to get back to the Stat Plots menu. This time, move down to Plot2. The properties you enter are almost exactly the same, except pick the Modified Box plot icon, the left one on the second row.

4 Press (ZOOM), and choose 9:ZoomStat. You're taken to the graphscreen without needing to press (GRAPH).

Your result should resemble the right side in figure 8.15. This is pretty descriptive already: you can see the median, minimum, maximum, Q1, and Q3 salaries in each case. The second Box plot—the Modified Box plot—shows that by eliminating the $18,720 salary as an outlier (plotted as a single point), you can see that the next-lowest salary is close to the first-quartile salary.

The ticks on the x axis are meaningless here, because they're too close together to be visible. To fix this, press (WINDOW), and then try setting Xmin=15000, Xmax=125000, and Xscl=5000. Press (GRAPH) to return to the graphscreen, and you'll see the pair of Stat Plots in figure 8.16. Much clearer! You can now see from the graph that the difference between Q1 and Q3 salaries is about four ticks, or $20,000, and that the median salary is about five ticks below the maximum salary, or $25,000.

The Modified Box plot tells you that the $18,000 salary is an outlier. In statistics terms, an outlier is usually defined as any point less than Q1 – 1.5 × (Q3 – Q1) or greater than Q3 + 1.5 × (Q3 – Q1), where the quantity (Q3 – Q1) is called the inter-quartile range (IQR). We can graphically estimate that the IQR is about $20,000, with Q1 at about $80,000 and Q3 at about $100,000. Therefore, any salary less than $80,000 – $30,000 = $50,000 or greater than $100,000 + $30,000 = $130,000 can be considered an outlier for this data set. Of course, this set is selected to mostly contain high salaries, and the results would be different if less-technical professions were chosen.

Although Box plots are a useful way to visualize the spread of a group of data samples and whether the data includes outliers, there are other important ways to examine a data set. It's often important to know if a data set approximates a Gaussian

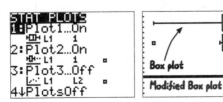

Figure 8.15   Creating a pair of Box plots. Plot1 is set to be a regular Box plot, whereas Plot2 is a Modified Box plot that includes an outlier. Figure 8.16 fixes the ticks on the x axis and explains the pieces of the plot.

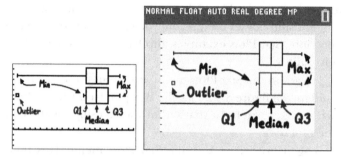

Figure 8.16   The same Box and Modified Box plots as in figure 8.15, with better `Xscl` **tick spacing and marked with explanations of each part of the plot. Notice that the Modified Box plot provides a much clearer picture of this data set than the Box plot, because it indicates that there are no samples between the outlier and the modified minimum. The right side shows the plots on a TI-84 Plus C Silver Edition; the left screenshot applies to all the other TI-83 Plus/TI-84 Plus-family calculators.**

or normal distribution, which the sixth and last Stat Plots type, the Normal plot, will tell us.

8.3.4   *Normal probability plots*

In probability, a normal distribution is defined by a so-called bell curve, with a peak at the most probable value for a sample, sloping off to the sides toward less-probable values for the sample. Normal distributions, also called Gaussian distributions, accurately approximate many real data sets. For example, SAT scores and IQ scores are usually normally distributed, with high probabilities for average scores and lower probabilities for very low and very high scores. Rainfall per month over the course of a year is sometimes normally distributed.

We'll deal more with normal distributions in chapter 9, along with a few of the other probability distributions your calculator can calculate and draw. If you're still confused about what a normal distribution is, or even what a distribution is, a math textbook or a knowledgeable math teacher would be a perfect resource. In this section, you'll use the Normal plot to determine whether the set of Olympian ages from table 8.4 in section 8.3.2 is normally distributed.

> **NORMAL**   In this section, *normal* doesn't mean "regular." The normal or Gaussian distribution is used throughout classic probability, and when graphed, it forms a classic bell-curve shape.

If the data plotted with a Normal plot is indeed Gaussian (or normal), then the plotted points appear as a straight line. The farther the data is from perfectly normal, the less linear the points appear. We'll give it a try with the data from table 8.4, so start by putting the data into a list. You might still have ₗAGES on your calculator from the example in section 8.3.2, but if not, put the 18 ages in L_1 or ₗAGES. The values are reproduced in table 8.6 so that you don't need to keep flipping back.

Table 8.6 The ages of 18 imaginary Olympic athletes. You can enter these into your calculator in a single 18-element list.

22	23	42	26	18	27
25	24	25	19	26	26
25	21	31	18	27	25

As always, the List Editor can help you put data into a list, or you can store the data to a list from the homescreen. Review how to use the List Editor in section 8.1 if you need to. Next, go to the Stat Plots menu via (2nd) (Y=). Make sure Plot2 and Plot3 are set to Off; if either one is On, go into the settings for that plot and set it to Off. Go into the Plot1 settings and set the Normal plot style (the right icon on the second row of icons), Data List to L_1 or ∟AGES (or wherever the Olympian age data is stored), Data Axis to X, and the mark to whatever you want.

In the previous examples, you learned that your existing window is rarely correct for a Stat Plot, so instead of pressing (GRAPH), go to the Zoom menu and choose 9:Zoom-Stat. You'll get the result shown on the left in figure 8.17. As you can see, these points don't resemble a straight line at all, so it's likely that these Olympians' ages aren't normally distributed. If you use almost the same list but omit the two oldest competitors (leaving you with 16 ages), the resulting graph on the right in figure 8.17 looks closer to linear (and therefore Gaussian).

You've now explored all six types of Stat Plots and tried out examples teaching each one in more depth. Up to this point in the chapter, you've learned to create numerical summaries of data using 1-Var Stats and 2-Var Stats and to visualize statistical data with Stat Plots. The next and final skill you'll learn in this chapter is fitting a line of best fit to a set of plotted data.

8.4   *Regression: fitting lines to data*

Regression refers to fitting a line to a data set, in the process finding an equation that could as nearly as possible be used to generate all the points in the data set. Your calculator has the tools to perform 10 different types of regression. We'll focus on two of the most important in this section, but I'll also introduce the other eight. The process for performing each type of regression is similar, and the way you use the results of regression to plot the resulting equation on top of a Stat Plot is also straightforward.

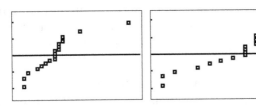

Figure 8.17 Determining if the set of 18 Olympic athletes' ages is normally distributed (left). Without the outliers at 31 and 42 years old (plotted on the right), this data might be closer to a normal distribution. The Normal plot type makes points appear to be in a straight line if the data is perfectly Gaussian.

I'll first show you linear regression, in which you fit a straight line to the data. You'll see an example where spotters along a marathon route record the times for a marathon runner to reach several milestones, and you want to calculate her average speed. The second type of regression you'll learn in depth is exponential regression; you'll apply it to understanding the trends in the rabbit colony from section 8.3.1. Finally, I'll summarize the remaining eight regression types and what you could use them for. If you have a TI-84 Plus C Silver Edition, a new regression tool called Quick-Plot & FitEQ is powerful and easy to use; you can flip forward to section 12.4 to learn how to use it.

The lowdown on fitting a function to a data set

Regression is mathematically complex to do by hand, but with your calculator, it's easy. Just follow these steps:

1 You need two equal-length lists of data, as you did for XYLine and Scatter plots. For these steps, assume that one set (the *x* values) is in L_1, and the other (the *y* values) is in L_2.

2 Go to the Calculate tab of the Statistics menu (STAT ▶), and look at all the options between LinReg(ax+b) and SinReg. Scroll down to the regression type you want, and press ENTER. If your chosen type fits poorly, you can always try again with a different type.

3 If you're using a non-MathPrint calculator, the command is pasted to the home-screen. Type L_1, L_2 after it, and press ENTER. If you're using a MathPrint calculator, a Stats Wizard may appear. Set L_1 as the Xlist and L_2 as the Ylist, move the cursor to Calculate, and press ENTER.

4 You see the equation of best fit, complete with the constants to plug in.

5 If you want the $r/r^2/R$ values (also called the *diagnostic variables*), press 2nd 0 to access the Catalog, x^{-1} to type D (because Alpha-Lock is already set inside the Catalog), and scroll down to DiagnosticOn. Press ENTER twice, and then perform the regression again.

The first type of regression you'll explore is called linear regression and involves fitting a straight line to a set of data samples.

8.4.1   Linear regression

With linear regression, you try to fit a line in the form $y = mx + b$ to a set of data samples. Needless to say, this only really works if the samples are already in more or less a straight line. I'll show you an easy version of this process, in which you fit a line to the time it takes a marathon runner to travel different distances. From this, you'll be able to see how fast she was running. The second example will be a step-by-step look at the process to quantitatively determine how normal (Gaussian) a data set is.

TIMING A MARATHON RUNNER

This example is admittedly similar to the example in section 1.1.5, but the concept is an important one, and it's worthwhile to reexamine the process of figuring out the slope of a line using linear regression. First, consider our marathon runner. She is running at roughly a constant speed so that she can pace herself through the 26.2-mile course. At various checkpoints along the route, five volunteers are stationed with stopwatches. They're cheap stopwatches, so they aren't synchronized. The five volunteers record the time the runner passes each of them, and they know how far they are from the starting line. Table 8.7 shows this data.

Table 8.7 The times a group of volunteers record on their stopwatches for a marathon runner's progress and how far each is from the starting line

Distance from start (miles)	Time recorded (hours:minutes)	In minutes
4	0:39	39
9	1:28	88
15	2:31	151
20	3:16	196
26.2	4:32	272

Enter the data in the distance column of table 8.7 into list L_2 and the time (in minutes) in the third column into L_1 (carefully note which one goes in L_1!). Figure 8.18 shows how this will end up looking in the List Editor. Speed is distance over time, so we'll draw a Stat Plot where we put the distances (L_2) on the y axis and times (L_1) on the x axis. To do this, press (2nd)(Y=), enter the Plot1 settings, and set Plot1 to On, with a Scatter type (the top-left icon), using Xlist:L_1 and Ylist:L_2. The left screenshot in figure 8.19 shows these settings, if you want to make sure you have things set up properly.

L1	L2	L3	1
39	4	------	
88	9		
151	15		
196	20		
272	27		
------	------		

L1(6)=

Figure 8.18 The times in minutes (L_1) for the marathon runner to reach certain milestones (L_2), as viewed in the List Editor

As you've done in previous examples, press (ZOOM) and choose 9:ZoomStat to simultaneously adjust the window and go to the resulting graph. Fortunately, as illustrated on the right in figure 8.19, these look like they're lined up pretty well. We'll calculate the line of best fit; its slope will be distance/time = miles/minutes, from which we can easily figure out miles per hour.

Press (STAT) (▶) to get to the Calculate tab of the Statistics menu, scroll down to 4:LinReg(ax+b), and press (ENTER). As mentioned in the sidebar "The lowdown on fitting

Figure 8.19 The marathon times and distances from table 8.7 plotted as a Scatter plot (right), along with the Plot1 settings that created it (left)

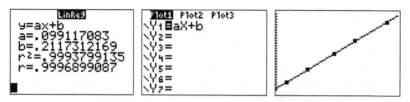

Figure 8.20   The linear equation of best fit for the observations of our marathon runner's progress (left). The regression tools all store the resulting constants to special lowercase variables, which can be found in the EQ tab of the Stats Vars menu, from ⌐VARS⌐ ⌐5⌐ ⌐▶⌐ ⌐▶⌐**. The center screenshot is the equation, and the graphed result is shown on the right.**

a function to a data set," the process for finding the line of best fit is slightly different depending on whether you're using MathPrint and whether the Stats Wizard option in the Mode menu of MathPrint calculators is set to On or Off. With MathPrint's Stats Wizard, enter Xlist:L_1, Ylist:L_2, leave the other options blank, and then move the cursor down to Calculate and press ⌐ENTER⌐ to see the resulting line of best fit. Without MathPrint, the LinReg(ax+b) command will be pasted to the homescreen; add L_1, L_2 after it as arguments. You should have this on your screen:

LinReg(ax+b) L_1, L_2

Press ⌐ENTER⌐, and you'll get the equation for the list of best fit.

> **R^2? R?**   If you generate your LinReg(ax+b) line of best fit and only see a and
> b values, you need to turn on diagnostics. Go to the Catalog via ⌐2nd⌐ ⌐0⌐,
> press ⌐x^{-1}⌐ (for D), scroll down to DiagnosticOn, and press ⌐ENTER⌐ twice. Rerun
> your regression tool, and you'll now get r^2 and r values as well.

MathPrint or not, you'll get the resulting best fit shown on the left in figure 8.20. See the callout titled "R^2? R?" if you only see values for y, a, and b. These numbers mean the line $y = 0.099x + 0.212$ is the best fit to try to go through all the points in the data set while remaining a straight line. In regression, the r^2 value (called the *coefficient of determination*) indicates how well a line fits the given data, where 1 is a perfect fit. An r^2 of 0.99938 means this is an extremely good fit.

This result tells us that the slope is 0.099, and we know that slope, always defined as rise/run, is miles/minutes here. We can take 0.099 miles/minute and multiply by 60 minutes/hour to get 5.94 miles/hour. Our marathon runner was jogging right along! Shall we make sure this line fits over the points as well as the r^2 value says it does? Let's graph this over the Stat Plot of the points:

1   Press ⌐Y=⌐. Clear out (or disable) any existing equations, as you learned to do
    in chapter 3.

2   If you want a faster way to do this step, read the sidebar "Graph the Regression
    Equation (ReqEQ) faster." Otherwise, read on. Type the equation Y_1=aX+b (or
    use another Y_n if Y_1 is occupied). Where are you going to get those lowercase a

and b constants? Press (VARS), choose 5:Statistics, and then press (▶)(▶) to get to the EQ tab of the menu. The a and b constants are filled with values when the LinReg(ax+b) tool is used. Each regression tool fills lowercase constants with the results of its calculations. You'll find that there are also r^2 and r variables in the same EQ tab of the Stats Vars menu, for example.

3 When you finish typing the equation, press (GRAPH) to view the result. Because you already used the ZoomStat tool when you created the Stat Plot, you don't need to do it again. Your results should match the right side of figure 8.20.

Graph the Regression Equation (ReqEQ) faster

Although it's a good idea to know that the statistics variables in the EQ tab of the 5:Statistics section of the Vars menu contain the coefficients from regression, you can save a lot of time by using one of the following tricks:

- On any calculator, press (Y=) after performing regression, pick a blank equation slot, and then press (VARS). Choose 5:Statistics, press (▶)(▶) to get to the EQ tab, and choose 1:ReqEQ. The entire regression equation is pasted.

- If you're computing the regression using a function like LinReg(ax+b) on the homescreen, add one of the Y= equations like Y_1 or Y_6 as an extra argument on the end. The equation is automatically filled with the resulting equation. You can find Y_0 through Y_9 under (VARS)(▶)(1) or, on a MathPrint calculator, (ALPHA)(TRACE).

    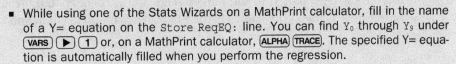
    LinReg(ax+b) L_1, L_2, Y_1

- While using one of the Stats Wizards on a MathPrint calculator, fill in the name of a Y= equation on the Store ReqEQ: line. You can find Y_0 through Y_9 under (VARS)(▶)(1) or, on a MathPrint calculator, (ALPHA)(TRACE). The specified Y= equation is automatically filled when you perform the regression.

As your graph proves, the line of best fit matches the observed times and distances extremely well; it looks like it passes through the center of each point. For data collected in the real world, it won't always be possible to get a fit quite this good, but if you measure and record carefully, you can often get a decent approximation.

The second type of regression we'll look at in depth is exponential regression.

8.4.2 Exponential regression

In section 8.3.1, you learned to plot Scatter and XYLine statistical plots. You used this new skill to plot the population of a colony of rabbits over six years, using population counts that are replicated in table 8.8. If you look closely, you'll see that the rabbit population appears to be four times as large as the previous year every time you recount the bunnies. Exponential regression tries to fit a line of the type $y = ab^x$ to the data, which seems like it would work here.

The steps to perform exponential regression (and indeed every type of regression on your calculator) are similar to the steps for linear regression. Assuming that you're a pro at the List Editor by now, put the Years Elapsed column from table 8.8 into list L_1 and the Number of Rabbits column into list L_2. You'll have two six-element lists that you can use for regression. You'll set up a Stat Plot to display the data later; for now, go to the Calculate tab of the Statistics menu via (STAT) (▶), and choose 0:ExpReg. As before, depending on whether you're using MathPrint, you'll be faced with either a Stats Wizard or the ExpReg command pasted to the homescreen.

Table 8.8   Observed population of a colony of rabbits over time. This is the same data you saw in table 8.3; here, we want to try plotting an exponential regression curve to the data.

Years elapsed	Number of rabbits
1	4
2	17
3	67
4	254
5	1,053
6	4,195

If you have ExpReg pasted to the homescreen, add L_1, L_2 after it, indicating that you want to use L_1 as the Xlist and L_2 as the Ylist. The complete command is

ExpReg L_1, L_2

If you're instead faced with a Stats Wizard taking up the screen, set Xlist and Ylist to L_1 and L_2, respectively, leave everything else as is, and move the cursor down to Calculate. Press (ENTER).

If everything goes according to plan, you'll see the results shown either in the center or left in figure 8.21. If you see the results on the left, missing the r^2 and r values, then refer back to the "R^2? R?" callout in section 8.4.1 for the solution. As you learned in the previous section, an r^2 value of 0.99899 means this is an extremely good fit.

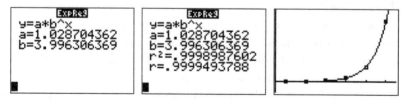

Figure 8.21   Fitting an exponential regression (ExpReg) line of best fit to the population of a colony of rabbits over time. The left screenshot shows the default ExpReg output, whereas the center shows diagnostics turned on. The right side shows $Y_1=ab^X$ graphed over the Stat Plot. $r^2 = 0.9998$ means it's nearly a perfect fit.

You can graph this result by going to the Y= menu and entering Y₁=ab^X. The statistics constants a and b can be found in the EQ tab of the Stats Vars menu: (VARS) (5) (▶) (▶). The graph you get won't resemble the right side in figure 8.21; go to the Stat Plots menu ((2nd) (Y=)) and set Plot1 to On, in Scatter mode (the first icon), and with Xlist:L₁ and Ylist:L₂. On your way to the graphscreen, stop off in the Zoom menu and choose 9:ZoomStat. *Now* you'll see the same thing as the right side in figure 8.21! A nearly perfect match, once again. Of course, if you have a TI-84 Plus C Silver Edition, your graph will be a little higher resolution and in color, as in figure 8.22, but otherwise identical.

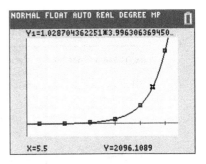

Figure 8.22 The exponential function fitted to the rabbits' population, as in figure 8.21. This is the same plot graphed on a TI-84 Plus C Silver Edition.

But how did I know that ExpReg would yield the right kind of equation to fit? I didn't; I made an educated guess. If I was wrong, I could have tried any other of the 10 total types of regression your calculator can do. In fact, to make sure you know what they all do, let me tell you about the rest.

8.4.3 More regression: the many options

Your calculator contains 10 automatic tools to fit functions to your statistical data. Table 8.9 contains all 10 of these functions, listed along with the general form of the equation to which they apply, and when that regression type is the correct choice based on looking at a Scatter plot of your data. All 10 require two lists: one containing x coordinates of points, the other containing y coordinates. All 10 paste the command to the homescreen on non-MathPrint calculators or display a Stats Wizard on MathPrint calculators.

Table 8.9 The 10 automatic regression tools in the Calculate tab of the Statistics menu ((▶) (STAT)), along with the function used to fit to the data and when that's a good choice

Regression function	General equation	When should you use this regression type?
LinReg(ax+b)	$y = ax + b$	Choose this if the data appears to form a nearly straight line.
QuadReg	$y = ax^2 + bx + c$	Good for parabolas.
CubicReg	$y = ax^3 + bx^2 + cx + d$	Try this for data that resembles a third-order polynomial. It may be a good option if you think QuadReg should work but it doesn't.
QuartReg	$y = ax^4 + bx^3 + cx^2 + dx + e$	If you have a roughly parabolic (or more complex) curve, and CubicReg isn't good enough, try QuartReg. Be sure you can show why the data makes sense fit to a quartic expression, though.

Table 8.9   The 10 automatic regression tools in the Calculate tab of the Statistics menu ([▶] [STAT]), along with the function used to fit to the data and when that's a good choice (*continued*)

Regression function	General equation	When should you use this regression type?
LinReg (a+bx)	$y = b + ax$	Exactly the same as LinReg(ax+b), except a and b are switched.
LnReg	$y = a + b \ln x$	Good if the data starts out going steeply upward and then nearly levels off.
ExpReg	$y = ab^x$	Nearly the opposite of LnReg: the data should appear to start off nearly level and quickly shoot up.
PwrReg	$y = ax^b$	The data may have a shape somewhat similar to ExpReg, but it shoots up much more slowly for large x values.
Logistic	$y = c/(1 + ae^{-bx})$	The logistic function has horizontal asymptotes at large positive and negative x values but is roughly diagonal near the origin.
SinReg	$y = a \sin(bx + c) + d$	Good for sinusoidal data, like a sine or cosine wave.

In addition, all 10 of these regression functions store their resulting values for constants like a and b to the statistics constants in [VARS] [5] [▶] [▶]. If you have a data set to which you want to fit a line, always follow these steps:

1 Enter the *x* values in L_1 and the *y* values in L_2 (or choose your own lists).
2 Create a Scatter plot from the 2nd Y= menu that uses your two lists. Choose 9:ZoomStat from the Zoom menu, and see what the resulting statistical plot looks like.
3 Based on the shape, pick a regression tool from table 8.9 and try it out. Is the r^2 value close to 1? If not, try a different regression tool. If you see no r^2 value, then run the DiagnosticOn command from the Catalog ([2nd] [0]) and try again.
4 If you're happy with the fitness of the result, go to the Y= menu and enter the function to graph. Remember to use the lowercase statistics constants from [VARS] [5] [▶] [▶]. Press [GRAPH], and observe how well your function fits the data.

Equally important, you *must* turn off Stat Plots when you've finished with statistics and want to return to normal graphing. One of the most frequent points of frustration with students who try to graph after playing with Stat Plots is the ERR:INVALID DIM error you get from deleting one of the lists from a Stat Plot without turning off the associated plot.

And now you've reached the end of the skills you need to manipulate and evaluate statistics on your calculator! We'll move on to the related field of probability next.

8.5   *Summary*

In this chapter, you worked through a complete introduction to the important statistical tools on your TI-83 Plus or TI-84 Plus graphing calculator. One of the most significant features that sets graphing calculators apart from scientific calculators, other than the obvious graphing facilities, is the ability to juggle and analyze large data sets. This chapter taught you how you can get that data onto your calculator in the first place via the List Editor. You then learned how to generate a summary of your data, including the five-number summary, average, sum, sum-squared, and more. Your next step was to summarize data in a more visual format via Stat Plots. We worked through six different types of plots, including some plotting two related lists and others summarizing a single list of data. We concluded with a look at how you can harness your calculator to fit a function to your data.

The tools on your calculator for statistics are vast, beyond even the scope of this chapter, but we've covered what you'll need for 95% of average high school statistics material. There's also a Manual Fit tool at the bottom of the Calculate tab of the Statistics menu, which is much less useful than the `LinReg` commands for fitting a straight line to data. The third tab of the Stat menu, titled Tests, contains a wealth of significance tests that figure out if data samples that deviate from an expected model are the result of randomness or important factors. These may be useful for more advanced math courses but are outside the scope of an introductory calculator math text.

We're now going to charge on to the probability tools your calculator includes. Whereas statistics deals with examining the results of experiments to determine patterns and relations, probability works with known patterns and relations.

Working with probability and distributions

This chapter covers

- Computing probability distribution functions and cumulative distribution functions
- Visualizing and graphing distributions
- Combinatorics and permutations
- Generating random numbers

In chapter 8, you learned all about statistics, where you take real-world samples and measurements and try to understand them. This chapter deals with the intimately related field of probability, which approaches finding patterns in numbers and data from the opposite perspective. With probability distributions, you define models of how you expect data to behave. For example, the Gaussian or normal distribution is used to define SAT scores, ensuring that most test takers get average scores and few get very high or very low scores. The binomial distribution can forecast how many tails you'll get if you flip a coin six times.

We'll start with the functions your calculator provides to calculate probability distribution functions (PDFs) and their integrals, called cumulative distribution functions (CDFs). Your calculator can calculate the PDF and CDF values for seven different distributions, three of which are discrete and four of which are continuous.

There are also one or two inverse distributions (depending on whether you have a MathPrint operating system) that your calculator can manipulate, as you'll discover. Next, you'll see how to plot the four continuous distributions and find the probability of a random value falling within a given range in each distribution. Your calculator can also help you calculate combinatorics, such as the number of different ways you could assign 25 desks in a classroom to 20 students. We'll discuss the three tools the TI-83 Plus/TI-84 Plus calculators include for combinatorics. Finally, we'll look at the random number–generating functions, which you can use to simulate experiments like flipping coins or rolling dice.

By the end of this chapter, you'll understand how to calculate and analyze properties of probability distributions. Let's start with the functions for calculating the values of PDFs at specific points and CDFs within given ranges.

9.1   *Calculating PDFs and CDFs*

A distribution function tells you the probability of any particular outcome or range of outcomes. It provides a way to model the process you're examining. For example, if the process is how students perform on a test, then your distribution might be a Gaussian (normal) distribution, or it might be something more complex. From the distribution, you could estimate how likely it would be for a student to get a particular grade, or how many students in a class would get above or below a certain score.

A *probability distribution function* tells you the probability of a single event, like a student getting B on a test or getting three heads out of five coin tosses. A *cumulative distribution function* lets you find the probability of at least or at most a certain set of events happening. For example, out of a class of 30 students, you could use the CDF to estimate how many would fail a test (get less than 60% correct). You could also find the probability that you would get no more than 2 tails when flipping a coin 10 times.

There are also two types of PDFs. There are *continuous PDFs*, which can take on infinitely many values within a certain range. For example, if you weigh a collection of watermelons, each watermelon might be 5 pounds, 5.001 pounds, 5.1282 pounds, and so on. There are also *discrete PDFs*, which can only take on a countable set of values. The number of seeds in each watermelon would follow a discrete PDF: you could have 2 seeds or 40 seeds or 251 seeds, but you couldn't have 40.5 or 39.88889 seeds. Your calculator can compute seven distributions: four continuous PDFs and three discrete PDFs:

Continuous PDFs	**Discrete PDFs**
1 Normal or Gaussian distribution	5 Binomial distribution
2 Student's T distribution	6 Poisson distribution
3 Chi square (χ^2) distribution	7 Geometric distribution
4 F distribution	

In this section, you'll first see all seven of these distributions in action. The continuous PDFs are mostly useful only for graphing, whereas the continuous CDFs let you calculate the probability of a data sample falling within a range. The discrete distributions are useful both as PDFs and CDFs, and you'll see real-world examples of both. I'll round out the section with a look at the one or two inverse distributions that your calculator can manipulate to find a value from a probability, instead of the other way around. We'll start with the seven PDFs.

PDFS AND CDFS ON THE TI-84 PLUS C SILVER EDITION   All the skills in this chapter are directly applicable to the color-screen TI-84 Plus C Silver Edition. The only differences are aesthetic; sidebars will point out the differences you need to know about.

9.1.1   *Probability distribution functions*

Your calculator can produce the value of seven different PDFs at any point along the functions. For the discrete PDFs, you can use these to find the probability of specific outcomes. For continuous PDFs, this is meaningless, because the probability of any single point along a continuous PDF is infinitely small. But you can use the continuous PDF functions on your calculator to draw graphs of those PDFs, as you'll learn in this section.

We should start with a table of all the continuous and discrete functions your calculator offers before getting into the nitty-gritty of using them. I'll show you graphs of some of the continuous distributions, and we'll work through an example testing the binomial distribution. The MathPrint operating system features make the process of using the seven functions in this section slightly easier but are by no means required for any of the distributions. All the PDFs can be found in the Distr menu, found via 2nd VARS. On most MathPrint calculators, the wizards shown in tables 9.1 and 9.2 will appear anywhere you use a PDF, whereas on non-MathPrint calculators, you'll have to fill in the arguments by hand.

> **PDFs in a nutshell**
> All PDF functions are found in the Distr tab of the Distr menu, accessed by pressing 2nd VARS. All seven of the PDF functions end in pdf(. The arguments to the PDF functions can be found in table 9.1 (for continuous PDFs) and table 9.2 (for discrete PDFs). If you're using a MathPrint calculator, a wizard guides you through choosing each of the arguments to the PDF function and then pastes the result to the home-screen. Without MathPrint, only the function name is pasted to the homescreen, and you must type the arguments manually.

CONTINUOUS PDFs

The four continuous PDFs your calculator offers are shown in table 9.1. As mentioned, none of these is particularly useful on its own, because the true probability of any single precise point along a continuous distribution is effectively zero. Consider a spinner from a board game: it can point to any point along a circle. You could mark the circle off into 360 one-degree increments, but it could still fall infinitely many places within each one-degree segment. Therefore, although the probability of falling into one of the 360 segments when spun would be 1/360, the probability of falling at an exact point would be infinitesimally small.

Table 9.1 The *continuous* PDFs available on your calculator. On non-MathPrint calculators, you use them as homescreen functions; most MathPrint calculators include wizards that help you use these functions. All italicized arguments should be replaced with numbers or variables. The screenshots show the MathPrint wizard on top and the function (and result) on bottom.

Distribution/function	Usage and arguments	In action

Gaussian (normal) normalpdf (	Calculates a probability p(x) from a Gaussian (normal) distribution. Defaults to mean $\mu = 0$ and standard deviation $\sigma = 1$ if those arguments are omitted.
	
	normalpdf (x, μ, σ)
		<pre>normalpdf
		x value: -0.2
		μ:0
		σ:1
		Paste
		normalpdf(-0.2,0
		,1)
		     .391042694</pre>

Student's *T* tpdf (	Calculates probability p(x) from the student's *T* distribution. The degrees of freedom *df* is an integer, equal to the number of samples minus 1. As degrees of freedom approaches infinity, this distribution converges to the normal distribution.
	
	tpdf (x, df)
		<pre>tpdf
		x value:1.2
		df:12
		Paste
		tpdf(1.2,12)
		     .1870490485</pre>

Chi square (χ^2) χ^2pdf (	Calculates probability p(x) from the χ^2 (chi square) distribution with *df* degrees of freedom.
	
	χ^2pdf (x, df)
		<pre>χ2pdf
		x value:0.15
		df:8
		Paste
		χ2pdf(0.15,8)
		 3.261598194ᴇ-5</pre>

F Fpdf (	Also known as the Fisher-Snedecor distribution; rarely used distribution to analyze variance in statistics. Arguments d_1 and d_2 are also called the numerator degrees of freedom and denominator degrees of freedom, respectively.
	
	Fpdf (x, d_1, d_2)
		<pre>Fpdf
		x value:1.1
		dfNumer:5
		dfDenom:2
		Paste
		Fpdf(1.0,7,5)
		     .4614764175</pre>

What you *can* do with these PDFs is graph them. Each of the four PDFs in table 9.1 represents a family of probability distributions, and you provide the arguments discussed in the table to pick the exact function out of the family. For example, whereas the student's *T* distribution is a whole family of functions, the student's *T* distribution for 10 data samples (which means 10 – 1 = 9 degrees of freedom) is a specific function in that family. Take a look at figure 9.1, which shows graphs of four instances of the four continuous probability distributions:

- The standard normal PDF, with mean $\mu = 0$ and standard deviation $\sigma = 1$
- The student's *T* distribution for 5 degrees of freedom
- The χ^2 distribution for 4 degrees of freedom
- The F distribution for numerator degrees of freedom $d_1 = 3$ and denominator degrees of freedom $d_2 = 2$

Want to replicate any of these graphs, or graph your own continuous PDFs? Just go to the Y= menu, move the cursor to an empty equation, and press ⟨ 2nd ⟩ ⟨VARS⟩. Choose the distribution of your choice, and then either fill in the arguments by hand while referring to table 9.1 (on non-MathPrint calculators) or use the wizard that appears (on MathPrint calculators). Use the variable X instead of a number for the x value. When you're satisfied, graph the result. To fix the window, refer to "Graphing continuous PDFs."

> **GRAPHING CONTINUOUS PDFS** It's difficult to pick a good window for graphing continuous PDFs. The 0:ZoomFit option in the Zoom menu can help a bit, but you'll likely want to manually adjust the window settings from the Window menu after you choose that option.

DISCRETE PDFS

There are three discrete PDFs as well, which analyze events that can only happen integer (discrete) numbers of times. Because the discrete PDFs compute resulting probabilities that are valid, and because the number of possible results (like the seeds in a watermelon) are countable, you can use the three PDFs your calculator offers directly. Table 9.2 shows all three in action, as well as the arguments necessary to use them. The example for the binompdf(function in table 9.2 predicts the likelihood of four boys among six siblings, if girls and boys are equally likely. The Poisson example gives the probability that a restaurant that normally gets 10 customers for lunch per hour gets only 4 in a given hour. The geometric example predicts how likely it is that it will take four tries to throw a wadded-up piece of paper into a faraway trash basket, assuming you can make the shot only 20% of the time.

From the discussion so far plus tables 9.1 and 9.2, you now know just about everything you need to use the PDFs your calculator offers. But it's always better to try new skills to make sure you understand them, so let's use two of the discrete PDFs to examine a game of soccer.

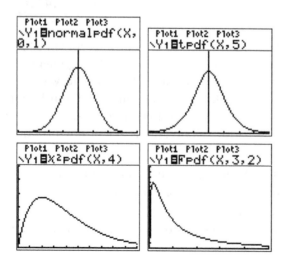

Figure 9.1 Graphing four different continuous PDFs. Left to right, top to bottom: the standard normal PDF, the student's *T* distribution for 5 degrees of freedom, the χ^2 distribution for 4 degrees of freedom, and the F distribution for $d_1 = 3$ and $d_2 = 3$.

Table 9.2 The *discrete* PDFs available on your calculator. All italicized arguments should be replaced with numbers or variables. The screenshots show the MathPrint wizard on top and the function (and result) on bottom.

Distribution/function	Usage and arguments	In action
Binomial binompdf(	Used to simulate a repeated experiment where two results are possible (flipping a coin, gender of a baby). Calculates the probability that the same outcome will be produced *outcome* (x value) times out of *trials*. You also specify the *probability* of the outcome you're looking for (for a fair coin, this would be 0.5 for heads or tails). binompdf(*trials*,*probability*, *outcome*)	**binompdf** trials:6 p:0.5 x value:4 Paste binompdf(6,0.5,4) 　　　　　　.234375
Poisson poissonpdf(	Given that some event occurs λ times on average per object, unit of space, or unit of time, calculates the probability it will happen *actual* (x value) times. For example, defects in a circuit board or cups of coffee sold per minute. poissonpdf(λ,*actual*)	**poissonpdf** λ:10 x value:4 Paste poissonpdf(10,4) 　　　　.0189166374
Geometric geometpdf(	Whereas the binomial distribution calculates the number of instances of the same event per trials (such as heads in coin tosses), the geometric distribution calculates the probability that it takes *trials* (x value) for the first instance of the event with *probability* to occur, given that there are only two possible outcomes. geometpdf(*probability*,*trials*)	**geometpdf** p:0.2 x value:4 Paste geometpdf(0.2,4) 　　　　　　.1024

EXAMPLE: PLAYING SOCCER

You enjoy playing soccer (or football, if you're from outside the United States). You and your friends decide to see how good each of you is at scoring, so you draw a line 50 yards from the goal. You've tried this before, so you know you can only make one out of every four shots from this far away. First, you want to predict how likely it is that it takes you exactly three attempts to make a goal.

From what you know of distribution, the geometric distribution is the right choice to figure this out. You know that your probability of making a goal on each attempt is $1/4 = 0.25$. You want to know if you'll make it in exactly three trials. Therefore, as you can see from table 9.2, you'll run the function

geometpdf(0.25,3)

Starting from the homescreen, press 2nd VARS to access the Distr menu. Scroll all the way down to E:geometpdf(, and press ENTER. If you're on a MathPrint calculator, you'll see a wizard that looks like the left side in figure 9.2; if so, enter p:0.25, x value:3, move the cursor to Paste, and press ENTER. If you're not on a MathPrint

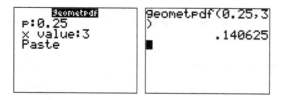

Figure 9.2   **Figuring out that there's a 14% chance it'll take you exactly three attempts to make a goal from 50 yards away, given that you can (on average) make that shot 25% of the time**

calculator, you'll see geometpdf(pasted to the homescreen, so add the arguments 0.25,3 and a closing parenthesis. Either way, press (ENTER) again to compute the answer, as shown on the right in figure 9.2. There's only a 14% probability that you'll make the shot in exactly three attempts (you multiply the probability by 100 to get the percent probability).

What if you want to find the odds that you'll make exactly two out of three attempts, still with a 25% chance that you'll make any given shot? For this, we need to use a binomial distribution. We want an outcome of two successes in three attempts, where the probability of success for each attempt is 0.25. Therefore, the arguments (from table 9.2) are

binompdf(3,0.25,2)

As before, go to the Distr menu via (2nd) (VARS); this time, choose A:binompdf(. The left side in figure 9.3 illustrates what to do if you get a MathPrint wizard, and the right side shows typing out the arguments without MathPrint. In either case, press (ENTER) when you've finished to get the result: there's also a 14% chance you'll make two out of three shots! Somewhat counterintuitively, you're equally likely to need three attempts to make one goal or to make exactly two out of three goals.

What if you want to know the probability of making at least two out of three goals? For that, you need a CDF, precisely the topic we're going to examine next.

9.1.2   *Cumulative distribution functions*

CDFs are the integrals of PDFs. Whereas PDFs compute the probability of a precise event, CDFs are used to compute the probability that an event falls somewhere within a range. You use your calculator's *continuous CDFs* to determine the likelihood that a data sample falls somewhere within its range of possible values, such as the probability that a student gets between 90% and 100% on a test. Your graphing calculator's *discrete CDFs* are used to determine the probability that a random sample takes at most a particular value: for example, that there are 30 or fewer seeds in any given watermelon.

   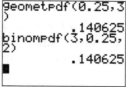

Figure 9.3   **Calculating the probability of making exactly two out of three shots in soccer to be 14%, given that you can make any single shot one-quarter of the time ($p = 0.25$). You use the binomial PDF, shown with its MathPrint wizard (left) and homescreen form (second line, right).**

Of course, you can also use your calculator to determine other properties from its CDFs. If you want to know the probability that a sample is less than a particular value for a continuous CDF, use negative infinity for the lower bound. If you want to calculate a discrete CDF within a range, subtract the value of the CDF at the lower bound from the value of the CDF at the upper bound. In this section, you'll learn all about using CDFs on your calculator. We'll start with the four continuous CDFs your calculator offers, which directly mirror the four PDFs you discovered in the previous section. You'll then learn about the three discrete CDFs. Throughout the discussion of both types of CDFs, we'll work through several relevant examples.

CDFs in a nutshell

All CDF functions are found in the Distr tab of the Distr menu with their PDF counterparts, accessed by pressing (2nd) (VARS). All seven of the CDF functions end in cdf (. The arguments to the CDF functions can be found in table 9.3 (for continuous CDFs) and table 9.4 (for discrete CDFs). If you're using a MathPrint calculator, a wizard guides you through choosing each of the arguments to the CDF function and then pastes the result to the homescreen. Without MathPrint, only the function name is pasted to the homescreen, and you must type the arguments manually.

CONTINUOUS CDFs

Your calculator has four continuous CDF functions, all found directly below their PDF counterparts in the Distr menu. As summarized in "CDFs in a nutshell," you can find them under (2nd) (VARS). Just as with PDFs, a wizard appears to help you fill out each function's arguments on MathPrint calculators. On non-MathPrint calculators, the function name is pasted to the homescreen when you choose a CDF from the Distr menu, and you must type the arguments manually.

INFINITY You can use the continuous CDFs on your calculator to calculate open-ended ranges, where you find the probability that a sample is less than or greater than some value. To do this, you can use negative infinity as the lower bound or infinity as the upper bound. Because your calculator doesn't understand infinity, you use 1E99 as positive infinity and ‾1E99 as negative infinity. These mean 10^{99} and -10^{99}, respectively, and are the largest and smallest numbers your calculator can process. You type the E symbol via (2nd) (,).

Details on all four continuous CDFs can be found in table 9.3, including their arguments and screenshots of each one in action. Note that whereas $p(x)$ represents the PDF, as in tables 9.1 and 9.2, $P(x)$ represents the value of the CDF. Although all these CDF functions take two bound arguments, which can be used to specify a finite interval like [−1, 1] or [0, 3.5], you can turn these into half-bounded intervals using your calculator's approximation for infinity. See the aside on "Infinity" for more information.

Table 9.3 The *continuous* CDFs available on your calculator. All italicized arguments should be replaced with numbers or variables. The screenshots show the MathPrint wizard on top and the function (and result) on bottom.

Distribution/function	Usage and arguments	In action

normal
`normalcdf(`
	Calculates a probability P(*upper*) – P(*lower*) from a Gaussian (normal) distribution. Defaults to mean $\mu = 0$ and standard deviation $\sigma = 1$ if those arguments are omitted.
	
	`normalcdf(`*lower,upper,μ,σ*`)`
		`normalcdf`
		`lower: -1E99`
		`upper: -0.2`
		`μ:0`
		`σ:1`
		`Paste`
		`normalcdf(-1E99,`
		`-0.2,0,1)`
		`        .4207403122`

Student's *T*
`tcdf(`
	Calculates probability P(*upper*) – P(*lower*) from the student's *T* distribution. The degrees of freedom *df* is an integer, equal to the number of samples minus 1.
	
	`tcdf(`*lower,upper,df*`)`
		`tcdf`
		`lower: -0.2`
		`upper: 1.2`
		`df:12`
		`Paste`
		`tcdf(-0.2,1.2,12`
		`)`
		`         .450937717`

Chi square (χ^2)
`χ²cdf(`
	Calculates probability P(*upper*) – P(*lower*) from the χ^2 (chi square) distribution with *df* degrees of freedom.
	
	`χ²cdf(`*lower,upper,df*`)`
		`χ²cdf`
		`lower:0.15`
		`upper:1E99`
		`df:8`
		`Paste`
		`χ²cdf(0.15,1E99,`
		`8)`
		`         .9999987583`

F
`Fcdf(`
	Computes P(*upper*) – P(*lower*) for the F distribution. Arguments d_1 and d_2 are also called the numerator degrees of freedom and denominator degrees of freedom, respectively.
	
	`Fcdf(`*lower,upper,d_1,d_2*`)`
		`Fcdf`
		`lower:0.5`
		`upper:1.1`
		`dfNumer:5`
		`dfDenom:2`
		`Paste`
		`Fcdf(0.5,1.1,5,2`
		`)`
		`         .2304772304`

EXAMPLE: WEIGHTS OF PUPPIES

When they are born, a particular breed of puppies usually weighs, on average, 120 grams. You study many different litters and discover that the weights of the newborn puppies follow a normal (Gaussian) distribution with a standard deviation of 10 grams. Because you're thinking of becoming a veterinarian, you research a disorder called *fading puppy and kitten syndrome*, which affects puppies that are born too small and must be carefully treated. To save puppies from the fatal consequences of this syndrome, you need to pay special attention to any puppy weighing less than 105 grams when it's born.

What percentage of puppies will weigh less than 105 grams at birth and thus need special care? You can find out with the normal CDF. You want to calculate the percentage of all puppies born that weigh less than 105 grams, so your upper bound is 105. There is no lower bound; we'll set it to negative infinity (-1E99). We know the

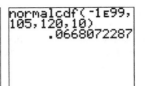

Figure 9.4 **Figuring what percentage of puppies of a certain breed are born underweight and thus at risk for health problems. The normal (Gaussian) CDF reveals it's about 6.7%.**

mean $\mu = 120$ and the standard deviation $\sigma = 10$. Therefore, we can use normalcdf(like this:

`normalcdf(-1E99,105,120,10)`

From the homescreen, go to the Distr menu using ⟨2nd⟩ ⟨VARS⟩, and choose 2:normal-cdf(. If you have a MathPrint calculator, a wizard will appear, as shown in table 9.3. Enter a lower bound of ⁻1E99, where the negative sign is ⟨(-)⟩ and E is ⟨2nd⟩ ⟨,⟩. Set the upper bound to 105, the mean to 120, and the standard deviation to 10. If your results match the left side in figure 9.4, press ⟨ENTER⟩ to paste the result to the home-screen and ⟨ENTER⟩ again to get a result. If you don't have a MathPrint calculator, the normalcdf(function will be pasted to the homescreen; fill in the arguments as shown above and at right in figure 9.4, and press ⟨ENTER⟩.

As you can see, you'll need to keep an eye on 6.7% of the puppies born to make sure they get enough food and care to thrive. You could also use the normcdf(function to find the percentage of puppies born at solid, healthy weights (say, lower = 110 grams and upper = 130 grams). You could find how many puppies would be born significantly overweight (lower = 135 grams, upper = 1E99 or infinity).

DISCRETE CDFS

There are three discrete CDFs that correspond to the three discrete PDFs you learned about in section 9.1.1. The three functions along with their arguments and screen-shots are shown in table 9.4. The biggest difference from the continuous CDFs is that each of these three functions takes a single point at which to calculate the CDF, with an implied lower bound of negative infinity. If you want to calculate a CDF on a finite bound [*lower,upper*], you need to separately calculate the CDF at the *upper* and *lower* bounds and then subtract the *lower* CDF from the *upper* CDF.

As you can see from table 9.4, the arguments for the discrete CDFs are exactly the same as the arguments to the associated discrete PDFs. The only difference is that the resulting probability computed by your calculator is the probability for at most x value rather than exactly x value. You could repeat the example at the end of section 9.1.1 to find out the probability that it will take you at most three attempts to make a goal (with the geometcdf). You could use the binomcdf(to calculate the likelihood that you make at most two goals in three attempts.

You can calculate the probability of *at least* x value instead of at most x value occurring by subtracting a CDF result from 1. Every CDF reaches $P(\infty) = 1$, so if p is the probability that some sample lies between $-\infty$ and x, $1 - p$ is the probability that it lies between x and ∞.

Table 9.4 The *discrete* CDFs available on your calculator. All italicized arguments should be replaced with numbers or variables. The screenshots show the MathPrint wizard on top and the function (and result) on bottom. The only difference between these and the PDF versions are that, whereas the PDFs calculate the probability the event will happen exactly `x value` times, these CDFs calculate the probability it will happen at most `x value` times.

Distribution/function	Usage and arguments	In action
Binomial `binomcdf(`	Calculates P(*outcome*) for the binomial distribution. Computes the probability that the same outcome will be produced at most *outcome* (`x value`) times out of *trials*. You also specify the *probability* of the outcome you're looking for (for a fair coin, this would be 0.5 for heads or tails). `binomcdf(trials,probability, outcome)`	binomcdf trials:6 P:0.5 x value:4 Paste binomcdf(6,0.5,4)) .890625
Poisson `poissoncdf(`	Calculates P(*actual*) for the Poisson distribution, the probability some outcome will happen at most *actual* (`x value`) times that usually averages λ times per object/unit time/unit space. `poissoncdf(λ,actual)`	poissoncdf λ:10 x value:4 Paste poissoncdf(10,4) .0292526881
Geometric `geometcdf(`	Calculates probability P(*trials*) that it takes at most *trials* (`x value`) for the first instance of the event with *probability* to occur, given that there are only two possible outcomes. `geometcdf(probability,trials)`	geometcdf P:0.2 x value:4 Paste geometcdf(0.2,4) .5904

To keep this section covering the many facets of PDFs and CDFs from getting any longer, let's quickly conclude with a look at the one (or two) inverse CDFs your calculator can evaluate.

9.1.3 Inverse CDFs

Whereas a regular CDF tells you the probability of an event based on a distribution, an inverse CDF tells you what event is based on the probability. That's very abstract, so let's try again with an SAT example. As I've mentioned, SAT scores are fitted to a Gaussian distribution, so you can use the normal CDF to figure out how many students get a 2100 or below out of 2400 possible points. You can use the inverse normal CDF to figure out, given a probability p that 80% of students get at most score x, what the value of x is. With the SAT example, given that $p(x) = 0.8$, you can use the `invNorm(` function to find that $x = 1790$, given that the mean score in 2011 was 1500 and the standard deviation was 344.

Every TI-83 Plus and TI-84 Plus can calculate the inverse normal distribution using `invNorm(`, found in the Distr menu under [2nd] [VARS]. It takes at least one argument, the probability p of the desired point along the CDF. With only one option, it calculates the inverse normal point from the standard Gaussian PDF, where mean $\mu = 0$ and

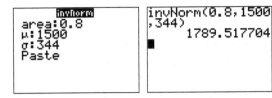

Figure 9.5 Estimating the maximum score for the lowest-scoring 80% of SAT test takers in 2011. The `invNorm(` function takes a probability and produces an input point along the CDF function.

standard deviation $\sigma = 1$. The second and third optional arguments are a different mean and deviation, such as $\mu = 1500$ and $\sigma = 344$ for the SAT statistics previously mentioned. In summary,

`invNorm(p, μ, σ)`

To replicate the previous SAT experiment, go to the Distr menu and choose `3:invNorm(`. If you have the MathPrint wizards, you'll see something like the left side in figure 9.5. Enter `0.8` for area (p), `1500` for μ, and `344` for σ. Move the cursor to `Paste`, and press ENTER twice. If you don't have MathPrint, the `invNorm(` function will be pasted to the homescreen; add the arguments `0.8,1500,344`, and press ENTER. In either case, you'll get the result demonstrated on the right in figure 9.5—that 80% of SAT test takers in 2011 got a 1790 or lower. This also implies that $1 - 0.8 = 20\%$ of students taking the SAT got above 1790.

If you have a TI-84 Plus calculator, including MathPrint calculators (but *excluding* all TI-83 Plus devices), you have access to a second inverse CDF function called `invT(`. As you might guess, it's the inverse CDF for the student's T distribution. Like the `invNorm(` function, it takes a probability p and produces the x value along the CDF that corresponds to that probability. Because the student's T also requires the number of degrees of freedom, this is the second argument:

`invT(p, df)`

As always, the function can be found in your TI-84 Plus calculator's Distr menu. As with the `invNorm(` function, `invT(` includes a wizard for MathPrint calculators or is pasted directly to the homescreen on non-MathPrint devices.

You can visualize the four continuous PDFs even more effectively with a collection of four drawing functions. In section 9.1.1, you saw sample graphs of the four continuous PDFs; now you'll learn how to simultaneously visualize the PDF and CDF results.

9.2   *Drawing distributions*

Understanding PDFs and CDFs with or without a calculator can be challenging, hence the detail in section 9.1 of this chapter. We always go through examples of each new skill you learn to make those new skills clearer, and you've previously seen that being able to visualize math concepts is even better than working through purely numerical examples. To help you further grasp the four continuous PDFs your calculator can compute, it offers four functions to draw those distributions on the graphscreen.

For each of the four distributions that can be drawn, you specify the parameters of the distribution, and the calculator draws the PDF. You also supply lower and upper bounds, as for a CDF; the calculator shades the area under the PDF between those bounds and shows you the area of the shaded region. From this, you can see the relationship between the PDF (the graphed line) and the CDF (the integral of the PDF). You could replicate these same results by graphing the PDF functions as in figure 9.1 and then use the $\int f(x)\,dx$ tool from the Calculate menu. The distribution drawing tools you'll learn about in this section make the process easier.

The list of four available functions is shown in table 9.5. Although the descriptions of each Shade function are identical to the descriptions of the CDFs in table 9.3, they're replicated for quick reference. In addition, the arguments to these Shade functions exactly match the arguments to the related CDF functions from table 9.3. Each graph in the third column of table 9.5 corresponds to the example arguments in the second column. Although the MathPrint wizards aren't shown, they're identical to the wizards in table 9.3.

Table 9.5   The CDF drawing functions available on your calculator found under (2nd) (VARS) (▶). The screenshots omit the MathPrint wizards (which are available for the drawing functions), instead showing sample plots. The graph windows have been manually set from the Window menu.

Distribution/function	Usage, arguments, example	Example graphed
Normal ShadeNorm(	Calculates and plots a probability $P(upper) - P(lower)$ from a Gaussian (normal) distribution. Defaults to mean $\mu = 0$ and standard deviation $\sigma = 1$ if those arguments are omitted. ShadeNorm(*lower*, *upper*, μ, σ) ShadeNorm(⁻1E99, ⁻0.2, 0, 1)	 Area=.42074 low=⁻1E99 up=⁻.2
Student's *T* Shade_t(	Calculates and graphs probability $P(upper) - P(lower)$ from the student's *T* distribution. The degrees of freedom *df* is an integer, equal to the number of samples minus 1. Shade_t(*lower*, *upper*, *df*) Shade_t(⁻0.2, 1.2, 12)	 Area=.450938 df=12 low=⁻.2 up=1.2
Chi square (χ^2) Shadeχ^2(	Calculates and draws probability $P(upper) - P(lower)$ from the χ^2 (chi square) distribution with *df* degrees of freedom. Shadeχ^2(*lower*, *upper*, *df*) Shadeχ^2(2.1, 1E99, 8)	 Area=.977792 df=8 low=2.1 up=1E99
F Shade**F**(	Computes and plots $P(upper) - P(lower)$ for the F distribution. Arguments d_1 and d_2 are also called the numerator degrees of freedom and denominator degrees of freedom, respectively. Shade**F**(*lower*, *upper*, d_1, d_2) Shade**F**(0.5, 1.1, 5, 2)	 Area=.230477 low=.5 up=1.1

Choosing a shade window

None of the four distribution drawing functions in table 9.5 can automatically set the graph window, and using any of the Zoom menu functions erases the plot. You must set up the window before you use the functions. Remember that no probability can be less than 0 or greater than 1, so `Ymin=0` and `Ymax=1` are a good start. Because the area, lower, and upper bounds are written at the bottom of the screen, try setting `Ymin=-0.3` so that they won't be written over the graph. The `Xmin` and `Xmax` values you choose will depend on your distribution and the parameters you provide to it.

If you have a TI-84 Plus C Silver Edition, you don't need to leave space at the bottom of the screen, because the area, lower, and upper bounds are written in the border below the graph area. The figures shown here compare `ShadeNorm(` on the TI-84 Plus C Silver Edition with the same operation on the black-and-white calculators.

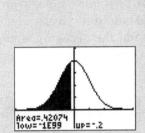
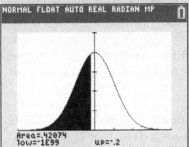

Using the `ShadeNorm(` function on a black-and-white TI-83 Plus or TI-84 Plus calculator (left) or a TI-84 Plus C Silver Edition (right). On the color-screen calculator, you don't have to leave space for the text when choosing `Ymin`.

EXAMPLE: IQ TESTING

Intelligence quotient (IQ) scores are distributed normally (as a Gaussian distribution), with a mean of $\mu = 100$ and a standard deviation $\sigma = 15$. Therefore, the "average" adult has an IQ of 100. One way of defining a genius is any individual with an IQ above 140. What if you want to calculate the percentage of the population that have above-average intelligence but aren't geniuses? You could use the `normalcdf(` function from section 9.1.2 with a lower bound of 100 and an upper bound of 140. To visualize the process (and results) more easily, let's use the `ShadeNorm(` command.

Start by setting up your graphing settings. Go to (Y=), and clear out (or disable) any equations present. If the axes are off, turn them on from the Graph Format (2nd) (ZOOM)) menu. We want to look at a distribution with a mean of 100 and a standard deviation of 15; let's set `Xmin=50`, `Xmax=150`, `Ymin=-0.01` (to leave space for the text `Shade-Norm(` adds), and `Ymax=0.04`. To make the ticks on the axes meaningful, set `Xscl=10` and `Yscl=0.005`. Of course, I didn't magically know that would define a good window. I started with `Ymin=-0.2` and `Ymax=1`, saw that the resulting graph wasn't very tall, and adjusted the window settings a few times. I retested the `ShadeNorm(` function after

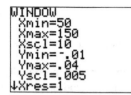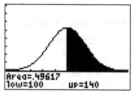

Figure 9.6 Using `ShadeNorm(` to graph the PDF of IQ scores and find out what percentage of the population are smarter than average (but not geniuses). The result is 49.6%, meaning 0.4% of the population are geniuses (because 50% of the area of a Gaussian distribution is above the mean).

each one to see if I had it right yet. You can see the final window settings on the left in figure 9.6.

Next, press 2nd VARS ▶ and choose 1:`ShadeNorm(`. On a MathPrint calculator, enter `lower:100`, `upper:140`, `μ:100`, and `σ:15`, and then move the cursor down to Draw and press ENTER. If you're working with a non-MathPrint calculator, the `Shade-Norm(` function will be pasted to the homescreen. Add the necessary arguments, as shown in the center in figure 9.6 and summarized in table 9.5, and then press ENTER:

`ShadeNorm(100,140,100,15)`

You'll see the resulting graph on the right side in figure 9.6. If you have a TI-84 Plus C Silver Edition, you'll instead see the graph in figure 9.7, which although fancier illustrates the same results. You can see that 49.6% of the area under the graph is shaded, as the text points out. This means that 49.6% of the population have above-average IQs but are not geniuses, leaving 0.4% of the population that are geniuses.

With the functions to calculate and graph PDFs and CDFs under your belt, you're ready to look into the other probability tools your calculator offers. The next set of skills covers combinatorics, in which you figure out the number of ways you can choose or arrange things.

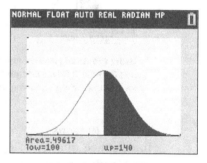

Figure 9.7   The result of the `ShadeNorm(` **command in figure 9.6 when run on a TI-84 Plus C Silver Edition. The only difference is that** `Ymin` **is 0 here, because the area and bounds are written in the border around the graph area.**

9.3   *Combinatorics*

Combinatorics is an important part of probability, involved with figuring out how many different ways you can permute, arrange, or choose objects or ideas from a collection. For example, if you have a bag containing six marbles of different colors, combinatorics tells you in how many different orders you could pick out the marbles, if you pick them one by one. If you're at a restaurant where you need to choose two of six possible appetizers and one of four entrées, combinatorics can help you find the answer to how many different meals you could select.

In this section, we'll look at the three different combinatorics tools your calculator provides, as well as examples of each:

- We'll start with nPr, which is used to compute the number of different ways you could permute the items in a collection, where order matters.
- You'll learn about nCr, which counts the number of possible unique subsets you could choose from a larger set, where order doesn't matter.
- You'll see the factorial (!) operator, a special case of the permutation operation.

Permutation is a good place to start. Consider a hungry student who likes frequenting local restaurants during the summer. He lives close to 12 different restaurants that he enjoys, but to avoid monotony, he wants to go to a different restaurant each day from Monday to Friday. This gives him 5 lunches to eat at 12 different restaurants. How many possible schedules could he set out for himself for the week? With permutation, both the restaurants he picks and the order he chooses matter.

PERMUTATION

The permutation operator is called nPr and is found in the Prb (fourth) tab of the Math menu. You pronounce nPr "*n* permute *r*," and because it's an operator (like + or ^), you place it between rather than before its operands. The number you put before the nPr operator (*n*) is the size of the list of options or items. For our famished student, $n = 12$, because he has 12 different restaurants to choose from. The number you place after nCr, *r*, is the number of items to be chosen. Our student would select $r = 5$, because he has 5 weekdays on which he wants to go out for lunch. Therefore, to figure out how many ways he could arrange his lunches, he would compute 12 nPr 5 on the homescreen, as shown in figure 9.8.

As you can see, there are over 95,000 different ways he could arrange his dining schedule. That's a lot! What if our intrepid student decides not to worry about the order in which he visits the restaurants and just wants to pick five? He just wants a set of 5 restaurants out of the 12, and the order no longer matters. You might think on

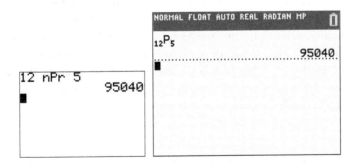

Figure 9.8 Calculating the number of ways 5 items randomly chosen from a set of 12 could be arranged in order. The example explores deciding what restaurants out of 12 possibilities to eat in for a week. On the right, the same computation on a TI-84 Plus C Silver Edition, which adds MathPrint-style nPr operations.

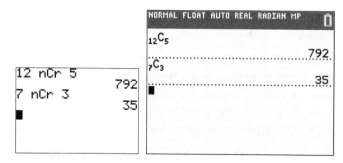

Figure 9.9   Top: Using the `nCr` (*n* choose *r*) operator to figure out how many different sets of 5 (unique) restaurants you could choose out of 12. Bottom: Having decided to take a break and just make a sandwich, seeing how many different sets of 3 condiments you could choose out of 7 options. On the right, the same calculations on a TI-84 Plus C Silver Edition, which adds MathPrint-style `nCr` operations.

this a bit and decide that this is probably a smaller set of possibilities, and you'd be right. How much smaller? The `nCr` operator will tell you.

COMBINATION

Whereas `nPr` means "*n* permute *r*," `nCr` means "*n* choose *r*." The `nCr` function is also found in the Prb (fourth) tab of the Math menu, and like `nPr`, it's placed between its operands. It also takes the operands in the same order: the number of items in the whole set of options first, then `nCr`, and then the number of items to choose. The student in our scenario is still pondering $n = 12$ possible restaurants from which he will pick $r = 5$. Therefore, using his trusty graphing calculator to continue his exploration, he computes 12 `nCr` 5. You can see his work on the top line in figure 9.9.

All this math and thinking of restaurants is making our student hungry, so he goes to the kitchen to whip up a quick sandwich. Confronted by a refrigerator full of 7 different condiments, he decides he only wants to choose 3 (because he's willing to be adventurous, any 3 will do). As you can see from the second line in figure 9.9, he grabs his calculator and finds that 7 `nCr` 3 gives him 35 different possible sets of condiments.

Sated by his delicious sandwich (he ended up with ketchup, horseradish, and ranch dressing, if you're curious), the student looks back at his list of restaurants and realizes that of the 12, there are really only 5 on the list that he loves. With 5 restaurants and 5 days of the week, he no longer needs to eliminate any restaurants! All he needs to do is pick in what order he wants to visit these fine establishments. He could compute 5 `nPr` 5, but there's an even faster way.

FACTORIAL

There's a special case of the permutation operation when $n = r$. It's called the *factorial* operator, and it looks like an exclamation point (`!`). The factorial operator is the fourth item in the Prb tab of the Math menu, accessed by pressing MATH ▶ ▶ ▶ 4. The factorial operator takes only one operand, not two (as you'd expect, because specifying both *n* and *r* would be redundant now). Computing n! is precisely equivalent to n nPr n, so figuring out on which of 5 days to schedule 5 different restaurants is as easy as computing 5!. You can see this calculation in figure 9.10.

Having narrowed his problem down to only 120 options, our student is satisfied that he can live with finding the proper order in which to visit his favorite restaurants. In fact, if he goes to each restaurant once a week, he can go in a different order every week for over two years (104 weeks)!

With all that theorizing out of the way, what if you want to use your calculator to generate random data, or even simulate flipping a coin or rolling a die? Your calculator includes functions to create all sorts of random numbers.

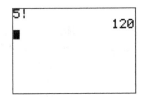

Figure 9.10 Computing 5!, read as "5 factorial." You can use the factorial operator to compute n nPr n, a permutation where you use all the items in the set of possibilities.

9.4 *Generating random numbers*

Random numbers are useful for all sorts of things. You could generate random numbers to see how accurate the probabilities you computed in sections 9.1 and 9.2 were. You could flip virtual coins, roll virtual dice, spin virtual spinners, even pick virtual cards. Your calculator can do this for you, with four or five included functions that produce different types of random numbers. In this section, you'll learn about all of them and what makes each one unique. As always, we'll walk through a few examples to show the features in action.

Although *random number* might sound like a descriptive enough term on its own, it's actually quite vague. For one thing, you need to specify whether you're working with random integers or numbers that can take on any decimal value. For another, you need to specify whether you're calculating uniformly distributed random values (where every value is equally likely to appear) or numbers following some other distribution. Your calculator includes four random-number functions (five for MathPrint calculators):

- rand produces a uniformly distributed random decimal between 0 and 1.
- randInt(a,b) generates a uniformly selected random integer between (and including) a and b.
- randNorm(μ, σ) calculates a normal (Gaussian) distributed decimal for the distribution with mean μ and standard deviation σ.
- randBin(n,p) computes a binomially distributed random integer between (and including) 0 and n for the distribution with n trials and probability of success p.
- randIntNoRep(a,b) returns a list of (b − a + 1) uniformly distributed random decimals, in which all numbers between and including a and b appear exactly once. MathPrint calculators (OS 2.53 and higher) only.

All four (or five) of these functions can be found in the Prb (Probability) tab of the Math menu, under (MATH) (▶) (▶) (▶). On the TI-84 Plus C Silver Edition, this tab is called Prob instead of Prb. Incidentally, this is exactly where you got the combinatorics functions in section 9.3.

Random number wizards

The TI-84 Plus C Silver Edition adds new wizards for the `randInt(`, `randNorm(`, `randBin(`, and `randIntNoRep(` commands, similar to the Stats Wizards you saw in chapter 8. When you select one of these four commands from the Prb/Prob tab of the Math menu, you'll see a wizard like this one. If you want a single random number, leave the n argument blank.

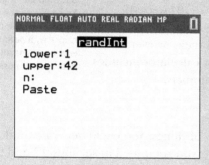

It would be easiest to start with `rand(`, the simplest of the random-number functions. This takes no arguments and generates a random decimal between 0 and 1. Its results are uniformly distributed, so if you were to collect 900 samples from `rand` and create a histogram (as from chapter 7), your bins would all hold almost exactly the same number of samples. `rand(` has another nifty trick up its sleeve; check out the sidebar "Seeding the random number generator." You can also see a set of six results from `rand(` in figure 9.11.

Seeding the random-number generator

Internally, your calculator uses the same random number–generation system for all four or five of the random-number functions. Although the numbers appear truly random, they are actually *pseudorandom*, meaning they're generated based on formulas. You can control the random numbers that your calculator returns by a process called *seeding* the generator.

A seed is any number; you set the seed via *seed*→rand (the `rand(` function in the Prb tab of the Math menu). For example, you can set the seed to 2 via 2→rand. If you set a seed and generate some random numbers, then set the same seed again and generate more random numbers, you'll get the same sequence of random numbers. This can be useful if you need random numbers but still want to be able to replicate your exact steps.

The next function is `randInt(`, which generates uniformly distributed random integers. The syntax is `randInt(a,b)`, where *a* and *b* are the lower and upper bounds on the numbers the function generates. You can simulate flipping a coin with `randInt(0,1)`,

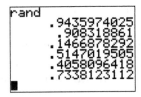

Figure 9.11 Testing the `rand(` **function, which has been run six separate times here. As you can see, each time you run it you get a different uniformly distributed random decimal.**

where 0 is heads and 1 is tails. Running that command produces random 0s and 1s. You could roll a virtual die with `randInt(1,6)` and pick a random card out of a deck with `randInt(1,52)`.

`randNorm(` and `randBin(` both generate random numbers following nonuniform distributions. `randNorm(μ, σ)` generates a random decimal with probabilities from the Gaussian distribution with mean μ and standard deviation σ. `randBin(n, p)` generates a random integer between (and including) 0 and n, indicating how many trials it takes to get n successes from a two-outcome test (like flipping a coin), where p is the probability of a success. As an example, illustrated in figure 9.12, you could generate random (but properly distributed) SAT scores by computing `randNorm(1500,344)`. Section 9.1.3 included other SAT score examples.

Lists of random numbers

`rand(`, `randInt(`, `randNorm(`, and `randBin(` can all return a list of random numbers instead of a single random number. To get them to do this, add another argument on the end indicating how many elements the list should have. Each element of the list will follow the requested distribution. The arguments for each function for this mode are as follows:

```
rand(elements)
randInt(a,b,elements)
randNorm(μ,σ,elements)
randBin(n,p,elements)
```

On MathPrint calculators, there's one more function, called `randIntNoRep(` (random integer, no repeats). This function takes no length argument and instead is used as

```
randIntNoRep(a,b)
```

As mentioned in the text, this creates a list ($b − a + 1$) elements long containing all the numbers between a and b, inclusive, exactly one time.

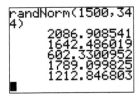

Figure 9.12 Using the `randNorm(` **function to generate random SAT-style scores. These follow the same distribution as real SAT scores out of 2,400 possible points, although they'd need to be rounded to the nearest 10 to be completely accurate.**

You can use all four (or five) of the random-number functions in larger mathematical expressions. For example, you could use randBin(and binompdf(together to calculate the probability of each random outcome of a binomial process in a single step. You could use randInt(or rand(to plug random values in to an equation. For something not very useful but a bit entertaining, try using one of the random-number functions in a graphed function.

With the conclusion of this section on random numbers, the material on probability and statistics we've been examining for the last two chapters is wrapped up with a neat bow. We'll look at a brand-new topic in the next chapter: financial tools.

9.5   *Summary*

You learned all about your calculator's probability tools in this chapter. We started with the probability distribution functions and cumulative distribution functions that your calculator can compute. You learned about four continuous PDFs and CDFs and three discrete PDFs and CDFs. You learned about graphing the continuous PDFs manually, and then about using the built-in drawing functions to calculate a CDF while plotting a PDF. We worked through a few examples from the CDF and PDF functions. After a brief glance at inverse PDFs, we moved on to combinatoric functions, permutations, and factorials. We concluded with the different functions your graphing calculator offers for generating random numbers. Now that we're at the end of probability and statistics, we'll move on to the financial features of TI-83 Plus and TI-84 Plus calculators to finish part 3 of this book.

Financial tools

10

This chapter covers

- Using your calculator to solve time-value of money (TVM) problems
- Analyzing interest, loans, mortgages, investments, and more

The math tools we've been dealing with in this book run the gamut from very useful to somewhat more abstract. The probability and statistics we've dealt with in the past two chapters have pretty clear connections to real-life situations, such as test scores, flipping coins, and data in chemistry experiments. Skills like parametric graphing don't connect as clearly with the everyday concerns of the real world. In this chapter, we'll look at your calculator's financial tools, which have among the most obvious real-world applicability of any of the advanced calculator skills you've learned.

The financial tools on your calculator can calculate interest, mortgages, amortization, and depreciation, all of which are important to big financial decisions. We'll start with an overview of the several facets of a TI-83 Plus/TI-84 Plus' financial toolset. You'll learn about the TVM Solver, which is what we'll be using for all of this chapter's examples. I'll explain the different variables used in the TVM Solver and what each one means. We'll briefly explore some other financial functions that are

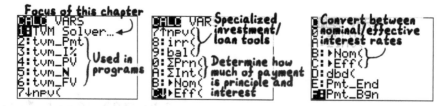

Figure 10.1 The 15 different options and tools in the Calculate tab of the Finance menu. This chapter will focus on the TVM Solver, although we'll briefly review a few other functions in section 10.2.3.

available but that we won't look at in any great depth in this chapter. Because the TVM Solver is pretty easy to use but versatile enough to cover a range of problems, we'll spend the majority of this chapter looking at those problems. You'll get to explore two problems covering interest on investments and two problems looking at the feasibility of taking out a mortgage from different angles.

By the time you reach the end of this chapter, you'll have the understanding to use the financial tools in your own life, as well as to help simplify the material in any basic finance class. To get you to that point, let's begin with an overview of the financial tools on your calculator, as well as the special financial variables they manipulate.

10.1 *Financial variables and tools*

All the financial tools and variables we'll be working with in this chapter are neatly organized in two tabs of a menu called, oddly enough, Finance. To find the Finance menu, you'll need to venture into the Apps (APPS) menu for the first time in this book. Although the Apps menu usually holds the names of applications, large programs that you can load from a computer or another calculator, the Finance menu always has a spot reserved at the top of the Apps menu. It's not technically an app, so it can't be deleted from your calculator or removed from the Apps menu. Anyway, press APPS and choose 1:Finance so you can get a good look at the Finance menu.

The first tab, Calculate (CALC), contains all the functions you can use to perform financial computations. You can see all 15 items in the Calculate tab in figure 10.1. We'll focus on the first item, 1:TVM Solver…, which can solve problems involving money borrowed or invested. I'll also briefly walk you through how you might use the bal(, ΣPrn(, and ΣInt(functions to further analyze mortgages, as well as convert between effective and nominal interest with ▸Nom(and ▸Eff(. The remaining functions and commands either are used in user-written programs that solve finance problems or are specialized, both of which are outside the scope of this chapter.

If you press ▶ from the Calculate tab of the Finance menu, you'll switch to the Variables (VARS) tab, shown in figure 10.2. Here you can see the seven variables used by the TVM Solver and other finance functions. All are related to borrowing and investing sums of money over time. To give you an advanced hint about the TVM Solver, you usually fill in six of these variables and ask the calculator to solve for the seventh missing variable. Here's what each of the seven means:

- N—The number of payments. For a 10-year loan paid monthly, N = 120. Notice that this isn't the same as the regular N variable.

Figure 10.2 The seven finance variables. The text explains more about what each of these seven variables is used for.

- I%—Percent interest for money invested or borrowed. Unlike most percentages on your calculator, where 0.05 would be 5%, you set I% to 5 to indicate 5%, or 3.5 for 3.5%.

- PV—The present value, which is the amount initially invested or borrowed.

- PMT—The amount paid at each payment.

- FV—The future value of the money, which is often 0 for loans (all paid up) or what you'll be solving for to see the yield of an investment.

- P/Y—Payments per year.

- C/Y—Number of times interest is compounded per year.

For the most common finance problems that you'll solve with your calculator's financial tools, all you need to know is how to use those seven variables with the TVM Solver. In the next section, we'll focus on using the TVM Solver effectively and then briefly touch on some of the more esoteric financial functions.

10.2 Solving finance problems

The TVM Solver on your calculator can be used to solve all sorts of problems, including payments and interest on loans, interest and yield on investments, and depreciation rates and values. Using it is straightforward: as summarized in more detail in the "TVM Solver in 60 seconds" sidebar, you go to 1:TVM Solver…, fill in six of the seven variables with known values, and solve for the missing variable. We'll walk through a series of four examples in this section, two of which involve investments and two of which concern mortgages (or loans). We'll conclude with a survey of the other important financial tools on your calculator and how you use them.

TVM Solver in 60 seconds

Start by pressing (APPS) and choosing 1:Finance and then 1:TVM Solver…. You'll see something resembling figure 10.3. Fill in six of the variables (see section 10.1 for the description of each variable), and choose whether payments are made at the end or beginning of each payment period. Move the cursor to the missing variable, and press (ALPHA) (ENTER) to solve for it. A black square appears on the left, next to the value computed.

The TVM Solver looks like figure 10.3 when you first use it. Like the Equation Solver (covered in chapter 2) and the Window menu, you use the (▼) and (▲) keys to move between items and use (CLEAR)/(DEL) and the number keys to erase existing values and type in new ones. To toggle between the END and BEGIN options for PMT, move the cursor to the desired option and press (ENTER).

AN IMPORTANT NOTE ON SIGNS   In the TVM Solver, money that you spend or put out is negative, and money that you get back is positive. For example, an amount invested in the PV slot is negative (you let go of money you invest), and the amount you get back at the end of the investment is positive. For loans and mortgages, the PV is positive, because you get the money that you borrow, and the PMT value is negative, because you need to give the bank money back to pay off the loan.

Figure 10.3   The TVM Solver. You fill in six of the seven variables, choose whether payments occur at the end or beginning of a pay period, and solve for the seventh variable.

Using the TVM Solver properly will be clearer once we work through some examples, so let's start with its most popular application: interest and yield on investments.

10.2.1   *Investments and interest*

The TVM Solver can solve any sort of problem where your money makes money—namely, investments. In this section, you'll work through two different investment examples. In the first problem, you'll figure out how much money you'll make from an investment, given that you know the initial investment amount, the interest rate, and the length of the investment. In the second example, you'll compute the interest rate you'd need to double your initial investment in five years.

FUTURE VALUE OF AN INVESTMENT

You're smart and careful with your money, and you manage to save quite a bit. Anticipating that you won't need to spend $20,000 of your savings for a few years, you invest it. The investment you choose is safe and fairly low-yield: the interest rate is 2%, compounded quarterly, and you get back your money plus interest after three years. To figure out how much you'll make at the end of two years, you turn to your trusty graphing calculator. You've used the TVM Solver many times before, so you fill in the values on the left side in figure 10.4.

Why pick the values you did?

- P/Y and C/Y are both 4. The interest is compounded quarterly (four times per year), and that interest is immediately added to the principle (the initial investment).

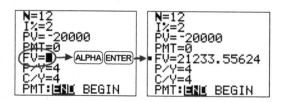

Figure 10.4   A $20,000 investment earns $1,233.56 over two years, compounded quarterly at 2%.

- Because your investment will accrue interest for three years, N = 12 (that's 3 years × 4 quarters). Be careful to always enter the number of payment periods as N, not the number of years.
- You won't be adding or removing any money from the investment during the three years, other than what interest adds, so PMT = 0.
- The interest rate is 2%, and therefore I% = 2 (not 0.02!).
- Your initial investment is $20,000, making PV = –20,000. It is important to remember to get the signs of your PV, PMT, and FV values correct. You're "losing" money when you invest, so PV is negative. You'll "gain" the original money plus the interest accrued at the end of the investment period, so you expect FV to be positive.

The interest is compounded at the end of each quarter, not the beginning, so you leave PMT at END. With the setup complete, you're ready to solve for the future value (FV) of your money at the end of the three years. Move the cursor to FV (as shown on the left in figure 10.4), and press (ALPHA) (ENTER) (solve). A value of 21233.55624 will appear next to FV: a positive number meaning you'll get back $21,233.56 after three years. Your three-year investment earned you $1,233.56.

How interest works

Compounded interest is computed through a well-known exponential formula. If you're taking a finance class or a math class where you're working with interest, you may recognize this formula. It computes the future value (*p*) given the initial value (*c*), the interest rate (*r*), the number of times the interest is compounded per year (*n*), and the number of years (*t*):

$$p = c \left(1 + \frac{r}{n}\right)^{nt}$$

p = future value, or what your calculator calls FV

c = initial value, present value, or PV

r = interest rate, expressed as a fraction instead of a percent (0.05 instead of 5%)

n = number of times the interest is compounded per year (C/Y)

t = number of years (your calculator uses N = t × C/Y)

You can also use the TVM Solver to figure out what kind of interest rate you'll need on an investment if you know how much you want to earn from the investment.

PICKING AN INVESTMENT

You can also solve an investment problem the other way around. You could decide how much you want to invest, how much money you want to make from the investment, and how long you want to invest for. Based on that information, you could figure out what interest rate you would need on your investment to meet your goal.

Figure 10.5   Figuring out that to double a $500 investment in 5 years, you need to find an interest rate of 13.88% (quite high!)

For this problem, you want to invest the modest sum of $500 and within five years get back $1,000, double your original investment. You find several investment opportunities where the interest will be compounded weekly, although each opportunity earns a different interest rate. You want to know what interest rate will let you double your money. Because you know the TVM Solver will help you find the answer, you pull out your calculator and open the TVM Solver from the Finance menu ((APPS) (1) (1)). You fill in the values shown on the left side in figure 10.5. P/Y and C/Y are both 52, because the interest is compounded weekly. You can type 5*52 (5 years of 52 weeks each) for N, and your calculator will replace it with the result, 260. As in the previous example, the PMT is 0 for an investment that you don't add to over time. PV is –500, because you're giving $500 to whatever you're investing in, and FV is 1000, because you want to get $1,000 back from your investment. As in the previous example, PMT is END, because the interest is compounded at the end of each week.

Fill in all the values as shown in figure 10.5, move the cursor to I%, and press (ALPHA) (ENTER). Your calculator will think for a second and spit out the result, marked by a square next to I%. As you can see, you would have to find an investment with a 13.88% interest rate to double your money in 5 years—a tall order indeed. If you scaled back your expectations, or considered a longer investment period, you might get a more realistic interest rate. Try setting FV to 650 instead of 1000, and you'll get a 5-year interest rate of 5.25%. Try doubling your money over 20 years instead (by setting N to $20 \times 52 = 1040$ and leaving FV at 1000), and you'll get an even more modest interest rate of 3.47%.

You've seen that the TVM Solver is handy to calculate properties of investments when you have money to spare. What about the reverse, when you're taking out a loan or mortgage where you need to borrow money and pay it back over time?

10.2.2   *Mortgages and loans*

Practically, mortgages and loans aren't quite the same thing. Both involve borrowing money, but with a mortgage, you have collateral against the money borrowed, you usually pay a flat amount when you take out the mortgage, and a mortgage is generally over a longer time period. But as far as your calculator is concerned, they're identical. In both cases, you're borrowing a fixed amount of money, you're charged an interest rate, you periodically make payments (often monthly), and you want to eventually reduce the money you owe to zero.

Because from the TVM Solver's point of view, mortgage and loan problems are identical, the skills you'll learn in this section apply to both types of calculations.

Although the first example uses a mortgage and the second example concerns a loan, the two could easily be interchanged. The only difference is that for the initial loan amount you put into PV (present value), you subtract the down payment, because you're not technically borrowing that money. The first problem will have you compute the monthly payments you'll be making on a 25-year mortgage. The second example asks you to calculate the maximum interest rate you can afford to pay, given the monthly payments you can realistically make.

COMPUTING MORTGAGE PAYMENTS

You take out a 25-year mortgage on a new house, and after the down payment, the loan amount is $450,000. You get a 3.5% interest rate on the mortgage, compounded monthly, and you'll also be making monthly payments on the mortgage. How much will each monthly payment be?

Because we're discussing this problem, you already know the TVM Solver can do the math for you. From the investment problems, you might even have some intuition into how to do it. Go to the Apps menu, choose 1:Finance, and then select 1:TVM Solver.... Fill in the values shown on the left side in figure 10.6. Start with the present value of the mortgage when you first take it out, PV = 450,000. The PV is positive because you're getting money at the beginning, unlike with an investment. The interest I% is 3.5 (not 0.035), FV = 0 (because you want the loan to be paid off after 25 years), and P/Y and C/Y are both 12 (monthly compounding and payments). You can type 300 or 12*25 for N; if you type the latter, your calculator will automatically simplify it to 300. Finally, move the cursor to PMT and press (ALPHA) (ENTER) (solve).

You can see from the right side in figure 10.6 that the resulting monthly payments are $2,252.81. Because signs are important in the TVM Solver, notice that PMT is negative, meaning you lose (pay) that $2,252.81 every month instead of getting that amount. Bonus problem: How much do you actually pay over 25 years to pay off the mortgage? You don't need any fancy financial tools for this; multiply PMT by N. You could type the numbers on the homescreen, but it would be more accurate to use the finance variables directly, as shown in figure 10.7.

Press (APPS) (1) (▶) to get to the Vars tab of the Finance menu, and choose 4:PMT. The PMT variable will be pasted to the homescreen. Type (×), and then return to the Vars tab of the Finance menu and choose 1:N. You'll have PMT*N on the screen, as shown in figure 10.7; press (ENTER). You end up paying $675,841.82 over the course of 25 years on your original $450,000 loan. As illustrated on the second line in figure 10.7, you can add that to the original $450,000 paid (via the PV variable, also in the Vars tab) to discover you lose an extra $225,841.82 to paying off the interest.

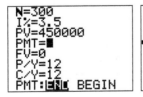
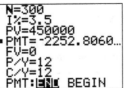

Figure 10.6 Finding that you need to pay $2,252.81 a month on a 25-year, $450,000 mortgage with 3.5% interest

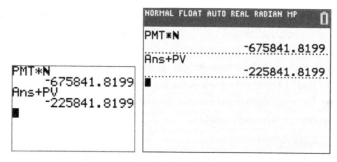

Figure 10.7 Calculating the total amount you pay in monthly payments on a 25-year mortgage. The second line adds the total amount to the present value (the amount borrowed) to determine how much you'll have paid in interest at the end of the 25 years. The two screenshots show the same thing; the right side is the result on a TI-84 Plus C Silver Edition, whereas the left side applies to the TI-83 Plus and TI-84 Plus calculators.

MAXIMUM INTEREST RATE ON A LOAN

You can also start with the monthly payments and compute the maximum interest rate you can afford on a loan. Because you're paying the interest instead of getting the interest (as you would with an investment), you want to find as low an interest rate as possible, unlike the second investment problem in section 10.2.1. In this case, you can afford $1,500 per month on a 10-year, $100,000 loan compounded monthly. What is the maximum interest rate that won't break your budget?

As with all the TVM Solver problems, start at the homescreen and press (APPS) (1) (1) to get to the 1:TVM Solver... tool. You'll be filling in the values shown on the left in figure 10.8. N is 10 × 12, or 120, because you'll be making monthly payments for 10 years. You'll be solving for I%, so skip it for now. PV is 100,000, PMT is –1500 (negative because you're giving instead of receiving the monthly payments), and FV is 0. Monthly payments and monthly compounding means P/Y and C/Y are both 12. Move the cursor back to I%, and press (ALPHA) (ENTER) to solve for I%.

The center screenshot in figure 10.8 shows the result: you could afford a loan with up to a 13.12% interest rate. That's extremely high, though, so let's fix the interest rate much lower and see what monthly PMT value you get. Set I% to 3, move the cursor

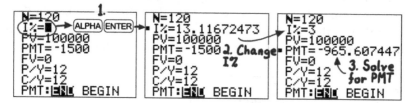

Figure 10.8 Calculating that if you can afford $1,500 per month for loan payments, you can afford a maximum of a rather steep 13.12% interest rate. If you limit your choices to a more manageable 3%, then your monthly payments drop to $965.61.

to PMT, and press (ALPHA) (ENTER) (solve). You'll see that a 3% interest rate means you'll need to pay $965.61 per month to pay off your loan.

Every problem that involves calculating the TVM can be solved with the TVM Solver the same way. Set up the six variables that you know, with negative PV, PMT, and FV values for money you pay out and positive values for money you get back. Move the cursor to the seventh missing value, and press (ALPHA) (ENTER) (solve) to find that value.

There are a few other tools, which I briefly mentioned in section 10.1 but haven't discussed yet.

10.2.3 *Other finance tools*

As mentioned in section 10.1 and shown in figure 10.1, the Finance menu contains many more tools than just the TVM Solver. Some of them are meant to be used in programs, but others are additional ways to solve finance problems. Although it's not likely that you'll need them unless you're in finance, it's worth knowing what extra financial tools your calculator offers.

Three functions help you understand more about mortgages and loans. All three functions require that you have already used the TVM Solver to set PV, **N**, I%, PMT, and FV. Here's what each of the three functions does and the arguments it takes:

- bal(n)—Given that the financial variables are already set, calculates how much of the *principle* is left to pay after n payments.
- ΣPrn(a,b)—Calculates the total amount of money paid back toward the mortgage or loan that went to paying the principle, between and including payment numbers a and b.
- ΣInt(a,b)—Like ΣPrn(but computes how much of the payments' total value went toward paying off the interest.

The end of this section will include a brief example using all three of these functions.

Nominal and effective interest rates are two related ways of measuring how much you earn on an investment (or savings) or pay on a loan. The nominal interest rate is usually the stated annual interest rate, such as a 5% APR (annual percentage [interest] rate) on a car loan. The effective interest rate is calculated using the nominal interest rate and the number of times the interest is compounded per year. The formula for converting between the two is a matter for your finance textbooks, but the functions to automatically convert between the two on your calculator are among the tools in this book:

- ▶Nom(rate,C/Y) converts an effective interest rate (rate) compounded C/Y times per year into a nominal interest rate.
- ▶Eff(rate,C/Y) does the opposite, converting a nominal interest rate (rate) into an effective rate compounded C/Y times per year.

As promised, let's take the 25-year mortgage example from this chapter and find out our financial standing after 10 years of payments.

BALANCE OF A MORTGAGE

In section 10.2.2, we worked through a problem with a 25-year, $450,000 mortgage. Given that it has a 3.5% interest rate, compounded and paid monthly, we determined that the monthly payments would be $2,252.81. In this problem, you'll continue that example to find out how much of the principle remains unpaid after 10 years and, of the payments made so far, how much went toward the principle and interest.

Start by returning to the TVM Solver and reentering the values from the original example. These were N = 300, I% = 3.5, PV = 450,000, FV = 0, P/Y = 12, C/Y = 12, and PMT set to END. Move the cursor back to PMT, and press (ALPHA) (ENTER); the left side in figure 10.9 illustrates what you should see. You needed to do this so all the finance variables would be properly set up. Quit back to the homescreen with (2nd) (MODE) so that you can test bal(, ΣPrn(, and ΣInt(.

As demonstrated in the center screenshot in figure 10.9, you want to give each of the three functions arguments that will make them examine the first 10 years of mortgage payments. For bal(, you specify how many payments have already been made to get the remaining principle balance, so 10 years × 12 payments per year. ΣPrn(and ΣInt(each take two arguments, the number of the first and last payments in the range we want to examine. We want to look at the total funds put toward paying off the mortgage between payment 1 and 10 × 12. Therefore, the three commands to enter are

```
bal(10*12)
ΣPrn(1,10*12)
ΣInt(1,10*12)
```

The bal(, ΣPrn(, and ΣInt(commands can all be typed by pressing (APPS) (1) (1) to get to the Calculate tab of the Finance menu, scrolling down to the function in question, and pressing (ENTER).

As you can see from figure 10.9, $315,129.54 of the original $450,000 remains unpaid after 10 years, even though you've already paid $270,336: $134,870.46 went toward the principle, whereas a *larger* sum, $135,466.27, paid off interest. Because you know the amount paid per payment from the PMT variable, and you know that 10 × 12 payment periods have passed, you can make sure your calculator has produced correct

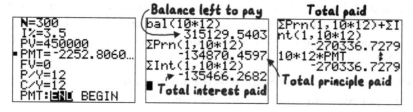

Figure 10.9 Calculating the balance of a mortgage's principle left to pay after 10 years, as well as the amount of the payments so far that has gone toward the principle and the interest. The center and right screenshots prove that the total funds paid toward interest and principle correctly sum to the total of all payments in those 10 years.

values for the portion paid toward the principle and interest. As shown on the right in figure 10.9, compute $\Sigma\text{Prn}(1,10*12)+\Sigma\text{Int}(1,10*12)$, and compare that to `10*12*PMT`. The two numbers should be the same, and they are.

The financial tools your calculator offers are straightforward; any complexity comes from the many different ways the tools can be used. You now have seen many examples of these tools in action, and you should be well prepared to solve any such academic or real-life financial calculations of your own.

10.3 Summary

This chapter introduced one of the toolsets most easily applied to the real world that your calculator offers: financial functions. We focused on time-value of money problems analyzed with your TI-83 Plus or TI-84 Plus' TVM Solver, exploring investments, loans, and mortgages. You learned how to solve for a minimum or maximum interest rate, figure out how much you'd need to pay per loan or mortgage payment, and compute the value of a long-term investment. We also looked at three functions that let you examine details of funds paid toward a loan or mortgage at any point while the mortgage is held and two others that convert between nominal and effective interest rates. You have all the skills you need to evaluate TVM problems on your own.

The conclusion of this chapter brings us to the end of part 3. Part 4 will begin with programming in chapter 11, a topic near and dear to my heart. My love of graphing calculators is deeply rooted in their power and capabilities as programmable devices, and I hope you'll pick up some of that enthusiasm as we walk through programming basics.

Going further with the TI-83 Plus/TI-84 Plus

This fourth and final part of this book covers some extra features and skills that although not immediately applicable to most math and science classes are still important. Your calculator is a powerful programming platform, and a broad introduction to what it can do starts off the part as chapter 11. If you have a new color-screen TI-84 Plus C Silver Edition, you'll want to read chapter 12 to learn about its unique tools and features. The final chapter of this book shows you how your calculator can connect to computers, calculators, sensors, and robots and looks forward toward the future of graphing calculators.

Part 4 starts with a chapter on programming, a condensed introduction designed to teach you enough to create simple math programs and games. I hope it will whet your appetite to explore my earlier book, *Programming the TI-83 Plus/TI-84 Plus*, and to make programs of your own.

Chapter 12 provides an overview of the TI-84 Plus C Silver Edition, the latest calculator in the TI-83 Plus/TI-84 Plus line. It offers a color screen and new math and graphing features, and this chapter will show you how to use the new tools to their fullest.

Chapter 13 ties the book together with a look at how your calculator can connect to other devices. You'll learn to download programs and apps to your calculator and how to share programs and variables with classmates' calculators. I'll show you how your calculator can connect to sensors for science experiments, control robots, and even network with other calculators. I'll leave you with a few thoughts on the future of graphing calculators and your own future in math, science, engineering, and technology.

Turbocharging math with programming

11

Programming is what made my personal passion for graphing calculators blossom. I started using a TI-82 in sixth grade and got my own TI-83 in seventh grade. I used calculators through about 12 years of school, and I've been helping people use graphing calculators for math for nearly the same amount of time. But discovering that a graphing calculator could be programmed like a computer helped me realize that far from being a specialized tool, a graphing calculator is actually a pocket computer—and quite a capable one at that.

Knowing how to do any sort of programming is an important skill to have, and graphing calculators can provide the perfect first step. Why should you learn calculator programming?

- Any kind of programming is great for refining your problem-solving skills and for teaching you to think more analytically.

- It's gratifying to develop an idea for a program and to successfully bring that idea to fruition.
- You may find that you enjoy the satisfaction of surmounting challenges, learning to optimize your programs to make them small and fast, and sharing your finished work with friends and users around the world.
- Calculator programs can give you a way to accelerate and check your math work and to gain a more intuitive understanding of the material.
- Calculator programming teaches you to think like a programmer and makes it easy to transition into almost any computer language.

From making math more fun and understandable to giving you a way to write games and learn computer languages, there's little reason not to experiment with calculator programming.

In this chapter, I'll give you a foundation for programming TI-BASIC, your calculator's built-in programming language. We'll start with a program called Hello World, the traditional first program taught to beginners in any language. Along the way, you'll learn what exactly a program is and how to create, edit, and run programs on your calculator. We'll continue with a Quadratic Formula solver, a popular type of program among math students and teachers alike. I'll then kick the chapter into high gear, showing you a broad swath of the programming commands available on your calculator and how you might use each one. We'll conclude by stepping back and reviewing what sort of programs you might want to create and how they can help you in math, on the SATs, and just having fun.

Of course, no single chapter can adequately cover something that normally takes an entire book. If this chapter piques your interest, I strongly recommend you take a look at another of my books, *Programming the TI-83 Plus/TI-84 Plus* (2012, Manning). First I need to give you a taste of why I love calculator programming, so let's start with your first program, a classic called Hello World.

11.1 *Hello World, your first program*

When you perform a series of math steps to solve a problem, you're using steps that you've been taught to get an answer. Typing in a few lines of math on your calculator's homescreen, you're giving your calculator instructions about how to help you calculate each of those steps. Although you may not realize it, from a series of homescreen calculations to a program that helps you check your work or speed up problems is a short leap. A *program* is a series of predefined instructions about how to manipulate data, use it, and act on it. On your calculator, *data* is often numbers, but it can be lists, strings, or even pictures.

The simplest kind of math program takes some input (say, the values of a, b, and c as variables A, B, and C), runs it through a set of calculations (for example, the Quadratic Formula), and prints out answers on the screen. Before I teach you how to do that, you need a few basic skills, all of which you'll learn in this section. First, you need to know how to create a new program on your calculator. Then I'll show you how to

Figure 11.1   The output (results) from your first program, Hello World, shortened to HIWORLD to fit on the screen. In this section, you'll learn about editing and running TI-BASIC programs while you create your first program.

give your program some contents, so that it will have something to do. Finally, I'll show you how to run the program (the result of your first program is shown in figure 11.1) and explain what happens when you do.

Let's get started with the first thing you need to know: what a program is and why you want to create one.

11.1.1 What's a program?

The easiest answer is that a program is a set of instructions to a computer (or in this case, your calculator). A program tells it how to automatically perform a set of steps. Applied to your calculator, this could be as simple as automating an annoying formula or as complex as an arcade game. Your calculator's programs are a series of instructions called *commands* that your calculator follows one at a time. In this section, you'll learn how to create the simplest possible program on your calculator.

There are hundreds or thousands of different programming languages, each of which has its own strengths and weaknesses. We'll be working with a language called *TI-BASIC*, which comes built-in on your TI-83 Plus or TI-84 Plus graphing calculator. The commands you'll use are similar to the math you've already been doing on the homescreen. TI-BASIC is called an *interpreted language*. This means you can immediately run a program after writing it, as opposed to a compiled language like C++ that requires an intermediate step between writing and running a program. TI-BASIC being an interpreted language also means your calculator will point you to any errors it finds in your program rather than crashing when you make mistakes.

Any program starts with an idea of what you want to create. For straightforward math programs, you first figure out what kind of math you want your program to perform and then what input data it will need and what output it will generate. Next, decide what variables will be necessary and what equations will be needed to calculate the values of the output variables from the input. Finally, write the program and test it.

The program you'll create in this section, Hello World, is about as simple as a program can get. It takes no input from the user (the person running the program) and performs no calculations. It does exactly one thing: display HELLO WORLD on the screen. Let's get to it.

11.1.2 Creating and writing a program

Once you know what sort of program you want to create, and you have a rough idea of how it will work, you can start writing it. You'll be working with TI-BASIC, your calculator's built-in language; you don't need a computer, a transfer cable, or indeed anything other than your calculator to write these programs. All your programming will take place inside the Prgm (Program) menu, which you can access with the (PRGM) key. Let's start there: quit to the homescreen if you were inside any other menu, and press (PRGM).

Creating and running programs, fast

1 Press (PRGM), move to the New tab, and press (ENTER).
2 Type the name of your program, which can be from one to eight letters and numbers in length and must start with a letter: for example, HELLO, FROGGER, or CALC2.
3 Press (ENTER) to create a new program with that name. You'll be in the program editor, where you can create your program by typing commands and math.
4 Quit with (2nd) (MODE) when you've finished creating your program.
5 Run your new program by pressing (PRGM), finding it in the Exec tab, and pressing (ENTER) (ENTER).

The Prgm menu has three tabs: Exec, Edit, and New (shown with the New tab highlighted in figure 11.2). If you choose any program from the Exec tab, that program's name is pasted to the homescreen; press (ENTER) again, and the program will run. The Edit tab contains the same list of programs as the Exec tab, but if you choose a program here, you'll go into the program editor, which lets you modify existing programs. Finally, the New tab is how you create a new program on your calculator. You can have as many programs as you want, as long as each program has a different name and there's enough space for your calculator to store them.

To create the Hello World program, go to the New tab in the Prgm menu, press (ENTER), and type the name HIWORLD. Remember that typing a long string of letters usually requires pressing (2nd) (ALPHA) to set Alpha Lock, but the New tab automatically starts with Alpha Lock set, indicated by the A cursor. You can type HIWORLD with the keys (^) (x²) (−) (7) (×) ( )) (x⁻¹). If you see Name=HIWORLD, as on the left in figure 11.3, press (ENTER) to go into the program editor. If the name isn't correct, you can use (CLEAR) or (DEL) to change it. Also, if you want to call the program something other than HIWORLD, that's fine too, as long as the name is one to eight characters long and starts with a letter.

```
EXEC EDIT NEW
1 Create New
```

Figure 11.2   The Prgm (Program) menu, showing the New tab selected. The Exec and Edit tabs list the programs you currently have on your calculator so you can run and modify them, respectively.

Figure 11.3   Creating a new program called HIWORLD. Entering the name (left) and typing the code for the program (right).

Inside the program editor, you'll see `PROGRAM:HIWORLD` at the top, which tells you which program you're editing. You want to type the command shown on the right side in figure 11.3:

`Disp "HELLO, WORLD"`

You can type `Disp`, a command used to display strings, numbers, lists, and matrices on the homescreen, by finding it in the program commands menu. While inside the program editor, press (PRGM), which opens a different set of menus than when you pressed it from the homescreen. Section 11.3 will teach you how to use the many commands in this menu. For `Disp`, press (▶) to get to the I/O tab, and choose `3:Disp`. Just as items you select in menus can be pasted into the Y= menu and the homescreen, the `Disp` command gets pasted into the program editor.

Next, add the string `"HELLO, WORLD"`. The double-quote symbol is (ALPHA) (+), the space is (ALPHA) (0), and you should know how to type the letters and the comma. When you finish, you should see something that looks like the right side in figure 11.3. Now you're ready to run your program!

11.1.3 *Testing the Hello World program*

Running a program makes your calculator follow the instructions you've given it via the commands in that program. For your Hello World program, the command `Disp "HELLO, WORLD"` asks the calculator to display a string on the screen, containing `HELLO, WORLD`. Because there are no more commands after that line, the program ends. If there were more lines, the calculator would keep executing the lines of the program, one by one.

To run the Hello World program, quit from the program menu by pressing (2nd) (MODE), if you didn't already. From the homescreen, press (PRGM), and staying in the first (Exec) tab, choose `HIWORLD`. If it's the only program you have on your calculator, this will be the only item in the Prgm menu; but if you have lots of programs, they'll be listed alphabetically, and you might have to scroll down to find `HIWORLD`. Once you find it, press (ENTER), which will paste `prgmHIWORLD` to the homescreen, as shown in figure 11.4. This tells the calculator to find the program named `HIWORLD` and run it. As with all functions and calculations on the homescreen, press (ENTER) to execute the program.

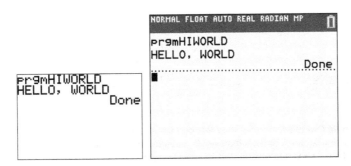

Figure 11.4 The Hello World program in action on a TI-84 Plus C Silver Edition (right) or any other TI-83 Plus or TI-84 Plus calculator (left). As you can see, it writes HELLO, WORLD to the homescreen and then prints Done.

You'll see the words HELLO, WORLD appear on the screen, as shown in figure 11.4 for the older TI-83 Plus and TI-84 Plus calculators and the new TI-84 Plus C Silver Edition. To signal that the program has run its course and reached the end, the word Done also appears on the right edge of the screen. If, however, you encounter an error such as ERR:SYNTAX, you'll have two options: 1:Quit and 2:Goto. If you choose Quit, you'll return to the homescreen, and on MathPrint calculators you'll see Error instead of Done. If you choose 2:Goto, then the calculator will open the program editor and show you roughly where in your program it thinks the mistake is.

The Hello World program is neither complicated nor a very good example of a useful math program, but it's a good first program to understand the mechanics of creating, editing, and running programs. Let's do an about-face and make a useful program to solve our favorite equation, the Quadratic Formula.

11.2 *Writing a Quadratic Formula solver*

A Quadratic Formula solver is a great first math program, and it's often the first math application that budding calculator programmers teach themselves. The Quadratic Formula is universally taught in algebra or geometry classes around the time when many students first receive their graphing calculators, and the program itself is short and simple. It demonstrates the framework of most short math programs: ask the user for values, calculate an answer by running those values through an equation, and display the results. Most important, when you finish typing what in this case is a short nine-line program, you have a tool that you can use in math class.

We've dealt with the Quadratic Formula in several previous chapters: it gives you the values of x that make a quadratic equation $ax^2 + bx + c$ equal to zero. Letters a, b, and c represent the three coefficients to a quadratic equation in math notation, corresponding to variables A, B, and C in TI-BASIC on your calculator. As a refresher, the general form of the Quadratic Formula is shown in figure 11.5, along with two examples worked through.

To solve the Quadratic Formula, a simple program should ask the user for values for a, b, and c, store them in A, B, and C, and then plug them into the Quadratic Formula solver and print out the roots. Unfortunately, there are complications. Suppose that $a = 1$, $b = 4$, and $c = 5$. When you do the math, you'll need to take the square root of the expression $4^2 - 4(1)(5) = 16 - 20 = -4$. As you know, taking the square root of a

$$x = \frac{-b \pm \sqrt{b^2 - 4ac}}{2a}$$

SOLUTION WITH REAL ROOTS
$a=1, b=2, c=1$

$$x = \frac{-2 \pm \sqrt{2^2 - 4*1*1}}{2*1} = \frac{-2 \pm \sqrt{0}}{2}$$

$$x = -1$$

SOLUTION WITH IMAGINARY ROOTS
$a=1, b=4, c=5$

$$x = \frac{-4 \pm \sqrt{4^2 - 4*1*5}}{2*1} = \frac{-4 \pm \sqrt{-4}}{2}$$

$$x = -2 \pm 1i$$

Figure 11.5 The Quadratic Formula for finding the roots of 0 = ax^2 + bx + c (top). The samples show a = 1, b = 2, c = 1 (left), which yields a single real root, and a = 2, b = 1, c = 2 (right), which yields distinct but imaginary roots.

negative number (here, −4) yields an imaginary result. Therefore, if $4ac > b^2$, then both roots are imaginary, because $b^2 − 4ac$ will be negative and the square root of a negative number is imaginary. If $b^2 = 4ac$, then the original quadratic equation has a double root, and if $b^2 > 4ac$, making $b^2 − 4ac$ greater than zero, the quadratic equation will have two distinct (different) real roots.

A Quadratic Formula solver more complex than the one we're creating here would detect double roots and imaginary roots and adjust accordingly. For your first math program, you'll write a simple solver that doesn't try to determine imaginary roots (but does warn you about them) and doesn't check for double roots. After you read this chapter and begin experimenting on your own (and perhaps give *Programming the TI-83 Plus/TI-84 Plus* a read), you'll be well equipped to modify this program yourself.

Let's start with creating and testing the Quadratic Formula solver.

11.2.1 Coding and testing the Quadratic Formula solver

In the spirit of having a handy tool to play with first and then learning the details of how it works, I'll first show you how to type and run the Quadratic Formula solver. You'll be mostly drawing on skills you've learned throughout this book, like typing numbers, letters, and symbols and finding functions inside menus. We'll then give the Quadratic Formula solver a spin with two sets of *a*, *b*, and *c* values.

Here's what the quadratic program looks like. You'll be creating a new program called QUAD and typing in these nine lines of source code:

```
PROGRAM:QUAD
:Prompt A,B,C
:If 4AC>B²
:Then
:Disp "IMAGINARY ROOTS"
:Else
:Disp (⁻B+√(B²-4AC))/(2A)
:Disp (⁻B-√(B²-4AC))/(2A)
:End
:Return
```

Before we go through how it works, test it. A few guidelines for typing this program are shown here:

- You can find If, Then, Else, End, and Return in the Ctl (Control) tab of the Prgm menu inside the program editor. Remember that (PRGM) displays a different set of tabs when you press it from inside the program editor instead of from the homescreen.
- In the Hello World example, you saw that Disp was in the second tab of the Prgm menu, I/O; Prompt is there too.
- The > symbol is in the Test menu, under (2nd) (MATH).
- Create this as a new program called QUAD, using the same process you went through for the Hello World program. Don't type the colons (:) at the beginning of each line, because the program editor displays those automatically.

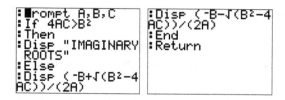

Figure 11.6 **The source code for the QUAD program, typed on a calculator. This is the same as the code presented in the text but shown on a calculator so you can make sure you typed it correctly.**

When you're satisfied that your program looks like the preceding code, you're ready to use it. If you're lost on typing any particular line, flip to section 11.2.2 for the line-by-line explanation of the code. Figure 11.6 shows this program typed on a calculator, if you want to see it in that form for comparison.

When you test the program, it will prompt you for three separate numbers: the values for the variables A, B, and C that it will plug into the Quadratic Formula solver. At each prompt, you can use the number, decimal point, and negative-sign keys to type a value; then press (ENTER). After you provide a value for C, the program will either display the two roots of the equation $ax^2 + bx + c$ or tell you the roots are imaginary.

Let's first try $a = 2$, $b = 1$, and $c = -3$, which correspond to the polynomial $2x^2 + bx - 3$. Press (PRGM) from the homescreen, pick QUAD, and, when prgmQUAD is pasted to the homescreen, press (ENTER) to run it. You'll be prompted for A, B, and C, as shown on the left in figure 11.6. Type (2) (ENTER) for A, (1) (ENTER) for B, and (–) (3) (ENTER) for C. If all is well, you should get the two roots 1 and –1.5, as shown on the left in figure 11.7. If anything goes wrong, such as an ERR:SYNTAX or another error message appearing, double-check that your code matches the code given. You can select the program from the Edit tab of the Prgm menu to view and modify its source code.

Let's also try values that will yield imaginary roots. Run the program again, and enter the values A=5, B=4, and C=3. This is the equivalent of finding the values of x where $5x^2 + 4x + 3 = 0$. If your results match the right side in figure 11.7, then the program is working properly. As we'll explore momentarily, the program recognizes that because B²-4AC ($4^2 - 4 \times 5 \times 3 = 16 - 60 = -44$) is less than zero, it will have to take the square root of a negative number, and thus both roots will be imaginary.

But how exactly is it figuring that out? I'll tell you, and I'll also explain a little more about typing each line of the program in case you got lost.

11.2.2 *Understanding the Quadratic Formula solver*

The best way to understand how the Quadratic Formula solver works is to do exactly what the calculator does when it runs the program: examine the program line by line.

Figure 11.7 **Testing the Quadratic Formula solver for a polynomial with two real, distinct roots (left) and imaginary roots the program detects but doesn't calculate (right)**

There are nine lines, plus the PROGRAM:QUAD at the top, and each plays a role in how the completed program works.

Let's start with the first line:

PROGRAM:QUAD

This first line isn't a piece of the source code; it's the name of the program. The TI-BASIC editor displays the name at the top of every program, so I did the same thing.

The first line of code of this sample program is a Prompt command:

[Line 1] :Prompt A,B,C

This instructs the calculator to prompt, or ask, the user for three variables named A, B, and C. Commands, sometimes also called functions, consist of a name and take one or more arguments. Indeed, commands are just like the math functions you've been using throughout this book. The arguments to a function can be inside parentheses or, as with Prompt, placed after the command. This particular Prompt has three arguments, A, B, and C. Users are asked to enter a number at each of the three prompts that appear, one each for A, B, and C. If they type anything that isn't a number, the calculator produces an error message. After this command runs, the three values the users entered are stored in variables A, B, and C. You can find the Prompt command in the I/O tab of the Prgm menu.

The second line of the program is a conditional statement, indicated by the If at the beginning of the line:

[Line 2] :If 4AC>B^2

Every If is followed by a statement that must evaluate to either true or false. True indicates the conditional statement that follows is correct, and false indicates it's incorrect. For example, if 4AC is greater than B^2, then the statement 4AC>B^2 is true; otherwise, it's false. Conditional statements dictate which pieces of the program, or code, are executed. If this case, the section between Then and Else is run only if the condition evaluates to true, whereas the section from the Else to the End is run only if the condition is false. If can be found in the Ctl tab of the Prgm menu.

The Then on the third line, therefore, marks the beginning of the code to run if the condition is true or if the roots will be imaginary because B^2-4AC will be less than zero. Then can be found under (PRGM) (2).

The fourth line displays the string "IMAGINARY ROOTS":

[Line 4] :Disp "IMAGINARY ROOTS"

As you learned, you can type Disp by pressing (PRGM) (▶) (3), and the quotation mark is (ALPHA) (+).

The Else on the fifth line marks the boundary between the true and false sections of code for the conditional on line 2. If the condition on line 2 is true, the calculator skips directly from Else to End and continues executing after End. If the condition is false, however, it skips directly from Then to Else and executes the code between Else and End instead of skipping over it. You can find Else in the Ctl tab of the Prgm menu.

Lines 6 and 7 apply the Quadratic Formula solver to A, B, and C, calculating the two possible roots:

```
[Line 6] :Disp (⁻B+√(B²-4AC))/(2A)
[Line 7] :Disp (⁻B-√(B²-4AC))/(2A)
```

The calculator needs two separate equations because it doesn't know what the ± we usually write in the quadratic formula is; you must explicitly tell it to calculate the + case and the − case. Remember to keep the negative ((⊟)) and subtraction ((−)) symbols straight.

The final two lines end the conditional statement and then end the program:

```
:End
:Return
```

End marks the end of the conditional that started with If on line 2 and continued with Then and Else. Return tells the calculator that the current program has completed and that it can "return" you to the homescreen (or, as you'll later learn, to another program that called this program). End is under (PRGM) (7), and Return is near the bottom of (PRGM), at item E. To save time, you can press (PRGM) and then (▲) until you reach it.

I encourage you to play around with this program, plug in different values for A, B, and C, and try to modify the program. Don't worry about breaking the program; if you mess it up terribly, you can easily retype it from the code in this book. See if you can get it to calculate those imaginary roots! The Quadratic Formula solver is handy in many math classes, so it might be something that finds a permanent home on your calculator.

You've now seen two programs in action: the Hello World program that introduced you to editing and running programs, and the Quadratic Formula solver that showed you how math programs can be made. We're now going to work through an intense crash course in the many programming-specific commands your calculator offers. As you've seen in this section, most programs are sprinkled with exactly the same kind of math you might find on the homescreen, and programming isn't such a huge departure from what you've been doing already.

11.3 A crash course in programming commands

Teaching you all about programming would (and does!) take an entire book, calculator programming in TI-BASIC included. But if you're willing to do some experimentation on your own to understand how programs are constructed, I can give you a quick introduction to some of the useful commands your calculator offers. Together with the math you already know from working through the rest of this book, you can use programs to solve and check problems faster. By the end of this section, you'll know most of the programming-specific commands available on your TI-83 Plus or TI-84 Plus calculator, along with some pointers on how to put them together into working programs.

I've divided the programming commands into four groups. The commands in each group are related in some way, either because they're used together or because they do similar things. You'll learn what each group of commands does and how to use them, and then we'll work through an example of each. Here are the four groups:

- *Input and output*—These are commands that ask the user for a value and then store that value into a variable, as well as commands that display things on the screen.
- *Conditionals*—These commands let the calculator make decisions by testing equalities and inequalities.
- *Menus, labels, and jumps*—Normally, programs execute linearly, meaning the calculator runs each line of the program one at a time, starting at the top and ending at the bottom. With these commands, you can make it jump around to a different part of the program.
- *Loops*—Sometimes you want to repeat a section of a program several times. These commands let you create loops that run a specific number of times and loops that continue until some conditional becomes true.

We'll start with input and output. The Hello World program used one of the output commands, `Disp`, and you saw both `Prompt` and `Disp` in the Quadratic Formula solver.

11.3.1 *Input and output*

Input and output commands are used to let the program communicate with the user, the person running the program on their calculator. Input commands let the user type in numbers or strings and store the values into variables that the program can use. Output commands display information back to the user. All the input and output commands you'll learn in this section work on the homescreen, not the graphscreen, but if you decide to pursue programming further, you'll find that you can make more advanced graphical programs on the graphscreen.

A list of the input and output commands you'll want to know for simple programs is provided as table 11.1. `Disp` and `Output` are used for output, whereas `Input` and `Prompt` are input commands. `ClrHome` is sort of an output command, in that it clears the screen to make room for more things to be displayed. `Prompt` is sort of an input command, in that it lets your program wait for the user to press (ENTER) before it will continue. The third column of table 11.1 shows an example of each command in action. All these commands can be found in the I/O tab (the second tab) of the Prgm menu, but only if you're inside the program editor already.

As you've seen throughout this book, examples help to make everything clearer, so let's work through an example that exercises some of these new commands. This program asks you to type your name and your age and displays them back.

Table 11.1   Input and output commands. These can all be found in the I/O tab of the Prgm menu if you're inside the program editor.

Command	Description	Usage
ClrHome	Clears the homescreen and resets the cursor for Disp to the top row.	`:ClrHome`

Disp	Displays a number, string, matrix, list, or line of text. If you separate several items with commas, each will go on a line of its own. Strings are left-aligned on the LCD screen; all other items are right-aligned.
	
	`Disp number`
	`Disp variable`
	`Disp string`
	`Disp item_1,item_2,…`
		`:Disp 32`
		`:Disp "HELLO, SARA"`
		`:Disp 5,L₁,[A],"CODE"`

Input	Displays a string and then waits for the user to type in a value to store in a string, variable, matrix, or list.
	
	`Input "STRING TO DISPLAY",variable`
	`Input variable`
		`:Input "VALUE:",X`
		`:Input "HOW MANY?",N`
		`:Input M`

Output	Displays a number, string, numeric variable, matrix, or list at a specified row and column on the homescreen. Row can be 1 to 8 characters; column can be 1 to 16 characters. On the TI-84 Plus C Silver Edition, the maximum row is 10 and the maximum column is 26.
	
	`Output(row,column,item_to_display)`
		`:Output(4,7,"ROSE")`
		`:Output(8,15,42)`
		`:Output(7,2,Str5)`

Pause	Stops execution and waits for the user to press (ENTER). Optionally, can be given a string, number, or variable to display during the pause. If the item is a long string, list, or matrix, the user can scroll left, right, up, and down.	`:Pause`
		`:Pause 3`
		`:Pause "PRESS ENTER"`
		`:Pause [C]`
		`:Pause ∟ALIST`

Prompt	Displays the name of a variable, and asks the user to enter a value for that variable. Works with numeric variables, strings, lists, and matrices.
	
	`Prompt variable`
	`Prompt variable1,variable2,…`
		`:Prompt X`
		`:Prompt Str8`
		`:Prompt [C]`
		`:Prompt L₄`

EXAMPLE PROGRAM: GREET

Let's try a program that uses Input, Prompt, Disp, and Pause. We'll call it GREET, because it will ask you for your name and age and then say hello to you. Here's the source code for this program:

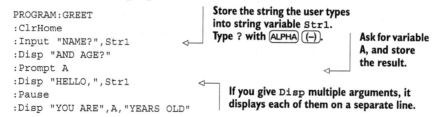

```
PROGRAM:GREET
:ClrHome
:Input "NAME?",Str1
:Disp "AND AGE?"
:Prompt A
:Disp "HELLO,",Str1
:Pause
:Disp "YOU ARE",A,"YEARS OLD"
```

Store the string the user types into string variable Str1. Type ? with (ALPHA) (–).

Ask for variable A, and store the result.

If you give Disp multiple arguments, it displays each of them on a separate line.

Figure 11.8 Testing the GREET program on a TI-84 Plus. I typed CHRISTOPHER for my name and 25 for my age. In the left screenshot, the calculator got to the Pause command; when you press (ENTER) to proceed past the Pause, the rest of the program (as shown on the right) is executed.

Try to type this short seven-line program on your own; you should know pretty much everything you need. The Str1 variable can be found under (VARS) (7) (1). If you need help creating a new program or running a program, you can refer back to section 11.1.

When you're satisfied that you've typed this program properly, press (2nd) (MODE) to return to the homescreen, and then find GREET in the Exec tab of the Prgm menu. Press (ENTER) once to paste prgmGREET to the homescreen, and press (ENTER) again to run the program. The program first asks you for your name, and when you type it and press (ENTER), it asks for your age. When you type your age and press (ENTER), you should see something like the left side in figure 11.8. The run indicator (dots in the upper-right corner) should be flashing on and off, which means the program is at a Pause command. Press (ENTER) to continue past the Pause, and the screen should change to the right side in figure 11.8. Of course, the name and age will be different.

What if you want your program to make decisions based on the values of variables? Let's look at conditionals, which do just that.

11.3.2 *Conditional statements*

A program that can only execute commands in sequence, the same way every time it's run, isn't a very powerful program. But if you can make the program examine the values of variables and execute different parts of the program depending on those values, you can make a program do a lot more. For example, the Quadratic Formula solver from section 11.2 makes a decision about whether the roots of the given polynomial will be real or imaginary. The GREET program we just looked at might display different greetings based on the age the user types in.

> **TRUE AND FALSE** Conditionals use tests like the ones you learned about in section 2.6. When your calculator computes something like 3=3, it gets the answer 1, which means true. Computing 4>5 produces the answer 0, which means false (because it's false to claim that 4 is greater than 5). In your programs you'd use something like X=3 for your conditions or even X>Y or N≤2X.

There are four commands involved in conditionals, listed in table 11.2. You need to use these commands together; you can create three types of conditional statements. I'll explain the three ways you can use conditionals, and then we'll look at an example of conditionals in action. Here are the three things you can do with conditionals (everything in italics like *condition* is just a placeholder for actual code):

- By itself, If *condition* executes the single following line when *condition* is true and skips the following line if *condition* is false.
- Code that looks like this runs all the lines between Then and End if *condition* is true or skips all of it if *condition* is false:

```
:If condition
:Then
:code run if condition is true
:can be any number of lines
:End
```

- If you want to run one set of code if *condition* is true and another set of code if *condition* is false, you can use code like this:

```
:If condition
:Then
:code run if condition is true
:can be any number of lines
:Else
:code run if condition is false
:can be any number of lines
:End
```

Table 11.2   Conditional and control-flow commands, all of which can be found in the Ctl tab of the Prgm menu when you're in the program editor. These all are used to let programs make decisions.

Command	Description	Usage

If	Evaluates a comparison or conditional statement and determines if it's true or false. If can be used to run or not run a single line of code, or, with Then/End or Else/Then/End, multiple lines of code.
	
	If *condition*
		`:If X<0`
		`:Disp "NEGATIVE"`
		`:If N=42`
		`:Then`
		`:X+1→X`
		`:3N→N`
		`:End`

Then	Separates the If statement from a block of two or more statements you want to run when the If's condition is true. The block must end with End.	`:If X>3 and X<6`
		`:Then`
		`:ClrHome`
		`:Disp "X IS 4 OR 5?"`
		`:End`

Else	Marks the end of the true block of code and the beginning of the false block of code for an If/Then/Else/End conditional. Also the end of the true block of an If/Then/End conditional.	`:If X=2`
		`:Then`
		`:Disp "X IS 2"`
		`:Else`
		`:Disp "X IS NOT 2"`
		`:End`

End	Marks the end of a Repeat, While, or For loop or the end of the false block for an If/Then/Else/End conditional.	`:For(R,⁻10,10,2)`
		`:Disp R`
		`:End`

Let's try a program that uses the most complex of the three conditional constructs to compare two different values the user enters. It will combine conditionals with input and output commands from section 11.3.1.

EXAMPLE: EQUALITY TESTER

The example in this section will compare two variables to see if they're equal. It will ask the user to type in two numbers and then display EQUAL or NOT EQUAL. Figure 11.9 illustrates how this program "flows" in a diagram. We'll call this program EQUAL-ITY, which at eight characters long is the longest name a TI-83 Plus or TI-84 Plus program can have. Here's the code for it:

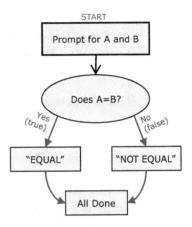

Figure 11.9　The flow of execution in the EQUALITY **program. It always first asks the user to type in values for** A **and** B**. Next, it makes a decision depending on whether the condition** A=B **is true or false. After it displays either** EQUAL **or** NOT EQUAL**, it finishes.**

```
PROGRAM:EQUALITY
:Prompt A,B
:If A=B
:Then
:Disp "EQUAL"
:Else
:Disp "NOT EQUAL"
:End
```

Type this code in program EQUALITY on your calculator, using the commands in the Ctl and I/O tabs of the Prgm menu. The = sign can be found in the 2nd Math menu, and you know where everything else is. When you're ready to give it a try, quit to the homescreen as with previous programs, enter the Prgm menu, and select EQUALITY. When the name is pasted to the homescreen, press (ENTER) to run the program.

Try out values that are equal, like 5 and 5 or –104.2 and –104.2. Try out unequal values, like 2.5 and √3. You'll see that equal values for A and B make only the code between Then and Else execute. If you enter different values, then only the code between Else and End runs, because A=B is false. Figure 11.10 shows two examples of the EQUALITY program in action, one on a TI-83 Plus/TI-84 Plus and one on a TI-84 Plus C Silver Edition.

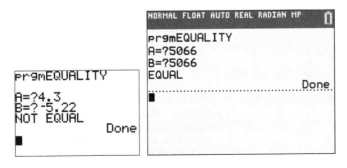

Figure 11.10　Using a program to test if two numbers are equal, to demonstrate conditionals in programs. The same program is run on a TI-84 Plus (left) and a TI-84 Plus C Silver Edition (right). The two numbers on the left aren't equal, whereas the two on the right are equal.

You still only know how to make programs that start at the beginning and end when they reach the bottom, although now you know how to make them skip over sections of code. What if you want a program to jump backward or to an arbitrary location in the code?

11.3.3 *Menus, labels, and jumps*

You've seen menus in every chapter of this book. *Menus* are lists of options that do something different depending on which option you choose. You can put a simplified form of these same menus in your TI-BASIC programs. Simplified how? In that they have only one tab, and they can't scroll (which means a maximum of seven options in a menu). When you choose an option in these menus, execution has to jump to some specific part of your program. Therefore, to use menus, you need something else: a way to mark specific lines of code in your program with names.

In this section, you'll learn about labels, jumps, and menus. You'll also see the two commands that make a program stop in its tracks, even if there are more lines of code after that command. The most important concept is that the Goto and the Menu(commands, both described in table 11.3, are forms of jumps. The Goto command takes the name of a Lbl as an argument and always jumps to the Lbl with that name (see figure 11.11). The Menu(command can have between one and seven options and can therefore jump to up to seven different Lbls depending on which option from the menu the user picks. The Lbl command is what acts as a marker or flag in the program. Every Lbl needs a unique name, which can be one or two letters or numbers.

Peruse table 11.3 for the syntax for Goto, Lbl, and Menu(. You'll also see two other commands, Return and Stop, which are used to end programs. The difference between the two is important only if you use subprograms, which I won't have space to teach you about in this chapter. You should almost always use Return where you want your program to stop. If the calculator goes past the last line of the program, it also automatically ends the program, so you don't have to put Return as the last line (although you can if you want).

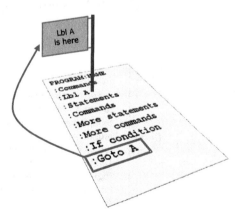

Figure 11.11   One way to think about labels and jumps. Labels are like a flag stuck in the program, marking a place that the calculator can jump to. A jump or Goto command tells it to find a specific flag and go to it.

Table 11.3 Labels, jumps, and menus, plus ways to end a program. These can all be found in the Ctl tab of the Prgm menu when you're inside the program editor.

Command	Description	Usage

Goto	Jumps forward or backward to a named label in the same program and continues executing there. Throws an error if the label isn't found.
	
	Goto *labelname*
		`:Goto NX`
		`:Lbl 1`
		`:...code...`
		`:Goto AA`
		`:Lbl NX`
		`:...code...`

Lbl	Marks a spot in the program to which a Goto can jump. Execution flows straight through this command if there is code before it.
	
	Lbl *labelname*
		`:5→M`
		`:Lbl A`
		`:M^4→M`
		`:If M<999999`
		`:Goto A`

Menu(	Draws a menu of one to seven items with a title. Lets the user use the arrows, number keys, and (ENTER) key to select an item. Each item in the menu, when selected, makes the program jump to a named Lbl.
	
	Menu("TITLE","OPTION 1",*label_1*
	[,"OPTION 2",*label_2*,...]
		`:Menu("MY GAME 1.0",`
		`➥ "PLAY",P,"HELP",`
		`➥ H,"QUIT",Q1)`

Return	Exits from the current program to the program that called it. If it was run from the homescreen or shell, returns there instead.	`:Return`
Stop	Exits from this program and every program that called this program back to the homescreen.	`:Stop`

These commands can be confusing if you haven't worked with other programming languages before, so let's look at an example. This one will ask you for three numbers and then perform one of three different calculations and show you the result.

EXAMPLE: PICKING AN EQUATION

This example program requests variables U, V, and W from the user. It then offers to calculate one of three different equations: U+V+W, UVW, or $(U+V)\sqrt{(W)}$. It uses a Menu(command for the options, which means it needs three different labels for the different equations. After displaying any of the three results, it uses Goto commands to go to Lbl Q, where it displays COMPLETE and then Return. This program has three different paths of execution it can take and four different named labels in the program: AA, BB, CC, and Q.

As always, we'll start with the code:

```
PRGM:MENU
:ClrHome
:Prompt U,V,W
:Menu("EQUATION:","U+V+W",AA,"UVW",BB,"(U+V)√(W)",CC,"SKIP",Q)
:Lbl AA
:Disp U+V+W
```

```
:Goto Q
:Lbl BB
:Disp UVW
:Goto Q
:Lbl CC
:Disp (U+V)√(W)
:Lbl Q
:Disp "COMPLETE"
:Return
```

> Goto Q followed
> immediately by Lbl Q would
> be a wasted command.

As with each of the previous example programs, type this on your calculator (as a program named MENU) so you can give it a try. Remember that all the programming commands are found in the first two tabs of the Prgm menu when you're inside the program editor, and that all the new commands from this section are in the first (Ctl) tab.

When you finish typing this program into your calculator, quit to the homescreen, pick the program named MENU, and run it. You'll first be asked to type in three numbers; I picked 5, 10, and 14.5, as you can see on the left side in figure 11.12. The menu that appears next is in the center of the same figure. I picked the third and most complex of the equations, which made the output shown on the right side in figure 11.12 appear. Notice that there's an extra option in the menu, SKIP, which if chosen jumps straight to Lbl Q. The other interesting thing to note is that the calculator will execute "through" a Lbl command, meaning if it encounters a Lbl in the course of normal line-by-line execution instead of from a Menu(or Goto command, it will ignore it and keep going.

You could make your program repeat the same section of code over and over by putting a Lbl at the beginning and a Goto at the end, but there are better ways to repeat the same code. In the following section, you'll learn about the three types of loop commands.

11.3.4 Loops

To repeat a section of code over and over, you use a type of programming concept called a loop. You can use loops on your calculator to create a section of code that is repeated a given number of times, such as 3, 10, or 9,001 times. You can also create loops that repeat while a condition is true or until some condition becomes true. You'll use three commands to create these loops on your calculator: For(, Repeat, and

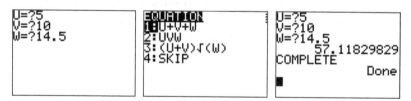

Figure 11.12 Testing the MENU program. It first asks you for values for U, V, and W using the Prompt command, shown on the left. The menu at the heart of the program is shown in the center, and the right side shows what happens if you pick the third option from the menu.

While. There's a fourth command that you use to mark the end of a loop: End (the same End used with If, Then, and Else).

I'll show you the three loop commands first, listed in table 11.4. Each one is placed at the start of a loop and tells the calculator how this loop should behave:

- The For(command is for loops that should run a specific number of times. More specifically, For(loops have start, end, and step values. What does this mean? You choose a variable (say, X), and the calculator runs the loop the first time (called an iteration) with X=start. When it reaches End, it loops back up to the For(line, adds step to X, and runs the loop again. It keeps adding step to X each time it loops, until X>end, when it stops.
- As the name suggests, While continues looping *while* its condition remains true. The condition is just like a condition used for If, and it can be true or false. While checks the condition before it runs the first iteration of the loop, so if the condition is false when it starts, it jumps directly to the code after the While's corresponding End.
- Repeat loops *until* its condition becomes true. Unlike While, it always runs the loop for at least one iteration, even if the condition is already true when it starts.

You can see more details about each loop command in table 11.4, along with arguments to the command and some sample code.

Table 11.4 Commands for creating loops. While, For(, and Repeat start loops, and End always marks the end of a loop. You can nest loops inside each other. All these commands can be found in the Ctl tab of the Prgm menu if you're inside the program editor.

Command	Description	Usage
End	Marks the end of a Repeat, While, or For loop.	:For(R,⁻10,10,2) :Disp R :End
For(	Loops a fixed number of times, modifying a variable called the loop variable on each iteration. For(loops end with an End command and can contain zero or more commands inside the body of the loop. For(*variable*,*start*,*end*[, *step*])	:For(X,1,10) :Disp X :End :For(M,3.0,0.5,⁻0.1) :N+M→N :End
Repeat	A loop that continues to execute until the specified condition becomes true ("repeat until..."). The condition is checked at the end of each iteration, so the loop always runs at least once. Repeat *condition*	:Repeat K=105 :getKey→K :End :Disp "ENTER PRESSED"
While	Begins a loop that loops only while the given condition is true. The condition is checked at the beginning of each loop, unlike Repeat, so it might be run zero times. While *condition*	:1→X :While X<999 :2X→X :End

Let's look at the fourth and final example in this intensive introduction to the important TI-BASIC programming commands you should know. You'll try out a program that counts to 10 three different ways, using For(, While, and Repeat loops.

EXAMPLE: COUNTING TO 10

On the surface, a program that counts to 10 isn't the most useful program you could possibly write, but it's good for demonstrating the similarities and differences between the three different types of loops. The For(loop is the easiest to understand, starting variable X at X = 1 and ending at X = 10, with a step of one per iteration. The While loop displays X, adds 1 to X in each iteration, and continues while X < 11. It stops when X gets to 11, so 10 is the last number it displays. The Repeat loop repeats until X > 10, so 10 is the last value displayed there too.

The code for the LOOPS program is shown here. The three loop commands can all be found in the Ctl tab of the Prgm menu if you're in the program editor. Remember from chapter 2 that the inequality symbols are in the Test menu, under 2nd MATH :

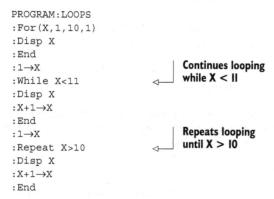

```
PROGRAM:LOOPS
:For(X,1,10,1)
:Disp X
:End
:1→X
:While X<11          Continues looping
:Disp X              while X < 11
:X+1→X
:End
:1→X
:Repeat X>10         Repeats looping
:Disp X              until X > 10
:X+1→X
:End
```

Once you type this program into your calculator, test it, as you have with all five programs thus far in this chapter. It should count to 10 three times, as you can deduce from examining the code:

- The first loop is the For(loop, which starts at the For(command and ends at the first End.
- The next loop is the While loop. You start by setting X to 1, its starting value, outside the loop. The loop continues while X < 11; inside the body of the loop, the program displays X and then adds 1. When X gets to 11, the program continues on the line after the second End.
- The final loop is the Repeat loop. Once again, you set X to 1 before the loop starts. The conditional on the loop is X > 10, which means it repeats until X > 10. The body of the loop is identical to the While loop: it displays X and then adds 1.

You can use loops for all kinds of programs of your own, from math algorithms to games and utilities. Together with the other commands you learned about in this section, you can create programs useful in situations from math classes to standardized tests, plus of course your own enjoyment and edification.

11.4 Putting it all together: programming, SATs, math, and more

Let's take a step back from the intricate details of programming. You know how to make your calculator do all kinds of math, and now you know how to make it do your bidding via programs. I've mentioned several times that you can use this for purposes as diverse as making programs to help you in math and games to entertain yourself and your friends. You've also seen my arguments about the importance of programming in general as a skill that everyone should know. Calculators are a great tool for learning programming, both for the sake of calculator programming itself and to understand how to think like a programmer. In this section, we'll look at how specifically this new skill can make your life better.

SAT PROBLEMS

Say you're taking the math portion of the SAT, and you encounter this question: "How many integers between 10 and 500 are divisible by both 3 and 4?" You could figure out a hard question like this by hand, and you should know how to do so. If you want to check yourself, though, you can write a two-minute calculator program to check your answer. Here's how I'd do this one:

```
:0→X
:For(A,10,500,1)
:If fPart(A/3)=0 and fPart(A/4)=0
:X+1→X
:End
:Disp X
```

Variable X tracks how many numbers are found.

The and command joins two conditionals together, and the compound conditional is true only if both halves are true.

What? Let me explain. You want to count something, namely the number of integers between 10 and 500 that are divisible by both 3 and 4. That sounds like you could loop from 10 to 500, stepping by 1; you'll use A for that. You'll use X to keep track of how many integers you found that match the given criteria. Inside the loop, you'll only add 1 to X if A is divisible by both 3 and 4. You use an If, of course, but the tricky part of this program is checking whether a number is divisible by some other number. You use fPart(, which you saw in section 2.4. It gets the fractional part of a number, so because 10/3 is 3.3333..., fPart(10/3) = 0.3333.... Whenever the fractional part of the quotient A/3 is 0, A is cleanly divisible by 3; the same idea is true for dividing by 4. The and joins two parts of a conditional. It can be found in the Logic tab of the Test menu (2nd MATH).

If you run this program, you'll find that there are 43 such numbers. If you get to be skilled at programming, this sort of quick throwaway program shouldn't take more than one or two minutes to write, and it might be a good way to use your time to check complex problems if you finish a section early. I remember when I took the SATs, my calculator was littered with such tiny programs afterward.

I should mention that there's another way math programs can help you on the SATs. At the time of writing, you're allowed to bring programs into the test on your calculator, so you can write yourself as many programs as you like that solve or check common problems. You can also find many such programs freely available online (see www.ticalc.org/pub and www.cemetech.net/programs).

MATH TESTS

If your teacher lets you use a graphing calculator on math tests, you can use the SAT technique for regular math tests as well. Anywhere you need to quickly check an answer that requires counting a lot of items or trying many possibilities is a good candidate for a throwaway program. The SAT math example is a problem where you need to count a lot of items. For a problem where you need to examine many possibilities, consider needing to find two numbers, *a* and *b*, where $a + b = 48$ and $ab = 495$. Your calculator can easily find those numbers for you:

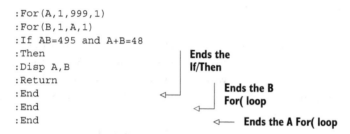

```
:For(A,1,999,1)
:For(B,1,A,1)
:If AB=495 and A+B=48
:Then                          Ends the
:Disp A,B                      If/Then
:Return
:End                                  Ends the B
:End                                  For( loop
:End                            Ends the A For( loop
```

This program will try every pair of numbers up to 999 × 999 to find the *a* and *b* values you need. It uses and in a conditional again and employs two nested For(loops. The outer one tries one value of A for lots of different B values. The inner loop tests all the Bs that could go with that A, from 1 to A. It stops at A instead of also going to 999 so that you test every possible pair of numbers once instead of twice.

LEARNING MATH CONCEPTS

You can spend more time perfecting and polishing programs to help you with math assignments, and the effort you spend creating such programs will help cement the concepts into your brain. If you create a program that solves some kind of problem, you must learn every detail of how to solve those problems to do so. Whether you create math programs primarily for the purpose of making your assignments easier or teaching yourself, in the end you'll wind up doing both.

WRITING GAMES

I won't deny that calculator gaming is an attractive distraction for generations of students, and I'm proud to say that I've contributed many games to the vast quantities out there. Lest writing calculator gaming seem like a total waste of time to your parents, you could point out that in writing games, you need to be able to formulate and hold complex program structures in your mind, trace how your code will work, and figure out what went wrong when you run across a bug. Calculator programming for math or for fun is no different than writing computer programs, leading to a final benefit.

THINKING LIKE A PROGRAMMER

In this day and age, programming is no longer a niche skill. Everyone in science, technology, engineering, and math needs to have at least a working familiarity with a handful of programming languages. Many other fields can benefit from learning to think with the logic and structure that programming entails. Even if you're not planning to go into a technical field, exploring programming might lead to a new career option or, at worst, a fun and relaxing hobby.

Unfortunately, we can't get any deeper into programming theory and practice in this book; otherwise this chapter would be even longer. It's up to you to take the next step toward teaching yourself more programming, or check out one of the resources in the next section.

11.5 Summary: taking programming further

I can't stress enough the value of exploring programming, and calculator programming in particular. To make taking the next step with programming easier, here are a few resources I recommend:

- Despite my obvious bias, I feel that my book *Programming the TI-83 Plus/TI-84 Plus* (2012, Manning) is a perfect introduction to programming skills and calculator programming. It's aimed at beginners to advanced programmers. It covers programming theory and practical programs for people who want to learn general programming concepts, as well as those who want to discover calculator programming specifically.
- If you want some programming help from friendly experts, I maintain a large membership on my website, Cemetech (www.cemetech.net). There are also several other great calculator programming communities out there.

I also want to reiterate that due to the confines of this chapter, I can't teach you anywhere near everything you need to know to have a complete set of calculator programming skills. For example, you can use many of the drawing commands in programs to make tools that automate graphing and games with fancy graphics. You can make programs call other programs to separate your largest programs into easier-to-read modules. You can learn Hybrid BASIC, a more powerful form of TI-BASIC, or z80 assembly, a more complex and powerful language still. The possibilities with programming, and especially calculator programming, are limitless and rewarding. I encourage you to pursue them.

As we near the end of this book, it's time to take a hard look at the TI-84 Plus C Silver Edition, the newest and fanciest member of the TI-83 Plus and TI-84 Plus family. I'll show you the new features of this large, color-screened calculator, from a new line-fitting tool to high-resolution color graphing.

The TI-84 Plus C
Silver Edition

This chapter covers

- The unique software and hardware of the TI-84 Plus C Silver Edition
- Special math and arithmetic tools of this color-screen calculator
- How to graph and visualize statistics on a high-resolution color screen

The first TI-83 graphing calculator rolled off Texas Instruments' production lines in 1996. It had a 96 x 64-pixel black-and-white screen. The TI-83 Plus was introduced three years later, with the same screen, RAM, and CPU. The TI-84 Plus arrived in 2004, with a faster processor and more Archive space than the TI-83 Plus but the same monochrome LCD screen. The TI-83 Plus/TI-84 Plus family of calculators was ripe for some major hardware changes, and 17 years after that first TI-83 was manufactured, the TI-84 Plus C Silver Edition came to partially fit the bill.

Photographed next to a TI-84 Plus Silver Edition calculator in figure 12.1, the new TI-84 Plus C Silver Edition's most obvious feature is a 320 x 240-pixel full-color LCD screen replacing the old monochrome LCD screen. To the chagrin of calculator enthusiasts and programmers everywhere, it has the same CPU and RAM as previous calculators, but the advantage of the high-resolution color screen for math is

Figure 12.1   The TI-84 Plus C Silver Edition (left) next to the TI-84 Plus Silver Edition (right)

undeniable. Graphs are crisper and more detailed, and you can tell multiple graphed equations apart by color. You get more options for how the graphscreen looks, and you can even draw and sketch in color.

THE TI-84+ C SE SYMBOL   Because this entire chapter covers the TI-84 Plus C Silver Edition, you won't see the usual symbol next to anything in this chapter. MathPrint-specific topics will still be marked with the MathPrint symbol.

The math and graphing tools of the TI-84 Plus C Silver Edition are, with few exceptions, identical to the older calculators. Even though menus can fit more items onscreen and there are a few new features, almost every tutorial and example for the TI-83 Plus and TI-84 Plus applies to the color-screen calculator. Indeed, all the skills and examples taught in this book can be used as is with a TI-84 Plus C Silver Edition. The new calculator does have some unique features, though, which this chapter will teach you about. Table 12.1 summarizes the new hardware and software features of the TI-84 Plus C Silver Edition compared with its most recent relative, the TI-84 Plus Silver Edition. The names are unfortunately confusingly close, but keep your eye out for the *C* (for color) and you'll be able to keep them straight.

Table 12.1   The major differences between the older black-and-white TI-84 Plus Silver Edition and the new color-screen TI-84 Plus C Silver Edition (pictured side-by-side in figure 12.1). Everything not listed here, such as calculus, arithmetic, algebra, and probability tools, is exactly the same between the different models.

TI-84 Plus Silver Edition	TI-84 Plus C Silver Edition
Powered by four AAA batteries and one coin cell backup battery	Powered by rechargeable battery
96 x 64-pixel black-and-white screen	320 x 240-pixel full-color screen

Table 12.1   The major differences between the older black-and-white TI-84 Plus Silver Edition and the new color-screen TI-84 Plus C Silver Edition (pictured side-by-side in figure 12.1). Everything not listed here, such as calculus, arithmetic, algebra, and probability tools, is exactly the same between the different models. *(continued)*

TI-84 Plus Silver Edition	TI-84 Plus C Silver Edition
15 MHz processor, 24 KB of user-accessible RAM	15 MHz processor, 21 KB of user-accessible RAM
1.5 MB of Archive for Apps and programs	3.5 MB of Archive for Apps and programs
Graphs in 7 black line styles	Graphs in 8 line styles and 15 possible colors
Manual data entry for finding a line of best fit	Point entry on the graphscreen to find a line of best fit
Up to 8 lines of calculations onscreen at once	Up to 10 lines of calculations onscreen at once

We'll start this chapter with the most basic differences—the changes for math and arithmetic on the homescreen. You'll see the new Mode menu, the OS-wide Catalog Help feature, and the changes to the Solver and MathPrint menus. We'll move on to the most visually appealing feature of the new calculator: color graphing. You'll work through an example of graphing two functions together in different colors, tracing along the functions, and examining their values in a table. Next, I'll show you the new tools and options for drawing in color, and we'll conclude with a handy new statistics tool.

Let's start with the new (but familiar) homescreen, Mode menu, and other algebra and arithmetic tools.

12.1   *Arithmetic and algebra*

Keystroke for keystroke, doing math on the TI-84 Plus C Silver Edition is identical to doing math on the earlier TI-83 Plus and TI-84 Plus calculators. Like the TI-84 Plus and TI-84 Plus Silver Edition, it has a MathPrint operating system, and like those other calculators, you can turn MathPrint on and off. The most obvious difference while doing math is that because the screen is larger, you can fit more math on the screen at once. A few other menus have been switched around, the Mode menu fits on one page, and new wizards have been added, but none of the arithmetic and algebra tools have changed significantly.

In this section, we'll look at the few differences between math on the TI-83 Plus/TI-84 Plus and the TI-84 Plus Silver Edition. All the algebra and arithmetic skills you learned in chapter 2 still apply, and you would be perfectly capable of using your TI-84 Plus C Silver Edition if you read chapter 2 and ignored this section entirely. But you'll learn some details in this section that might make using the color-screen calculator a bit faster. We'll start with what calculations look like on the homescreen and the aesthetic overhaul of the Mode menu. We'll continue with the new MathPrint features and then move on to the OS-wide Catalog Help tool. I'll conclude with a quick example of using the Solver on the TI-84 Plus C Silver Edition that you can try out on your own calculator.

We should begin with the new look for math on the homescreen.

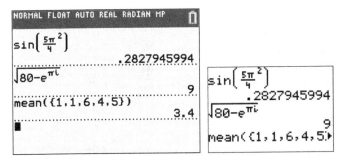

Figure 12.2 A set of three calculations on the homescreen of the TI-84 Plus C Silver Edition (left) and the same calculations on the TI-84 Plus Silver Edition with MathPrint enabled (right). You can see that the results are identical, but more math fits on the color-screen calculator's LCD screen.

12.1.1 The homescreen and the Mode menu

To reiterate a lesson that I'll be repeating throughout this chapter, you don't need to learn anything new to use the TI-84 Plus C Silver Edition properly. All the menus look enough like their TI-83 Plus/TI-84 Plus counterparts that you can easily follow along with the exercises and lessons in the remainder of this book. The keystrokes to type math are exactly the same. To see how literally true this is, take a look at figure 12.2. Both screenshots were taken with MathPrint enabled, and both calculators compute the same answers for the algebra performed. The only obvious difference, other than the higher resolution, is the top status bar on the TI-84 Plus C Silver Edition

The status bar at the top of the TI-84 Plus C Silver Edition's homescreen (annotated in figure 12.3) tells you at a glance what modes your calculator is in. These are the same modes you can change from the Mode menu. For example, MP tells you you're in MathPrint (instead of Classic) mode, and Auto means the calculator will automatically decide whether answers should be displayed as fractions. The TI-83 Plus/TI-84 Plus only show the current settings in the Mode menu, so this new status bar might help you avoid accidentally using Degree mode when you want to be in Radian mode or using a three-decimal-place Fix mode when you want to be in Float mode. Refer to chapter 2 if you need a refresher in what all these modes mean.

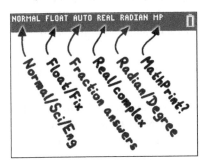

Figure 12.3 What each of the items on the TI-84 Plus C Silver Edition's status bar means. Together, they tell you the current mode the calculator is in, including Degree or Radian, Real or a+b*i* (complex), normal or Scientific mode, fraction or decimal answers, and MathPrint or Classic formatting.

To change any of the options shown on the status bar, head to the Mode menu, shown in figure 12.4. Although at first it looks much different from the Mode menu screenshots in chapter 2, it actually contains all the old options compacted onto a single screen. You can still control how numbers are calculated and displayed, how complex numbers are handled, whether MathPrint is enabled, and much more. There's a single new setting, with options Thick, Dot-Thick, Thin, and Dot-Thin. If you choose any of these options, the line style for all Y= equations will be set to whichever option

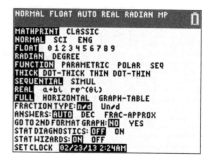

Figure 12.4   The TI-84 Plus C Silver Edition Mode menu

you choose. You can still return to the Y= menu and change the line style for any equation independently, as you'll learn in section 12.2.

Just as the only major differences in the Mode menu are how it looks, very few changes have been made to MathPrint.

12.1.2 *MathPrint features*

Almost all the MathPrint features on the TI-84 Plus C Silver Edition are the same as their TI-84 Plus counterparts, but with higher-resolution menus. The F1 through F4 menus (accessed via (ALPHA) (Y=) through (ALPHA) (TRACE)) look fancier, and a new tab has been added to the Math menu for typing fractions. A few new MathPrint wizards for probability have joined their statistics counterparts. This section will show you each of these new MathPrint upgrades and tell you what you need to know to use them for everyday math.

ONSCREEN BUTTONS   The TI-84 Plus C Silver Edition adds many menus where text appears at the bottom of the screen, enclosed in a black box. These are called *onscreen buttons*. For example, figure 12.5 shows a set of four buttons. These buttons correspond to the five small buttons directly below the screen: (Y=) (WINDOW) (ZOOM) (TRACE) (GRAPH). If you press any of these five keys when onscreen buttons are shown, they click the onscreen buttons instead of performing their usual function (like opening the Y= menu or displaying the graph).

First, MathPrint includes a special set of four menus you can use to access MathPrint-specific features on the homescreen. You can see the TI-84 Plus C Silver Edition form of these menus, which we briefly discussed in chapter 2, in figure 12.5. Here's what each one is for:

- *Frac* ((ALPHA) (Y=))—Inserts fraction templates, or converts between proper, improper, and mixed fractions.
- *Func* ((ALPHA) (WINDOW))—Inserts a selection of precalculus, calculus, and probability functions. Each of these includes a special MathPrint-friendly printed form, and items 6–9 (*n*th roots through the factorial function) are new for the TI-84 Plus C Silver Edition.

- *Mtrx* (ALPHA ZOOM)—Types a MathPrint matrix.
- *YVar* (ALPHA TRACE)—Types 1 of the 10 Y variables, Y_1 through Y_0.

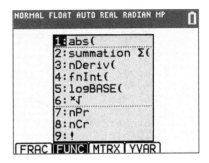

Figure 12.5   The four shortcut menu tabs available with MathPrint; the text describes what each one does.

The Frac tab of the MathPrint shortcut menu tabs has migrated into the Math menu. The Math menu on the TI-83 Plus and TI-84 Plus, up to and including OS 2.55 MP, has only four tabs. The TI-84 Plus C Silver Edition adds a fifth Frac tab, with the same contents as the F1 (ALPHA Y=) menu, as shown in figure 12.6. From here, you can insert a fraction template, into which you can type a numerator and denominator (and for the mixed-fraction template, a whole number). You can also convert between fractions and decimals and between proper or improper and mixed fractions.

Searching through the TI-84 Plus C Silver Edition's operating system for more changes, the thorough student would find four new wizards for four of the functions in the Prob tab of the Math menu. Like the Stats Wizards for the tools in the Calc tab of the Stat menu, these new wizards help you use randInt(, randNorm(, randBin(, and randIntNoRep(if you don't exactly remember the arguments each of those functions takes. An example of the wizard for the randNorm(function is shown on the right in figure 12.6. Of course, you can also refer back to chapter 9 if you need help with those probability functions.

Speaking of getting help remembering the arguments for functions, the TI-84 Plus C Silver Edition includes a calculator-wide Catalog Help feature. It will jog your memory if you forget the exact order of arguments for a complicated function, although it won't teach you everything you need to know about functions.

12.1.3 *OS-wide Catalog Help*

A downloadable App for the TI-83 Plus and TI-84 Plus called Catalog Help shows the arguments for functions listed in the Catalog (2nd 0). The TI-84 Plus C Silver Edition

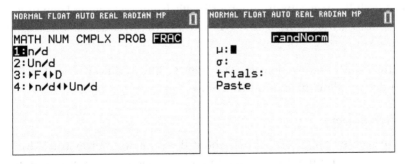

Figure 12.6   The new fifth tab of the Math menu on the TI-84 Plus C Silver Edition (left) with one of the new Probability Wizards (right)

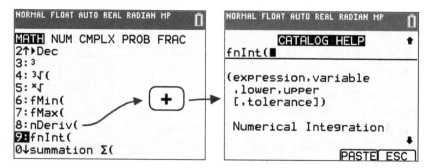

Figure 12.7   Using the Catalog Help feature to find the arguments for the `fnInt(` integration function. The top status bar turns from gray to green to indicate that you're in the Catalog Help tool.

took this concept and ran with it, weaving the Catalog Help feature throughout the entire operating system. Simply put, press ⊕ at almost any function in any menu, and the Catalog Help appears for that function, as demonstrated in figure 12.7. Although this isn't always enough information to figure out a function you've never seen before, it can be exactly the reminder you need when you can't quite remember the arguments to add after a function.

To use the Catalog Help feature, find the function you need in any of the calculator's menus, and press ⊕. The Catalog Help feature can also help you with some symbols and operators like ᵀ (the matrix transpose operator). If nothing happens when you press ⊕ over a menu item, it means Catalog Help has no entry for that particular item (in which case, jog to this book!). When the Catalog Help screen appears, it's marked by the status bar turning green and the words CATALOG HELP at the top. You can read the explanation and do one of three things:

- Press (GRAPH) (corresponding to the onscreen ESC button in figure 12.7) to leave the Catalog Help tool without pasting that function.
- Press (TRACE) (corresponding to the onscreen PASTE button in figure 12.7) to immediately paste the function into whatever text-entry screen you originally came from, including the homescreen.
- Most usefully, type your arguments directly from the Catalog Help tool, with the reference right in front of you. When you're happy with the function and arguments, press (TRACE) (for PASTE).

There's a final spiffy feature that the TI-84 Plus C Silver Edition offers for arithmetic, algebra, and general math: an improved Solver.

12.1.4   *The Equation Solver*

Way back in section 2.6.1, you learned about the Equation Solver (or Solver), which finds the value of an unknown variable in an algebraic equation with one unknown.

The major limitation of the Solver is that you had to get 0 on one side by itself, putting equations in the form

```
equation=0
```

For example, you could use the Solver on $3x - 4 = 0$, but you had to rearrange $x = 4 - 2x$ before you could plug it into the Solver.

The Solver on the TI-84 Plus C Silver Edition removes this limitation. You can take any equation with one unknown variable and plug it directly into the Solver. First, you enter the Solver by choosing `B:Solver…` from the Math tab of the Math menu. Type in one side of your equation as `E1:`, and then press ⏷ and type the other side as `E2:`, demonstrated on the left in figure 12.8. Next, press GRAPH, corresponding to the onscreen `OK` button. Here, you can modify the value where the calculator will start guessing (`X`) and the bound or range in which the answer might be. Because your calculator doesn't know what infinity is, the very small and very large values –1E99 and 1E99 (or -10^{99} and 10^{99}) are used as negative and positive infinity. If all is well on this second page, shown on the right in figure 12.8, then press ALPHA ENTER (`Solve`) to solve the equation.

For a quick demonstration, let's try the equation $3x - 8 = 40$ from chapter 2. Figure 12.8 shows how you can solve this using the Equation Solver. You enter `E1:3X-8`, `E2:40` and press ALPHA ENTER with the cursor over `X=` on the right side in figure 12.8. Lo and behold, your answer appears: `X=16`. In addition, the Equation Solver shows proof that it found the right answer: when it tries plugging the value $x = 16$ it found into both sides of the equation, it gets `E1-E2=0`, which means `E1=E2`. On the older calculators, this was labeled `left-rt=`.

Math on this new, bigger screen is handy, but it may be more fun to explore graphing in color. Let's look at the next graphing features that the high-resolution color screen makes possible, first with a complete example and then with a methodical walk through the TI-84 Plus C Silver Edition's new graphing features.

12.2 Graphing features

With the high-resolution color screen of the TI-84 Plus C Silver Edition, it should come as no surprise that graphs are clearer and easier to read. The color screen lets

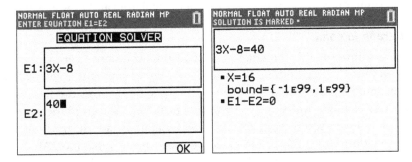

Figure 12.8   Using the Solver (or Equation Solver) to solve for *x* given the equation 3*x* − 8 = 40

you configure equations in different colors, and the higher resolution means you can see more details in functions. To use these new features, you really only need to know what I already taught you in chapters 3 and 5. You enter equations the same way, you graph the same way, you zoom the same way. The Graph Format and Calculate menus are in the same place, and you can still use the Table tool to explore *x* and *y* values.

In this section, I'll show you a specific example of graphing on the TI-84 Plus C Silver Edition so that you can get a feel for the necessary steps. We'll enter two equations, modify the graph format, and then graph and trace the equations and explore the Table tool. We'll then move on to a more methodical look at the new features of the Y= menu, the Graph Format menu, and the Window menu. By the end of this section, you'll know about everything that sets the graph features of the TI-84 Plus C Silver Edition apart from those of the TI-83 Plus and TI-84 Plus calculators.

TI-84 Plus C Silver Edition graphing in a nutshell

Graphing on the color-screen TI-84 Plus C Silver Edition is almost exactly the same as on the TI-83 Plus and TI-84 Plus calculators. You can read chapters 3 and 5 to learn all about graphing on your calculator, other than the special color features showcased in this section:

1. Go to the Y= menu, and enter your equation(s). Move the cursor all the way to the left and press (ENTER) if you want to change the line color and style.
2. Press (GRAPH) to graph your equations.
3. If you don't see the right part of the graph, you can zoom in, zoom out, or restore the standard window (ZStandard) from the Zoom menu. You can control the coordinates of the graphscreen edges from the Window menu.
4. You can change how the graphscreen looks from the Graph Format menu, under (2nd) (ZOOM).
5. Move the cursor along graphs with the (TRACE) feature, calculate properties with the Calculate ((2nd) (TRACE)) menu, or view the table with (2nd) (GRAPH).

We should start with your first color graph on the TI-84 Plus C Silver Edition so you can see how similar it is to graphing on the older calculators and how easy it is.

12.2.1   *Your first graph in color*

You'll need to follow roughly the same steps every time you want to graph an equation on your TI-84 Plus C Silver Edition, so I think we'd better start with a full example. In the next section, I'll show you a few of the color-specific features the new calculator sports, but this example will show you the practical steps for graphing on the TI-84 Plus C Silver Edition. You'll learn to enter two equations, adjust graph formatting, graph the equations, trace them, and examine them in the Table tool. All these skills are merely slightly modified forms of the steps you followed in chapters 3 and 5.

Let's begin with the two equations you'll be graphing, two variations on a standard sine function. Go to the Y= menu, which should display Y_1 through Y_9. If it doesn't, go to the Mode menu and choose FUNC. If any equations are already entered in the Y= menu, you should either disable them by moving the cursor to any highlighted   symbol and pressing (ENTER) or delete those equations. Enter these two equations (they don't have to be Y₁ and Y₂):

```
Y₁=6sin(X/2)
Y₂=5sin(X/3)
```

You can see these two equations entered in figure 12.9.

When you're satisfied that you entered the two equations correctly, you can graph them. To make them extra easy to see, let's add a grid behind them. Press (2nd) (ZOOM) to reach the Graph Format menu, which will look a bit different than the Graph Format menu that chapter 3 focused on; see Figure 12.10. Use the arrows keys to move the cursor to GridLine, and press (ENTER) to turn on the grid and set it to a grid of lines. Now you're ready to graph the two equations, so press (GRAPH).

You'll see the graphed equations on the left in figure 12.11. Not too shabby! The two lines are easy to see, and the grid means you can figure out (for example) that the blue line with the larger amplitude, the $y = 6\sin(x/2)$ function, goes through roughly (3,6). If you want to follow along the functions more accurately, press (TRACE). The (◀) and (▶) keys move the cursor along the function, the (▼) and (▲) keys switch between the two graphed functions, and (ENTER) recenters the graph on the trace cursor if you go off the top or bottom of the screen.

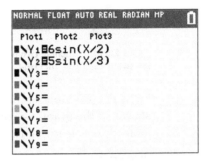

Figure 12.9 Two sine equations to be graphed entered in the TI-84 Plus C Silver Edition's Y= menu

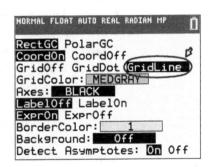

Figure 12.10 The Graph Format menu, where you set the grid mode to GridLine

Speaking of the detail about the functions' values, chapter 3 showed you the precise x and y values you can find in the table. This works just as it did on the TI-83 Plus and TI-84 Plus, albeit with more colorful numbers. If you press (2nd) (GRAPH), you'll see the Table view on the right in figure 12.11. You can scroll up and down to see the values of Y₁ and Y₂ as X changes, and if you want to jump to another part of the table, you can use the TblSet menu at (2nd) (WINDOW):

- TblStart changes the first x value shown in the table.
- ΔTbl controls the spacing between x values in the table.
- If you set Indpt to Ask and Depend to Auto, you can type in x values to get the associated y values. For the normal scrolling Table view, change Indpt to Auto.

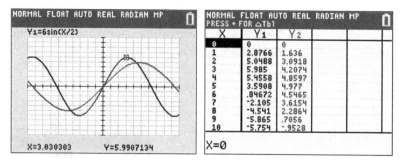

Figure 12.11   Graphing two functions on the TI-84 Plus C Silver Edition (left), and reviewing the Table tool (right)

From this example (combined with chapters 3 and 5), you already know how to do almost all the graphing you'll need for math and science. You can take the example a bit further to learn more.

GOING FURTHER

After you've followed the steps in this section to graph two sinosoids in color and explore their properties, you might want to try a few ideas for next steps:

- *Zoom the graph*—Use the options in the Zoom menu to reframe the graphs. Chapter 3 includes more details on the Zoom tools.
- *Edit the Window*—Change the area of the graph shown using the (WINDOW) settings. Chapter 3 explains more about the Window.
- *Shade the graphs*—You can shade above or below graphs, or change the color or line style, from the Y= menu. Go to (Y=), move the cursor to the leftmost column next to Y_1 or Y_2, and press (ENTER) to bring up the Style menu. When you're satisfied, save your modifications and return to the graph.
- *Calculate function properties*—Press (2nd) (TRACE) to open the Calculate menu, which lets you find minima and maxima and calculate derivatives and integrals. Chapters 3 and 7 provide more details about this.

Now that you've worked through an example of most of the things you'll need for everyday TI-84 Plus C Silver Edition graphing, let's take a more methodical look at each of the new graphing features.

12.2.2 *TI-84 Plus C Silver Edition graphing features*

It's important to continue noting that each of the features in this section in some way distinguished the TI-84 Plus C Silver Edition from the earlier TI-84 Plus and TI-84 Plus Silver Edition calculators. The TI-84 Plus C Silver Edition shares most of its features with the earlier calculators, and chapters 3, 5, and 7 explore those graphing features in great depth. If you have a color-screen calculator and you're looking to learn basic graphing skills, you should look at chapter 3 and then move to chapters 5 and 7.

In this section, we'll examine three specific areas of TI-84 Plus C Silver Edition graphing that make it stand out. First, I'll show you the many new graphing styles. The older calculators could graph with a thin or thick black line and draw just the line or shade above or below the graph. The TI-84 Plus C Silver Edition throws 15 possible line colors into that mix. We'll look at the several additional options in the Graph Format menu to make your graphs clearer and more readable and then move on to the one new item in the Window menu.

GRAPHING STYLES

As I explained in section 3.3.3, the black-and-white TI-83 Plus and TI-84 Plus can display graphs in seven different styles. You can graph with a thick or a thin line, shade above or below a function, or even make an animated circle trace out your functions. The TI-84 Plus C Silver Edition can graph in those same styles and adds 15 different colors to your options. You can see the Graph Style menu in figure 12.12.

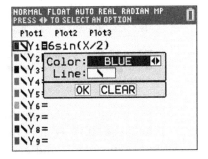

Figure 12.12 The Graph Style menu. You can change the color and line style for each of the 10 Y= functions by moving the cursor to the color next to each function name (like Y₁) and pressing ENTER.

To access the Graph Style menu, move the cursor as far left as it will go in the Y= menu, putting a box around the icons for the color and the line style, and press ENTER. The box in figure 12.12 will pop up. Use the ◄ and ► arrow keys to change the line color for the function, or press ▼ followed by ◄ and ► to change the line style. When you're happy with the color and line style, move the cursor to the onscreen OK button and press ENTER.

Whereas the TI-83 Plus and the TI-84 Plus had seven possible line styles, the TI-84 Plus C Silver Edition has eight line styles. Instead of a single dotted-line style, there are now two:

- ▪ ⸫Y₁ *(thin dotted line)*—Plots a graph as a series of single pixels. Use a color that contrasts well with the background; otherwise this is hard to see.
- ▪ ⸫Y₁ *(thick dotted line)*—Uses thick dots that nearly blend together into a line. If you want to graph more quickly than normal, this looks a lot like a solid line but graphs more than twice as fast.

Graphing in color is cool, and the ability to see your functions differentiated by color can make it easier to differentiate functions on a crowded graphscreen. Compared to a TI-84 Plus or Silver Edition, the TI-84 Plus C Silver Edition also offers more ways to customize how the graphscreen looks, from the axes to the background to the grid.

GRAPH FORMAT OPTIONS

In chapter 3, you learned that there are several graph formatting options you can control from the Graph Format menu (2nd ZOOM). You saw how to set rectangular or polar coordinates, show or hide coordinates while moving the cursor around the graphscreen, turn the grid and axes on and off, and so on. A TI-84 Plus C Silver Edition has all those options, plus quite a few more.

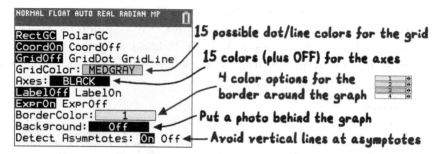

Figure 12.13 **The new options in the Graph Format menu, from the color and style of the grid to the axes color, background color, and border color, and whether to detect asymptotes**

You can see the defaults for the Graph Format menu on the TI-84 Plus C Silver Edition in figure 12.13. Four of the options are identical to their TI-83 Plus/TI-84 Plus counterparts, two (Grid and Axes) are modified, and four (GridColor, BorderColor, Background, and Detect Asymptotes) are completely new. These four options work just as they did on the TI-83 Plus/TI-84 Plus, as described in chapter 3:

- RectGC/PolarGC—Show graph coordinates in rectangular (x,y) or polar (r,θ) form.
- CoordOn/CoordOff—Show or hide the current graph coordinates when moving the cursor around the graphscreen with the arrow keys.
- LabelOff/LabelOn—Hide or show the x-axis and y-axis labels.
- ExprOn/ExprOff—Show or hide the equations for graphed functions when you're tracing them.

The modified and new options are all relatively straightforward:

- GridOff/GridDot/GridLine—On the calculators with black-and-white screens, the only options are no grid or a grid of dots. On the TI-84 Plus C Silver Edition, you can have a grid of dots or lines. The dots and lines are at the intersection of every set of integer coordinates, as you can see in figure 12.14.
- GridColor—Changes the color of the grid lines or dots. A light gray works well on a white background with dark graphed functions. There are a total of 15 possible colors; use the ◀ and ▶ keys to choose the grid color.
- Axes—Sets the color of the axes. There are 15 color options plus Off (which erases the axes). Use the ◀ and ▶ keys to flip between the options.
- BorderColor—There are four possible colors for the wide band around the graphscreen area. Use the ◀ and ▶ keys on this option to change colors.
- Background—You can load image files on the TI-84 Plus C Silver Edition. Images are photos or diagrams that you can graph over. You can use the Source-Coder tool (http://sc.cemetech.net) to convert your own photographs into image files.
- Detect Asymptotes—On all TI-83 Plus and some TI-84 Plus calculators, vertical asymptotes in graphed functions cause vertical lines to (incorrectly) appear on

the graph. Turning on the Detect Asymptotes feature prevents this, although it slows down graphing slightly.

One other new setting controls how the graph is displayed and used; it's found in the Window menu.

GRAPHING OVER PICTURES

You can load photographs onto the TI-84 Plus C Silver Edition and graph over them. Most calculators ship with five built-in Image files. If you press (2nd) (ZOOM) to go to the Graph Format menu and then move the cursor down to Background:, you should find that options Image1 through Image5 contain picture files, whereas Image6 through Image0 are likely empty (indicated by an *X* through a turquoise rectangle).

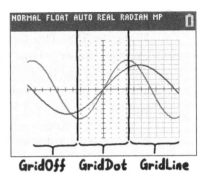

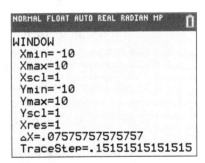

Figure 12.14 The three grid styles: GridOff, GridDot, and GridLine. The dots or lines are at the intersection of every integer *x* and *y* coordinate.

You can load more Image files onto your calculator using TI-Connect or from a friend's calculator. TI-Connect can also convert photographs into Image files for the calculator, or you can use a third-party tool like SourceCoder (http://sc.cemetech.net)

WINDOW SETTINGS

With a single exception, the Window menu on a TI-84 Plus C Silver Edition is identical to the Window menu on an earlier calculator. But because the screen is higher resolution, the entire menu fits on the screen at once without scrolling, illustrated in figure 12.15. The single new setting in the Window menu is TraceStep, which defines how far in the positive or negative *x* direction the cursor moves while you're tracing functions.

By default, your calculator automatically forces TraceStep to 2*ΔX, as figure 12.15 demonstrates. The ΔX value defines how much *x* increases or decreases by when you move one pixel right or left

Figure 12.15 The TI-84 Plus C Silver Edition's Window menu. Notice the new TraceStep setting.

on the graphscreen. Therefore, the default TraceStep moves the trace cursor by two pixels left or right when you press (◄) or (►). You can change this by setting the TraceStep to a specific value, like 0.5, 1, or 10. You can also set TraceStep to a multiple of ΔX, such as 5ΔX; you can paste in the ΔX symbol from the Window variables ((VARS)(1)) menu.

You learned in chapter 5 that you can draw, annotate, and sketch on the graphscreen. As you might hope from a color-screen calculator, the TI-84 Plus C Silver Edition adds color graphing features.

12.3   *Drawing in color*

Using the TI-84 Plus C Silver Edition's drawing tools is almost entirely the same as using the drawing tools on the TI-83 Plus and TI-84 Plus. The only difference is that you can change the color (and in some cases thickness) of lines, circles, text, points, and more. For general drawing skills, you should reread section 5.4 of this book. This section will cover the TI-84 Plus C Silver Edition's extra drawing features.

Chapter 5 taught you that there are two ways to use your calculator's drawing features: on the graphscreen and on the homescreen. You can also use drawing functions in programs, but that's covered in *Programming the TI-83 Plus/TI-84 Plus* in far more detail than I could ever fit here. I'll first show you the new Style menu that controls the color and style of lines, shapes, text, and points, two forms of which are shown in figure 12.16. I'll then show you updated versions of the tables from chapter 5 that summarized the syntax for your calculator's drawing tools.

If you're drawing on the graphscreen, you follow exactly the same steps that chapter 5 outlined. You go to the graphscreen, press (2nd) (PRGM) to access the Draw menu, and then select one of the tools there. This drops you back onto the homescreen, where you can use the arrow keys and the (ENTER) key to draw. The only thing the TI-84 Plus C Silver Edition adds is a new Style menu, which you can access by pressing the onscreen STYLE button (via the (GRAPH) key). From this menu, you can change line, point, and text colors and line and point styles. Use the (◄) and (►) keys to modify style options; (▲) and (▼) to move between the Color, Line/Mark, OK, and CLEAR fields; and (ENTER) or (CLEAR) to save or cancel your changes.

If you want to use the new color drawing features from the homescreen so that you can specify exact coordinates, you'll need to know the new arguments in table 12.2 and table 12.3. These tables are similar to tables 5.1 and 5.2, which explain how each of the Draw and Point tabs commands work and how they can be used from the homescreens of black-and-white calculators. Table 12.2 shows the extra arguments to many of the commands in the Draw tab of the Draw ((2nd) (PRGM)) menu. These

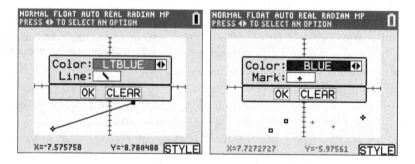

Figure 12.16 Two variations on the Style menu for graphscreen drawing. The menu on the left appears for lines and circles, and the menu on the right appears for points. You access these menus by clicking the onscreen STYLE button (via the (GRAPH) key) after choosing a drawing tool from the Draw menu.

extra arguments let you use different colors, line styles, and point styles, just like the Style menu for graphscreen drawing.

Table 12.2 The homescreen syntax for the TI-84 Plus C Silver Edition drawing functions in the Draw tab of the Draw menu. These can all be found in the Draw (2nd PRGM) menu. The color tokens are in the Color tab of the Vars menu.

Command	TI-84 Plus C Silver Edition homescreen syntax

`Line(`	`Line(<x₁>,<y₁>,<x₂>,<y₂>)`
	`Line(<x₁>,<y₁>,<x₂>,<y₂>,erase,color,style)`
	
	erase is 0 (erase) or 1 (draw). Color is one of the colors from the Color tab of the Vars menu (you can't type out R-E-D!). `Style` is 1 for a thin line or 2 for a thick line.
	
	Example: `Line(‾1,0,8.2,8,1,RED,2)`

`Horizontal`	`Horizontal <y coordinate>`
	`Horizontal <y coordinate>,<color>,<style>`
	
	See `Line(` for color and style.
	
	Example: `Horizontal 1.5,LTBLUE,2`

`Vertical`	`Vertical <x coordinate>`
	`Vertical <x coordinate>,<color>,<style>`
	
	See `Line(` for color and style.
	
	Example: `Vertical ‾4,YELLOW,1`

`Tangent(`	`Tangent(<func>,<x coord>)`
	`Tangent(<func>,<x coord>,<color>,<style>)`
	
	See `Line(` for color and style.
	
	Example: `Tangent(3X²,1.25,MAGENTA,2)`

`Circle(`	`Circle(<center >,<center y>,<radius>)`
	`Circle(<center >,<center y>,<radius>,<color>,<style>)`
	
	See `Line(` for color and style.
	
	Example: `Circle(2,‾1,4,GREEN,2)`

`Text(`	`Text(<row>,<column>, "STRING")`
	
	To change the `Text(` color, you must use the `TextColor(<color>)` command before using `Text(`. `TextColor(` can be found in the Catalog (2nd 0).
	
	Example:
	`TextColor(BLUE)`
	`Text(57,1,"GRAPH TITLE")`

You can also specify new point types and point colors for the six point and pixel commands in the Point tab of the Draw menu. Whereas the TI-83 Plus and TI-84 Plus had only three point types, the TI-84 Plus C adds a fourth. It also adds the expected color argument. Because the Pxl (pixel) commands only turn a single pixel on or off, the only extra argument they take is a color.

Table 12.3   Point and pixel commands, all in the Point tab of the Draw menu

Command	Homescreen syntax
Pt-On(Pt-Off(Pt-Change(	Pt-On(<x>,<y>) Pt-On(<x>,<y>,<type>,<color>) Pt-Off(and Pt-Change(take the same arguments. Type can be 1–4, where 1 is a small dot, 2 is a box, 3 is a cross, and 4 is a single pixel. Color is a color from the Color tab of the Vars menu. Example: Pt-On(5,1.2,3,ORANGE)
Pxl-On(Pxl-Off(function Pxl-Change(	Pxl-On(<row>,<column>) Pxl-On(<row>,<column>,<color>) Pxl-Off(and Pxl-Change(take the same arguments. Example: Pxl-Off(30,52,BROWN)

As I prefaced this brief overview, the drawing tools are largely the same as on older calculators, other than the new color options. If you're lost with this explanation, flip back and reread section 5.4; then return to this section to review the color-specific options. And speaking of features that haven't changed much beyond a judicious injection of color, let's look at the final major area of TI-84 Plus C Silver Edition changes: statistics features.

12.4   Statistics features

The statistics features on the TI-84 Plus C Silver Edition are very similar to their counterparts on the older TI-83 Plus and TI-84 Plus calculators. In a theme that seems to be running through this entire chapter, the major change is the addition of color. But there's also one new feature for calculating a line of best fit through a set of points that will make your life a lot easier. In chapter 8, you learned how to enter lists of data using the List Editor, plot those points on the graphscreen, and then use one of the line-fitting tools to find a function to fit your data. The new line-fitting tool on the TI-84 Plus C Silver Edition, called QuickPlot & Fit-EQ, combines all three of these steps into a single tool.

    This section will start by walking you through an example of using the QuickPlot & Fit-EQ tool to fit a parabola to a set of five points. You'll see how the tool can accelerate the previously tedious process of fitting lines to data. I'll also tell you about its limitations, including its inability to accept very precise data values. The latter half of the section will explore the changes to manual statistics plots, namely the ability to color your plots. You'll see that beyond learning to use the new QuickPlot & Fit-EQ tool, there are few extra skills you'll need to learn for statistics on the TI-84 Plus C Silver Edition beyond what chapter 8 taught you.

    Let's start with the biggest change, the QuickPlot & Fit-EQ tool, and how you can use it to speed up fitting functions to data.

12.4.1 *Using QuickPlot & Fit-EQ*

The statistics features of your calculator took an entire chapter to cover, and even then we only went through a broad, shallow overview of what your calculator can do with statistics. This section will add one more tool to your utility belt of statistics functions: the QuickPlot & Fit-EQ tool. With this little gem, you can get data into lists, plot the data in a statistical plot, and fit a line to the data, all at once. This section will work through a full example, from entering the points to saving the data and the fitted function for later use.

QuickPlot & Fit-EQ: a quick guide

1 Go to (STAT) (▶) (▲) (the bottom of the Calc tab of the Stat menu) and choose QuickPlot&Fit-EQ.
2 Plot all your data points, one by one, pressing (ENTER) after each one. If the window is wrong, quit the tool, adjust the window, and start over.
3 After you enter at least two points, you can press (GRAPH) to click the FITEQ onscreen button. Choose a function type, and your calculator will fit a line to the data.
4 If you want to save the data to lists, or the fitted function to a Y= equation, press (GRAPH) again to click the STORE onscreen button.

Let's jump right in without further ado, and you'll see the steps as we go along. If you just need a quick guide, then direct your attention to the sidebar "QuickPlot & Fit-EQ: a quick guide." If you have time for an example, then begin by setting the standard zoom (via (ZOOM) (6)), disabling any graphed functions from the Y= menu, and turning off any enabled Stat Plots. You can start up the QuickPlot & Fit-EQ tool by going to the bottom of the Calc tab of the Stat menu, finding E:QuickPlot&Fit-EQ, and pressing (ENTER), as shown on the left in figure 12.17. Your calculator will switch to the graph-screen so that you can, as it hints in the lower-left corner, drop points.

Before you start dropping points, make sure you're happy with the plot style. You can press (GRAPH) (corresponding to the onscreen STYLE button) to open the Style

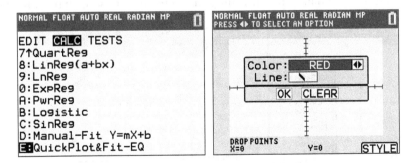

Figure 12.17 Starting the QuickPlot & Fit-EQ tool (left), and setting the Stat Plots style (right). These features are both unique to the color-screen TI-84 Plus C Silver Edition.

menu. From this menu, illustrated on the right in figure 12.17, you can set the color for the points and fitted line and the style for the fitted line. When you're happy with your choices, move the cursor down to OK and press (ENTER). Now you can drop those points; table 12.4 lists the coordinates of the five points. Use the arrow keys to move the cursor around the screen, and press (ENTER) to place each point. Notice that you can't get to *exactly* the coordinates listed, although you can get close.

Table 12.4   The rough *x* and *y* coordinates of the five points you'll drop for the QuickPlot & Fit-EQ statistical tool

x coordinate	y coordinate
−5	−7
−4	−3
−2	−1
0.5	−5
1.5	−10

When you've placed two points, you'll see the onscreen STYLE button change to FITEQ, meaning two points are enough for a simple fit (namely, a linear fit). After you've placed all five of the points in table 12.4, you'll have something resembling the left side in figure 12.18, so press (GRAPH) to open the FITEQ menu. Because these points look to be arranged in a rough parabolic shape to me, you should try 3: QuadReg. The Quadratic Regression tool, as chapter 8 taught, fits an equation of the form $y = ax^2 + bx + c$ to the data. After a split-second spent fitting the line, you'll get the parabola shown on the right in figure 12.18, complete with the equation printed at the top of the screen.

As you can see, the fit was close, and you already have both a line of best fit and that function graphed over your statistical data. In a few keystrokes, you entered your data (by placing points), picked a type of fitting function, and asked your calculator to fit that function to the data. The only thing that remains is to save all this information

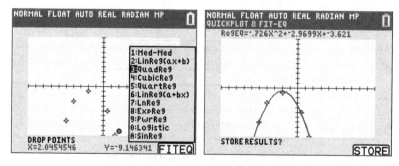

Figure 12.18   Choosing a function to fit to the dropped points (left), and examining the resulting function of best fit (right) using the QuickPlot & Fit-EQ tool

for later. You can see that the FITEQ onscreen button has now changed to a STORE button, which seems like a reasonable thing to choose. Press [GRAPH] to click STORE, and you'll get the menu shown in figure 12.19. From here, you can do three things: store the points to a pair of lists, set up a Stat Plot from these points, and save the function fitted to the data into a Y= equation.

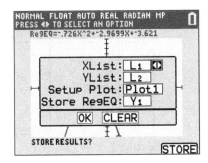

Figure 12.19 Storing the data and resulting function from the QuickPlot & Fit-EQ tool for later use. You can also set up a Scatter Stat Plot at the same time.

Use arrow keys to adjust any of these options, and then move the cursor down to OK and press [ENTER]. The points will be stored to the lists, the Stat Plot you chose will be set up as a Scatter plot and enabled, and the specified RegEQ will be filled in with the function of best fit. If you change your mind and don't want to save the results after all, you can move the cursor to CLEAR and press [ENTER], or tap the [CLEAR] key.

This new QuickPlot & Fit-EQ tool is fast and powerful, but its inability to accept exact typed point coordinates may be a deal breaker for you. You might also have too much data to patiently enter those points one by one, or you might already have your data in lists. In that case, you should fall back on the statistics skills you learned in chapter 8; you don't even need to learn anything new, although the few improved features I'll point out in the next section are welcome icing on the cake.

12.4.2 *Using manual Stat Plots*

One of the first lessons you learned in chapter 8 was how to set up the List Editor and use it to put data into lists. You'll be happy to hear that nothing has changed with that, and that using those lists of data to create Stat Plots to which you can fit functions hasn't changed a bit. The only noticeable differences are effects of the high-resolution screen and its newfound color. This section will briefly show you the effects of the screen on the List Editor and the Stat Plot menus.

We'll start with the List Editor. Section 8.1 showed you that it could display up to three columns of lists at a time and up to six elements of each list. If you wanted to see more, you could scroll up and down or side to side. An example of the List Editor on a TI-83 Plus is shown on the right in figure 12.20. The TI-84 Plus C Silver Edition's 320 x 240–pixel resolution means you can fit more on the screen at once. If you look at the left side in figure 12.20, you'll see that the new List Editor can show 11 items of each of 5 lists at once, a noticeable improvement over its older sibling. Why will that help you with math? Well, for one thing, you won't have to scroll as much, and if you can see more of the data onscreen at once, you're less likely to accidentally skip or repeat data as you're typing it in.

The other noticeable change in the tools related to creating manual Stat Plots is the addition of color options in the Stat Plots menu. If you press [2nd] [Y=], you'll see

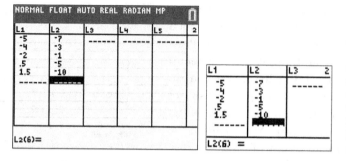

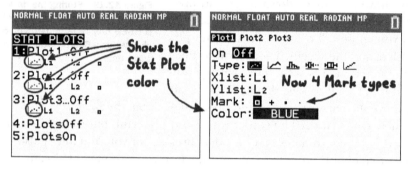

Figure 12.20 The List Editor on the TI-84 Plus C Silver Edition (left) and the older TI-83 Plus and TI-84 Plus calculators (right). Although the two List Editors work exactly alike, the high-resolution screen on the TI-84 Plus C Silver Edition can fit more data at once.

Figure 12.21 New color options in the Stat Plots menu (left) and the Stat Plot editor (right). Also notice that you have one extra choice for the Stat Plot point style.

the menu on the left side in figure 12.21. Like its predecessors, the TI-84 Plus C Silver Edition shows you a summary of the current Stat Plots, including what type of plot each is set to, whether it's on or off, and which list(s) it uses. As you can see from figure 12.21, the only change on the new calculator is that the plot type symbol now changes to the color set for the given Stat Plot. Choose a Stat Plot to edit its details, and as you can see on the right in figure 12.21, you can set the color of the plot points and lines. If the plot includes points (such as the Scatter type), you now have four instead of three different choices for the Mark (point) type.

And that's all there is to it. You use the Stat Plot and manual regression tools just as you did in chapter 8, so if you've gotten rusty (or skipped that chapter), feel free to flip back and review. With this final glance at colorful statistics, we've reached the end of the major changes you need to know about that set the TI-84 Plus C Silver Edition apart.

12.5   Summary

After 17 years of making calculators with reliable, recognizable monochrome screens, Texas Instruments has taken a tentative step toward color screens in the TI-83 Plus/TI-84 Plus series. Although the first calculators haven't overhauled the aging CPU and RAM underneath, the color screen by itself offers an easier, clearer way to visualize math. The new rechargeable battery will help you feed that backlit color screen's thirst for power and will eliminate the endless sets of AAA batteries that it would decimate. This chapter walked you through the big differences you need to know about to use the TI-84 Plus C Silver Edition as an effective math tool. Perhaps the most important lesson of this chapter is that behind the fancy color screen, the calculator hasn't really changed much, and everything else in this book still applies to the new calculator. Sure, graphing has color options, the homescreen fits more math, and you can compute lines of best fit faster than ever, but behind all that it's the same trusty TI-84 Plus calculator. If you have questions about any features on the new calculator, you should combine the new lessons in this chapter with the more in-depth examples and skills taught in the rest of this book.

So what special features *did* this chapter teach? We started with the area of the calculator you probably use the most: the homescreen. You saw how arithmetic and algebra have stayed the same, and how in spite of a few extra bells and whistles added to MathPrint, math on the new calculator is largely the same as on its predecessors. We moved on to the colorful graphing features, working through a full example of graphing in color. We then explored the new color graphing features one by one. The third topic of interest was drawing in color from the graphscreen and the homescreen, which you saw wasn't too different than drawing on the black-and-white calculators. Finally, I showed you the new statistics features, focusing mainly on the QuickPlot & Fit-EQ tool. As you finish this chapter, you should have a good sense of what new features the TI-84 Plus C Silver Edition offers and which of the older calculators' features are still intact.

Indeed, with the conclusion of this chapter, we are nearing the end of what I want to teach you about your graphing calculator. The final chapter of this book will broaden your horizon to the graphing calculator as more than a tool for computation.

Now what?

13

This chapter covers

- Your graphing calculator as more than a math tool
- How your calculator can connect to computers, calculators, and sensors
- What's next for you and for graphing calculators

In the past 12 chapters, we dove deeply into almost all your graphing calculator's features. You've seen everything from arithmetic to calculus, stopping at algebra, precalculus, statistics, and probability along the way. You've learned how to use your calculator as a powerful tool for math and science. In this final chapter, I want to round out your calculator expertise with a few extra skills, many of which aren't directly math-related. Some of these new skills stem from the calculator's programmability, which chapter 11 showed you could be used to write useful math programs or entertaining games. The other features we'll explore make use of your graphing calculator's ability to connect to other devices.

We'll start with how you can connect your calculator to computers or to other calculators. You can transfer lists, matrices, programs, and Applications (Apps) to and from other calculators and to and from computers. We'll continue with a related skill, finding and using popular Apps for your calculator. Once you find the ones you want, you'll use your newfound skills to transfer those Apps to your device, where they'll join the Apps preloaded on your calculator. I'll spend a few pages telling you more about how to create and share your own programming projects with the internet at large and why you'd want to do so. Finally, I'll show how you can explore your calculator as a controller for sensors and robots and conclude with some thoughts on what's next for your graphing calculator as your own academic tool.

Because almost everything we'll discuss in this chapter involves connecting your calculator to computers and other calculators, let's start with what you need to have and need to know to do so.

13.1 Connecting your calculator

As you know by now, your calculator can hold all kinds of files and variables, such as lists, matrices, pictures, and programs. Although you can create and use these on your calculator without connecting it to anything else, there are a few instances in which you'll want to transfer files to and from your calculator. For example, say you store a lot of data from a chemistry experiment in a matrix or a list. You could retype it by hand into a classmate's calculator, but transferring the list would be the better and faster solution. If you wrote a cool program for your calculator, you could transfer it to your computer and email it to a friend across the world, who could then test it on their own calculator.

In this section, I'll teach you how to transfer files between your computer and your calculator. You'll see the software and hardware that you need to upload and download files to and from your calculator, which depends on what kind of calculator and computer you have. We'll also walk through the basics of transferring data between two calculators, including how it's done and what you'll need. Let's get started with moving files and data between your calculator and computer.

13.1.1 Transferring files to and from computers

Once you get everything set up, transferring files between your calculator and your computer is straightforward. You need one piece of hardware to connect your calculator with your computer and one piece of software that tells your computer how to communicate with your graphing calculator. The only complexity comes from choosing the right software and hardware for your calculator and computer. You'll be able to

- Copy matrices, lists, programs, Apps, and pictures to your computer to back them up or share them
- Take screenshots of your calculator's LCD screen for reports, presentations, and lessons
- Upgrade your calculator's operating system
- Load matrices, lists, programs, Apps, and pictures onto your calculator

I told you that you need one hardware accessory and one piece of software to get your computer and calculator to talk to each other. To make things easy, table 13.1 shows exactly what you need. Find your calculator along the left side in table 13.1 and your computer's operating system on the top row, and the cell where they meet lists what you need. A mini-USB cable is a standard USB-to-mini-USB cable and is usually packaged with any new TI-84 Plus-family calculator. A SilverLink has a small cylindrical plug on one end (a smaller version of the plug on your headphones), a USB connector on the other end, and an oblong silver box in between. You need to buy a SilverLink separately from your calculator.

Table 13.1   The software and hardware you need to connect a particular calculator to a particular type of computer. Find the cell in the correct row and column: those are the two things you need. The text explains what mini-USB and SilverLink cables are and where to find TI-Connect and TILP II. As you can see, Windows and Mac OS users can use the official TI-Connect software, whereas Windows, Mac OS, and Linux users can all use TILP II.

	Windows or Mac OS	Windows, Mac OS, or Linux
TI-82	No TI-Connect support	TILP II 1.17 or later with a SilverLink cable
TI-82 Stats.fr, TI-83, TI-83 Plus, or TI-83 Plus Silver Edition	TI-Connect 4.0 or later with a SilverLink cable	TILP II 1.17 or later with a SilverLink cable
TI-84 Plus, TI-84 Plus Silver Edition, or TI-84 Plus C Silver Edition	TI-Connect 4.0 or later with a mini-USB cable	TILP II 1.17 or later with a mini-USB cable

Table 13.1 mentions two different pieces of software, TI-Connect and TILP II 1.17. TI-Connect is Texas Instruments' official (free) suite for transferring files between computers and calculators, taking screenshots, and more. You can find TI-Connect in the Downloads section at http://education.ti.com. If you prefer to use free open-source software created by the community, or if you run Linux, you can use TILP II, from http://lpg.ticalc.org/prj_tilp/. Both software options support all the major TI graphing calculators and any of the different cables used to connect the calculators to computers.

INSTALLING AND STARTING TI-CONNECT

We'll focus on installing and using TI-Connect, because it's TI's official software. If you choose to explore TILP II instead, chances are you're sufficiently tech savvy to figure out how to install it from its documentation. Anyway, you first need to make sure you have the proper cable. Any TI-83 Plus-family calculator can only use the SilverLink, sold separately from the calculator for about $20 from many office-supply stores. Any TI-84 Plus-family calculator can use a standard mini-USB cable, which is sold with the calculator. Once you have the proper cable, you can install the software; don't plug in the cables until after you install TI-Connect.

Go to http://education.ti.com, find the Downloads section, and look for software. When you find TI-Connect 4.0, download it and install it. You'll need administrator or superuser privileges on your computer to complete the installation. It's okay if your computer warns you about any unsigned drivers; allow it to continue. When the software is completely installed, plug your cable into your computer and your calculator

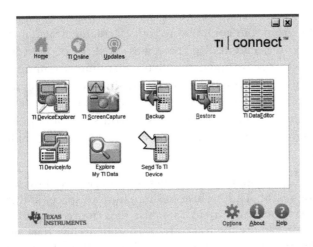

Figure 13.1 The main TI-Connect 4.0 menu. From here, you can see the contents of your calculator, take a screenshot, back up or restore your calculator's data, and edit lists and matrices on your computer. The older TI-Connect 1.6 looks slightly different.

into the cable, and then run the TI-Connect software. You'll start at a menu that resembles figure 13.1.

You can transfer files to and from your calculator, take screenshots, and edit variables from the TI DeviceExplorer section. Double-click the TI DeviceExplorer icon. There might be a small dialog that searches for your calculator the first time you open the TI DeviceExplorer; it will find the calculator attached via USB regardless of whether you're using the SilverLink or a mini-USB cable. If your calculator isn't found, try a different USB port, and make sure your calculator's batteries aren't low. The DeviceExplorer tool looks like figure 13.2. It enumerates all the files and data on your calculator in an expandable list and includes a toolbar full of other icons.

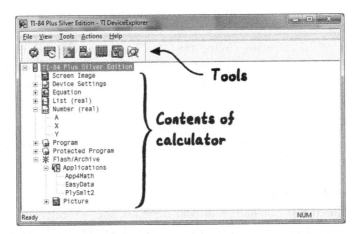

Figure 13.2 A sample view of the TI DeviceExplorer, showing all the files on a TI-84 Plus Silver Edition calculator. You can drag files into this screen to load them onto your calculator, drag them out to save them onto your computer, and click the camera icon to take a screenshot of your calculator's LCD screen.

TRANSFERRING FILES

To transfer a program or file from your computer to your calculator, drag it into the TI DeviceExplorer window. Valid files end in .8xp (programs), .8xl (lists), .8xi (pictures), .8xk (Apps), .8xm (matrices), .8xs (strings), and .8xu (operating system upgrades), among others. TI-Connect will warn you if you're overwriting existing files and give you the option to skip that transfer or replace the file on the calculator. It will also let you know if your calculator's memory is full. To save yourself from opening the TI DeviceExplorer in Windows, you can also right-click a file in any folder and choose Send to TI Device.

> **RAM OR ARCHIVE?**   You can choose to transfer files to the Flash/Archive section or to the calculator's RAM. The Archive has much more space, and its contents survive RAM clears, but you have to unarchive files (move them from Archive to RAM) before you can use them. To archive and unarchive data and programs, go to the Memory menu via ⟮2nd⟯ ⟮+⟯, and press ⟮2⟯⟮1⟯ to get to Memory Management → All. Press ⟮ENTER⟯ next to any data you want to move between Archive and RAM. Files prefixed with an asterisk (*) are in Archive; files without an asterisk are in RAM.

To transfer a program or file from your calculator to your computer, find it in the TI DeviceExplorer window. You might need to expand sections of the list shown in the main window by clicking the small ⟮+⟯ icons. Once you find the file or files that you want, drag them from the TI DeviceExplorer window into a folder on your computer. Alternatively, you can select a file and then choose File > Copy to PC.

There are a few other useful tools in the TI DeviceExplorer window:

- Clicking the camera icon takes a screenshot of your calculator's screen. You can choose to save the screenshot as an image and then use it in a report or presentation.
- If you have any of the calculators in the TI-84 Plus family, you can click the clock/calendar icon to change the current time and date stored on the calculator.
- To upgrade your calculator to the latest operating system version, you can choose Tools > TI OS Downloader.

If you just want to transfer files between two different calculators, you need neither software nor a computer-to-calculator cable. All you need is a calculator-to-calculator cable and a few minutes; I'll show you how it's done.

13.1.2 *Transferring files between calculators*

To transfer files between two calculators, all you need are the two calculators and a link cable. The cables for connecting two calculators are a bit different than the cables for connecting a calculator to a computer. If either (or both) of the calculators is in the TI-83 Plus family, you need to use an I/O unit-to-unit cable, distinguished by a cylindrical gold connector on each end. The plugs look like smaller headphone plugs, and they fit into the bottom of a TI-83 Plus or the top-left of a TI-84 Plus. If both the

Figure 13.3 Setting up the receiving calculator in a calculator-to-calculator transfer. Select 1:Receive from the Receive tab of the Link (2nd XTθn) menu.

calculators you're connecting are in the TI-84 Plus family, you can use the mini-USB-to-mini-USB cable that comes with TI-84 Plus calculators.

Connect the two calculators with the unit-to-unit cable. Access the Link menu on both calculators by pressing (2nd) (XTθn). You'll need to make one of the calculators the receiver and the other the sender. The receiver passively accepts anything the transmitting calculator sends, and the sender picks the variables, data, and programs from its own memory to send to the receiver. From the Link menu on the receiver, go to the Receive tab and press (ENTER), as shown in figure 13.3. The word Waiting... will appear on the screen. If for any reason you need to stop the transfer, hold the (ON) key for a few seconds.

Next, on the transmitting calculator, choose the 2:All- option from the Send menu. This option lets you pick as many files as you want, including lists, strings, matrices, pictures, Apps, and programs, to send to the receiver. In figure 13.4, for example, lists L₂ and L₃ will be sent to the connected calculator. You can even transfer things like the current window and Table tool settings. Press (ENTER) to select a file to send (which will place a square next to the item), and press (ENTER) again if you want to deselect any previously selected item. When all the files you want to send have small squares next to them, press (▶) to get to the Transmit tab, and then press (ENTER). If there are any problems, the receiving calculator will warn you that you're risking overwriting an existing program or that its memory is full.

You now know how to transfer files between your calculator and your computer and how to copy variables and data between two calculators. What if you want to find some new Apps and programs from the wide world of the internet to try? That's our next topic of discussion.

13.2 Finding and using Apps and programs

Since 1996, the year when the first TI-83 calculator rolled off Texas Instruments' production lines, enterprising students and teachers have been creating software for the devices. In the intervening years, the collected works of these enthusiasts have grown to vast proportions, with some 20,000 individual programs available for the graphing

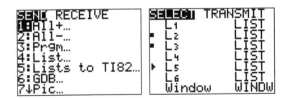

Figure 13.4 Setting up the sending calculator in a calculator-to-calculator transfer. Select 2:All- from the Receive tab of the Link (2nd XTθn) menu, choose the items to send, and then go to the Transmit tab.

calculators and dozens of Apps. Texas Instruments itself has published many well-known Apps for the calculators, some of which come preloaded on the TI-83 Plus and TI-84 Plus models. In this section, I'll give you an overview of where to find these programs and Apps and which ones might be particularly appealing to you.

APPS AND PROGRAMS   Apps and programs are both software that you load onto your calculator to give it new features and functionality. *Programs* are always found in the Prgm ((PRGM)) menu. Your calculator can run many programs by itself, though some games require a type of App called a *shell*. *Apps* are usually bigger and more complex than programs and are listed under the (APPS) key on your calculator. Apps are always self-sufficient and don't require anything else on your calculator to run properly.

With few exceptions, programs and Apps for TI calculators are entirely free. You download the files from the internet and then use TI-Connect or TILP II to load them onto your calculator. To make things easier, most of the programs and Apps that you download include instructions in the form of a readme.txt file or other documentation, but the steps for using programs and Apps don't vary much. I recommend three main places to search for files:

- For official Apps, Texas Instruments' own website is a good source. Go to http://education.ti.com, find the Downloads section, and look for Apps. Most of Texas Instruments' Apps are math and science tools.
- ticalc.org has long collected almost every calculator program released by enthusiasts. You can find programs and Apps at www.ticalc.org/pub.
- My own website, Cemetech, has a more modest but growing collection at www.cemetech.net/programs.

There are tens of thousands of TI-83 Plus and TI-84 Plus programs and games out there, far too many for me to recommend the best for your education and entertainment. But the Apps selection is much more limited, so it's worthwhile to discuss some of the outstanding choices.

DELETING FILES AND APPS   Your calculator likely came with many Applications in the Apps ((APPS)) menu, some of which you might want to delete to free up space. You might also no longer want some of the programs and other data on your calculator. To delete items, go to the Memory Management submenu via (2nd) (+) (2), and choose 1:All. Press the (DEL) key next to any item you no longer want.

POPULAR APPS

Texas Instruments and the extensive community of graphing calculator enthusiasts have together generated over 100 Apps for the TI-83 Plus and TI-84 Plus families. Most of them are useful and well written, but a few stand out as particularly helpful. The name in parentheses after each App is its name in the Apps menu, and links to all these Apps can be found at http://cemete.ch/t9025:

- *Bubble Bobble* (Bubble) from ticalc.org is a fun port of a classic Nintendo game.
- *Doors CS* (DoorsCS7/DoorsCS8) from ticalc.org is a *shell* (made by me), used to run programs and games that require the special features it gives to programmers.
- *Graph3* (Graph3) from ticalc.org is the best existing 3D graphing application for the TI-83 Plus/TI-84 Plus calculators. A rumored 3D grapher called *Graph3Dc* might be available by publication time for the TI-83 Plus C Silver Edition.
- *Periodic Table* (Periodic) from Texas Instruments puts an interactive periodic table on your calculator, tells you vital data about each element, and lets you graph and export atomic mass, number of protons and neutrons, and more.
- *Probability Simulator* (Prob Sim) from Texas Instruments can simulate tossed coins, rolled dice, drawn cards, and more and can graph and export the results.
- *Puzzle Pack* (PuzzPack) from Texas Instruments includes four fun puzzle and arcade games that will hold your attention for hours.
- *Science Tools* (SciTools) from Texas Instruments helps you work with significant figures, unit conversion, and vector arithmetic.
- *Symbolic* (Symbolic) from ticalc.org can simplify algebraic equations and perform some symbolic differentiation, and this App adds csc(, sec(, and cot(functions.

There are many more great Apps, and new ones are being written every year, especially with the continuation of the TI-84 Plus family in the form of the TI-84 Plus C Silver Edition.

If you enjoyed chapter 11 and want to continue pursuing programming, you might be intrigued to learn how you can become a more advanced programmer and share your own programs with the world.

13.3 *Writing and publishing your own programs*

Chapter 11 introduced some of the motivation behind writing your own programs for TI graphing calculators. You get to learn or refine programming skills, an important feather in your cap in a world where many technical jobs in engineering, science, computer science, and similar fields require knowing how to program. While planning and writing a program, you exercise your ability to think logically: you need to be able to hold an overview of your whole program in your head and plan how the pieces will fit together. Finally, educational programs often have direct applicability to helping you in math or science class, whereas games are fun to play.

In this section, I'll show you a few tools and resources to help you program faster and better. Programming TI-BASIC on your calculator is convenient and portable, because everything you need is already built in to a device you can slip in a pocket or backpack. But there are online and downloadable tools and documentation that can make your life easier. In addition, there are communities with friendly calculator programmers who would be happy to help you learn more and give you feedback on your projects. Finally, there are archives where you can upload your own completed programs for posterity.

Let's first look at the categories of programming tools that can help you code more efficiently.

13.3.1 *Programming tools*

Two types of tools make it easier to write graphing calculator programs. An *emulator* is a piece of software that lets you run a virtual device on another device; figure 13.5 shows screenshots of two emulators. Just as an emulator lets you use a virtual calculator, an Integrated Development Environment (IDE)—also known as an editor—lets you edit TI-BASIC (or z80 ASM) programs on your computer. Many emulators and IDEs have been developed since the first TI-83 became available; this section highlights a few selected options.

First up are emulators, which let you run a virtual calculator on your computer, or in some cases on your smartphone or a web browser. There are many calculator emulators, including one made by Texas Instruments. Two of the most used are these:

- *Wabbitemu*—An emulator that runs on your computer, emulates the TI-83 Plus and TI-84 Plus calculators, and works in Windows (http://wabbit.codeplex.com).
- *jsTIfied*—An online emulator written in JavaScript that emulates the TI-83 Plus and TI-84 Plus calculators (including the TI-84 Plus C Silver Edition), among others. Works on computers, iPads/iPhones/iPods, and other smartphones and tablets (www.cemetech.net/projects/jstified).

To use an emulator, you need a ROM image, a copy of your calculator's operating system. Legally, you must get the ROM image from your own calculator. The best tool for the job is called ROM8x (www.ticalc.org/pub/dos/rom8x.zip).

ROMS, EMULATORS, AND LEGALITY   At press time, there is concern about the future of free community-made emulators. In the future, you may be required to use only emulators that Texas Instruments sells, such as the company's SmartView software.

The other type of tool you might want is an IDE. For TI-BASIC, two options exist: SourceCoder and TokenIDE. You haven't heard much about z80 assembly in this

Figure 13.5   TI-83 Plus/TI-84 Plus emulators: Wabbitemu (left) and jsTIfied (right)

book, other than that it's a more powerful, more complex language than TI-BASIC that your calculator can also use. For z80 ASM, the Doors CS SDK and WabbitCode are both good options.

- *SourceCoder*—An online TI-BASIC IDE, connected to the jsTIfied emulator. Can turn .8xp into text source code and vice versa, and can edit lists, pictures, matrices, and other files (http://sc.cemetech.net).
- *TokenIDE*—An offline TI-BASIC IDE with syntax highlighting and other advanced features; also includes a sprite editor (http://cemete.ch/DL515).
- *Doors CS 7 SDK*—A complete z80 ASM assembly toolkit for TI-83 Plus/TI-84 Plus calculators; works well with the Notepad++ text editor (http://cemete.ch/DL470).
- *WabbitCode*—Part of the Wabbitemu project (http://wabbit.codeplex.com).

No programmer should code in a vacuum, because one of the best ways to learn is to ask questions of experts and try to understand and modify existing code. On the flip side, once you've put a lot of effort into a project, it's only natural to want to share the finished product with the millions of graphing calculator owners.

13.3.2 Forums and archives

Although you might work hard to learn programming and try hard to resolve glitches in your programs, you may find yourself with a problem you don't know how to fix. You might also discover that you're stuck on a particular command or concept that doesn't make sense to you, no matter how many times you stare at it being used in programs. When that happens, your best recourse is to reach out to experts and to other beginner programmers. One of the best things about the graphing calculator programming community is that its members are, on the whole, friendly and willing to help out new users. The forum members on my website, Cemetech (www.cemetech.net/), have for over a decade been helping thousands of users with calculator programming, computer and web programming, and DIY hardware and electrical engineering. Programmers ranging from newbies to experts come to discuss programming and show off their projects. Cemetech also has program archives where you can submit your own completed projects so that calculator users can download and use them.

There are various other discussion forums online as well, with varying degrees of experience and numbers of users. In addition, a few assorted websites specialize in programming help in different languages. All these websites offer both forums and program archives:

- *TI-Planet*—French projects and programming help (http://tiplanet.org)
- *TI-Freakware*—TI-89/83 Plus/84 Plus help and tutorials (http://tifreakware.net)
- *Omnimaga*—TI-Nspire/83 Plus/84 Plus programming help (www.omnimaga.org)
- *MaxCoderz*—Inactive reference for z80 ASM (www.maxcoderz.org)

The flagship calculator community downloads website, ticalc.org (www.ticalc.org), has great archives you can submit your programs to, but it unfortunately lacks onsite general discussion boards.

Your calculator can be a tool for calculations and graphing in math, science, and standardized tests. It can also be used to learn programming and to write math programs and games. Did you know that it can also connect to sensors, control robots, and network with other calculators?

13.4   *Sensors, robots, and hardware*

Texas Instruments' calculators are primarily used as tools for math. But their programmability might have already suggested to you that these devices have more in common with your cell phone than a simple four-function solar calculator. Your calculator can also interface with all kinds of hardware:

- You already saw how it can communicate with *computers* and other *calculators* to transfer files and data.
- You can use *sensors* and *probes* connected directly to your graphing calculator to measure light, voltage, and temperature. With some extra hardware (shown in figure 13.6), the calculator can measure distance, velocity, and acceleration and can talk to many other types of sensors.
- Your calculator can control *robots*. There's an existing calculator-based robot platform, or you could build your own.
- You can *network* calculators to share programs, play network games, or chat in the same room or from around the world.

In this section, I'll tell you a little more about each of these capabilities and let you explore them further on your own.

DATA COLLECTION AND SENSORS

The Calculator-Based Laboratory (CBL) was a calculator-sized device introduced by Texas Instruments in 1994. On its own, it could record temperature, light levels, and voltage over time. If you connected your calculator to the black-and-yellow CBL, you could move the data to your calculator to analyze it, graph it, and try fitting curves to the data. A newer version called the CBL2 was introduced in 2000; it's built to work with many of the sensors created by a company called Vernier. These additional sensors can measure everything from color to conductivity to gas concentration, among

Figure 13.6   Texas Instruments' CBL2 (left) is used to collect voltage, temperature, and light data over time. The CBR2 (right) can record distance, velocity, and acceleration and transfer the data to a graphing calculator.

many others. If you're a science teacher, you can explore how the CBL2 can make your students' calculators log and graph data during experiments. If you're a student looking to perform experiments for projects on your own, try asking your science teacher if they have a CBL/CBL2 available to try out.

Vernier, the company that makes extra probes for the CBL2, manufactures a few sensors that can connect directly to the mini-USB port on the TI-84 Plus-family of calculators. To measure distance, speed, and acceleration, you can use a gadget similar to the CBL called the Calculator-Based Ranger (CBR). It includes an ultrasonic sensor, and it can transfer data it records to an attached calculator for analysis. The CBR was introduced in 1997; a successor called the CBR2, which includes a mini-USB port to connect to TI-84 Plus-family calculators, was added in 2004. Using the CBR devices, you can test and graph the kinematics equations, which relate the position, velocity, and acceleration of moving objects.

ROBOTS

If robots are more your speed, you might want to experiment with Norland Research's Texas Instruments' Calculator-Controlled Robot, a platform with two wheels and a front bump sensor. You connect it to your calculator's link port and can use TI-BASIC programs to control the robot. Alternatively, the astute electronics whiz might be able to use an Arduino or other microcontroller to communicate with their graphing calculator. The calculator could then instruct the microcontroller to turn motors on and off or return sensor data. My website has Arduino code that lets it speak the TI-83 Plus/TI-84 Plus's language (http://cemete.ch/t4471).

LINKING AND NETWORKING

You already know that your calculator can transfer files to and from other calculators. If you pursue TI-BASIC, you'll discover that you can use a command called GetCalc(to write simple two-player games running on two linked calculators. If you want to make more advanced games, some of the Hybrid BASIC libraries described in my book *Programming the TI-83 Plus/TI-84 Plus* can help. There's also a networking protocol called CALCnet (also created by me) that lets more than two calculators talk among themselves, as shown in figure 13.7. I wrote a chat program, a few games, and a file-transfer program to demonstrate its capabilities, and several other programmers explored the same.

Figure 13.7 Six calculators connected via a CALCnet network, with a seventh to soon be linked in

You too could write multicalculator programs and games, using unit-to-unit linking, CALCnet, or even your own protocol. Once you start exploring calculator programming, there's not much that you *can't* do. With that important lesson, I want to leave you with a few final words and thoughts about everything you've learned in this book, what's next for graphing calculators, and what's next for you.

13.5   *Final thoughts*

You started this book by learning about the basics of your TI-83 Plus or TI-84 Plus graphing calculator as an academic tool. Starting practically with 2 + 2, we worked with arithmetic, algebra, graphing, precalculus, and calculus. You saw the many different graphing modes and tools that set your graphing calculator apart from a scientific or engineering calculator. We worked through countless problems and examples in probability, statistics, and finance to help you learn those calculator features. The final chapters of this book broadened your horizons about the non-math/science things your calculator can do and be, from a pocket computer for programming to a data-collection tool for experiments. You saw some of the unique features of the latest TI calculator, the TI-84 Plus C Silver Edition.

In these chapters, we covered all these skills that the vast majority of students and teachers might need to know for class. You learned most of your calculator's features, and Texas Instruments' own manuals can fill in the few remaining esoteric skills that didn't warrant coverage here. So where do you go from here? For one thing, you'll get into the rhythm of using your calculator as an extension of yourself, a tool that you no longer really have to think about. You might have already reached that point, in fact. For another thing, you may eventually move on to no longer needing your trusty TI-83 Plus or TI-84 Plus for class. In college, students taking nontechnical courses often stick with these graphing calculators, but scientists and engineers may need a calculator like the TI-89 or the TI-Nspire CX CAS (or another CAS-based calculator). A CAS (or computer algebra system) lets calculators work with symbolic equations, one of the things you discovered in the algebra and calculus chapters that your TI-83 Plus/TI-84 Plus can't do. It can solve numeric equations, but it can't simplify symbolic equations or figure out symbolic derivatives and integrals.

But I hope you'll hold on to your calculator, because you never know when you might need to graph some data, calculate financial TVM problems, or write a quick program to help yourself solve a real-life problem. Because I'm so enthusiastic about calculators as math and programming tools, I hope you too will end up in a science, technology, engineering, or math (STEM) career where you can help lead another generation of technological revolution. Math, science, and engineering can be fun subjects if taught well to interested students, and I hope some of the examples we covered in this book helped to inspire a passion for technical subjects.

It's uncertain where the future of graphing calculators will go. The TI-84 Plus C Silver Edition, in all its color-screen glory, seems like a more advanced graphing calculator, but actually has the same processor and memory under the hood as the TI-84 Plus

Silver Edition, with the color screen slapped on top. As powerful smartphones and tablets become more prevalent, even among students, the role of graphing calculators in the classroom will probably shrink and possibly even disappear. As a calculator enthusiast, I dread that day, but as an electrical and computer engineer, I'm excited to see what new technology will put the nails in the graphing calculator's coffin.

If you have any questions about math and science on your calculator, programming, or technology, don't hesitate to get in touch with me via this book's forum or my own forum, Cemetech. Good luck in all your academic endeavors, especially in math and science!

appendix A
The SATs and
your calculator

The SATs are the most important test in many young students' lives. This three-and-a-half-hour test is one of the major components of many college applications and measures aptitude in math, reading, and writing. Although a calculator isn't required for the math portion of the test, a majority of SAT test-takers use one, and most use TI graphing calculators. But it's important to know how to make your graphing calculator serve as a helpful tool. You need to know which questions you should try to use your calculator with and which questions are cleverly phrased to be solvable with little to no math. This appendix will demonstrate what you need to know to effectively use your TI-83 Plus or TI-84 Plus calculator for the SATs through sample problems.

You'll encounter two main types of math problems on the SATs. Most are multiple-choice questions, where you pick the correct answer from five possibilities. There are also some "student-produced response" questions, where you must perform a calculation and come up with an exact answer that you write down and bubble on your test sheet. With both types of questions, you must be careful while solving the problem quickly. For multiple-choice questions, the wrong answers are often designed to either look correct or be values you'd get if you did the problem the wrong way. For the student-produced response questions, you have nothing to guide you as to whether your answer is possible or totally off base.

This appendix will start with a few general problem-solving approaches for SAT math problems. We'll talk about different types of problems you might encounter and which ones you should use your calculator to solve. Many problems that look like they'll require a lot of arithmetic have a tricky but simple answer, because the SAT is designed to be doable even if you have no calculator, so we'll discuss how to identify those. Next, we'll solve five sample multiple-choice questions, focusing on problems that might require a calculator, but including a few problems where a calculator wouldn't help you. Finally, I'll show you five sample student-produced response questions and how to solve them.

We'll start with a look at general strategies for taking the SAT math test.

A.1   Solving SAT math problems

For the math portions of the SAT, you're allowed to use many types of scientific and graphing calculators to help solve the problems. Among the calculators allowed are your trusty TI-82, TI-83, TI-83 Plus, or TI-84 Plus-family graphing calculators. This appendix demonstrates how to solve 10 SAT math problems with your calculator, but the lessons must be taken in the context of solving problems as a whole. How can you approach each math problem, break it into manageable pieces, and solve it?

When you first confront a problem, you shouldn't immediately jump into solving the problem. I like to approach problems like this:

1 *What is the problem asking for?* Without knowing what it's asking you to find, you could easily start solving for the wrong thing and waste precious time.

2 *What does the problem provide?* Taking the information the problem gives you and what it's asking you to figure out together, you can figure out how to approach the problem.

3 *How should you solve it?* Given your knowledge of logic and math, figure out how to solve for what the problem wants. Often SAT math problems don't actually require that you do any computation.

4 *Solve it!* As you solve the problem, you'll be able to decide whether or not your calculator will help you solve the problem.

Many SAT problems follow similar patterns, so the more practice problems you do, the better prepared you'll be for the test. You'll start recognizing the patterns in the problems, which will help you figure out how to solve each category of problems more quickly. And completing questions quickly is key.

As many other SAT resources will point out to you, you have limited time to complete each problem, and problems have varying difficulty. If you can finish all the easy problems fast, you'll have more time to spend on the problems you're struggling with and more opportunity to narrow down your choices and do intelligent guessing if you're not sure what the answer is. If you know when to effectively use your calculator for a problem and when your calculator isn't going to help you, you'll likely be able to save yourself time. This appendix walks you through deciding whether to use your calculator on 10 sample problems and then follows through with solving each problem.

A.1.1   Math problem categories

The math problems on the SAT can be grouped into four categories, according to the College Board: general math and arithmetic, algebra, geometry, and statistics and probability. From a general standpoint, your calculator will help you on problems where you need to do one of the following:

- Calculate percentages, ratios, or probabilities with large numbers.
- Compute products of large numbers, squares, or square roots.
- Plug values into functions.

On the other hand, there are plenty of problems where your calculator wouldn't help you at all, including problems where you need to

- Solve logic ("reasoning") problems.
- Look for patterns in the problem that prevent you from needing to perform calculations, even if the numbers appear large or complicated.
- Apply algebra that would be slower to type into your calculator than to solve by hand.

The SAT is designed to be possible even if you have no calculator, so you know you're making a problem more complicated than it needs to be if you end up using advanced features of your TI-83 Plus or TI-84 Plus. On the other hand, you should be comfortable and familiar with your calculator when you go into the test, so make sure you're using your graphing calculator whenever you work on practice problems and practice tests.

A.1.2   Reference programs

One advanced feature of your calculator that *can* help you is its ability to store and run programs. You're not required to clear your calculator's memory, so you can bring any programs and data stored on your calculator with you that you want. Chapter 13 of this book teaches you how to load programs on your calculator as well as good places to find programs. There are some programs written specifically to help you with SAT problems and others that provide general algebra and geometry reference materials. I recommend the Cemetech and ticalc.org archives in particular.

But keep in mind that if such programs are to be helpful to you during the test, you must be familiar with what they contain and how to use them ahead of time. If you spend too much time familiarizing yourself with new programs or writing your own programs, you might have better spent your time just practicing problems. On the other hand, if you take the time to write your own SAT helper program, you'll have a quick reference you can legally use during the test, and writing the program is a form of practice as well.

In most cases, your calculator will be a way to perform arithmetic. We'll start looking at sample problems with multiple-choice questions that demonstrate this.

A.2   Multiple-choice questions

Multiple-choice math problems on the SAT can seem daunting, but a few strategies can help you approach them with less anxiety. Although this book teaches calculator skills rather than SAT or math lessons, and while this appendix focuses specifically on how your calculator can help you on the SAT, you can't solve SAT math problems with your calculator without also keeping general test-taking skills in mind. In this section, you'll apply these skills to figure out how to go about solving five multiple-choice questions. You'll see that although most of the problems can be solved more quickly with a calculator, all five are doable even without a calculator. Without further ado, let's jump into the multiple-choice problems.

PROBLEM 1: TERMS IN A SEQUENCE

Question: Given the following sequence, in which the first term is 6 and each subsequent term is 8 more than the last, what is the 12th term?

6, 14, 22, 30,...
(A) 86
(B) 94
(C) 96
(D) 102
(E) 104

Use a calculator? The trick to this question is not the math but recognizing that getting the 12th element requires adding 8 a total of 11 times, not 12 times. If you want to formally express this series: $S(n) = 6 + 8(n-1)$ for $n?1$. The first element is 6, the second element is $6 + 8$, the third is $6 + 8 * 2$, the fourth is $6 + 8 * 3$, and so on. You want the 12th element, so you can compute $6 + 8(12 - 1) = 6 + 8 * 11$.

Solve it: This is a simple arithmetic expression, 6+8 (12–1). Type it via ⑥ ⊕ ⑧ ⟮ ① ② ⊖ ① ⟯ . You'll get 94, so the answer is **(B) 94**.

PROBLEM 2: AVERAGE OF AVERAGES

Question: If the average of variables *a* and *b* is 12, and the average of variables *c* and *d* is 12, then what would the average of *a*, *b*, *c*, and *d* be?

(A) 6
(B) 9
(C) 12
(D) 24
(E) Impossible to determine

Use a calculator? Although there are variables and numbers in this problem, it's a misdirection: the only thing necessary is a bit of logic.

Solve it: Averaging (taking the arithmetic mean of) a set of numbers involves adding them and then dividing the sum by the size of the set. This means that if the average of *a* and *b* is 12, then $(a + b) / 2 = 12$, or $a + b = 24$. By the same logic, $c + d = 24$, even though we don't know the individual values of *a*, *b*, *c*, or *d*. We can therefore conclude that the sum of *a*, *b*, *c*, and *d* is 48, so the average of *a*, *b*, *c*, and *d* is $48 / 4 = 12$. The answer is thus **(C) 12**.

Be careful to take the size of each set into account for problems like these. If the average of *m* and *n* was 10, and the average of *r*, *s*, and *t* was 14, then the average of *m*,

n, r, s, and t would not be 12. Instead, the sum would be m + n + r + s + t = 10 * 2 + 14 * 3 = 62. The average would be 62 / 5 = 12.4.

PROBLEM 3: TRIANGLE AREA

Question: What is the largest possible area for a triangle where one of the three sides has length 20, and another side has length 12?

  (A) 480
  (B) 240
  (C) 192
  (D) 120
  (E) 96

Use a calculator? This problem has three components. First, because you know the lengths of two sides but not the third, and you don't know which two sides you have, you need to decide how you could assign these lengths to triangle sides for the largest possible triangle. Second, you're not told if this is a right, obtuse, or acute triangle, so you need to think about which option will yield you the largest triangle. You can use your calculator for the final area calculation, but the numbers are small enough that you could also do it in your head or on paper. You'll use the triangle area formula $a = 0.5 * b * h$.

Solve it: First, you need to decide which legs have lengths 12 and 20. It would make sense that you choose the shortest legs to have those lengths, so that you can get a longer length for the third leg. For the triangle type, a right triangle will give you the largest area (see figure A.1 for proof). Finally, because you picked the two short legs to have lengths 12 and 20, you don't you need to find the length of the hypotenuse.

From figure A.1, a right triangle is the best option to maximize the triangle's area, and you know that the equation $a = 0.5 * b * h$ will give you the area of the triangle. The answer therefore is a = 0.5 * 12 * 20 = 120, so you'd choose **(D) 120**.

PROBLEM 4: BUYING A COMPUTER

Question: As you head off to college, you need a new laptop for your schoolwork. You finally find a good laptop with a regular price of $800. Luckily, it's on sale for 10% off,

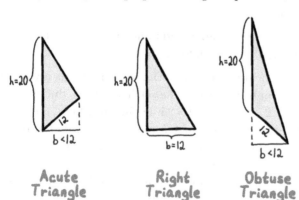

Figure A.1   Three possible triangles with legs of length 12 and 20, showing that a right triangle offers the largest possible area. For the acute and obtuse triangles, the length of the base is less than 12, so the total area will be less than 0.5 * 20 * 12. The right triangle has area a = 0.5 * 20 * 12 = 120.

and the store offers you an extra 10% off that sale price. However, you find it online for $800 and 20% off. How much will you save by buying it online?

(A) $0 (same price)
(B) $4
(C) $6
(D) $8
(E) $10

Use a calculator? This is a perfect candidate for quickly computing the answer on your calculator. To compute 20% off of $800, you can calculate 80% of $800, or 0.8 * 800. To compute 10% off of 10% off $800, you can compute 800 – 0.1*800 and then subtract 0.1 times that, but there's an easier way: 0.9 * (0.9 * 800).

Solve it: First, calculate 20% off of $800. You could compute `800-800*0.2` on your calculator, but it's simpler to calculate 80% of $800 via `800*0.8`. You can see the result, $640, on the first line in figure A.2. Next, calculate the result of taking an extra 10% off a sale price of 10% off $800. You can take 90% of 90% of $800 and get the same result: `0.9*(0.9*800)`. The second line in figure A.2 shows that the result is $648. Subtract $640 from $648 (which you probably don't need your calculator for), and you find that you save an extra $8 by buying your laptop online. The answer is **(D) $8**.

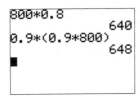

Figure A.2   Computing 20% off an $800 computer (top line) and 10% off of 10% off the $800 computer (second line). Your calculator shows you that you save $8 more by accepting a straight 20%.

PROBLEM 5: EQUATION OF A LINE

Question: Given the (x, y) coordinates of points on a line in table A.1, which of the following could be the equation of the line?

(A) $y = x + 1$
(B) $y = 2x - 1$
(C) $y = 2x + 1$
(D) $y = 2x + 2$
(E) $2y = x + 1$

Table A.1 (x, y) coordinates of points on a line for Problem 5

x	y
1	4
2	6
4	10
8	18

Use a calculator? At first glance, this seems like something you could graph or at least solve via a Stat Plot and linear regression (see chapter 8). But if you did, you'd be overcomplicating things for yourself. All you need to do is apply the equation of a line, $y = mx + b$, twice. You could even figure the equation out by inspecting table A.1, but I still recommend you check your result algebraically.

Solve it: You could use any two points from table A.1; let's use (1, 4) and (4, 10) for this sample solution. First, plug $x=1$ and $y=4$ into $y = mx + b$:

$$4 = m(1) + b$$
$$4 - b = m$$

Now plug the point (4, 10) as $x = 4$ and $y = 10$ as well as $4 - b = m$ into $y = mx + b$:

$$10 = (4 - b)4 + b$$
$$10 = 16 - 4b + b$$
$$-6 = -3b$$
$$b = 2$$

Finally, plug this back into $4 - b = m$ to get $m = 4 - 2 = 2$. Because m = 2 and b = 2, the final answer is **(D) $y = 2x + 2$**.

If you want to see what your calculator would do if you happened to take the hard route and try to perform linear regression, take a look at figure A.3. As you can see, the calculator comes up with the same result we derived in a few lines of algebra, $y = 2x + 2$. Always keep in mind that the SAT gives you less than 2 minutes per problem and is designed to be possible even without a calculator, so you likely won't ever be required to do something as complex as linear regression during a test.

You've seen five multiple-choice SAT math problems and how to answer them. As we discussed each one, you learned that immediately applying your calculator to solving the problem isn't the best approach. Instead, it's better to think about what the problem is asking and how you will solve it and then pick up your calculator only if arithmetic is involved or you want to graphically check an answer.

You can apply the same approach to the SAT's student-produced response questions.

A.3   *Student-produced response questions*

Student-produced response questions require you to write in an exact numerical answer on your SAT answer sheet. You have four spaces for each answer, into which

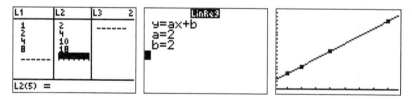

Figure A.3   Computing the equation for a line given four points and linear regression. Chapter 8 explains more about Stat Plots and linear regression. As noted in the explanation of Problem 5 in the text, you wouldn't be expected to perform such complex steps during the SAT.

you can write a 0 to 9, a decimal point, or a division symbol. Therefore, .667, 1/23, and 8422 are all possible answers you could write on your answer sheet. Negative answers, integers larger than 9999, decimals with more than three digits, and fractions with more than three digits are impossible, so your answer couldn't be 10001, ⁻5, .0004, or 40/41. For these problems, you need to double-check your answer carefully, because you don't have the guidance of five possible options to help you make sure your answer makes sense.

In this section, we'll look at five sample student-produced response questions that might appear on the math portion of the SAT. They cover combinatorics, equations of lines, averages, probability, and more. As we go through each problem, you'll see the typical approach you should take to SAT math problems, which should be familiar from the previous section: first decide how you'll solve the problem, judge whether your calculator will help you solve it, and then solve it. If you have time, you should always go back and check your answers, and for many problems, your calculator can provide a good way to do that.

Let's start with the first of the five student-produced response questions.

PROBLEM 6: PICKING COURSES

Question: Sara is trying to pick out college history courses. She is a history buff, so she wants to pick two courses to take in a semester, but the school offers eight different courses. If she can pick any two of those eight courses, how many possible combinations could she choose?

Use a calculator? This sounds like a combinatorics problem, which you can solve by hand or accelerate with a calculator. It's as simple as using the n choose r formula:

$$nCr = \binom{n}{r} = \frac{n!}{r!(n-r)!}$$

Solve it: Use the nCr function described in section 9.3. Sara will evaluate the $n=8$ possible courses she could take and choose $r=2$ of them. To solve this problem, type 8, press (MATH) (▶) (▶) (▶) (3) (ENTER) to type the nCr command, and add 2 on the end, yielding 8 nCr 2. The left side of figure A.4 shows how this might look on your calculator. If you have a TI-84 Plus C Silver Edition with MathPrint enabled, you can use the nCr template from the Func shortcut menu ((ALPHA) (WINDOW)). The right side of figure A.4 illustrates what this looks like.

In either case, the result is 28 possibilities for pairs of courses that Sara could pick. You could do this same problem by hand by expressing each factorial as a product, which would allow you to cancel many terms before performing the final calculation. Once you recognize that this is a combinatorics problem where you will need to use n choose r, it's probably faster to use your calculator.

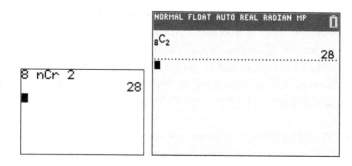

Figure A.4   Computing 8 choose 2 on the TI-84 Plus C Silver Edition (right) and all other TI-83 Plus and TI-84 Plus calculators (right). In either case, the result is 28.

PROBLEM 7: MAGAZINE SUBSCRIPTIONS

Question: A student is an avid reader of science magazines. He subscribes to three different magazines, one of which has a new issue every week, the second of which has monthly issues, and the third of which has quarterly issues (one every three months). After six years of receiving each of these magazines in the mail and stacking them on a bookshelf, how many total science magazines does he have?

Use a calculator? To solve this problem, you'll need to figure out how many issues the student gets per year of each of the magazines and then multiply by 6 and add up the resulting sum. You could do this by hand, but if you already have your calculator out, you can do it very quickly.

Solve it: First, figure out how many issues per year he gets of each magazine. The weekly magazine delivers 52 issues per year, the monthly magazine delivers 12 issues per year, and the quarterly magazine publishes 4 issues per year. Multiply by six years, and you get `6*(52+12+4)` or just `6(52+12+4)`. Plug the expression into your calculator and press ENTER, and it spits out the answer: 408 magazines.

   A slightly more roundabout solution method would be to figure out how many issues six years of each magazine would be. Six years of the first magazine would be `6*52` issues, six years of the second would be `6*12`, and six years of the last would be `6*4`. Add the three sums in a single line via `6*52+6*12+6*4`, and you get the same answer, `408`.

PROBLEM 8: POINT ON A LINE

Question: A point P lies on the line $y + 7 = 2(x-1)^2$. If the x-coordinate of point P is 3, what is the y-coordinate?

Use a calculator? You can easily do this by hand, but it's equally quick to do on a calculator if you want to check your answer. Subtract 7 from both sides to get $y = 2(x-1)^2 - 7$, and then plug in x.

Solve it: You can plug in x directly without needing to use your calculator's variables. Compute $2(3-1)^2-7$ via [2] [(] [3] [−] [1] [)] [x^2] [−] [7]. As you might also be able to deduce by inspection, the answer is 1, because $2(3-1)^2 - 7 = 2(2)^2 - 7 = 8 - 7 = 1$.

Just because a function is involved, don't assume that you need to graph this equation. Most SAT problems that include plotted graphs require you to pick out the correct graph to match a given function, not to create your own graph given a function. Just for the sake of completeness, the graph of $y + 7 = 2(x - 1)^2$ is shown in figure A.5. If you were given this on the SAT, you could use it to check your answer by making sure the (x, y) point $(3, 1)$ that you computed appeared on the graph.

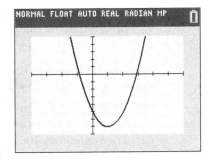

Figure A.5 Graphing $y + 7 = 2(x - 1)^2$ as $Y_1 = 2\,(X-1)\,2-7$ on a TI-84 Plus C Silver Edition. As discussed in Problem 8, you probably won't need to graph functions during the SAT, although it might come in handy for checking answers.

PROBLEM 9: COLLEGE ENROLLMENT

Question: A small college proudly states in its 2012 brochure that it has had an average enrollment of 1,450 students enrolled between 2008 and 2012. In an unfortunate accident, its enrollment figures for 2008 are lost, and it only has the 2009 through 2012 figures, shown in table A.2. Help the college fix its records: how many students were enrolled in 2008?

Table A.2 Five years of college enrollment at a small college for Problem 9

Year	Number of enrolled students
2008	(lost)
2009	1440
2010	1450
2011	1480
2012	1505

Use a calculator? This seems like a prime candidate for a problem you can solve easily with your calculator. You know the average of five numbers and all but one of the five numbers, so you can use the fact that $(x + 1440 + 1450 + 1480 + 1505) / 5 = 1450$ to solve for x.

Solve it: The formula for the average tells you that the sum of the numbers to be averaged divided by the number of values gives you the average. Here, that expression is

$$(x + 1440 + 1450 + 1480 + 1505) / 5 = 1450$$

where x is the unknown 2008 enrollment figure. You can rearrange this to get x on one side by itself:

$$1450 * 5 - (1440 + 1450 + 1480 + 1505) = x$$

Plug `1450*5-(1440+1450+1480+1505)` into your calculator, and press (ENTER). As you can see from figure A.6, the result is 1,375. Enrollment sure picked up over five years!

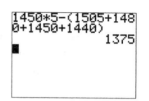

Figure A.6 Computing the 2008 enrollment for a small college. The average enrollment over five years as well as the annual enrollment in four of the five years are known, so the missing value may be computed.

PROBLEM 10: PRINCIPAL FOR A DAY

Question: To promote school spirit, a local high school decides to hold a Principal for a Day lottery, where any sophomore, junior, or senior student can take over the school for a day. The school has 100 seniors, 120 juniors, and 140 sophomores. In the hopes that older students would use the position more responsibly, every senior is entered into the lottery two times, but each junior and sophomore is entered once. What are the odds that a senior will become Principal for a Day?

Use a calculator? This probability-based question will require computing how many lottery entries are from seniors and then dividing that by the total number of lottery entries. That sounds like math that your calculator can easily do.

Solve it: First, compute the number of entries from seniors. There are 100 seniors and 2 lottery entries per senior, so 100 * 2 entries from seniors. The total number of entries is (2 * 100 + 1 * 120 + 1 * 140), because each senior is entered twice and each junior and sophomore is entered once. You can see from figure A.7 (or a quick mental or scratch-paper calculation) that there are 460 total entries. Therefore, there is a 200/460 probability that a senior will become Principal for a Day.

You could simplify that to 100/230, or 10/23; although the student-produced response grids allow you to answer in fractional form, there are only four spaces, and 10/23 takes five spaces. As you can see in figure A.7, you need to divide 10/23 (or 200/460) to get a decimal answer, .435. Notice that I rounded to the third decimal to fit on the SAT answer sheet.

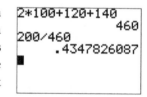

Figure A.7 Computing the probability that a senior will become Principal for a Day at a local high school. On the actual SAT, the numbers will likely be chosen to produce a simpler decimal answer.

In general, the student-produced response questions require more arithmetic, and all five of the problems presented in this section were more easily solved by letting a calculator do the math for you. Notice that with the exception of the combinatorics problem, Problem 6, none of the questions required more than simple four-function arithmetic to complete.

Having reviewed these 10 multiple-choice and student-produced response questions with you, my final piece of wisdom to impart is that the best preparation for the SATs is practice. I didn't have an SAT tutor or take SAT classes; my preparation was studying with all the sample questions and practice tests I could get my hands on, and I was able to get an extremely high score. I also recommend that you make sure you're as familiar with the format of the test, including the length, number of sections, and common types of questions, as you are with the material itself.

appendix B
Calculator skills
summary

This appendix provides a brief but thorough reference for your calculator's most important features. It covers everything from arithmetic and graphing through statistics and programming, plus all the skills in between. Much of the material in this appendix is repeated in sidebars and tables throughout the book, so if you want to quickly learn about a specific calculator feature, you can also jump to the relevant section in this book's chapters.

This appendix covers the following material:

- To review how to perform **arithmetic** and basic math, use your calculator's keypad, change modes, solve equations, and use variables and lists, flip to section **B.1**.
- For **graphing** skills, including how to draw function, parametric, polar, and sequence graphs, go to section **B.2**. You can also find pointers on finding minima, maxima, zeroes, and intersections of functions, using the Table tool, and drawing.
- For **precalculus** skills like using real, complex, and imaginary numbers, using trigonometric functions, and computing limits, refer to section **B.3**.
- For **calculus**, **statistics**, **probability**, and **finance** tools, go to section **B.4**.
- To review **programming** commands, read section **B.5**.

B.1 *Arithmetic and basic calculator skills*

With these tips, you'll be able to quickly get started using your calculator for arithmetic. Table B.1 shows some special key combinations for negative numbers, imaginary numbers, and more:

- Type your calculation, and then press (ENTER) to get the answer. (ENTER) is the equivalent of = on simpler calculators.
- You can clear a line and start over with (CLEAR).
- You can go to a previous equation to modify or recalculate it with (▲) (Math-Print only) or (2nd) (ENTER) (all calculators).
- Delete characters from anywhere in an equation with (DEL), move the cursor around with (◀) and (▶), and insert characters in the middle of a line by pressing (2nd) (DEL). Normally, typing in the middle of a line will overwrite the characters that are already there, not push them over.
- Any function that starts with an opening parenthesis must also have a closing parenthesis.
- To type an exponent, you type the number to raise, press (∧), and then type the power to raise it to. If the exponent is an expression instead of just a number, you might want to wrap it in parentheses.

Table B.1   Some special key combinations and what they do

Key combination	Types	What is it?
(−)	−	The negative symbol placed before negative numbers.
(2nd) (∧)	π	The constant pi (3.14159…).
(x⁻¹)	⁻1 (exponent)	Takes the inverse of a number or expression.
(2nd) (x²)	√(	Takes the square root of a number or expression.
(2nd) (,)	E	Multiplies a number by 10 to a power. 4.5E3=4.5*10³=4500; E4=104=10000. For the related topic of how your calculator displays numbers with exponents as answers, check section 2.5.
(2nd) (÷)	e	The constant e (2.71828…).
(2nd) (LOG)	10^(	Raises 10 to a power.
(2nd) (LN)	e^(	Raises e (2.71828…) to a power.
(2nd) (.)	i	The imaginary number i, √−1.
(2nd) ((−))	Ans	The result of the last calculation performed.

B.1.1   *Other important keys*

Remember these four important keystrokes, used to turn your calculator on and off and change the contrast (darkness/brightness) of the screen. If you turn the calculator on and the screen is still blank, try making the screen darker; the contents might just be too light to read:

ON —Turns your calculator on

2nd ON —Turns your calculator off

2nd ▲ —Makes the screen darker (hold the arrow key)

2nd ▼ —Makes the screen lighter (hold the arrow key)

B.1.2 Using Alpha-Lock

One special combination is 2nd ALPHA. When you press and release 2nd and then press ALPHA, you turn on Alpha-Lock mode. This means you can type with the ALPHA mode stuck on, as if you were pressing ALPHA before every subsequent key (without actually doing so!). This is useful for typing text, because the ALPHA function for most keys is a letter, a space, or another symbol. To turn off Alpha-Lock mode, press ALPHA again.

B.1.3 Answers as fractions

Your calculator prefers to display all answers as decimals. But it can also try to simplify them to fractions for you; depending on whether you're using MathPrint, you'll go about it in different ways.

On any calculator, MathPrint or not, enter your equation as usual and press ENTER. If a decimal appears at the right edge of the screen and you want to convert it to a fraction, press MATH to open the Math menu and select 1:▶Frac. Ans▶Frac will be pasted to the homescreen; press ENTER to generate the fraction. If no fraction appears, then your calculator can't figure out a fractional equivalent.

Have a MathPrint calculator and want to make it always display fractions instead of decimals? Get to the Mode menu by pressing MODE, scroll down until you see the ANSWERS: line, move the cursor over to FRAC, and press ENTER. To undo this later, switch ANSWERS: back to AUTO or DEC.

B.1.4 Functions

What is a function on your calculator? Functions look like abs(-0.5) or randInt(1,6). A function performs some calculation or algorithm on one or more arguments:

- Arguments are either numbers or more complex mathematical expressions, which can include other arguments.
- Most functions can be found in menus.

Table B.2 shows you where you can find your calculator's most important functions. Table B.3 shows where you can find special arithmetic functions that aren't mentioned beyond chapter 2.

Table B.2 Finding math functions

Menu	Access key(s)	Functions	Covered in...
(None)	SIN COS TAN	sin(, cos(, tan(, sin⁻1(, cos⁻¹(, tan⁻¹(	Section 6.2

Table B.2 **Finding math functions** *(continued)*

Menu	Access key(s)	Functions	Covered in...
Math	[MATH]	fMin(, fMax(, nDeriv(, fnInt(, Σ(, logBASE(	Chapter 3 (fMin/ fMax), section 6.4 (logBASE), chapter 7 (calculus functions)
Num (numbers)	[MATH]	abs(, round(, iPart(, fPart(, int(, min(, max(, lcm(, gcd(, remainder(	Chapter 2
Cpx (complex numbers)	[MATH]	conj(, real(, imag(, angle(, abs(	Section 6.1
Prb (probability)	[MATH]	rand, randInt(, randNorm(, randBin(	Section 9.4
Angle	[2nd] [APPS]	R▶Pr(, R▶Pθ(, P▶Rx(, P▶Ry(	Section 5.2
Draw	[2nd] [PRGM]	ClrDraw, Line(, Horizontal, Vertical, Tangent, DrawF, Shade(, DrawInv, Circle(, Text(	Section 5.4
Statistics	[STAT]	SortA(, SortD(, many more	Chapter 8
List Operations	[2nd] [STAT]	SortA(, SortD(, dim(, Fill(, seq(, cumSum(, ΔList(, Select(, augment(, List▶matr(, Matr▶list(	Section 4.2
List Math	[2nd] [STAT]	min(, max(, mean(, median(, sum(, prod(, stdDev(, variance(	Section 4.2
Matrix Math	[2nd] [x^{-1}]	det(, dim(, Fill(, identity(, randM, augment(, many more	Section 4.3

Table B.3 **Common arithmetic functions**

Function	Arguments	Description
abs(	abs(*number*)	Calculates the absolute value of the number in question. On MathPrint calculators, this shows up as absolute value bars instead of a function: $\lvert 3.1 \rvert$.
round(	round(*number, decimal places*)	Rounds the given number to the specified number of decimal places (see section 2.4.1). You can specify zero to nine decimal places.
iPart(	iPart(*number*)	Returns just the integer part of a number: iPart(3.1) = 3, iPart(3.9) = 3, and iPart(¯3.9) = –3.

Table B.3   Common arithmetic functions *(continued)*

Function	Arguments	Description
fPart(	fpart(*number*)	Returns just the part of a number after the decimal point: fPart(3.1) = 0.1, fPart(3.9) = 0.9, and fPart(⁻3.9) = –0.9.
int(	int(*number*)	Rounds a number down to the nearest integer. For positive numbers, this is the same as iPart. But it rounds in the opposite direction for negative numbers: int(3.9) = 3, but int(⁻3.9) = 4 and int(⁻3.1) = 4.
min(	min(*a*,*b*)	Returns whichever of *a* or *b* is smaller.
max(	max(*a*,*b*)	Returns whichever of *a* or *b* is larger.
lcm(	lcm(*a*,*b*)	Calculates the LCM of *a* and *b*.
gcd(	gcd(*a*,*b*)	Calculates the GCD of *a* and *b*.
remainder(	remainder(*a*,*b*)	Calculates the remainder when *a* is divided by *b*. Only Math-Print calculators have this function.

B.1.5   *The Memory menu*

Your calculator has memory it uses to hold everything from variables and strings to programs and Applications. There is RAM, the smaller but volatile area where lists, variables, and equations you're actively using are stored. This is also the Archive, a larger storage area where you can save items for later use. With the exception of Applications and some programs, Archived variables must be moved from Archive to RAM ("unarchived") before they can be used.

Your calculator's Memory menu is used to archive and unarchive programs and variables, delete items from RAM or Archive, and clear memory. You access the Memory menu by pressing (2nd) (+); the main Memory menu is shown in figure B.1. To delete, archive, or unarchive variables, choose 2: Mem Mgmt/Del…, and then pick the type of variable you want to organize from the new menu that appears. Archived variables appear with an asterisk (*) next to their names. Press (ENTER) next to a variable to move it between RAM and Archive or (DEL) to delete it. On a TI-83

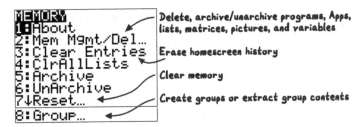

Figure B.1   The options in the top level of the Memory menu, accessed via (2nd) (+)

(non-Plus) or TI-82, (ENTER) deletes variables, and there is no such thing as the Archive or archived variables.

As mentioned in chapter 2, you can reset the calculator and delete all variables in RAM, Archive, or both by choosing 7: Reset... from the Memory menu. You can also perform various other memory-management tasks, like clearing the homescreen history, clearing lists, creating or unpacking groups, or viewing your calculator's OS and ID information.

B.1.6   Solving equations

To use the Solver to find the solution(s) to an equation with one unknown variable, use this process:

1   Find the Solver at the bottom of the Math menu.
2   Rearrange your equation to get 0 on one side and enter it. Use X as the unknown variable, even if it's a different variable in the original.
3   Press (ENTER), enter a guess next to X= (optional), and press (ALPHA) (ENTER).
4   If you get an error, try a different guess; if you still get an error, then the equation may have no solution.
5   If you get an answer and the equation has more than one answer, enter a different guess and see if the Solver converges to a different answer.

The Equation Solver on the TI-84 Plus C Silver Edition is a bit different. Section 12.1.4 demonstrates how to use it.

SOLVING A SYSTEM OF EQUATIONS WITH A MATRIX

A handy matrix trick lets you solve a system of equations with m equations and n unknowns using an m x $n+1$ matrix. Arrange each equation so that the coefficients to the unknown variables appear in order, with all the unknowns on the left of the equal sign and the constants on the right (shown in figure B.2). Fill the coefficients into a matrix, and then use the rref(function to put the matrix in Reduced Row-Echelon Form (a process called Gaussian Elimination). If the system is solvable, each row of the matrix will give you the value of one of the unknowns.

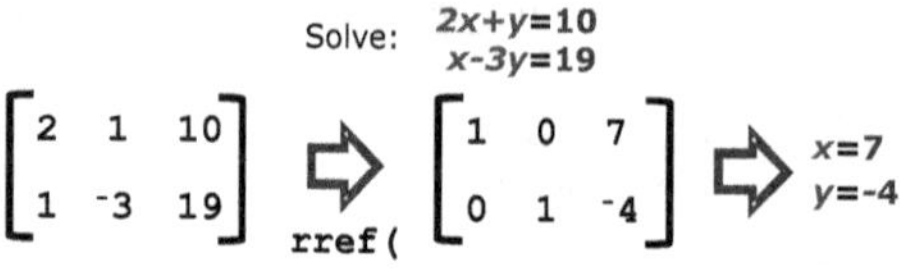

Solve: $\begin{aligned} 2x+y&=10 \\ x-3y&=19 \end{aligned}$

$$\begin{bmatrix} 2 & 1 & 10 \\ 1 & \text{-}3 & 19 \end{bmatrix} \underset{\text{rref(}}{\Rightarrow} \begin{bmatrix} 1 & 0 & 7 \\ 0 & 1 & \text{-}4 \end{bmatrix} \Rightarrow \begin{aligned} x&=7 \\ y&=\text{-}4 \end{aligned}$$

Figure B.2   Solving a system of two equations with two unknowns using a matrix and the rref(function

B.1.7   Variables

Variables are buckets with names you can store numbers in and later get numbers out of. There are numeric variables, which hold single values. There are list variables, which hold sets or series of numbers. And there are matrices, which hold arrays of numbers. See chapter 4 for more about variables, lists, and matrices.

NUMERIC VARIABLES

Using variables is easy:

- You store values into variables using the (STO▸) key, with the value to store typed before the → symbol that the key types and the name of the variable typed after. For example:

  3.75→M

- To use a value stored in a variable, use that letter in an equation where you might otherwise use a number.

- To type the variables' letters, press (ALPHA) and then the key that has the letter you want in green. The M variable is (ALPHA) (÷), for example.

LIST VARIABLES

List variables hold lists, containing up to 999 numbers. The most commonly used lists for general math are L_1 through L_6, typed with (2nd) (1) through (2nd) (6). Functions that you can use with lists are shown in table B.4:

- To store a list to a list variable, type the list, then press (STO▸), and then type the name of the variable to store the list to. For example:

  {1,4,9,16}→L_5

- List variables aren't the same as regular variables that each store a single number. You can't store a list in the A, M, or X variables. You can have lists in Ans, but you'll need to store Ans to a list (like Ans→L_2) to keep it.

- You can use a list variable anywhere you might otherwise use a list, just as you can use a numeric variable anywhere you might use a number. Your calculator will substitute in the list what the list variable contains.

- To use a single number from a list (an element), the syntax is list(*index*), where *index* is the element number to pluck out. See section 4.2.3 for an example.

- To remove all the elements in a list variable, use the ClrList command from (STAT) (4). It can take one or more list variables as arguments, such ClrList L_4 or ClrList L_1, L_3, L_5.

Table B.4   Some list-wise operations in the List Ops menu

Function	Description	Example(s)

SortA(
 SortD(
	Sorts a list variable's elements into ascending (A) or descending (D) order. Only works on list variables, and stores the resulting list back to the variable on its own.	SortA(L_1)
		         Done
		 SortD(L_3)
		         Done

dim(	Gets the length (dimension) of a list or resizes a list. If you make a list smaller, items get chopped off; if you make it bigger, the new elements are filled with zeroes.	{1,2,3}→L_2
		     {1,2,3}
		 dim(L_2)
		     3
		 4→dim(L_2)
		     4
		 L_2
		     {1,2,3,0}

Table B.4   Some list-wise operations in the List Ops menu *(continued)*

Function	Description	Example(s)

Fill(	Sets every element of a list variable to a given number. The number comes first and then the name of the list variable. The list must already have at least one element; otherwise, you'll get an ERR:INVALID DIM error.	Fill(8,L$_2$)
		                              Done
		L$_2$
		                    {8,8,8,8}

cumSum(	Returns a list holding the cumulative sum of a list. The first element is the first element of the list by itself. The second element is the sum of the first two elements of the original list, the third element is the sum of the first three elements, and so on.	cumSum({1,1,1})
		                    {1,2,3}
		cumSum({4,¯4,0})
		                    {4,0,0}

ΔList(	Generates a list where each element is the difference between adjacent elements in the input list.	ΔList({2,4,6}) {2,2}
augment(	Concatenates (joins) two lists together. The function returns the new larger list; you can store it to a list variable if you need to save it.	augment({1,2},{8,9}) {1,2,8,9}

B.2   Graphing and drawing

Graphing calculators excel at graphing and drawing, one of the main family of features that sets them apart from scientific calculators. This section provides a brief overview of your calculator's major graphing features, from Function, Parametric, Polar, and Sequence mode to finding properties of functions and drawing. Refer to chapters 3 and 5 for more detailed information.

B.2.1   Function graphing

Here's how you graph a simple $y = f(x)$ function, such as $y = x^2 + 1$, in four easy steps:

1 Press (MODE) and make sure FUNC (or FUNCTION, on a TI-84 Plus C Silver Edition) is white text on a black background. If it isn't, move the cursor over FUNC and press (ENTER).

2 Press (Y=) to get to the menu where you enter equations to graph. Use the arrow keys and (CLEAR) to remove any equations already entered.

3 Type your own equation next to Y$_1$= (use X for the independent variable x in equations, where X is the (XTθn) key), and press (GRAPH).

4 Use the Zoom menu to zoom in and out, and press (TRACE) followed by the (◄) and (►) keys to scroll left and right along the graph.

B.2.2   Parametric graphing

Parametric graphs specify pairs of x and y values in terms of an independent variable t:

- To switch to Parametric mode, press (MODE), move the cursor to PAR, and press (ENTER).
- When you go to the Y= menu, you'll see pairs of functions you can enter, such as X$_{1T}$ and Y$_{1T}$. You must enter equations in pairs.

- When you press the (XTθn) key in PAR, it types a T instead of an X, because T is the independent variable for parametric graphing.
- As in normal (Function/Rectangular) mode, in Polar mode the Zoom menu options discussed in section 3.3.1 can be used to adjust what you see in the graph.
- To adjust the range and granularity of T values plugged into the parametric functions, use the Window menu.

B.2.3 Polar graphing

Polar graphs define points by their radius and angle from the origin:

- To switch to Polar mode, press (MODE), move the cursor to POL, and press (ENTER).
- When you go to the Y= menu, you'll see six single functions you can enter, from r_1 to r_6.
- When you press the (XTθn) key in POL, it types a θ instead of an X, because θ is the independent variable for polar graphing.
- As with Parametric and Function (Rectangular) modes, the Zoom menu options discussed in section 3.3.1 can be used to adjust what you see in the graph.
- To adjust the range and granularity of θ values plugged into the parametric functions, use the Window menu.

B.2.4 Sequence graphing

Sequence graphs usually deal with integers and are often recursive:

- To switch to Sequence mode, press (MODE), move the cursor to SEQ, and press (ENTER).
- When you go to the Y= menu, you'll see one setting (*n*Min) and three pairs of items. u(*n*), v(*n*), and w(*n*) are the sequences to be graphed, and u(*n*Min), v(*n*Min), and w(*n*Min) are lists of initial values, necessary for recursive sequences.
- When you press the (XTθn) key in SEQ, it types an *n* instead of an X, because *n* is the independent variable for sequence graphing.
- To type recursive functions, you might need to type u(*n*-1), u(*n*-2), v(*n*-1), and similar expressions. The sequence equation letters u, v, and w can be typed with (2nd)(7), (2nd)(8), and (2nd)(9), respectively.
- As for every other mode, the Zoom menu options discussed in section 3.3.1 can be used to adjust what you see in the graph. ZoomFit is particularly useful for sequences.
- The Window menu for Sequence mode has a lot of options. *n*Min and *n*Max control the range of *n* values that are plugged in to the sequences. There's no such thing as *n*Step, because *n* always increases by 1. There are also settings for the coordinates of the edges of the screen, as in every graphing mode.
- The PlotStart and PlotStep options in the Window menu control which values of the sequences are shown on the graph. This won't change the values that are calculated, though, which is controlled by *n*Min and *n*Max.

B.2.5   *Finding a maximum, minimum, or zero of a graphed function*

Your calculator can easily find the minimum or maximum of any Cartesian (FUNC-mode) function or points where the graph crosses the *x* axis:

1. Graph the function; then press (2nd) (TRACE) and choose 2:zero, 3:minimum, or 4:maximum.

2. If you have more than one function graphed, use the (▲) and (▼) keys to choose the function to examine.

3. Use the (◄) and (►) keys to move the cursor along the graphed function to select a left and right bound on the region where the zero, minimum, or maximum lies. Press (ENTER) when you get the cursor to the correct location.

4. After you select the left and right bounds, the calculator will ask you to guess where the zero, minimum, or maximum is. It isn't important that you be very accurate with the guess unless the function is complex, but it will help your calculator find the zero, minimum, or maximum faster. If you choose a guess outside the bounds you picked, you'll get an error, ERR:BOUND.

5. When you press (ENTER) after making your guess, your calculator will think for a bit and spit out the *x* and *y* coordinates of the point.

B.2.6   *Finding the intersection of two functions*

If you are in FUNC (FUNCTION) mode, you can find the intersection of any two graphed functions:

1. Choose 5:intersect from the Calculate menu ((2nd) (TRACE)).

2. Select the two graphed functions for the intersection you want to find. You can use the (▲) and (▼) keys to move between functions and press (ENTER) to make your selection final.

3. Your calculator will ask you to guess the approximate intersection point; then press (▼).

4. If the two functions intersect near the guess, you'll get the (*x*,*y*) coordinates of the point of intersection.

B.2.7   *Using the Table tool*

The Table tool lists independent and dependent variable values for graphed functions:

1. To access the Table tool, press (2nd) (GRAPH). The arrow keys scroll up and down, as well as left and right, if you have more than two equations entered.

2. To change the table settings, go to the Table Setup menu by pressing (2nd) (WINDOW). The Indpnt option controls whether X values are automatically filled in according to TblStart and ΔTbl or whether you manually type in each X value you want to appear in the table.

3. If you set the Depend option in the Table Setup menu to Ask, then you have to press (ENTER) in the Y₁, Y₂, ... columns to make values appear (which is as confusing as it sounds, perhaps good for guessing and checking?).

B.2.8 Drawing

You can draw on the graphscreen, either to annotate graphs or to sketch diagrams and pixel art. Table B.5 discusses drawing tools that you can use on the graphscreen or from the homescreen. Table B.6 describes functions that let you turn individual pixels on and off.

Table B.5 Drawing functions in the Draw tab of the Draw menu. You must first go to the graphscreen, press (2nd) (PRGM) and select the function you want, and then use it. You can also go to the homescreen instead to use many of these functions. If you have a TI-84 Plus C Silver Edition, you should instead refer to table 12.2 in section 12.3.

Command	What it does	Homescreen syntax
Line (	Draws a line between two points. On the graphscreen, move the cursor to the first point, and press (ENTER); move it to the second point, and press (ENTER) again.	Line(<x1>,<y1>,<x2>,<y2>) Example: Line(-1,0,8.2,8)
Horizontal	Draws a horizontal line across the whole screen. Move the line to where you want it, and press (ENTER) to make it permanent.	Horizontal <y coordinate> Example: Horizontal 1.5
Vertical	Draws a vertical line down the whole screen. Move the line to where you want it, and press (ENTER) to make it permanent.	Vertical <x coordinate> Example: Vertical -4
Tangent (	Draws a line tangent to a given function at a given x point. Always assumes that functions are rectangular (FUNC) functions, even if the calculator isn't in Function mode. On the graphscreen, you select the function and then the point.	Tangent(<func>,<x coord>) Example: Tangent(3X²,1.25)
Circle (	Draws a circle with a center and radius. On the graphscreen, select the center, press (ENTER), and then choose a point on the edge of the circle.	Circle(, <center y>,<radius>) Example: Circle(2,-1,4)
Text (	Writes out text. Move the cursor where you want the top-left corner of the text to be, and start typing (no need to press (ENTER)). Remember to press (ALPHA) if you want to type letters. For entering Text (on the homescreen, row and column are pixels from the top-left of the screen, which is row 0, column 0. The bottom-right is row 62, column 94.	Text(<row>,<column>, "STRING") Example: Text(57,1,"GRAPH TITLE")
Pen	Somewhat like drawing with an Etch-a-Sketch. Move the cursor to where you want to start, press (ENTER) to put the "pen" down, and move the pen to draw a black line behind it. You can press (ENTER) to lift the pen and move it to a new spot to draw again.	(You cannot use the Pen as a home-screen command)

Table B.6   Point and pixel commands, all in the Points tab of the Draw menu

Command	What it does	Homescreen syntax
Pt-On(Pt-Off(Pt-Change(	Once you enable this tool, you can freely move the cursor around the graphscreen. Every time you press ⟮ENTER⟯, it will turn the point on (to black), turn it off (to white), or change it. From the homescreen, uses (*x,y*) coordinates. If you omit <type>, it will draw a single dot. You can put in 2 for type for a square and 3 for a cross.	Pt-On(<x>,<y >,[<type>]) Pt-Off(<x>,<y >,[<type>]) Pt-Change(<x>,<y>,[<type>]) Example: Pt-On(5,1.2)
Pxl-On(Pxl-Off(Pxl-Change(	Can't be drawn on the graphscreen; only for use as a homescreen function. Like Text(, takes pixel coordinates. Row and column are pixels from the top-left of the screen, which is row 0, column 0. The bottom-right is row 62, column 94.	Pxl-On(<row>,<column>) Pxl-Off(<row>,<column>) Pxl-Change(<row>,<column>) Example: Pxl-Off(30,52)

B.3   Precalculus

Chapters 2, 4, and 6 discuss graphing calculator features on the TI-83 Plus and TI-84 Plus calculators to help you with precalculus-level math. This section will review using complex and imaginary numbers, working with trigonometric functions, and finding limits.

B.3.1   Complex and imaginary numbers

The quick-and-easy of complex and imaginary numbers on your graphing calculator centers on three skills:

- *Changing between a+bi mode and Real mode*—You can use the imaginary symbol *i* in both modes. But you must be in *a+bi* mode to take the square root of negative numbers. You can change modes in the Mode menu.
- *Typing* $\sqrt{(-1)}$—Your calculator has a way to type the *i* symbol that represents $\sqrt{(-1)}$: ⟮2nd⟯ ⟮.⟯ (*i*).
- *Using complex number–related functions*—All the functions your calculator provides for manipulating complex numbers are in the CPX tab of the Math menu (CMPLX on the TI-84 Plus C Silver Edition). Five of the commands are particularly useful: conj(, real(, imag(, angle(, and abs(.

For a list of functions that can be used to manipulate real, imaginary, and complex numbers, take a look at table B.7.

Table B.7   Commands to work with real, complex, and imaginary numbers, all of which can be found in the CPX tab of the Math menu. The first three are particularly important.

Command	What it does	Example usage
conj(	Takes a complex number, negates the imaginary part only, and returns the result.	conj(5+2*i*) 5-2*i*

Table B.7 Commands to work with real, complex, and imaginary numbers, all of which can be found in the CPX tab of the Math menu. The first three are particularly important. *(continued)*

Command	What it does	Example usage
`real(`	Returns only the real part of a complex number (including 0 if there is no real part).	`real(5+2i)` 5
`imag(`	Returns only the imaginary part of a complex number without the *i* (including 0 if there is no imaginary part).	`imag(5+2i)` 2
`angle(`	Finds the angle of a complex number represented in the complex plane (which is outside the scope of this book). Depends on the current angle mode (Radian or Degree).	`angle(5+2i)` .3805063771
`abs(`	Calculates the magnitude of a complex number. Given a complex number *c*, this is equivalent to $\sqrt{(\text{real}(c)^2 + \text{imag}(c)^2)}$ This is the exact same abs(command used to get the absolute value of positive and negative real numbers.	`abs(5+2i)` 5.385164807

B.3.2 A quick guide to trig functions

The sine, cosine, and tangent functions are available directly from the keypad, without going into any menus. You type `sin(`, `cos(`, and `tan(` with ⟨SIN⟩, ⟨COS⟩, and ⟨TAN⟩, respectively, and then add a number or expression and a closing parenthesis (⟨) ⟩). You can use trig functions on the homescreen, in graphed equations, in programs, and anywhere else you can use numbers and variables.

For secant, cosecant, and cotangent, you must use `sin(`, `cos(`, and `tan(`. Recall the definitions from your math class:

- $\sec(x) = 1/\cos(x)$
- $\csc(x) = 1/\sin(x)$
- $\cot(x) = 1/\tan(x)$

The results of `sin(`, `cos(`, and `tan(` depend on whether you're in Radian or Degree mode. $\sin(90) = 1$ if you're in Degree mode, but $\sin(90) = 0.894$ in Radian mode. You can change the angle mode by pressing ⟨MODE⟩, moving the cursor over RADIAN or DEGREE, and pressing ⟨ENTER⟩. To check the current mode, press ⟨MODE⟩ and see if RADIAN or DEGREE is highlighted.

B.3.3 Finding limits with graphs and the Table tool

Although your calculator can't compute exact limits, you can use a graph with the Table tool to compute approximate limits. For the full details and an example, see section 6.3:

1. Enter the function you're taking the limit of as a Y= equation, after checking that your calculator is in Function mode.
2. Graph the equation, and adjust the window so that you can see the discontinuity in question. Try to guess the value of the function very close to the discontinuity; ⟨TRACE⟩ may help here.

3 Adjust the `TblSetup` variables to display values near the discontinuity in the Table tool, and then press `2nd` `GRAPH` to access the Table. The values should give you a good guess for the limit as the function approaches the discontinuity, which should confirm the guess you made from looking at the graph.

B.4 *Other tools*

Your graphing calculator can also help you with calculus, statistics, probability, and finance. This section summarizes the most important skills for each topic. For more information, you can refer to chapter 7 for calculus, chapter 8 for statistics, chapter 9 for probability, and chapter 10 for finance.

B.4.1 *Calculus*

Chapter 7 details all the calculus tools included in your graphing calculator. It can't compute symbolic derivates or integrals, but it can help you find numeric integrals (area under a curve) and numeric derivatives (value of a derivative at a point).

COMPUTING DERIVATIVES

As with integrals, your calculator can find the value of a derivative on the graphscreen or on the homescreen. Like integrals, you can only find the numerical derivative of a function at a specific point, not the equation for the symbolic derivative. But section 7.2 will show you how to graph the derivative function without knowing the exact equation. The two ways to calculate a derivative at a point are as follows:

- *On the graphscreen*—Graph an equation, and then go to the Calculate menu (`2nd` `TRACE`) and choose `6:dy/dx`. You'll be asked to pick a function only if you have more than one equation graphed. Next, move the cursor left and right to choose the point where you want to calculate the derivative; you can also simply start typing an *x* coordinate. Press `ENTER` to get the result.
- *On the homescreen*—Use the `nDeriv(` function from the Math menu. You specify the function (either directly or as a variable from `VARS` `▶` `1`) as the first argument, the letter of the independent variable as the second argument, and the point at which to find the derivative as the third argument:

  `nDeriv(equation,X,x-coordinate)`

COMPUTING INTEGRALS

Your calculator can calculate numerical integrals on the graphscreen or homescreen. To calculate an integral on the graph screen, type a function in the Y= menu, and then press `GRAPH`. If you're satisfied with the graph, press `2nd` `TRACE` to access the Calculate menu, and choose `7:∫f(x)dx`. You'll be asked to pick the equation only if you have more than one equation graphed. You can then move the cursor to select the left and right bounds of the integral or use the number keys to type the *x* coordinates. Press `ENTER` after selecting each bound. After you pick both edges of the definite integral, the area will be shaded and the value displayed (see figure 7.10).

To calculate the same integral on the homescreen, press (CLEAR) or (2nd) (MODE) to return to the homescreen after you graph the equation in question. Press (MATH), and choose 9:fnInt(from the first tab of the Math menu. You'll need to enter the equation, the independent variable, the x value of the left bound, and the x value of the right bound. For example, fnInt(Y₁,X,⁻5,0) (Y₁ is in (VARS) (▶) (1)). Figure 7.12 shows more; here are the arguments to fnInt(in a nutshell:

```
fnInt(equation,X,lower bound,upper bound)
```

B.4.2 *Statistics and probability*

A full set of instructions and examples for working with statistics and probability is provided in chapters 8 and 9.

DRAWING STAT PLOTS

These steps are nearly the same for all six Stat Plots menu types. Section 8.3.1 contains the most detailed guide to creating a statistical plot (Stat Plot), so if you get stuck, try skimming it:

1 Put the data to be plotted in one or two lists. Any built-in or custom list will do. Scatter and XYLine plots take two lists; Histogram, Box, Modified Box, and Normal plots all take a single list.

2 Go to the Stat Plot menu via (2nd) (Y=), turn on one of the Stat Plots, and choose which plot style/type you're using. Also select the one or two lists holding the data. In most cases, you can ignore the Freq: option or set it to 1.

3 View the plot via (GRAPH). It's often helpful to automatically adjust the Window settings by using the ZoomStat option in the Zoom menu.

4 Turn off the Stat Plots when you're finished with statistics and want to return to normal graphing. Otherwise, you may get an ERR:INVALID DIM error when you try to graph.

FITTING A FUNCTION TO A DATA SET

Regression is mathematically complex to do by hand, but with your calculator, it's easy. Just follow these steps:

1 You need two equal-length lists of data, as you did for XYLine and Scatter plots. For these steps, assume that one set (the x values) is in L₁, and the other (the y values) is in L₂.

2 Go to the Calculate tab of the Statistics menu ((STAT) (▶)), and look at all the options between LinReg(ax+b) and SinReg. Scroll down to the regression type you want, and press (ENTER). If your chosen type fits poorly, you can always try again with a different type.

3 If you're using a non-MathPrint calculator, the command is pasted to the homescreen. Type L₁,L₂ after it, and press (ENTER). If you're using a MathPrint calculator, a Stats Wizard may appear. Set L₁ as the Xlist and L₂ as the Ylist, move the cursor to Calculate, and press (ENTER).

4 You'll see the equation of best fit, complete with the constants to plug in.

5 If you want the $r/r^2/R$ values (also called the diagnostic variables), press (2nd) (0) to access the Catalog, press (x⁻¹) to type D (because Alpha-Lock is already set inside the Catalog), and scroll down to DiagnosticOn. Press (ENTER) twice; then perform the regression again.

DISTRIBUTION FUNCTIONS (PDFs AND CDFs)

All PDF functions are found in the Distr tab of the Distr menu, accessed by pressing (2nd) (VARS). All seven of the PDF functions end in pdf(. The arguments to the PDF functions can be found in table 9.1 (for continuous PDFs) and table 9.2 (for discrete PDFs). If you're using a MathPrint calculator, a wizard will guide you through choosing each of the arguments to the PDF function and then will paste the result to the homescreen. Without MathPrint, only the function name will be pasted to the homescreen, and you must type the arguments manually.

All CDF functions are found in the Distr tab of the Distr menu with their PDF counterparts, accessed by pressing (2nd) (VARS). All seven of the CDF functions end in cdf(. The arguments to the CDF functions can be found in table 9.3 (for continuous CDFs) and table 9.4 (for discrete CDFs). If you're using a MathPrint calculator, a wizard will guide you through choosing each of the arguments to the CDF function and then will paste the result to the homescreen. Without MathPrint, only the function name will be pasted to the homescreen, and you must type the arguments manually.

B.4.3 *Finance: the TVM Solver*

Your calculator's finance tools center around the TVM (Time-Value of Money) solver. You learn all about this feature in chapter 10, but here's what you need to know to use it fast.

Start by pressing (APPS) and choosing 1:Finance and then 1:TVM Solver…. Fill in six of the variables (see section 10.1 for the description of each variable), and choose whether payments are made at the end or beginning of each payment period.

In the TVM Solver, money that you spend or put out is negative, and money that you get back is positive. For example, an amount invested in the PV slot will be negative (you let go of money you invest) and the amount you get back at the end of the investment will be positive. For loans and mortgages, the PV is positive, because you get the money that you borrow, and the PMT value will be negative, because you need to give the bank money back to pay off the loan.

Move the cursor to the missing variable, and press (ALPHA) (ENTER) to solve for it. A black square will appear on the left next to the value computed.

B.5 Programming

Your calculator has powerful built-in programming tools. For more information, refer to chapter 11 or the companion volume, *Programming the TI-83 Plus/TI-84 Plus*. This section contains a summary of your calculator's programming commands. Table B.8 contains input and output commands, table B.9 describes conditional and control-flow commands, table B.10 has jump and menu commands, and table B.11 has loop commands.

Table B.8 Input and output commands. These can all be found in the I/O tab of the Prgm menu if you're inside the program editor.

Command	Description	Usage
ClrHome	Clears the homescreen and resets the cursor for Disp to the top row.	:ClrHome
Disp	Displays a number, string, matrix, list, or line of text. If you separate several items with commas, each will go on a line of its own. Strings are left-aligned on the LCD screen; all other items are right-aligned. Disp *number* Disp *variable* Disp *string* Disp *item_1,item_2,...*	:Disp 32 :Disp "HELLO, SARA" :Disp 5,L₁,[A],"CODE"
Input	Displays a string and then waits for the user to type in a value to store in a string, variable, matrix, or list. Input "STRING TO DISPLAY",*variable* Input *variable*	:Input "VALUE:",X :Input "HOW MANY?",N :Input M
Output	Displays a number, string, numeric variable, matrix, or list at a specified row and column on the homescreen. Row can be 1 to 8 characters; column can be 1 to 16 characters. On the TI-84 Plus C Silver Edition, the maximum row is 10 and the maximum column is 26. Output(*row,column,item_to_display*)	:Output(4,7,"ROSE") :Output(8,15,42) :Output(7,2,Str5)
Pause	Stops execution and waits for the user to press ENTER. Optionally, can be given a string, number, or variable to display during the pause. If the item is a long string, list, or matrix, the user can scroll left, right, up, and down.	:Pause :Pause 3 :Pause "PRESS ENTER" :Pause [C] :Pause ∟ALIST
Prompt	Displays the name of a variable, and asks the user to enter a value for that variable. Works with numeric variables, strings, lists, and matrices. Prompt *variable* Prompt *variable1,variable2,...*	:Prompt X :Prompt Str8 :Prompt [C] :Prompt L₄

Table B.9 Conditional and control-flow commands, all of which can be found in the Ctl tab of the Prgm menu when you're in the program editor. These all are used to let programs make decisions.

Command	Description	Usage
If	Evaluates a comparison or conditional statement and determines if it's true or false. If can be used to run or not run a single line of code, or with Then/End or Else/Then/End, multiple lines of code. If *condition*	:If X<0 :Disp "NEGATIVE" :If N=42 :Then :X+1→X :3N→N :End

Table B.9   Conditional and control-flow commands, all of which can be found in the Ctl tab of the Prgm menu when you're in the program editor. These all are used to let programs make decisions. *(continued)*

Command	Description	Usage

Then	Separates the If statement from a block of two or more statements you want to run when the If's condition is true. The block must end with End.	`:If X>3 and X<6`
		`:Then`
		`:ClrHome`
		`:Disp "X IS 4 OR 5?"`
		`:End`

Else	Marks the end of the true block of code and the beginning of the false block of code for an If/Then/Else/End conditional. Also the end of the true block of an If/Then/End conditional.	`:If X=2`
		`:Then`
		`:Disp "X IS 2"`
		`:Else`
		`:Disp "X IS NOT 2"`
		`:End`

End	Marks the end of a Repeat, While, or For loop or the end of the false block for an If/Then/Else/End conditional.	`:For(R,⁻10,10,2)`
		`:Disp R`
		`:End`

Table B.10   Labels, jumps, and menus, plus ways to end a program. These can all be found in the Ctl tab of the Prgm menu when you're inside the program editor.

Command	Description	Usage

Goto	Jumps forward or backward to a named label in the same program and continues executing there. Throws an error if the label is not found.
	
	Goto *labelname*
		`:Goto NX`
		`:Lbl 1`
		`:...code...`
		`:Goto AA`
		`:Lbl NX`
		`:...code...`

Lbl	Marks a spot in the program to which a Goto can jump. Execution flows straight through this command if there is code before it.
	
	Lbl *labelname*
		`:5→M`
		`:Lbl A`
		`:M^4→M`
		`:If M<999999`
		`:Goto A`

Menu	Draws a menu of one to seven items with a title. Lets the user use the arrows, number keys, and (ENTER) key to select an item. Each item in the menu, when selected, makes the program jump to a named Lbl.
	
	Menu("TITLE","OPTION 1",*label_1*
	[,"OPTION 2",*label_2*,...]
		`:Menu("MY GAME 1.0",`
		`  "PLAY",P,"HELP",`
		`  H,"QUIT",Q1)`

Return	Exits from the current program to the program that called it. If it was run from the homescreen or shell, returns there instead.	`:Return`
Stop	Exits from this program and every program that called this program back to the homescreen.	`:Stop`

Table B.11 Commands for creating loops. `While`, `For(`, and `Repeat` **start loops, whereas** `End` **always marks the end of a loop. You can nest loops inside each other. All these commands can be found in the Ctl tab of the Prgm menu if you're inside the program editor.**

Command	Description	Usage

`End`	Marks the end of a `Repeat`, `While`, or `For` loop.	`:For(R,⁻10,10,2)`
		`:Disp R`
		`:End`

`For`	Loops a fixed number of times, modifying a variable called the loop variable on each iteration. `For` loops end with an `End` command and can contain zero or more commands inside the body of the loop.
	
	`For(variable,start,end[, step])`
		`:For(X,1,10)`
		`:Disp X`
		`:End`
		`:For(M,3.0,0.5,⁻0.1)`
		`:N+M→N`
		`:End`

`Repeat`	A loop that continues to execute until the specified condition becomes true ("repeat until..."). The condition is checked at the end of each iteration, so the loop always runs at least once.
	
	`Repeat condition`
		`:Repeat K=105`
		`:getKey→K`
		`:End`
		`:Disp "ENTER PRESSED"`

`While`	Begins a loop that loops only while the given condition is true. The condition is checked at the beginning of each loop, unlike `Repeat`, so it might be run zero times.
	
	`While condition`
		`:1→X`
		`:While X<999`
		`:2X→X`
		`:End`

appendix C
Something went wrong

In an ideal world, everything would work the first time. Sadly, we don't live in a perfect world, and your graphing calculator is no exception. Although the TI-83 Plus and TI-84 Plus-family calculators are designed to be resilient to you making mistakes, you'll occasionally find yourself with errors that you don't know how to fix. This appendix is designed to help you out of these jams. There are two broad categories of problems you might encounter while trying to use your calculator.

The first category encompasses "big" problems: the calculator won't turn on at all, you can't type anything, or the math you're performing is returning nonsensical answers. The calculator can't provide any feedback to help you figure out what's wrong, because it doesn't realize anything is wrong. To solve those, take a look at section C.1 of this appendix.

The second category of issues you might encounter consists of smaller problems that display error messages. In these cases, your calculator is alerting you that it can't move forward with what you've asked it to do, and it's trying to help you solve the problem. The error messages it gives are often hard to understand, though, so section C.2 clarifies what those error messages mean and how to fix them.

We'll start with the bigger problems: issues that prevent you from doing anything with your calculator.

C.1 Troubleshooting big problems

Big problems that stop you from using your calculator properly at all are particularly frustrating because there are no error messages. Without any error messages to point you in the right direction, it's hard to figure out how to start troubleshooting the issue. This section helps you troubleshoot four types of errors:

- Your calculator won't turn on at all, or the screen is totally blank (section C.1.1).
- When you type on the keypad, nothing happens, or you're stuck with a blinking cursor (section C.1.2).

- Features don't work the way you expect: the Y= screen is messed up, the home-screen looks weird, and more (section C.1.3).
- The results of your math or graphs aren't anything near what you'd expect them to be (section C.1.4).

These four categories cover the most common problems that TI-83 Plus/TI-84 Plus users encounter, and I'll show you how to resolve each of them.

If you're reading this, you probably are trying to solve a specific issue you're having with your calculator, so skip to the appropriate subsection. You might also be studying what to do in case anything ever does go wrong, in which case read on.

C.1.1 My calculator won't turn on

Graphing calculators tend to be built sturdily, meant to survive years bumping around in students' backpacks. They're quite hard to break, and if your calculator won't turn on at all, it isn't necessarily permanently damaged. Here are some troubleshooting steps to help determine what went wrong:

- *Low contrast*—You can change the contrast (brightness/darkness) of the screen. If you turn the contrast all the way down, it might look like it isn't turning on. Press ⟨ON⟩, then ⟨CLEAR⟩, and then ⟨2nd⟩; release it, and hold the ⟨▲⟩ (up arrow) key. If a flashing cursor gradually appears, all is well.

- *Dead batteries*—If increasing the contrast doesn't help, your batteries might be dead. For most TI-82, TI-83, TI-83 Plus, and TI-84 Plus calculators, you'll need to change the four AAA batteries. If you have a TI-84 Plus Edition, your calculator has a rechargeable battery; plug it into a computer or a charger via USB and wait for it to charge. You won't have to change the button-cell backup battery frequently, if at all.

- *Corrupted memory*—If replacing the batteries doesn't help either, try forcing a RAM clear (you'll lose variables in RAM). For a TI-84 Plus C Silver Edition, press the small RESET button with the tip of a pen. For all other calculators, remove one of the AAA batteries. Hold down the ⟨ON⟩ key, and, keeping it held down, reinsert the missing battery. Tap the ⟨CLEAR⟩ key, and finally release the ⟨ON⟩ key. The RAM Cleared screen should appear.
- *Corrupted OS*—As a last resort, you can force your calculator to invalidate its operating system, which will require you to load a new one. Remove one of the AAA batteries, hold down the ⟨ON⟩ key, and, keeping it held down, reinsert the missing battery. Tap the ⟨DEL⟩ key, and finally release the ⟨ON⟩ key. The message Waiting for OS should appear on the screen. You'll need to use a unit-to-unit cable and a friend's calculator or a computer with the TI-Connect software installed to send a new operating system to your calculator.

If all these steps fail, then there may indeed be something wrong with your calculator's hardware. TI-83 Plus and TI-83 Plus Silver Edition calculators in particular sometimes have a flaw in a cable connecting the screen and main circuit board inside the calculator that causes the screen to stop working after several years of use. This usually starts manifesting itself as a garbled or static-y screen and eventually degrades into a blank or all-black screen. If this happens to you, there's not much you can do unless you know how to solder. If you do know how to solder, visit http://cemete.ch/t5161 for repair instructions.

C.1.2   I can't type anything

If you can turn your calculator on but none of the keys work, then you most likely have a stuck key. When one of the keys is stuck down, your calculator will have trouble reading other keys. Depending on which key is stuck, you might not be able to press any other keys. The obvious solution to this problem is to unstick the stuck key. If you've recently spilled something sugary or sticky on your calculator, you can use a cotton ball dipped in isopropyl alcohol to dissolve sticky substances on the sides of your keys. Just be sure to use a damp (not dripping) cotton ball so that no liquid gets inside your calculator. If you're comfortable taking your calculator apart, which will require a Torx-6 screwdriver and Phillips screwdriver and will void your warranty, you can also clean the holes in the case that the keys fit into.

In rarer cases, leaking batteries can permanently damage the calculator's main circuit board in such a way that some keys will no longer work. Unless you have soldering and circuit-debugging experience, you'll be unable to fix this and should get a new calculator.

C.1.3   My settings are messed up

In all the examples in this book, I've made an effort to anticipate common problems you might have while trying to follow along. For example, in graphing examples, I advised you to check which graphing mode you were in before you started entering equations. When you're using your calculator on your own, though, you don't have anyone to remind you what settings to change. You could flip back to the chapter that taught you the original skill, but to save you time, here are a few troubleshooting steps to try:

- *The Y= equations are the wrong type.*
  Make sure you're in the correct mode. Press (MODE) and choose FUNC, PAR, POL, or SEQ, and then return to the Y= menu.
- *I can't see the graph.*
  Did you press (GRAPH) and you can't find the graphed equation, or are you looking at the wrong part? Reset the default zoom by choosing 6:ZStandard from the Zoom menu.
- *My axes are gone.*
  If you're missing axes or other graph formatting options are wrong, press (2nd) (ZOOM) for the Graph Format menu and adjust the settings.
- *I'm stuck in a split-screen mode.*
  Press (MODE) and choose FULL instead of the HORIZ or G-T split-screen mode.

- *Answers are always in scientific notation.*

  If you always get answers like 2E0 or 1.5E1 instead of 2 or 15, you've enabled Sci or Eng mode. Go to the Mode menu, and choose NORMAL by moving the flashing cursor over the word and pressing (ENTER).

- *Answers always have the same number of decimal points.*

  You might always get the same number of decimal points after numbers, even if they're integers. You accidentally set one of the Fix modes. Go to the Mode menu and choose FLOAT.

When in doubt, the Mode and Graph Format menus are the best places to look for settings that might have gone amiss. If all else fails, you can reset all default settings without clearing your memory. Press (2nd) (+) to get to the Memory menu, choose 7:Reset…, choose 2:Defaults…, and then confirm your choice with 2:Reset.

C.1.4   *My math is coming out wrong*

Do your answers make no sense? If so, then one of the settings that controls numeric answers might be in an unexpected state. If you always get answers in scientific notation (like 3.2E1) or your answers always have the same number of decimal points, then look at the tips in section C.1.3. Otherwise, try these troubleshooting steps:

- *Trig answers are wrong.*

  If you're getting weird answers for sin(, cos(, and tan(, you might be in the wrong angle mode. Go to the Mode menu, and see if you're in Degree or Radian mode; if you're in the wrong mode, change it. If you have a TI-84 Plus C Silver Edition calculator, the current angle mode is always shown at the top of the screen for easy reference.

- *Complex numbers look odd.*

  If you expect complex numbers like 2+3*i* and get something like 3.6e^(0.983*i*), you're in re^(θ*i*) mode. Go to the Mode menu, and choose a+b*i* mode instead.

If neither of these options describes your particular problem, you're probably entering the problem wrong. Your calculator follows preprogrammed rules of math and will do exactly the computations you tell it to do. Beware of math like this:

4/2*2

You might expect this to equal 1, because 2 * 2 = 4, and 4 / 4 = 1. But although PEMDAS (order of operations) suggests that multiplication comes before division, the two operations have equal precedence. This means your calculator will first divide 4 / 2 and get 2 and then multiply the result by 2 and get a final answer of 4 (see figure C.1). To fix this, wrap the 2*2 in parentheses. By the same token, always remember to divide the Quadratic Formula by (2A), not 2A; otherwise, you'll end up with 2 in the denominator and A in the numerator.

Not all calculator errors are these so-called "big" problems. Most of the issues you encounter with your calculator will probably produce error messages that help

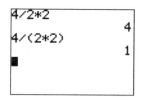

Figure C.1 The importance of remembering that multiplication and division have equal precedence, meaning division can be done before multiplication if it comes first in the expression. Using parentheses forces your calculator to do the multiplication first.

you understand what went wrong. I'll now show you how to decode and fix these error messages.

C.2 Decoding error messages

When it realizes that you've made an error of some sort, your calculator will warn you with an error message. All error messages resemble figure C.2: they display the type of error and give you the option to cancel or (sometimes) go to the error and fix it. These error messages are far from self-explanatory, though, and you may need help to understand what happened. In this section, you'll first see tips for solving the most common errors, including SYNTAX, DOMAIN, UNDEFINED, and more. I'll then show you a table of almost all the errors you're likely to encounter while using your calculator, plus what causes those errors and how to fix them.

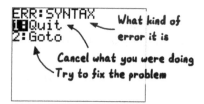

Figure C.2 How most error messages look. The name of the error is shown at the top, along with the option Quit (cancel what you were doing) or, sometimes, Goto (go to where you made a mistake and try to fix it).

Let's start with the most common error messages and how to fix them.

C.2.1 Common error messages

Your calculator has dozens of error messages it can display, to warn you about everything from entering a math expression that doesn't make sense to trying to use a list that doesn't exist. There are a handful you'll see much more often than the others, though, and this section will explain these error messages in more depth.

ERR:SYNTAX

You'll probably see ERR:SYNTAX more than any other error message. Simply put, it means you typed a math expression that doesn't make sense. Here are a few examples of what you might have typed:

- *Two operators next to each other*—3+*5 doesn't mean anything, nor does 4//2. Fill in the missing numbers or take out the extra operator.
- *Nonsensical numbers*—3..4 isn't a valid number, for example. Interestingly enough, 34. and .34 are both valid.

- *Operators missing their operands*—²+3 (squared plus 3) and 3√() don't make mathematical sense, because you're not squaring or taking the square root of anything. Fix the missing operand.

- *Confused negative and subtraction symbols*—You need to use ⊟ for subtraction and ⊝ for negation. -5 (that's the subtraction symbol) will produce a syntax error, because your calculator will read it as "(nothing) minus 5." Type ⁻5 (the negative symbol) instead.

- *Mismatched parentheses*—If you have more closing than opening parentheses, your calculator won't know what to do. Make sure every closing parenthesis matches an opening parenthesis.

- *Missing commas between function arguments*—Each argument to a function must be separated by a comma. If you miss commas, your calculator won't be able to figure out which arguments are which. If you give the wrong number of arguments or use invalid arguments, you'll get an ERR:ARGUMENT or ERR:DATA TYPE instead.

All the other mistakes you might make to get an ERR:SYNTAX message follow the same general theme: you entered an expression that the calculator doesn't understand. Check it over carefully.

ERR:INVALID DIM OR ERR:STAT PLOT

Perhaps the most common problem students ask me on Cemetech is how to fix ERR:INVALID DIM or ERR:STAT PLOT messages that they get when they try to graph something. The answer is usually that a Stat Plot was enabled accidentally, which makes the calculator try to draw a Stat Plot that wasn't set up properly (see chapter 8).

To fix this, go to the Y= menu, move the flashing cursor up to whichever of Plot1, Plot2, or Plot3 is white text in a black box, and press ENTER to disable it. Alternatively, you can press 2nd Y= to get to the Stat Plots menu and choose 4:PlotsOff.

You can also get these two error messages from other issues. If you try to perform element-wise math on lists or matrices with unequal sizes, for instance, you'll get the ERR:INVALID DIM message. See section C.2.2 for more on the INVALID DIM and STAT PLOT errors and sections 4.2 and 4.3 for more about lists and matrices.

ERR:DOMAIN

Several places where you're asked to enter a value, that number can only fall within certain bounds, called the *domain* of the number. If you enter a value outside those bounds, you'll get the ERR:DOMAIN message. Alternatively, if only integers or positive numbers are allowed, and you provide a decimal or negative number, this error might occur. Here's a list of examples, although there are many more possibilities than those mentioned here:

- You provided a decimal number for an argument that only accepts integers. For example, randInt(1.3,4) will generate this error.

- You provided a negative number for an argument that only accepts positive numbers. For example, round(9.81,⁻1) will produce this error, because you can't round numbers to a negative number of digits after the decimal point.

- You provided a value outside the valid range of input values to a function. For example, you can only take the $\sin^{-1}($, $\cos^{-1}($, and $\tan^{-1}($ of values between -1 and 1. You can't use the Pxl-On(, Pxl-Off(, and Pxl-Change(functions on off-screen pixels.

Double-check what values the function in question allows and adjust the arguments.

ERR:NONREAL ANS

To save students who haven't yet learned about complex-numbers confusion, your calculator won't produce complex numbers as answers in Real mode. Instead, it displays ERR:NONREAL ANS. To resolve this, go to the Mode menu and switch to a+bi or re^(θi) mode, and then try your calculation again.

If your expression wasn't meant to produce a complex number, you probably accidentally took the square root of a negative number. Check your expression again.

ERR:DATA TYPE

Your calculator can store and use many different types of data: real numbers, complex numbers, lists, matrices, pictures, strings, Y= equations, programs, and more. Many functions require numbers, lists, matrices, or other values as arguments, but they can only accept one type of data. If you give them the wrong type of data, such as a matrix where a single number is expected, you'll get this error.

You might have made this mistake by way of a simple typo, or you might have forgotten what types of arguments a specific function needs. For the former case, double-check the expression you entered. For the latter case, refer to the appropriate chapter of this book (or the calculator's included guidebook, for esoteric or rarely used functions) and find what type of values the function or tool expects.

ERR:UNDEFINED

If you try to use a variable like A, X, L_1, ∟LIST, [C], Str5, or Pic7 without first creating it and filling it with data, you can't use that variable for math or in your calculator's tools. This is a fairly logical error, because the calculator can't work with data it doesn't have. This error might also be caused by using the wrong variable after putting your data in or defining a different variable.

To fix this error, either define the variable in question and try again, or switch to the correct variable.

C.2.2   *Other error messages*

Your calculator has many more error messages than just those described in section C.2.1. To help you track down exactly what happened when something goes wrong, it offers dozens of possible error messages, many of which are shown in table C.1. If you can't find a description of your error message in section C.2.1, then see if this table helps. A few rarely seen error messages are omitted; if you encounter them, you can find explanations in the calculator's official manual.

Table C.1   A full list of error messages that may appear on the TI-83 Plus or TI-84 Plus, what causes each error, and how to fix it. Note that the Error column omits the `ERR:` **that appears before each error name. Refer also to section C.2.1 for more detail on common errors.**

Error	Cause	Fix
ARCHIVED	You tried to use a variable, a list, a matrix, a picture, a string, or an equation that's archived, or you tried to run a program that's archived.	Unarchive the variable in question from the Memory Management menu. Press `2nd` `+` to access the Memory menu; then choose option `2`. Press `ENTER` next to variables labeled with an asterisk (*) to move them from Archive to RAM, if there is space. (See also section B.1.4 in appendix B.)
ARCHIVE FULL	You tried to archive a variable, but the archive is already full.	Try deleting archived items from the Memory menu, or delete Apps that you don't use.
ARGUMENT	You gave a function the wrong number of arguments, or you left out the comma(s) between function arguments. See section B.1.3 or section 2.4 for more about functions.	Give the function in question the correct arguments in the correct order. Refer to the chapter of this book that explains the function. If you have a TI-84 Plus C Silver Edition, find the function in its menu and press `+` to see the arguments it expects.
BAD GUESS	You're finding a minimum, maximum, or zero from the Calc menu and chose a guess that's not between the lower and upper bounds. You're using the Equation Solver and picked a guess not between the lower and upper bounds.	Fix the guess, or fix the bounds. This can also rarely happen if a function has discontinuities, in which case try a different guess.
BOUND	In any function or tool that requires you to enter a lower bound and upper bound, you entered an upper bound that's below the lower bound.	Make sure your upper bound is always larger than your lower bound.
DATA TYPE	You used one type of variable or data where another was expected, like a matrix or list where only a number is allowed. This can happen with functions or with variables: for example, if you try to store the list $\{2,3,4\}$ to matrix `[A]`.	Check which data types are allowed, and use the proper type. The three most frequently confused types are numbers, lists, and matrices, but incorrect use of strings, pictures, Y= equations, and other variables can also cause this error. (See also section C.2.1.)
DIM MISMATCH	You tried to perform list-wise or matrix-wise math on lists or matrices with unequal sizes.	Change the sizes of the lists or matrices in question, or use different lists or matrices. (See also section C.2.1.)

Table C.1 A full list of error messages that may appear on the TI-83 Plus or TI-84 Plus, what causes each error, and how to fix it. Note that the Error column omits the `ERR:` that appears before each error name. Refer also to section C.2.1 for more detail on common errors. *(continued)*

Error	Cause	Fix
DIVIDE BY 0	You attempted to divide by zero. Your calculator can't represent the negative or positive infinity (or undefined value) that division by zero generates.	Change your equation or expression. Note that division by zero is allowed in graphed equations; a blank space will be left in the graphed function.
DOMAIN	A function or tool only allows values within certain ranges, and you provided a value outside those ranges.	Fix the value(s) in question. If necessary, refer back to the chapter where the function or tool was introduced to see what values are valid. (See also section C.2.1.)
ILLEGAL NEST	You tried to use `seq(` inside itself, or you tried to use `fnInt(` or `nDeriv(` as an argument to itself more than once.	Remove nested `seq(`, `fnInt(`, or `nDeriv(` functions. This error will happen even if the nested function is inside a separate equation variable such as Y_1 when used from Y_2.
INVALID	This is a very general error, used to cover a lot of possible cases of using the wrong variable in the wrong place or forgetting to define some equation.	Check if you're using the Y variable or any of the Window variables inside a Y= equation. Check that you entered all equations and initial conditions properly for SEQ-mode equations.
INVALID DIM	You tried to use a list with zero elements. You tried to graph with a Stat Plot accidentally enabled. You tried to access a list element outside of a list (for example, $L_1(4)$ when L_1 has only three elements).	Change the size of the list(s) or matrice(s) involved, or turn off the Stat Plot in question. (See also section C.2.1.)
ITERATIONS	The Equation Solver or TVM solver got stuck while trying to find a solution.	For the Equation Solver, try setting narrower bounds or a different guess.
MEMORY	Your RAM is full, or there's not enough free RAM for a calculation to complete.	Delete variables like lists, matrices, programs, and pictures from RAM, or move them from RAM to Archive. See section B.1.4 for more details.
NO SIGN CHNG	The Equation Solver or the TVM solver believes the equation or financial problem given is unsolvable.	For the TVM solver, try adjusting the values of FV, PV, N, and PMT.
NONREAL ANS	An expression involved complex numbers or the square root of a negative number, but your calculator is in Real mode.	Switch to $a+bi$ or $re^{\wedge}(\theta i)$ mode from the Mode menu. (See also section C.2.1.)

Table C.1 A full list of error messages that may appear on the TI-83 Plus or TI-84 Plus, what causes each error, and how to fix it. Note that the Error column omits the ERR: that appears before each error name. Refer also to section C.2.1 for more detail on common errors. *(continued)*

Error	Cause	Fix
SINGULAR MAT	You tried to invert a non-invertible matrix using the $^{-1}$ operator or $^-1$. You can only invert square matrices and only when the determinant of the matrix is nonzero. This error can also occur while using the SinReg (regression tool.	If inverting a matrix, fix your matrix values to give it a nonzero determinant. If using SinReg (, adjust the data points to make a solution possible.
SINGULARITY	The Equation Solver encountered an undefined value on the input equation.	Fix the input equation, bounds, or guess. The Solver can't solve some equations with discontinuities near the solution.
STAT	Lists used with statistics tools contain invalid or insufficient data.	Make sure you entered all the relevant data, you didn't make a mistake entering values, and you're using the lists containing your data with the statistics tool in question.
STAT PLOT	You accidentally turned on a Stat Plot.	(See also section C.2.1.)
SYNTAX	You typed a mathematical expression with errors.	(See section C.2.1 for more details on what causes this and how to solve it.)
TOL NOT MET	A function or tool has a tolerance (bounds within which it can declare an answer correct) that was not met. The Equation Solver and fnInt (function may produce this.	Change the tolerance argument to a larger number, or try a different function or bounds.
UNDEFINED	You tried to use a numeric variable, a list variable, a matrix variable, or another type of variable that doesn't exist.	Declare the variable before you use it. (See also section C.2.1.)
WINDOW RANGE	You defined a Window that doesn't make sense. For example, Ymax is less than Ymin or Tstep = 0.	Use the Window menu or the variables in (VARS) (1) to fix the Window.
ZOOM	You tried to zoom in or out too far, or you made a mistake using the ZBox tool.	Zoom in the opposite direction, or make sure you're defining a rectangle with the ZBox tool.

index